Principles of accounts

E F Castle
B Com, FCA

N P Owens
BA (Soc) Hons, ACIS, M Inst AM

Ninth Edition

Revised by Geoffrey Whitehead BSc (Econ)

THE M & E HANDBOOK SERIES

PITMAN PUBLISHING
128 Long Acre, London WC2E 9AN
A Division of Longman Group UK Limited

First published 1966
Ninth edition 1994

© Macdonald & Evans Ltd 1966, 1969,
1971, 1974, 1978, 1981, 1983
© Longman Group UK Limited 1991, 1994

British Library Cataloguing in Publication Data
Castle, E.F. (Eric Frank)
  Principles of accounts. –9th ed.
  1. Accounting
  I. Title II. Owens, N.P. Norman Percival 1927–
  III. Whitehead, Geoffrey 1921–
  657

ISBN 0 7121 1711 3

Founding Editor: P.W.D. Redmond

Printed and bound in Singapore

Contents

Preface

This book has been prepared with examinations in mind. To this end its aim is to give a grounding in the basic principles of accounts, and in so doing to enable the student of average ability to apply those principles to problems that will confront him/her in the examination.

The aim of the first four chapters is to present an outline picture of an accounting system, and to justify the reason for and the purpose of any system of accounting.

Changes in legislation and techniques are inevitably reflected in the syllabuses of examining bodies and we have revised and modified the text in the light of current practice and have included material now covered by a wide variety of examining bodies.

Examination questions have been brought up to date, and for students working on their own we have endeavoured to maintain a logical presentation. The size of the book, and the large number of questions set, makes the supply of fully worked answers impossible, but the abbreviated answers have been extended to include most of the vital sub-sections, and the wording of the questions has been checked to ensure that ambiguous elements have been eliminated.

We hope that this revised edition will enable the text to be of greater benefit to a wider student body and we thank all those who have helped us with useful suggestions.

A book of this size, covering a wide section of accounts, must omit detail, but we have endeavoured to include all relevant matters in sufficient depth to promote a thorough understanding and to develop competence in examinations.

EFC
NPO

It has been a great pleasure to work through this tried and tested *Handbook*, updating and re-working the many examples. The only real change made to the text is the transposition of the traditional English Balance Sheets into the correct and natural style with assets on the left and liabilities on the right. This change was recently introduced into the Companies Act 1985 as part of the harmonisation with European Balance Sheets. It thus corrects the error imparted into British Law as long ago as the Companies Act of 1856, which started off the 'traditional English Balance Sheet' to the perpetual confusion of UK students. Let us hope that Simon Stevin of Bruges who invented the Balance Sheet in 1536 (and got it wrong) is resting more quietly in his grave. We salute him for his sublime thought, however incorrect

GW

1

Starting a business: a Balance Sheet at dawn on Day 1

1. What is a Balance Sheet?

Every business starts on a given day, and we will call the moment of commencement 'Dawn on Day 1'. At that moment the proprietor, or proprietors if it is a partnership, or the shareholders if it is a limited company, contribute the capital to start the business. The capital may be in money form, or it may be partly in money and partly in the form of existing assets such as land, premises, tools and equipment etc. It is essential to list these assets, whatever form they take, so that the opening position is clear, and it is usual to present them in the form of an **Opening Balance Sheet**, where the assets are listed on one side, and are set against the liabilities. There may be only one liability, in which case it will be the capital owed by the business to the proprietor. However, there may be other liabilities even at Dawn on Day 1. For example the proprietor may have arranged a loan for the business from a bank, or a finance house, and possibly a mortgage secured on the premises. We shall learn more about the various assets and liabilities in a moment. First let us answer our question 'What is a Balance Sheet?' The answer is:

> **A Balance Sheet is a piece of paper, which shows the assets of a business (the things the business owns) listed on one side, and the liabilities (the things the business owes) listed on the other.**

It has been called a snapshot of the affairs of a business, at a given moment in time. The snapshot we are about to take is the position at Dawn on Day 1. We can draw up a Balance Sheet at any time once a business has got under way, but the essential time to draw up a Balance Sheet is at the last moment of the last day of the financial year, which may be a calender year – 31 December each year, or the anniversary of the commencement date, or very often companies choose 31 March, which is the end of the tax year for companies. Apart from an Opening Balance Sheet, most Balance Sheets are drawn up on the last day of the financial year.

Thus, the Balance Sheet of a business is essentially a statement of the assets and liabilities of the business at a particular date.

2. Starting a business

Assume that A. Beck has been left £18,000 in his aunt's will and wishes to start a retail business. The first step will be for him to put the money in a *business bank account*. If he does this on 1 January he could produce a Balance Sheet as follows:

A.BECK: BALANCE SHEET AS AT 1 JANUARY 19___

Assets	£	Liabilities	£
Cash at Bank	18,000	Capital (A. Beck)	18,000

3. Form of the Balance Sheet

You will see that the assets have been listed on the left-hand side of the Balance Sheet and the liabilities on the right-hand side. These are the correct sides, under the Companies Act 1985, which was passed to assist in the harmonisation of accounts in the European Community, and is the system used by all other European nations. In the United Kingdom, for historical reasons which need not concern us here, the assets were for over a hundred years entered on the right-hand side and the liabilities on the left. To make matters worse, the accountancy bodies started to present Balance Sheets in a style called vertical style, and this style will be explained and used later in this book. Actually a Balance Sheet in vertical style is a contradiction in terms — a balance must by its very nature be horizontal — as the Statue of Justice on the Old Bailey in London testifies to all those whose rights and wrongs are weighed on her scales.

Leaving such matters on one side, why are the assets properly placed on the left-hand side and the liabilities on the right? Because the assets have all received value from the proprietors of the business, and any account that receives value is debited (a word which means 'entered on the left-hand side'). All accounts which give value are credited — so the Capital Account of the proprietor is credited (a word which means 'entered on the right-hand side'). The first rule in accounting, as we shall see is:

Always debit an account that receives goods, or services, or money.
Always credit an account that gives goods, or services, or money.

4. A Balance Sheet at 'Dawn on Day 1'

Let us imagine that A. Beck had been thinking of setting up in business for some time and had been collecting together various things he would need, and making a few arrangements. The legacy from his aunt is a fortunate addition to his affairs but we will suppose that besides the legacy he has the following things: (*a*) he has arranged for the use of some premises and has paid the first month's rent of £400. (*b*) He has a motor van, valued at £1,350 and some tools and equipment worth £1,850, although he owes one supplier £300 for one particular piece of equipment. The firm is of course a creditor of A. Beck (a person to whom Beck owes money). Its name is Electro-switch Ltd. He has some stock that he will be able to sell which he bought in a bankruptcy sale for £950, and he has £150 in cash. He has also arranged the purchase of a machine for £30,000 on which he has paid £2,000 deposit and the rest is being paid by a loan from Friendly Bank PLC. To draw up A. Beck's Balance Sheet at Dawn on Day 1 we list the assets and liabilities as follows:

Assets	£	Liabilities	£
Machinery	30,000	Loan A/c	28,000
Tools and Equipment	1,850	(Friendly Bank PLC)	
Motor Vehicles	1,350	Creditors	300
Stock for re-sale	950		
Rent in Advance	400		
Cash at Bank (legacy)	18,000		
Cash in hand	150		
	£52,700		£28,300

The assets and liabilities must balance, but manifestly they do not because we have left out the liability that the business owes to the proprietor who has set up the business by contributing the assets. This is the difference between the two totals, £52,700 - £28,300 = £24,400. This figure is sometimes referred to as the **net worth** of the business to the owner of the business. It may also be called **'owner's funds'**. The total worth of the business is £52,700 (the total of the assets) but £28,000 of the funds for the machinery were provided by an outsider (Friendly Bank PLC), while £300 of the tools and equipment were provided by a creditor, Electro-switch Ltd. The value of the business to the owner of a business (the net worth) is therefore £24,400, and it is this sum that is credited to Capital Account as a liability of the business to the owner of the business.

If we set out the figures listed above in a well-presented Balance Sheet it is usual to clarify the presentation with the use of some sub-headings. They are shown below, but we must first explain them.

5. Fixed assets and current assets

All the assets that are contributed at the start of a business play some part in the business's activities but some are for long-term use (called fixed assets) and others are for short-term use (current assets). The dividing line between the two is a useful life of one year. Fixed assets have a useful life longer than one year — machinery, tools and equipment and motor vehicles, in this case. Current assets are expected to be used up in this current year (either because they are consumable items like stationery (or in this case 'rent') or because we hope to turn them into cash (selling the stock, for example).

6. Current liabilities, long-term liabilities and capital

In rather the same way liabilities are divided into current liabilities (payable in less than one year) and long-term liabilities (payable over a period of years). One liability (the capital) is not repayable until the close of business on the last day — which may be many years away, and possibly — in the case of companies — generations from now. It is often called 'permanent capital' to make this point clear.

A. BECK: BALANCE SHEET AS AT 1 JANUARY 19__

Fixed assets	£		*Capital*	£
Machinery		30,000	At start	24,400
Tools and Equipment		1,850		
Motor Vehicles		1,350		
		33,200		
			Long-term liability	
Current assets	£		Loan A/c	
Stock for			(Friendly Bank PLC)	28,000
re-sale	950			
Rent in Advance	400		*Current liability*	
Balance at Bank	18,000		Creditor	300
Cash in hand	150			
		19,500		
		£52,700		£52,700

7. The purpose of business activity

The purpose of business activity is to create wealth by playing some part in the provision of goods and services which satisfy human 'wants'. The general term for business persons is 'entrepreneurs', a word derived from the French, and meaning 'people who undertake activities of various sorts'. As a reward for their enterprise, entrepreneurs hope to earn profits — because they charge more for the goods and services they provide than the costs of production incurred. Not all are successful, as the bankruptcy notices in the local and national press show. Where firms make profits the capital of the business is increased (except to the extent that the proprietor draws out the profits earned as 'drawings'). Where firms make losses the capital is eroded by the loss, and if the losses are so great that the capital is eroded completely the firm or company must cease trading.

8. Profit as an increase in both assets and liabilities

Consider the change in the affairs of A. Beck if he sells the stock he has on 1 January (the cost price of which is £950), for a total of £1,250 cash, during the day. He now has no stock, but an extra £1,250 cash instead. The assets of the business have risen by

£300, so profit clearly means an increase in the assets of the business (to £53,000). This would unbalance Beck's Balance Sheet, were it not for the fact that profits belong to the entrepreneur, because they are the reward for enterprise. Therefore the business now owes to the owner of the business not only the original capital of £24,400 but a further sum — the profit of £300.

The new Balance Sheet, after this single transaction, would read:

A. BECK: BALANCE SHEET AS AT 2 JANUARY 19__

Fixed assets		£	Capital	£
Machinery		30,000	At start	24,400
Tools and Equipment		1,850	Add profit	300
Motor Vehicles		1,350		24,700
		33,200	Long-term liability	
Current assets	£		Loan A/c	
Stock	—		(Friendly Bank	
Cash at Bank	18,000		PLC)	28,000
Cash in hand	1,400			
Rent in Advance	400		Current liability	
		19,800	Creditor	300
		£53,000		£53,000

The reader might like to work out what the situation would have been had Beck sold the stock for only £600 — it having deteriorated over the time when he was collecting his ideas together in preparation for entry into the enterprise sector of the economy.

9. Effect of transactions on the Balance Sheet

As is evident from the above example, *profit must always be represented as an increase in the assets* of the business. This is also an increase in the amount of capital, since capital represents the amount which the business owes to the proprietor.

(a) *Every business transaction, whether profitable or otherwise will have an effect on the Balance Sheet,* and since all transactions have a twofold aspect, both sides of the Balance Sheet must always agree.

(b) *The effect of transactions will* therefore be either:
- (*i*) to increase both assets and liabilities;
- (*ii*) to reduce both assets and liabilities:
- (*iii*) to increase some assets and reduce others;
- (*iv*) to increase a liability and reduce others.

10. Further transactions of A. Beck

Let us continue the transactions of A. Beck from 2 to 8 January and see how we can develop the idea of altering the figures in a Balance Sheet.

During this period A. Beck:

(a) bought stock costing £500 on credit from a wholesaler, C. Smith (in the Balance Sheet stock will increase by £500 and creditors will rise by the same amount on the liabilities side).

(b) took £100 from the Bank Account for his own use (this is termed 'Drawings'). When the proprietor draws money out in this way, he may be said to be reducing his capital, but a better way to regard 'Drawings' is as 'drawings in expectation of profits made'. It is therefore better to regard drawings as reducing the profit available to the entrepreneur. In this case assets are being reduced — cash at Bank will go down by £100 and profits will be reduced, on the liabilities side.

(c) sold goods costing £300 for £600 on credit to B. Jones and has not yet received payment (stock will go down by £300 and a *new item — Debtors —* amounts owing to the business — will be introduced as a Current Asset).

> NOTE: This item will also bring in a profit element of £300 and Capital must be increased by this amount, as the profit becomes available to the proprietor.

(d) Beck wins a prize in a national competition and uses the £3,000 to pay off some of his loan from Friendly Bank PLC The loan decreases by £3,000 and Beck's capital increases by £3,000.

> NOTE: Each of these transactions illustrates one of the types of transaction in **9** above.

We now have a Balance Sheet as follows:

A. BECK: BALANCE SHEET AS AT 8 JANUARY 19___

Fixed assets	£	Capital	£
Machinery	30,000	At start	24,400
Tools etc	1,850	Add new capital	3,000
Motor Vehicles	1,350		27,400
	33,200		£
		Add profit	600
		Less Drawings	100
			500
Current assets	£		27,900
Stock	200	Long-term liability	
Debtors	600	Loan A/c	
Cash at Bank	17,900	(Friendly Bank PLC)	25,000
Cash in hand	1,400	Current liability	
Rent in Advance	400	Creditors	800
	20,500		
	£53,700		£53,700

NOTE: Stock rose by £500 and fell by £300.

11. Balance Sheet interpretation

Examinations frequently test candidates' understanding of the Balance Sheet by asking them to calculate some basic figures from the Balance Sheet. Unfortunately terms can have more than one meaning, and some ambiguity can arise as a result. In this section we will use the Balance Sheet of A. Beck as at 8 January to discuss these figures.

Capital employed. There are three common measures of this term, which are explained later in this book. For the moment we will only use one definition.

Capital employed is the total of the assets of the business — in A. Beck's case £53,700. Since the business has £53,700 of assets, someone must have provided the capital to finance them, and we can see that the funds were provided partly by the proprietor's capital (27,900); partly by the bank (25,000) and partly by the creditors (800).

Capital owned. Capital owned means the capital owned at the Balance Sheet date by the proprietor. It is defined as the total of the Balance Sheet less the external liabilities. We can see that this figure is £27,900. It is also called the **net worth** of the business to the owner of the business.

Liquid funds. The word 'liquid' means 'in cash form'. Liquid funds means the Cash at Bank + Cash in hand = £19,300. (*Note:* The assets are shown arranged in the order of permanence, with the most permanent items first and the most liquid items last.)

Fixed capital. That part of the capital that is tied up in fixed assets, in this case £33,200.

Working capital. The amount of capital that is available to meet the day-to-day expenses of running the business. The fixed capital is not available (it is tied up in fixed assets) and some of the current assets are already committed to paying the current liabilities, as they become due in the weeks ahead. Therefore the working capital is current assets – current liabilities = £20,500 – £800 = £19,700.

Liquid capital. The amount of readily available funds to meet the day-to-day expenses of the business. This is a more stringent test of the financial soundness of the business. Since the stock is not readily available (we cannot be sure we can realise it as a liquid asset), liquid capital is: (Current assets – stock) – current liabilities = £20,300 – £800 = £19,500.

This is not very different from working capital in this case but where a business has a great deal of stock it can appear to have plenty of working capital but actually be very short of liquid capital.

12. Bringing out net working capital on the Balance Sheet

By a slight re-arrangement of the Balance Sheet it is possible to bring out the net working capital and the net assets of the business. Accountants often do this because it shows up the financial position more clearly. All that is necessary is to bring the current liabilities over to the assets side, and deduct them from the current assets. The Balance Sheet of A. Beck as at 8 January, when rearranged in this way, appears as shown below.

A. BECK: BALANCE SHEET AS AT 8 JANUARY 19__

Fixed assets	£	Capital	£
Machinery	30,000	At start	24,400
Tools etc	1,850	Add new capital	3,000
Motor Vehicles	1,350		27,400
	33,200		£
		Add profit	600
		Less Drawings	100
			500
Current assets	£		27,900
Stock	200		
Debtors	600	Long-term liability	
Rent in Advance	400	Loan A/c	
Cash at Bank	17,900	(Friendly Bank PLC)	25,000
Cash in hand	1,400		
	20,500		
Less			
Current liabilities			
Creditors	800		
Net working capital	19,700		
Net assets	£52,900		£52,900

13. Capital expenditure and revenue expenditure

All expenditure is either capital expenditure or revenue expenditure.

(a) *Capital expenditure* is expenditure on assets which are durable, and last a long time (longer than one year) and therefore give reasonably permanent service to the business and make a long-term contribution to the profit-making capacity of the business. The commonest examples of capital expenditure are expenditures on land, buildings, plant and machinery, fixtures and fittings, office equipment and motor vehicles. They are the fixed assets of the business. Even fixed assets wear out in time, and have to be reduced in value to the extent of the 'fair wear and tear' suffered. This is called the depreciation of assets. More rarely, assets can appreciate in value, for example land and buildings may appreciate, as changes of taste and fashion affect the values in a neighbourhood.

(b) *Revenue expenditure* is expenditure on items which have a relatively short life (less than one year). There are three types of revenue expenditure: (*i*) purchases of goods for re-sale in the course of normal trading activities, or of raw materials in manufacturing activities (*ii*) purchases of consumables, to be used up in the course of business — such as stationery, cleaning materials, etc. (*iii*) overhead expenses, such as rent, rates, light, heat, etc.

By contrast to capital expenditure and revenue expenditure we can have **capital receipts** (funds provided by the proprietor, or by external borrowing) and **revenue receipts** (profits of the business such as rent received, discount received, commission received, etc).

Progress test 1

1. What is a Balance Sheet?   **(1)**

2. What is capital?   **(4) and (6)**

3. What is working capital and what does it do?   **(11)**

4. How do you find: (*a*) working capital; (*b*) capital owned; (*c*) capital employed?   **(11)**

5. Distinguish between fixed assets and current assets.   **(5)**

6. What are liquid funds?   **(11)**

7. What is profit?   **(7) and (8)**

8. What effect will profit have on: (*a*) the assets of a business; (*b*) the capital of a business?   **(8)**

9. What effect do drawings have on the Balance Sheet?   **(10)**

10. What is a liability?   **(1)**

11. What do you understand by the terms: (*a*) debtors; (*b*) creditors?   **(10)** and **(4)**

12. Explain how it is possible for the capital employed in a business to be greater than the amount of the capital owned. **(11)**

13. How would you distinguish capital expenditure from revenue expenditure?   **(13)**

Specimen questions

1.   The following balances remain in the ledger of H. Christian at 30 June.

Bank Overdraft £600; Sundry Debtors £550; Delivery Van £2,700; Stock £7,250; Furniture & Fittings £3,850; Sundry Creditors £1,340; Premises £48,000; Mortgage on Premises £42,000; Cash in hand £150.

Draw up a Balance Sheet at 30 June in such a form as to show clearly the following totals: (*a*) fixed assets; (*b*) current assets; (*c*) current liabilities; (*d*) long-term liabilities; (*e*) capital of H. Christian.

2.   On 31 December S. Turner had the following assets and liabilities.

Motor vehicles £7,830; Furniture and fittings £5,585; Trade debtors £1,980; Stock £12,240; Cash in hand £240; Balance at bank £4,670; Trade creditors £2,560; Expense creditors £45. Loan (fifteen years) from JK Loans Ltd £20,000; Premises £68,250; Mortgage on premises £35,800.

Draw up Turner's Balance Sheet in such a way as to show within the Balance Sheet the: (*a*) total fixed assets; (*b*) total of current assets; (*c*) total of current liabilities; (*d*) Net working capital; (*e*) net assets; (*f*) capital of S. Turner.

3.   The Balance Sheet of L. Fletcher, a trader, at the commencement of the financial year is shown in the first column below, in vertical style, with the liabilities shown first, and the assets below.

		£	£	£	£	£	£
			(a)	(b)	(c)	(d)	(e)
Capital	–	8,400	8,400				
Creditors	–	700	700				
		9,100	9,100				
Equipment	–	4,000	4,000				
Stock	– –	1,300	1,300				
Debtors	–	600	550				
Cash at bank	–	3,200	3,250				
		9,100	9,100				

Copy the above on to your answer paper. Show in the appropriate columns the Balance Sheet after each of the following transactions (the Balance Sheet after the first transaction is shown in column (a)):

(a) received a cheque from a debtor for £50 which was paid into bank;

(b) sold on credit for £120 goods from stock which had cost £80;

(c) paid by cheques £300 owing to creditors;

(d) sold equipment book value £100 for £120 which was paid into bank;

(e) L. Fletcher drew a cheque for £50 for private expenses and took goods from stock for his own use which had cost £20 but for which he paid £25.

4. Explain the distinction between capital and revenue expenditure. State under which heading you would classify each of the following items incurred by a manufacturing business and give reasons for your decision in each case:

(a) cost of a freehold building;

(b) legal charges on the purchase of a freehold building;

(c) replacement of furniture which has been destroyed by fire;

(d) relaying floors destroyed by dry rot. *(RSA)*

5.   Brown sets up in business as a trader. With a capital of £8,000 he buys equipment for use in the business which cost £5,000 leaving the balance in the bank. He buys on credit a stock of goods for sale which cost him £7,000. During the first month's trading:

(a) he sells part of his original stock for £5,000 cash, which is paid into the bank, and the remainder is sold for £6,000 on credit terms, the buyer to pay for the goods in the following month;

(b) he pay £7,000 to the suppliers of the original stock and purchases further goods, on credit terms, at a cost of £8,000.

(c) he pays out of the bank £600 for wages and office expenses of £120. Further expenses for the month amounting to £80 remain unpaid;

(d) he sells some goods (which cost £900) for cash £1,100.

Prepare a statement to show the capital employed at the beginning of the month and the sources of that capital, and a further statement showing how Brown's capital changed (if it did change) after each of the transactions (a), (b), (c) and (d).

2

The theory of double entry

1. What is double entry?

Most accountancy students have heard the term 'double-entry book-keeping' and before we study it in detail it is helpful to see the way the double-entry system arises in actual business life. Turn to p.17 and you will see a diagram of the whole system. It is in five parts:

1. The first thing that happens in business life which calls for accounting records is that someone makes out a business document which relates to a transaction between our business and some other business. The document may be an invoice (about the supply of goods or services) or a credit note (about the return of goods or an allowance made off the price the goods or services). It may be a cheque, or a receipt, or a petty cash voucher of some sort or it may be a more formal document such as a lease, or a bankruptcy notice.

2. These documents may then be recorded in some permanent record such as a Journal (Day Book). Such Day Books are called 'Books of Original Entry'. Alternatively the documents themselves are retained as a permanent record, either in a lever arch file or some other sort of binder.

3. Entries are then made from these permanent records into the main book of account called the Ledger. It may be a bound book, or a loose-leaf book, or an electronic ledger stored in the memory-base of a computer. Every 'page' in a ledger is called an 'account' and keeps a record of one person or thing only. This is explained more fully later, but examples would be the Cash Account (keeping a record of our cash), the Light and Heat Account keeping a record of moneys spent on light and heat and

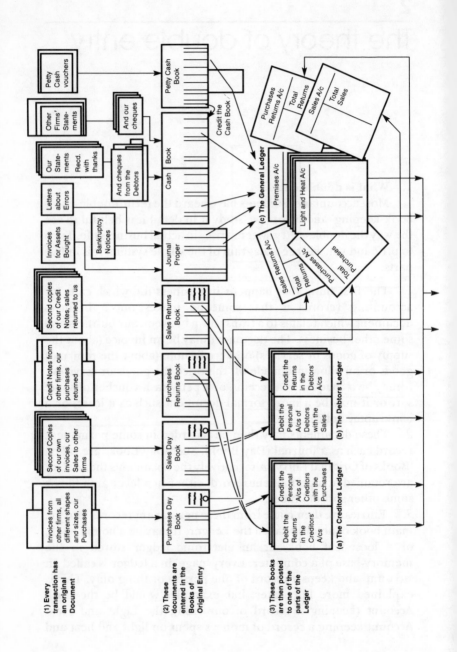

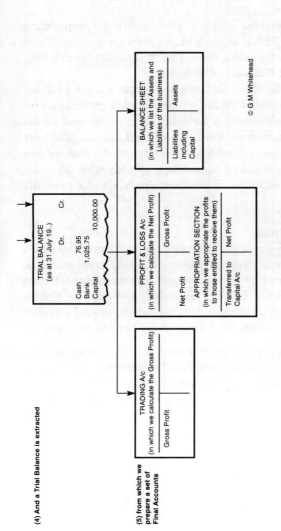

(4) And a Trial Balance is extracted

TRIAL BALANCE (as at 31 July 19..)		
	Dr.	Cr.
Cash	76.95	
Bank	1,025.75	
Capital		10,000.00

© G M Whitehead

(5) from which we prepare a set of Final Accounts

TRADING A/c
(in which we calculate the Gross Profit)

Gross Profit

PROFIT & LOSS A/c
(in which we calculate the Net Profit)

	Gross Profit
Net Profit	

APPROPRIATION SECTION
(in which we appropriate the profits to those entitled to receive them)

Transferred to Capital A/c	Net Profit

BALANCE SHEET
(in which we list the Assets and Liabilities of the business)

Liabilities including Capital	Assets

Figure 2.1   *How the double-entry system works*

Tom Smith Account keeping a record of our transactions with Tom Smith.

For convenience the ledger may be split into a number of parts, the most usual division being into three sections — a Debtors Ledger, a Creditors Ledger and a General Ledger. Some businesses also have a Private Ledger — particularly partnership businesses.

4. The fourth stage of the double-entry system is the preparation of a Trial Balance. This is a check to see if we have done all our book-keeping properly with a double entry for every transaction. If we have the Trial Balance will balance.

5. Finally, from the Trial Balance we prepare a set of Final Accounts, which calculate whether we have made a profit or a loss. In doing so we also produce a Balance Sheet at the end of the trading period for which we have just worked out the profit (or loss). What began as a jumbled collection of documents has finished up in a neat set of accounting records with an exact understanding of our financial position. Study Fig. 2.1 carefully at this point.

2. Basic book-keeping

Theoretically we could go on developing a system under which the Balance Sheet was constantly altered to take account of the changes brought about by our many business transactions. Such a system would, however, be very unwieldy, and thus we need a system of book-keeping designed to record the *twofold aspect* of every business transaction. Such records are kept in a *Ledger*.

(a) A Ledger is a book full of pages called 'accounts'. Each account has two sides: left-hand *debit;* right-hand *credit.*

(b) *Accounts in the Ledger are classified as follows.*

   (i) *Real* accounts: these always represent something we can see, touch or move. They are the assets of the business.

   (ii) *Personal* accounts: these are headed with the name of a person, business or firm. These persons are either debtors of the business or creditors of the business.

   (iii) *Nominal* accounts: these record transactions for which we have nothing tangible to show, e.g. expenses such as rent, rates, heat, etc. Alternatively they may be profits, such as commission received.

(c) *This classification enables us to establish definite rules.*
   (i) *Real* accounts: we DEBIT the real account when we purchase an asset, and we CREDIT it when we sell a worn-out asset, or depreciate it in value.
   (ii) *Personal* accounts: we DEBIT the receiver of goods, or services or money, and we CREDIT the giver of goods or services or money.
   (iii) *Nominal* accounts: we DEBIT *losses and expenses* and we CREDIT *profits and gains.*

(d) *When faced with any transaction, ask yourself* three questions.
   (i) What *two* accounts are affected? Give them a *name*.
   (ii) What *types* of accounts are they? Classify them, e.g. real, personal or nominal.
   (iii) Which one is to be *debited* and which *credited*? If you are certain that one is to be *debited,* then the other MUST be *credited.*

(e) *When entering a transaction in the Ledger* (referred to as 'posting' the Ledger from the permanent record of the documents) always use the name of the *other account* in the account you are posting.
   Applying these principles to the case of A. Beck we would show:

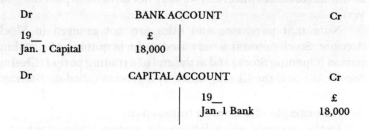

Dr	BANK ACCOUNT		Cr
19__	£		
Jan. 1 Capital	18,000		

Dr	CAPITAL ACCOUNT		Cr
		19__	£
		Jan. 1 Bank	18,000

NOTE: that the *name* of the other account appears in each account against the entry made. This is the basis for a 'built-in' system of cross referencing each entry made.

3. Cash and credit transactions

Not all transactions in business involve immediate payment by cash or cheque, and by far the greatest number of transactions are on credit. This means that payment will be made at a later date. The normal period of credit is one month, and accounts have traditionally always been settled at the end of each month. Today businesses are so large that most firms operate a system of *cyclical billing*, in which about 5 per cent of accounts are sent out each day. This spreads the work out over the month, and debtors are asked to pay within 30 days of the statement date. This also eases cash flow problems — some money comes in every day.

4.   'Purchases' and 'Sales'

The terms 'purchase' and 'sales' have a special meaning in accountancy. They refer to items which are purchased in order to be sold again at a later date, or items purchased to be manufactured into items which are sold as the normal stock-in-trade of a trading business.

Purchases are debited in the Purchases Account whenever we buy items for re-sale or manufacture into finished goods for re-sale. Purchases Account has received goods to the value debited.

Sales are credited in the Sales Account, either daily if they are cash sales, or monthly if they are sales on credit (because we collect all the sales together in a Sales Day Book which we post to the ledger once a month). Sales Account is credited because it has given goods to the value recorded to our customers (though as far as our debtors are concerned we may not have been paid the cash yet).

Note that purchases and sales are not entered in Stock Account. Stock Account is only used at the beginning of a trading period (Opening Stock) and at the end of a trading period (Closing Stock). We find the Closing Stock by a process called *stock-taking*.

5.   An example of a month's transactions

In the example which follows the various transactions have been taken to the Ledger accounts directly, without first being recorded in any Book of Original Entry. The opening position has been shown in accounts 1–5 and then the rest of the month's activities have been outlined. The full records for the month are then shown, accounts 1–5 being repeated.

Example _____

A. Pitt started in business on 1 January 19__ with £50,000 capital which he paid into the business bank account. On that date he purchased shop premises by cheque £34,000 and equipment and machinery by cheque £1,600. He also purchased stock (record this in Stock Account, since it is his initial purchase of Opening Stock) by cheque for £2,000. Record these opening entries (*see* below).

Note: The numbers L1, L2, L3 etc. are called folio numbers. The word 'folio' means page (actually a double-sided page — from the Latin *folium* — leaf). The L stands for Ledger — so the Capital A/c is the first page in the ledger, the Bank A/c is page 2 in the ledger and so on. Pages in the Journal would be numbered J1, J2, etc. and if we had a special Purchases Day Book they would be labelled PDB1, PDB2, etc. Folio numbers are widely used to cross reference from one book to another.

		CAPITAL A/C		L1
				£
		19__ Jan. 1 Bank		50,000

			BANK A/C		L2
19__	£	19__			£
Jan. 1 Capital	50,000	Jan. 1	Premises		34,000
		1	Equipment etc.		1,600
		1	Stock		2,000

		SHOP PREMISES A/C		L3
19__		£		
Jan. 1 Bank		34,000		

		EQUIPMENT & MACHINERY A/C		L4
19__		£		
Jan. 1 Bank		1,600		

		STOCK A/C		L5
19__		£		
Jan. 1 Bank		2,000		

The month's transactions then continued as shown below. Make the double entries necessary, balance off the accounts at the end of the month and draw up a Trial Balance as at 31 January 19__.

Jan. 2   Purchased goods on credit from G. Hall (£450) and I. John (£550).
Sold goods on credit to A. Bland (£200) and C. Deighton (£250).

Drew £350 from the Bank to use as office cash.

Jan. 3 Sold goods on credit to A. Bland £350.

5 Cash sales £1,504.

6 Bought van from Abel Garages Ltd, £3,925, on credit.

8 Purchased goods from G. Hall £220, on credit.

10 Paid postage £7 in cash.

12 Paid salaries from cash £240.

13 A. Pitt took goods costing £50 for his own use, at selling price.

15 Paid £96 by cheque for repairs to machinery.

16 Cash sales £2,765. Paid to Bank £3,000.

19 Sold goods to C. Deighton, on credit £875.

20 Cash sales £1,682. Paid into bank £1,000.

22 Paid for office stationery in cash £36. Paid for cleaning expenses £56 in cash.

23 Purchased goods from I. John £471, on credit.

24 Sold goods to A. Bland £980, on credit.

26 Paid salaries in cash £240.

27 Cash purchases £120.

29 Received cheque from A. Bland in full settlement of the amount owing by him.

30 Paid G. Hall by cheque to settle the amount owing to her.

31 Paid rates by cheque £326. Cash sales £3,214. Banked £2,500. A. Pitt drew £600 in cash for personal use.

Notes: In exercises of this type, as in real life, you have to make up your mind what the double entries are for each transaction. These hints may help you to understand the entries made in the accounts which follow.

Jan. 2 When we purchase goods G. Hall gives us the goods (credit G. Hall) and our Purchases Account is debited. The same is true of the transaction with I. John.

When we sell goods on credit to A. Bland, Bland receives the goods (debit the receiver) and our Sales Account is credited. The same applies to the transaction with C. Deighton.

When we draw cash from the Bank and put it in the office cash box (or till) Bank Account gives the money (Credit Bank A/c) and Cash Account receives the money (debit Cash A/c). From now on we will only refer to new items, not already explained.

Jan. 5 Cash Sales. Usually cash sales are entered and banked every day but we are only doing it every few days (on Jan. 5, Jan. 16, Jan. 20 and Jan. 31). Cash Account receives the money (debit Cash A/c) and Sales Account gives the goods to the customer (credit Sales A/c).

Jan. 6   This is the purchase of an asset. Debit Motor Vehicles A/c (always debit the asset account when you buy an asset) and credit the supplier Abel Garages Ltd.

Jan. 10   Cash Account gives the £7 for stamps (credit Cash A/c) and debit Postage A/c (one of the losses of the business – a nominal account).

Jan. 12   Debit Salaries A/c, credit Cash A/c.

Jan. 13   Inland Revenue Department requires traders who take goods for own consumption to pay the selling price for them (except in one or two special cases). This is called 'drawings in kind'. Debit Drawings A/c of the proprietor, who receives the goods. Credit Sales A/c (he sold them to himself).

Jan. 15   Debit Repairs to Machinery A/c; credit Bank A/c.

Jan. 16   The 'paid to bank' transaction requires us to debit Bank A/c (it receives the money) and credit Cash A/c (it gives the money).

Jan. 27   If you purchase goods for re-sale for cash you have to credit Cash A/c (it gives the money) and debit Purchases A/c (which receives the goods, for sale at a later date).

Jan. 31   The drawings mentioned this time is drawings in cash. Credit Cash A/c (it gives the money) and debit Drawings A/c (the proprietor receives the money).

		CAPITAL A/C	L1
		19__	£
		Jan. 1 Bank	50,000

		BANK A/C	L2

19__		£	19__		£
Jan. 1	Capital	50,000	Jan. 1	Premises	34,000
16	Cash	3,000	1	Equipment etc.	1,600
20	"	1,000	1	Stock	2,000
29	A. Bland	1,530	2	Cash	350
31	Cash	2,500	15	Repairs to Machinery	96
			30	G. Hall	670
			31	Rates	326

		SHOP PREMISES A/C	L3
19__		£	
Jan. 1	Bank	34,000	

EQUIPMENT & MACHINERY A/C   L4

19__			£
Jan. 1	Bank		1,600

STOCK A/C   L5

19__			£
Jan. 1	Bank		2,000

PURCHASES A/C   L6

19__			£
Jan.	2	G. Hall	450
	2	I. John	550
	8	G. Hall	220
	23	I. John	471
	27	Cash	120

G. HALL A/C   L7

19__			£	19__			£
Jan.	30	Bank	670	Jan.	2	Purchases	450
					8	"	220

I. JOHN A/C   L8

				19__			£
				Jan.	2	Purchases	550
					23	"	471

A. BLAND A/C   L9

19__			£	19__			£
Jan.	2	Sales	200	Jan.	29	Bank	1,530
Jan.	3	Sales	350				
	24	Sales	980				

SALES A/C L10

			£
19__			
Jan.	2	A. Bland	200
	2	C. Deighton	250
	3	A. Bland	350
	5	Cash	1,504
	13	Drawings	50
	16	Cash	2,765
	19	C. Deighton	875
	20	Cash	1,682
	24	A. Bland	980
	31	Cash	3,214

C. DEIGHTON A/C L11

19__			£
Jan.	2	Sales	250
	19	Sales	875

CASH A/C L 12

19__			£	19__			£
Jan.	2	Bank	350	Jan.	10	Postage	7
	5	Sales	1,504		12	Salaries	240
	16	"	2,765		16	Bank	3,000
	20	"	1,682		20	Bank	1,000
	31	"	3,214		22	Office Stationery	36
					22	Cleaning Expenses	56
					26	Salaries	240
					27	Purchases	120
					31	Bank	2,500
					31	Drawings	600

MOTOR VEHICLE A/C L13

19__			£
Jan.	6	Abel Garages Ltd	3,925

ABEL GARAGES LTD A/C L14

			£
19__			
Jan.	6	Motor Vehicles	3,925

POSTAGE A/C   L15

19__			£
Jan. 10	Cash		7

SALARIES A/C   L16

19__			£
Jan. 12	Cash		240
26	"		240

DRAWINGS A/C   L17

19__			£
Jan. 13	Sales		50
31	Cash		600

REPAIRS TO MACHINERY A/C   L18

19__			£
Jan. 15	Bank		96

OFFICE STATIONERY A/C   L19

19__			£
Jan. 22	Cash		36

CLEANING EXPENSES A/C   L20

19__			£
Jan. 22	Cash		56

RATES A/C   L21

19__			£
Jan. 31	Bank		326

6. Balancing off accounts

In the above example all the entries for the month have been made, but the accounts need 'balancing off' or 'closing'. This is done by finding the 'difference', or balancing figure, by subtracting the total of one side from the total of the other side. This balance is then added on the smaller side and carried down to the other side. Since this is usually done at the close of business, on the last day of the month the balance is taken down to start the following day, the first day of the new month.

In accounts with only *one* entry it is not necessary to balance off the account and bring down a balance, since the entry itself automatically becomes the balance on the account, as with, for example, the Capital A/c in the example given.

Where an account has more than one item on one side and no entries on the other side it is customary just to total the side in question in pencil. This total then becomes the figure to be used in drawing up a Trial Balance (*see* below).

In the example given accounts L1, L3, L4, L5, L13, L14, L15, L18, L19, L20 and L21 will not need any action at all. Their balances are clear already. Accounts L6, L8, L10, L11, L16 and L17 just need adding up and the totals pencilling in very small.

Accounts L7 and L9 will be found to be clear, and simply need to be closed off as shown below (only L7 is shown).

G. HALL A/C

L7

19__		£	19__		£
Jan. 30	Bank	670	Jan. 2	Purchases	450
			8	"	220
		£ 670			£ 670

The account is closed off, but there is no balance to bring down. To prevent anyone at a later date trying to make an entry on the spare line below Jan. 30 it is customary to rule in an elongated Z in the details column (below the word Bank).

Accounts L2 and L12 need to be balanced off fully, as shown below (only L2 is shown).

BANK A/C   L2

19__		£	19__		£
Jan. 1	Capital	50,000	Jan. 1	Premises	34,000
16	Cash	3,000	1	Equipment etc.	1,600
20	Cash	1,000	1	Stock	2,000
29	A. Bland	1,530	2	Cash	350
31	Cash	2,500	15	Repairs to Machinery	96
			30	G. Hall	670
			31	Rates	326
			31	Balance c/d	18,988
		£ 58,030			£ 58,030
19__		£			
Feb. 1	b/d	18,988			

NOTES:

(a) The two sides total £58,030 and £39,042. The difference is therefore £18,988.

(b) This balance is inserted on the smaller side (in value), so that both sides now total £58,030.

(c) The balance is then carried down to the opposite side, which in this case means there is a debit balance on the Bank A/c (in other words we have £18,988 in the bank). Students who feel worried about the last statement, because they feel that having a debit balance on the Bank A/c means that they are overdrawn at the bank must be careful here. When you get a bank statement from the bank showing you have a debit balance that is the record from the bank's point of view. If we think of the bank's record of the Bank A/c shown above, it will be the other way round. From the bank's point of view A. Pitt is a creditor, with a credit balance of £18,988, which is what is left of the £50,000 deposited on 1 January.

(d) Note that we need a very large Z to fill in the unused lines below the word 'Cash'. Since such Z lines are very difficult to put into a printed book they will be ignored in future in this text.

(e) Note that c/d means 'carried down' and b/d means 'brought down'.

(f) Always make sure you bring down any balance when you close an account. It is a major error to leave the account looking as if it is clear, when really there should be a balance brought down. We are now ready to check our month's work, with a Trial Balance of A. Pitt's books.

7. The Trial Balance

A Trial Balance may be defined as a list of the balances on the accounts of a business at a given moment in time. It is usually prepared monthly to check the accuracy of the book-keeping. If we leave it any longer and the Trial Balance fails to balance it is very difficult to find the errors. When the two sides of the Trial Balance come to the same total it is said to agree, and we know that, on the face of it, our posting of the transactions to the Ledger (as far as debits and credits are concerned) is correct.

It can be regarded as a convenient check on our posting, but it does not prove that the Ledger is absolutely correct. For example, it will not disclose five kinds of errors.

(a) *Original errors.* If a document has an error in it the error will be entered on both the debit and credit sides somewhere in the accounts and the error will not show up on the Trial Balance.

(b) *Errors of principle* — where we enter an item in a wrong account. For example we may enter the purchase of an asset in Purchases Account, when it is not an item for re-sale.

(c) *Compensating errors* — where we have made two mistakes of equal amount on opposite sides of two different accounts;

(d) *Errors of omission* — where we have left a transaction out entirely — i.e. both debit and credit. This often happens when invoices or credit notes are lost on their way to the Accounts Department.

(e) *Errors of commission* — where we do something wrong. For example, debit D. Smith's A/c instead of D. Smythe's A/c. Such an error will not show up on the Trial Balance.

The Trial Balance of A. Pitt would be as follows, using the balances from our sample exercise.

A. PITT: TRIAL BALANCE AS AT 31 JANUARY 19__

Folio	Account	Dr	Cr
L1	Capital		50,000
L2	Bank	18,988	
L3	Shop Premises	34,000	
L4	Equipment and Machinery	1,600	
L5	Stock	2,000	
L6	Purchases	1,811	
L8	I. John		1,021
L10	Sales		11,870
L11	C. Deighton	1,125	
L12	Cash	1,716	
L13	Motor Vehicles	3,925	
L14	Abel Garages Ltd		3,925
L15	Postage	7	
L16	Salaries	480	
L17	Drawings	650	
L18	Repairs to Machinery	96	
L19	Office Stationery	36	
L20	Cleaning Expenses	56	
L21	Rates	326	
		£ 66,816	£ 66,816

NOTES:

   (a) The Trial Balance always shows the date on which it was drawn up.

   (b) Those accounts with debit balances are listed in the debit column. Note that they are all either assets or losses (expenses).

   (c) Those accounts with the credit balances are listed in the credit column. Notice that they are all either liabilities or profits (but in this case there is only one 'profit' — the sales figure.

   (d) If the totals are the same the Trial Balance is said to 'agree' *prima facie* (at a first view). Actually we could have errors still hidden in it, as explained above.

Progress test 2

1. Explain the five stages of double-entry book-keeping as outlined in Fig. 2.1.
2. What are the characteristics of a Ledger Account? **(2)**
3. Name the two sides of an account. **(2)**
4. What do you understand by: (*a*) real account; (*b*) personal account; (*c*) nominal account? **(2)**
5. What are the rules for making entries in real accounts when we buy an asset or sell a worn-out asset? **(2)**
6. What are the rules for making entries in personal accounts? **(2)**
7. What are the rules for entering losses and profits in nominal accounts? **(2)**
8. What is meant by 'closing an account'? **(6)**
9. What is a Trial Balance? **(7)**
10. Describe the five types of errors, which do not show up on a Trial Balance. **(7)**

Specimen questions

1. R. Keen starts business on 1 September 19—, when he pays £25,000 of his private money into the Business Bank A/c. He also has an opening stock of goods for re-sale worth £1,800, and £500 in cash.

19—

Sept. 2 He acquires equipment for £3,500 and pays by cheque.
3 He acquires a small second-hand motor-van for £500 and also pays by cheque.
4 He buys goods for re-sale for £2,000 and pays by cheque.
10 Cash sales to date £2,460. Banked £2,000.
13 Buys goods valued at £400 from F. Lloyd, on credit.
15 Sells goods on credit to S. Williams, value £850.
16 Pays rent £200 for the month by cheque.
17 Pays wages £160 to an assistant, in cash.
18 Buy's goods for re-sale, worth £700 from T. Jones on credit.
20 Pays F. Lloyd the £400 outstanding, by cheque.

21 Sells goods worth £560 to A. Adams, on credit.
24 Sells goods worth £580 to S. Williams, on credit.
30 Pays assistant's wages: £160 in cash.
Pays general expenses £70 in cash.
He draws £500 out of the business for his personal expenditure in cash.
Cash sales £3,840. Banked £3,000.

You are required to enter the above transactions in the appropriate accounts and extract a Trial Balance at 30 September 19—.

2. T. Rooke started business on 1 January 19—, with Premises £55,000, motor vehicle £3,275, stock £8,500, fixtures & fittings £2,850, cash in hand £100 and cash at bank £4,295. Open the accounts necessary to start his books. During the month he undertook the following transactions.

19—
Jan. 2 Acquired a till for shop use £342.00, paying by cheque.
4 Bought goods for re-sale £785.60 on credit from A. Supplier.
5 Paid general rates of £460, by cheque.
7 Cash sales for week, £4,325. Paid into bank £3,500.
9 Bought goods for cash £236.50.
13 Paid assistant's wages £80 cash. Paid motor expenses by cheque £86.50.
16 Purchased goods, value £950 from A. Supplier on credit.
17 Sold goods valued £426 to F. Philips on credit.
20 Cash sales for week £3,950. Paid assistant's wages £85 cash. Paid into bank £3,250.
23 Purchased goods, value £995 from A. Supplier on credit.
24 Paid £1,735 to A. Supplier by cheque. Sold goods on credit to E. Carr £385.
27 Cash sales for week £4,125. Paid assistant's wages £85. Paid into bank £3,500.
30 Purchased goods £1,315 from A. Supplier on credit. Received cash of £200 from F. Philips, on account.

You are required to enter the above transactions in the appropriate accounts and extract a Trial Balance at 31 January 19—.

3. From the following information, open the Ledger Accounts of Alice Wood; find her capital, post the transactions to the Ledger and extract a Trial Balance at 31 October 19—.

Her financial position on 1 October was as follows:

Cash in hand £42; bank £4,350; premises £58.000; equipment £4,200; stock £5,950; debtor L. Cross £72; creditor B. Banks £946.50.

Oct 2 Purchased goods for resale from F. Small £425.50, on credit.

4 Sold goods to M. Mullen £328.60 on credit.

5 Received rent for part of premises sub-let – by cheque £450.

6 Returned goods to F. Small £38.50.

7 M. Mullen returned goods £42,60.

8 L. Cross paid £50 on account by cheque.

9 Cash sales £4,236.75. Banked £3,500.

9 Paid wages from cash £240.50.

12 Cash sales £3,785. Paid £3,000 into bank.

14 Sold goods to C. Crisp £425, on credit.

15 Purchased goods for resale £224, for cash.

16 Paid commission, by cheque £95. Paid wages from cash £240.50.

18 Bank notified A. Wood that they had charged her account with charges of £62.50.

19 Purchased goods for resale, by cheque £854.20.

19 Paid carriage inwards, by cheque £26.32.

22 Sold goods for cash £4,295. Paid into bank £4,000.

23 Sold goods to L. Cross £105 on credit. Paid wages from cash £240.50. Paid carriage outwards, by cheque £18.50.

25 Wood took £620 from bank and £15 goods at sales price for his own use. Both items count as Drawings.

27 Paid advertising, by cheque £84.60.

28 C. Crisp paid his account, by cheque £403.75. Balance to be regarded as discount allowed.

30 Paid salaries, by cheque £650.00.

3
Finding the profits of the business

1. The Final Accounts of a business

The profits of a business are found by drawing up a set of Final Accounts. The vast majority of businesses are trading businesses, and their sets of Final Accounts consist of a Trading Account (where we work out the **gross profit** on trading), and a Profit and Loss Account to which we take the gross profit and reduce it by deducting the overhead expenses of the business (thus discovering the **net profit**, or clean profit).

Where a business is a manufacturing business it cannot begin to trade until it has manufactured its goods to trade with. Such businesses have a set of Final Accounts which consist of a Manufacturing Account, a Trading Account and a Profit and Loss Account.

Where a business does not trade, but only offers a service (such as a professional consultancy, accountants, etc.) there is no Trading Account, and it is usual to call the Profit and Loss Account by a different name. This may be a Revenue Account, or an Income and Expenditure Account. In such an account the fees received (income) are set against the expenses, to find the net profit (sometimes called a surplus).

Finally, to round the picture off, we may say that where the business is owned by more than one person (for example by partners, or shareholders in a company) there has to be an account in which the profits can be shared out. This is called an Appropriation Account (though it is sometimes referred to as the Appropriation Section of the Profit and Loss Account).

This account of 'Final Accounts' would not be complete without saying that when all these calculations have been made and the profits have been given to the proprietor (or proprietors) we are left with a number of accounts which are still open — all the expense accounts having been closed off in the course of the 'Final Accounts' process. These accounts that are still open are listed on a Balance Sheet, which is a statement of the affairs of the business on the last day of the financial year for which the profits have just been prepared.

For the purposes of this chapter we will deal with the simplest case, the Final Accounts of a trading business, in which we find first the gross profit in the Trading Account and then the net profit in the Profit and Loss Account.

2. Gross profit

This is essentially the difference between the *cost price* and the *selling price* of goods.

Example _____

Selling Price £550 – Cost Price £500 = Gross Profit £50

_____

The word 'gross' implies that this profit on trading is larger than the true profit (the net profit) because the overheads of the business have not yet been deducted. Net profit is explained later in this chapter.

3. Stock

Stock has a special meaning in accounts. It refers only to the initial value of stock held at the start of a business, or at the start of a new financial year. Purchases of stock made at other times of the year are not referred to as 'stock', but as 'purchases'. In accounts the *cost price* of the goods will have been taken to a *Purchases Account*, and the *selling price* will be recorded in the *Sales Account*. Only the *initial purchase* of goods for resale will have been taken to a *Stock Account*.

(a) To find the gross profit we must concern ourselves with the value of *stock on hand* at the end of the financial period.
(b) This 'closing' stock will be valued at cost price or net realisable value (whichever is the lower) and will be based on a physical check of the stock on the premises.

The accountancy bodies have agreed this method of valuing closing stock and have published it as one of their Statements of Standard Accounting Practice (SSAP). It means that almost all stock will be valued at cost price, but if stock has deteriorated in value it may be valued at the 'net realisable value'. This is the sum it is estimated we can get when we sell it, less any costs of disposal (for example an auctioneer's commission). The method of valuation is in line with one of the principles of accounting — the prudence principle. This principle argues that a prudent businessperson never takes a profit until he/she has actually made it (and so we value anything at cost price only), but also takes a loss whenever we believe we have suffered one (so stock which has deteriorated must be valued at the deteriorated value, not the cost value (which is higher).

4. Finding gross profit

Gross profit is found in two stages, as follows:

(a)

Opening stock at start of business (or year)	£ 9,500
Plus Purchases (at cost price)	32,500
	42,000
Less Closing stock (valued as explained above)	7,750
thus arriving at 'cost of stock sold'	£34,250

(b) If these goods have been sold for £73,800 then gross profit will be £73,800 − £34,250 = £39,550.

Gross profit is often expressed as a percentage. We can express it as a percentage of the sales figure (which is called the turnover). Expressed in this way we use the formula:

$$\text{Gross profit percentage} = \frac{\text{Gross profit}}{\text{Turnover}} \times 100$$

$$\text{In this case it is} \quad \frac{£39,550}{£73,800} \times 100$$

$$= 53.6\%$$

This is called the **margin of profit**.

If expressed as a percentage on cost we have:

$$\text{Gross profit percentage on cost} = \frac{\text{Gross profit}}{\text{Cost of stock sold}} \times 100$$

$$= \frac{£39,550}{£34,250} \times 100$$

$$= \underline{\underline{115.5\%}}$$

This is called the **mark-up**.

> NOTE: One of the commonest causes of failure in business is not adding a sufficiently large mark-up on goods purchased for re-sale. This is the same as saying the profit margin is too low. You cannot cover your overhead expenses on a 25 per cent or 30 per cent profit margin. You need much more. For example, most publishers work on a 'five-times' mark-up, and many businesses work on a 'ten times' mark-up.

5. Estimating profit

A retailer will have some idea of what his/her gross profit ought to be, since he/she will work on the basis of a mark-up, e.g. buying at one price and selling at a price, say, twice as great as this cost price.
Future profit can thus be estimated.

Example
If total sales for one *month* are £10,000 and gross profit is 100 per cent greater than cost price which is 50 per cent of selling price) then gross profit for the *month* is £5,000.
If sales can be maintained at this level for twelve months, then the gross profit for the year will be £5,000 x 12 = £60,000.

6. Gross profit and the Trading Account

A Trading Account collects the balances on those accounts directly concerned with the trading process.

(a) This is an account — therefore the principles of double entry still apply, i.e. items debited to Trading Account must have corresponding credits elsewhere.

(b) Accounts directly concerned are: Purchases, Sales, Stock, Purchases Returns and Sales Returns.

(*i*) *Purchases and Sales Accounts* reflect what has happened during the period. They are *nominal* accounts providing convenient totals. These are closed by transferring them to the Trading Account.

Debit Trading Account. *Credit* Purchases Account
Credit Trading Account. *Debit* Sales Account

(*ii*) Purchases Returns Account and Sales Returns Account have the total figures for their returns for the year. The double entries to transfer those balances to the Trading Account are as follows:

Debit Purchases Returns Account, to clear the account, and credit Trading Account.
Debit Trading Account and credit Sales Returns Account, to clear the account.

We shall see in a moment that for the sake of an improved presentation in the Trading Account we do in fact not stick to strict double-entry, but use an 'accountants' licence', and deduct some items from the opposite side. For example, we show the Purchases and Purchases Returns as follows:

Purchases	23,856
Less Returns	1,058
Net purchases	22,798

More of this later, but it is useful to recognise at an early stage that *deductions* on the *debit* side of an account are *credits*; similarly, deductions on the *credit* side of an account are *debits*.

(*iii*) Stock requires special treatment. Remember that throughout the year the figure showing on the Stock Account is the opening stock at dawn on Day 1 of the new financial year. We shall close this off with a double-entry:

Debit the Trading Account with the opening stock figure, and credit Stock A/c to close the account.

We must now do a stock-taking check and arrive at a figure for Closing Stock. This is brought on to the books by a double entry:

Debit Stock Account to open the account for the coming year and credit Trading Account.

Actually we shall use the special presentation method referred to above instead of keeping to strict double entry.

NOTE: The closing stock *must* also appear as an asset in the Balance Sheet

We can follow both these double entries best by considering an example.

Example

At 31 December D. Walker's accounts show the following balances, among others:

Purchases £23,856; Purchases Returns £1,058; Sales £76,152; Sales Returns £778; Stock in hand (1 January) £8,915. A stock-taking at 31 December revealed that stock in hand at the end of the financial year was £13,453.

If we draw up the Trading Account sticking to the rules of strict double entry we would have a Trading Account as shown below.

TRADING ACCOUNT OF D. WALKER FOR YEAR ENDING 31 DEC. 19__

	£		£
Opening stock	8,915	Sales	76,152
Purchases	23,856	Purchases Returns	1,058
Sales Returns	778	Closing stock	13,453
Gross profit	57,114		
	£ 90,663		£ 90,663

The closed-off accounts will appear as shown below (but of course Stock Account has also been re-opened).

STOCK A/C

19__	£	19__	£
Jan. 1 Balance b/d	8,915	Dec. 31 Trading A/c	8,915
19_ 1 Trading A/c	13,453		

PURCHASES A/C

19__	£	19__	£
Dec. 31 Balance b/d	23,856	Dec. 31 Trading A/c	23,856

SALES A/C

19__	£	19__	£
Dec. 31 Trading A/c	76,152	Dec. 31 Balance b/d	76,152

PURCHASES RETURNS A/C

19__	£	19__	£
Dec. 31 Trading A/c	1,058	Dec. 31 Balance b/d	1,058

SALES RETURNS A/C

19__	£	19__	£
Dec. 31 Balance b/d	778	Dec. 31 Trading A/c	778

If we exercise our right to improve the presentation by deducting Purchases Returns from Purchases, Sales Returns from Sales and Closing Stock from 'Total stock available' we have a Trading Account as shown below.

TRADING ACCOUNT OF D. WALKER FOR YEAR ENDED 31 DEC. 19__

	£		£
Opening stock	8,915	Sales	76,152
Purchases	23,856	*Less* Sales Returns	778
Less		Net turnover	75,374
Purch. Ret.	1,058		
Net purchases	22,798		
Total stock available	31,713		
Less Closing stock	13,453		
Cost of goods sold	18,260		
Gross profit	57,114		
(to Profit and Loss A/c)			
	£ 75,374		£ 75,374

This method is preferred, and it will be seen that it produces exactly the same gross profit as the previous Trading Account.

Since gross profit appears as a *debit* in the Trading Account, this must be matched by a *credit* entry somewhere. The net profit is *carried down* to the *credit side* of the next account, which is called the *Profit and Loss Account*.

7. Net profit: expenses and the Profit and Loss Account

The Profit and Loss Account *continues the Final Accounts* by taking into account:

(a) *items of expense* that will further reduce the gross profit;
(b) any *gains* from sources other than those directly concerned with the normal trading of the business, e.g. a trader may let part of his premises at an annual rental of £800. This £800 would be *rent income*, and as such would increase his profit.

Example _____

Referring again to the nominal accounts in the Ledger of D. Walker suppose that other nominal accounts read as follows: Salaries Account £17,560; Repairs Account £496; Insurance Account £856; Travelling Account £752; Light and Heat Account £2,586; Telephone Expenses Account £1,235; Wages Account £11,560; Commission Received Account £1,420 and Rent Received Account £800.

We need not show the closing-off of all these accounts as the losses or profits are transferred to the Profit and Loss Account, but if we take one example of a loss (Salaries Account) and one of a profit (Rent Received Account) it will show what happens.

The Salaries Account has a debit balance of £17,560. The double entry is:

Credit Salaries Account to close the account for the year.
Debit Profit and Loss Account with the loss.

The Rent Received Account has a credit balance of £800. The double entry is:

Debit Rent Received Account (to close the account for the year).
Credit Profit and Loss A/c to take the profit into the calculation of net profit.

These accounts would look as shown below, and the other accounts would be similar. The Profit and Loss Account would reveal the true **net profit**.

SALARIES A/C

19__	£	19__	£
Dec. 31 Balance b/d	17,560	Dec. 31 Profit and Loss A/c	17,560

RENT RECEIVED A/C

19__	£	19__	£
Dec. 31 Profit & Loss A/c	800	Dec. 31 Balance b/d	800

PROFIT & LOSS A/C OF D. WALKER FOR THE YEAR ENDED 31 DECEMBER 19__

	£		£
Salaries	17,560	Gross profit (from	
Repairs	496	Trading A/c)	57,114
Insurance	856	Commission Recd	1,420
Travelling	752	Rent Recd	800
Light & Heat	2,586	Total	59,334
Telephone Exp.	1,235		
Wages	11,560		
Total	35,045		
Net profit (to	24,289		
Capital A/c)			
	£ 59,334		£ 59,334

(a) The net profit of £24,289 is a balancing figure inserted on the debit side of the Profit and Loss Account to enable the two sides to agree with each other. This *debit* must be reflected by a credit entry somewhere.

(b) *Ask yourself the questions:*

    (*i*) To whom does this profit belong? It belongs to D. Walker

    (*ii*) How can we give this to him? By crediting his Capital Account.

(c) The Capital Account of D. Walker will now appear as follows:

CAPITAL A/C (D. WALKER)

		£
	19__	
	Jan. 1 Balance b/d	50,000
	Dec. 31 Profit and Loss	24,289

> NOTE: Some accountants prepare a single continuous Trading and Profit and Loss Account. This makes no difference to the book-keeping, since the Trading Account simply appears as the top half of the account, the gross profit being carried down to start the second part, which is really the Profit and Loss Account.

---

8. Drawings

At the end of the year the Drawings Account will show a considerable sum drawn out by the proprietor for his/her personal use. This may be drawings in cash, or drawings in kind. The total in D. Walker's case is £16,500. Remember drawings are usually described as 'Drawings in expectation of profits made', and a prudent businessperson would draw as little as possible. The Drawings Account must now be cleared off into the Capital Account.

The double entry is:

Debit the Capital A/c, the proprietor is deemed to be receiving the money although in fact he received it over the year in numerous small amounts.

Credit Drawings Account to clear the account ready to start a new year.

DRAWINGS A/C

19__		£	19__		£
Jan. 1– Dec. 31	Sundry Drawings	16,500	31	Capital A/c	16,500

CAPITAL A/C

19__		£	19__			£
Dec. 31	Drawings	16,500	Jan. 1	Balance b/d		50,000
31	Balance	57,789		Profit and		
					Loss A/c	24,289
		£ 74,289				£ 74,289
			19__			£
			Jan. 1	Balance		57,789

(d) The closing balance on Capital Account can also be shown in tabulated form in the Balance Sheet.

Example ————————————————————————————

	£
Capital Jan. 1	50,000
Add Net profit	24,289
Less Drawings	16,500
	7,789
	57,789

9. The Final Balance Sheet

Having prepared the Trading and Profit and Loss Accounts by transferring certain amounts to them, we find that there are still some accounts which remain in the Ledger which have not been closed and on which we must bring the balances down.

(a) These balances which remain on the Ledger accounts will now be grouped together and shown as balances on a sheet of paper; hence the expression 'Balance Sheet'.

(b) If we set out the Trial Balance of D. Walker and mark those accounts whose balances have been transferred, we can see at a glance those balances which remain.

TRIAL BALANCE OF D. WALKER AS AT 31 DECEMBER 19__

Account	Dr £	Cr £	Cleared to:
Capital A/c		50,000	Changed to £57,789
Drawings A/c	16,500		Capital A/c
Purchases	23,856		Trading A/c
Purchases Returns		1,058	Trading A/c
Sales		76,152	Trading A/c
Sales Returns	778		Trading A/c
Stock at start	8,915		Changed to Closing Stock £13,453
Salaries	17,560		Profit & Loss A/c
Repairs	496		Profit & Loss A/c
Insurance	856		Profit & Loss A/c
Travelling	752		Profit & Loss A/c
Light and Heat	2,586		Profit & Loss A/c
Telephone Expenses	1,235		Profit & Loss A/c
Wages	11,560		Profit & Loss A/c
Commission Received		1,420	Profit & Loss A/c
Rent Received		800	Profit & Loss A/c
Debtors (Sundry accounts)	2,950		
Creditors (Sundry accounts)		876	
Mortgage on Premises		25,000	
Bank Loan		15,000	
Premises	55,000		
Plant and Machinery	18,000		
Fixtures and Fittings	2,800		
Motor Vehicles	3,750		
Cash in hand	557		
Cash at Bank	2,155		
£	170,306	170,306	

The reader should note the following points:

(a) All the items cleared to Trading A/c and Profit and Loss A/c led to the discovery of the net profit for the year.

(b) This net profit was added to the Capital Account, and the drawings were deducted from the Capital Account as the Drawings Account was cleared. As a result the Capital Account balance had changed to £57,789.

(c) Another account that had changed was the Stock Account; it now carries the Closing Stock figure not the Opening Stock figure.

(d) These two accounts, and all the other unclosed accounts, are to be carried to the Balance Sheet and appear as shown below.

D. WALKER'S BALANCE SHEET AS AT 31 DECEMBER 19__
(in correct European style)

	£			£
Fixed assets		Capital at 1 Jan. 19__		50,000
Premises	55,000	*Add* Net profit	24,289	
Plant and Machinery	18,000	*Less* Drawings	16,500	
Fixtures and Fittings	2,800			7,789
Motor Vehicles	3,750	Net worth to the owner		57,789
	79,550			
		Long-term liabilities		
Current assets	£	Mortgage	25,000	
Stock	13,453	Bank Loan	15,000	
Debtors	2,950			40,000
Cash at Bank	2,155			
Cash in Hand	557	*Current liabilities*		
	19,115	Creditors		876
	£98,665			£98,665

10. Listing the balances

Note that in the Balance Sheet shown above we have the assets listed on the left-hand side in the **order of permanence**, with the most permanent item (Premises) first, followed by the other fixed assets. Motor vehicles come last, as they are the easiest of the fixed assets to dispose of. Current assets are less permanent than fixed assets, and (hopefully) will be turned into cash within one month. Such assets are said to be more liquid (more easily turned into cash) than fixed assets. The most liquid items of all are cash at bank and cash in hand, which are already in liquid form.

We also have the liabilities in the order of permanence. The most permanent liability is the capital (it will only be repaid when the proprietor ceases to trade). Long-term liabilities are repayable over a long period (more than a year) while current liabilities are due for payment very soon, and certainly in less than a year.

We thus return at the end of the financial year to our starting-point — the Balance Sheet, i.e. a statement of the assets and liabilities of the business set out in a particular form.

It only remains for us to expand on these basic principles by introducing other accounts as the business grows in size to illustrate how other matters are dealt with in the accounts, and in particular their effect upon the Final Accounts and Balance Sheet.

Progress test 3

1. Given that opening stock is £500, purchases £6,000, sales £9,350 and closing stock £480, set out a Trading Account to find the gross profit.

Express this gross profit as a percentage of: (*a*) selling price; (*b*) cost price. **(4)**

2. If opening stock is £750, purchases £8,400, sales £19,700 and gross profit 25 per cent of the selling price, find the value of the closing stock. **(4)**

3. If opening stock is £250, sales £8,000, closing stock £300 and gross profit 20 per cent of selling price, find the value of the purchases. **(4)**

4. When opening stock is £700, purchases £9,200, closing stock £780 and gross profit is 100 per cent of cost price, find the value of sales. **(4)**

Specimen questions

1.   Set out a Trading Account, a Profit and Loss Account and a Balance Sheet from the following Trial Balance extracted at the end of May 19__, to show the result of the month's trading activities.

	£	£
Premises	56,000	
Capital		66,316
Bank	2,112	
Cash	304	
Sales		13,224
Purchases	4,000	
Van	2,000	
Equipment	6,000	
Stock, May 1	8,000	
Salaries	1,480	
Repairs	208	
Drawings	460	
Trade creditors		1,024
	£80,564	80,564

Stock on 31 May was valued at £7,840.

2.   T. William's financial year ended 31 August 19_6. His Trial Balance at that date included the following items:

Sales	£101,952
Sales Returns	1,140
Stock at Sept. 1, 19_5	4,134
Stock at Aug. 31, 19_6	5,442
Gross profit for year	55,203

You are required to calculate the: (*a*) purchases for the year; (*b*) cost of goods sold during the year; (*c*) gross profit percentage to sales. (Answer correct to 2 decimal places).   (*RSA*)

3.   Prepare a Trading and Profit and Loss Account and a Balance Sheet from the Trial Balance of M. Cooper at the end of December:

	£	£
Capital at start		8,326
Freehold Property	51,500	
Creditors		1,876
Debtors	2,536	
Sundry Expenses	170	
Purchases	26,033	
Telephone Expenses	1,565	
Sales		107,828
Stock at 1 Jan.	11,617	
Light and Heat	840	
Drawings	9,560	
Purchases Returns		1,254
Sales Returns	1,328	
Salaries and Wages	19,284	
Repairs	462	
Insurance	280	
Travelling Expenses	162	
Discount Allowed	360	
Commission Received		5,284
Rent Received		4,640
Mortgage on Premises		20,000
Loan (Finance House)		8,000
Fixtures	4,600	
Motor Vehicles	5,850	
Cash in hand	495	
Cash at Bank	4,726	
Plant & Machinery	15,840	
	£157,208	157,208

Closing Stock was valued at £14,592.

4. A. Limpet produced the following figures for the year ended 30 April 19_8:

Stocks 1 May 19_7 £4,355, 30 April 19_8 £1,365; sales £80,405; purchases £47,330; returns inwards £405; returns out £320; net expenses £20,000.

(a) You are required to prepare an abridged Trading and Profit and Loss Account for year ended 30 April 19_8, showing:

   (i) cost price of goods sold;
  (ii) turnover;
 (iii) calculation of percentage gross profit on cost;
 (iv) calculation of percentage gross profit on turnover;
  (v) calculation of percentage net profit on turnover.

(b) If the turnover increased by 25 per cent in the following year and the rate of gross profit remains the same, draw up an estimated Trading and Profit and Loss Account.

Assume that general expenses increase by 4 per cent (compound) for every £10,000 increase in turnover and that all stock is sold.

4
More about Final Accounts

1. Further points on the Trading Account

In preparing the Trading Account in Chapter 3 we only referred to six items, from five accounts. These were the 'Opening Stock' and 'Closing Stock' figures from the Stock Account, and the Purchases Account, the Purchases Returns Account, the Sales Account and the Sales Returns Account. There are actually one or two more items that can appear in the Trading Account and a word about them is necessary.

(a) *Carriage Inwards*. The effect of carriage paid on *goods purchased* is to increase the purchase price of the goods.

(i) *When we pay the carriage: debit* Carriage Inwards Account; *credit* Bank.

(ii) *In the Final Accounts, we transfer this cost to the Trading Account: debit* Trading Account; *credit* Carriage Inwards Account. In debiting the Trading Account it is usual to add this figure to the purchases figure, as it is virtually an increase in the cost of the goods purchased for re-sale.

NOTE: By contrast Carriage Outwards is carriage paid on goods sold. It is regarded as an overhead expense, since the trader is *not forced* to provide this service; it is an expense which he chooses to bear.

(i) *When we pay this carriage: debit* Carriage Outwards Account; *credit* Bank.

(ii) *In the Final Accounts, it is transferred to the Profit and Loss Account: debit* Profit and Loss Account; *credit* Carriage Outwards Accounts. The treatment of Carriage In and

Carriage Out can be seen in the sample exercise later in this chapter.

(b) *Customs duty on imported goods for re-sale.* Where goods are imported they frequently have to bear import duties and these are a further example of an increase in the cost of the purchases made. When the tax is paid the double entry is:

(*i*) Debit the Customs Duty Account which is receiving the sums paid (actually of course the recipient is HM Customs and Excise Department and the Customs Duty Account is a nominal account, receiving the money 'in name only')!

(*ii*) Credit Bank A/c, which is giving the money.

(*iii*) In the Final Accounts we shall transfer the total duty paid to the Trading Account (adding it to the Purchases) and clear the nominal account off, i.e. debit Trading Account; credit Customs Duty Account.

(c) *Stocktaking.* In examinations 'Closing Stock' is usually shown as a footnote to the Trial Balance, since the Final Accounts can not be prepared without this figure. In real life the figure for Closing Stock has to be found. Two methods are used to calculate its value.

(*i*) Large businesses keep separate records akin to costing records. These are called '**perpetual inventory**' methods.

(*ii*) Small businesses take a physical inventory of the stock.

Even large businesses with 'running stock records' must occasionally do a physical check, for pilfering may occur at any time and a store-keeper who is under pressure may also issue stock without updating the bin card or other 'perpetual inventory' record.

Physical inventory. In many businesses the physical inventory is preceded by a stock-taking sale, to clear shop-soiled or damaged items or unfashionable items, and thus reduce the work of stock-taking. Such a sale may reveal bad buying, a large proportion of 'shelf warmers' having been purchased by one particular buyer. Stock sold off in this way earns a smaller profit than usual, and unsold items at the end of the sale may even be sold at a loss, or be thrown away.

When the physical inventory starts it is usual to draw up a list of all the items normally kept in stock, to minimise the chance of omissions. The stock is then counted and valued. The method of valuation, 'cost price or net realisable value' NRV has been explained already (*see* 3:3). In practice this rule is applied to individual items of stock and is not a blanket value applied to all the stock.

Example

At the end of financial period a business has three items of stock, as follows:

	Cost	NRV
	£	£
A	100	120
B	80	60
C	210	280
	£ 390	£ 460

The closing stock will be valued as follows:

A at cost	£100
B at NRV	60
C at cost	210
	£370

(d) *Overheads shown in the Trading Account.* It is quite common for an accountant to charge some of the overhead expenses to Trading Account. For example, where a Manufacturing Account is not being used but overhead expenses are incurred in taking goods purchased into stock and perhaps in such activities as breaking bulk and re-packing prior to sale an element of Wages or supervision expenses may be entered in the Trading Account. Selling and distribution expenses are held to be items for the Profit and Loss Account, however, and most overheads will also be Profit and Loss Account items. We may therefore say that a fully developed Trading Account would be as shown:

T. SMART: TRADING FOR YEAR ENDED 31 DECEMBER 19__

	£		£
Opening Stock	5,850	Sales	117,650
Purchases	29,754	*Less* Returns In	3,650
Add			
Carriage In	496		114,000
Customs Duty on			
Imported Goods	3,854		
	34,104		
Less Returns Out	1,104		
	33,000		
Total stock available	38,850		
Less Closing Stock	11,795		
Cost of stock sold	27,055		
Warehouse Wages	13,585		
Warehouse Expenses	11,254		
Cost of sales	51,894		
Gross Profit (To P/L A/c)	62,106		
	£ 114,000		£ 114,000

2. Further points on the Profit and Loss Account

The Profit and Loss Account shows the income and expenditure of the business on its two sides, the income on the credit side and the expenditure on the debit side.

(a) *Income.* The gross profit, the main source of income of a trading business appears on the credit side.

Other items of income include:
 (*i*) rent income (often termed Rent Received);
 (*ii*) Interest Received;
 (*iii*) Commission income (Commission Received);

(*iv*) Discounts Received.

(b) *Expenditure or expenses*. These are debit items and are usually grouped under three headings in the Profit and Loss Account.

- (*i*) *Administrative expenses* include rent, rates and insurance, lighting and heating, salaries, office expenses, repairs and (usually) general expenses.
- (*ii*) *Selling and distribution expenses* include advertising, van expenses, travelling expenses, commission (also bad debts and discounts allowed), and carriage outwards.
- (*iii*) *Financial charges* include interest paid on loans and bank charges.

(c) *Wages and salaries*. Special mention should be made of wages and salaries, as often the position is not absolutely clear with this item.

When wages are incurred on improving or producing the goods sold they are charged to Trading Account as part of the cost of sales. If incurred on distribution, as a shop assistant or van driver, they are charged to Profit and Loss Account as a selling or distribution expense.

If both wages and salaries are given separately:

- (*i*) wages will be debited to Trading Account;
- (*ii*) salaries will be debited to Profit and Loss Account.

If one composite figure termed wages and salaries is given, this is debited to the Profit and Loss Account.

3. Example of Final Accounts prepared from a Trial Balance

From the following Trial Balance extracted from the books of A. Woods, prepare the Trading and Profit and Loss Accounts for the year ended 31 October 19__ and a Balance Sheet as at 31 October 19__.

A. WOODS — TRIAL BALANCE AS AT 31 OCTOBER 19__

	Dr	Cr
Cash	492	
Bank	3,370	
Purchases	25,330	
Sales		78,528
Returns Inwards	316	
Returns Outwards		521
Carriage Inwards	589	
Carriage Outwards	712	
Customs Duty on Imported Purchases	1,594	
Stock at start	4,950	
Interest Payable	812	
Drawings	9,575	
Premises	65,800	
Equipment	21,200	
Rent Received		2,024
Wages	17,375	
Salaries	14,660	
Commission Received		1,510
Advertising	2,814	
Capital A/c A. Woods		62,740
Debtors and Creditors	286	427
Motor Vehicles	9,250	
Mortgage on Premises		30,000
Loan — Helpful Finance		7,250
Light and Heat	1,250	
Rates and Insurance	2,625	
	£183,000	183,000

Stock on 31 October 19__, £7,134

Answer

A. WOODS—TRADING AND PROFIT AND LOSS ACCOUNTS
FOR THE YEAR ENDED 31 OCTOBER 19__

	£		£
Opening stock	4,950	Sales	78,528
Purchases	25,330	*Less* Returns Inwards	316
Add Carriage In	589	Net turnover	78,212
Customs Duty	1,594		
	27,513		
Less Returns Out	521		
	26,992		
	31,942		
Less Closing Stock	7,134		
Cost of stock sold	24,808		
Wages	17,375		
Cost of Sales	42,183		
Gross profit c/d	36,029		
	£78,212		£78,212
Administrative expenses:		Gross profit b/d	36,029
Salaries	14,660	Rent Received	2,024
Light and Heat	1,250	Commission Received	1,510
Rates and Insurance	2,625	Total	39,563
Selling Expenses:			
Advertising	2,814		
Carriage Outwards	712		
Financial charges:			
Interest Payable	812		
	22,873		
Net profit to			
Capital A/c	16,690		
	£ 39,563		£ 39,563

BALANCE SHEET AS AT 31 OCTOBER 19__

	£			£
Fixed assets			Capital at start	62,740
Premises	65,800		*Add* Net profit 16,690	
Equipment	21,200		*Less* Drawings 9,575	
Motor Vehicles	9,250			7,115
	96,250			69,855
Current assets			*Long-term liabilities*	
Closing Stock	7,134		Mortgage 30,000	
Debtors	286		Loan 7,250	
Bank	3,370			37,250
Cash	492		*Current liabilities*	
		11,282	Creditors	427
		£ 107,532		£ 107,532

Progress test 4

1. What items usually appear in a Trading Account? **(1)**

2. How do you deal with carriage inwards in the Trading Account? **(1)**

3. How do you deal with returns inwards? **(3)**

4. How do you deal with returns outwards? **(3)**

5. How is carriage outwards treated? **(3)**

6. Where do overhead expenses appear in the Final Accounts? **(2)**

7. How do you treat wages and salaries? **(2)**

Specimen questions

1. From the following trial balance of P. Syers prepare Trading and Profit and Loss Accounts for the year ended 31 March 19_1 and Balance Sheet as at that date:

	£	£
Capital April 1, 19_0		17,517
Drawings	11,250	
Stock on hand April 1, 19_0	3,875	
Purchases and Sales	24,923	166,758
Sales Ret. and Purchases Ret.	1,758	1,605
Carriage In	328	
Carriage Out	2,749	
Customs Duty on Purchases	1,925	
Wages (Trading A/c)	21,724	
Warehouse Expenses (Trading A/c)	5,284	
Salaries (offices)	19,365	
Rent and Rates	11,721	
Office Expenses	4,565	
Heat and Light	729	
Insurance (fire)	1,320	
Motor Vehicles	11,580	
Motor Expenses	640	
Office Equipment	5,965	
Cash in hand	321	
Debtors and Creditors	762	1,384
Bank balance	9,754	
Mortgage on Premises		45,000
Fixtures and Fittings	6,285	
Computers etc	13,256	
Premises	65,000	
Commission Received		4,925
Rent Received		3,800
Discount Allowed and Received	495	636
Advertising	2,795	
Selling Expenses	13,256	
	£ 241,625	241,625

Stock in hand at 31 March 19_1 £5,624

2. The following trial balance was extracted from the books of E. Smith, a sole trader, on 31 March, 19_7

	£	£
Capital April 1, 19_6		66,925
Drawings	17,580	
Stock on hand April 1, 19_6	5,956	
Purchases and Sales	34,279	163,425
Sales Ret. and Purchases Ret.	1,425	1,279
Carriage In	494	
Carriage Out	875	
Customs Duty on Purchases	1,356	
Wages (Trading A/c)	11,248	
Warehouse Expenses (Trading A/c)	5,865	
Salaries (offices)	29,320	
Business Rates	2,760	
Office Expenses	2,359	
Heat and Light	1,234	
Insurance (fire)	625	
Motor Vehicles	17,565	
Motor Expenses	2,350	
Office Equipment	19,716	
Cash in hand	1,250	
Debtors and Creditors	1,594	876
Bank balance	11,726	
Mortgage on Premises		36,000
Fixtures and Fittings	3,850	
Computers etc	8,640	
Premises	72,500	
Commission Received		994
Rent Received		1,586
Discount Allowed and Received	494	626
Advertising	3,854	
Selling Expenses	12,796	
	£ 271,711	271,711

Stock on 31 March 19_7 was £11,265.

Prepare a Trading and Profit and Loss Account for the year ended 31 March 19_7 and the Balance Sheet as at that date.

3. The following trial balance of J. Kennedy, although it adds up to the same total on both sides, is incorrect. You are asked to:

(a) draw up a corrected Trial Balance;
(b) Prepare the Final Accounts and Balance Sheet as at 31 March 19_5

	£	£
Capital April 1, 19_4		16,982
Drawings		15,624
Stock on hand April 1, 19_4	7,215	
Purchases and Sales	43,626	184,758
Sales Ret. and Purchases Ret.	1,758	395
Carriage In	1,124	
Carriage Out		568
Customs Duty on Purchases		8,808
Wages (Trading A/c)	11,280	
Warehouse Expenses (Trading A/c)	5,360	
Salaries (offices)	19,716	
Business Rates	3,840	
Office Expenses	5,250	
Heat and Light	620	
Insurance (fire)	495	
Motor Vehicles	12,010	
Motor Expenses	3,810	
Office Equipment	5,850	
Cash in hand	495	
Debtors and Creditors	1,762	4,858
Bank balance	4,250	
Mortgage	25,000	
Fixtures and Fittings	6,500	
Computers etc	8,725	
Premises	58,400	
Commission Received		2,650
Rent Received		3,450
Discount Allowed and Received	726	845
Advertising	3,950	
Selling Expenses	7,176	
	£ 238,938	238,938

Stock at 31 March 19_5 was £8,275.

5
More about stock

1. A closer look at cost

Where items are large and varied, e.g. a stock of secondhand cars, the cost of each item can be easily ascertained. When stock consists of numerous items of a similar nature acquired over a long period, the cost/value is more difficult to ascertain. This is particularly acute in periods of rising prices, and general principles of identifying cost must be applied. There are four main methods of ascertaining cost/value:

(a) first in, first out (FIFO);
(b) last in, first out (LIFO);
(c) weighted average cost (WAC);
(d) base stock.

2. First in, First out (FIFO)

This assumes that goods sold would be taken from the stock acquired at the earliest date of purchase. Goods forming part of the closing stock will be valued at the price paid for the latest goods acquired.

3. Last in, first out (LIFO)

Under this method sales are related to the goods most recently acquired and the stock valuation is based on the prices paid for the earliest goods acquired.

In times of inflation a much lower valuation of stock is arrived at when using LIFO as opposed to FIFO, since the prices used to value the stock may be those operating a long time ago.

4. Weighted average cost (WAC)

Whatever the actual cost, each item is deemed to cost the same. This figure is arrived at by dividing the total cost by the total number of units of stock. Each additional purchase requires a recalculation to update the average cost then applying.

Example

		£	£
100	units bought at £2 each	200	
50	units bought at £14 each	700	
So: 150	units cost a total of		900
60	units sold at a WAC of £6 each $\left(\text{i.e. } £\frac{900}{150} \right)$		360
90	units remaining deemed cost		540
10	units bought at £16 each		160
100	units deemed cost		£700

Any further goods sold before any additional purchases are made would be deemed to cost £7 each.

5. Base stock

This means that a certain quantity of stock is considered normal and unless there are violent fluctuations in stock levels, this figure is accepted and is based on the original cost. In effect it is LIFO carried back to the start of the business. In times of inflation this method gives a very low valuation and this is considered by many to be a commendable feature of this method.

6. Different methods compared

Different methods of arriving at the value of stock will result in different figures for gross profit. Since the closing stock for one year is the opening stock for the next, such differences will tend to even themselves out. In the first period of trading, however, substantial differences can occur.

Example

A trader has the following transactions for the six months to 30 June, 19_2:

19_2		Quantity	Price per unit £
Jan. 1	Purchases	600	1.00
Feb. 1	Purchases	200	1.40
15	Sales	200	1.50
Apr. 1	Sales	500	2.00
15	Purchases	300	1.50
Jun. 1	Purchases	300	2.10
15	Sales	100	2.50

Find the value of the closing stock under FIFO, LIFO, weighted average, and base stock methods, then prepare comparative Trading Accounts for the six months ended 30 June, 19_2.

Answer

19_2		Quantities In	Quantities Out	Bal.	FIFO In	FIFO Out	FIFO £	LIFO In	LIFO Out	LIFO £	Weighted average In	Weighted average Out	Weighted average £
Jan. 1	Purchases	600		600	600		600	600		600	600		600
Feb. 1	Purchases	200		800	280		880	280		880	280		880
15	Issues		200	600		200	680		280	600		220	660
Apr. 1	Issues		500	100		540	140		500	100		550	110
15	Purchases	300		400	450		590	450		550	450		560
Jun. 1	Purchases	300		700	630		1,220	630		1,180	630		1,190
15	Issues		100	600		140	£1,080		210	£970		170	£1,020

The value of the closing stock under the three methods is: FIFO, £1,080; LIFO, £970; weighted average, £1,020.

Using the base stock method, closing stock is valued at £600, being the original cost of 600 units.

The comparative Trading Accounts would appear thus:

TRADING ACCOUNT FOR THE SIX MONTHS TO 30 JUNE, 19–2

		FIFO £		*LIFO* £		*WA* £		*Base* £
Sales		1,550		1,550		1,550		1,550
Less Cost of sales:								
Purchases	1,960		1,960		1,960	1,960		
Less Closing stock	–1,080		–970		–1,020	–600		
		–880		–990		–940		–1,360
Gross profit		£670		£560		£610		£190

7. Stock adjustments

Very often it is impracticable to take a physical check of stock on the last day of the financial period, and, to arrive at the value of stock on hand, a check is made at a more convenient date, i.e. a few days before or a few days after the end of the financial period.

Careful records are kept of the stock movements during the intervening days, and in this way the value of the closing stock on the last day of the financial period can be calculated.

Example

Jay's financial year ends on 31 December 19__. It was found more convenient to take stock on 27 December when the stock on hand, valued at cost, was £3,750.

During the four days 28–31 December, the following records of stock movements were obtained:

Sales £200; sales returns £20; purchases £160; purchases returns £15.

Jay's profit margin is 25 per cent of the selling price on all goods. Calculate the value of stock on hand on 31 December 19__.

Stock at cost price 27 Dec.		£3,750	
Add Purchases			
28–31 Dec.	£160		
Less Returns Out	15		
		145	
		3,895	
Deduct Sales Dec.			
28–31	£200		
Less Returns In	20		
	180		
Less 25% profit	45		
Sales at cost price		135	
Stock at cost price 31 Dec.		£3,760	

(Having been purchased *after* the stocktaking, this item will be *included* in stock at 31 Dec.)

(Having been sold after the stocktaking, these goods will *not* be *included* in stock at 31 Dec.)

NOTE: If the stocktaking had been postponed until, say 5 January, then of course we would *add* back sales (at cost price), since these goods would have been on the premises on 31 December, and *deduct* purchases made before the taking of stock.

8. Summary of principles

The main points in deciding what goods are in stock on the last day of the financial year can be summarised as follows.

(a) Stock taken *before* the end of the year: *add* net purchases and *deduct* net sales (after adjusting to cost price).
(b) Stock taken *after* the end of the year: *add* net sales (after adjusting to cost price) and *deduct* net purchases.

NOTE: In the example shown, we were told the margin of profit on sales (25 per cent in this case). Sometimes in examinations we are told the mark-up on cost. Thus a 25 per cent mark-up on cost, by the usual formula:

$$\text{Selling Price} = \text{CP} + \text{mark-up}$$
$$= 100\% + 25\%$$
$$= 125\%$$

Therefore the selling price of goods (say £850) includes $\frac{25}{125}$ of profit

$= \frac{1}{5} = 20$ per cent.

So a 25 per cent $\left(\frac{1}{4}\right)$ mark-up is a 20 per cent $\left(\frac{1}{5}\right)$ margin.

The rule is:

100% mark-up is 50% margin on sales price

$\frac{1}{2}$ on mark-up is $\frac{1}{3}$ margin

$\frac{1}{3}$ "   "   " $\frac{1}{4}$ margin

$\frac{1}{4}$ "   "   " $\frac{1}{5}$ "   etc.

9. Insurance claims

Questions are frequently posed in examination papers to test a candidate's knowledge of the principles involved in valuing the stock at the close of business for the purpose of the annual accounts, and also for the calculation of the value of stock destroyed, e.g. in a fire, as the basis for a claim against an insurance company.

At this stage problems will require a knowledge of the normally accepted commercial practice that would be applied in the event of a claim being made, or as the basis for the valuation of the closing stock.

NOTE: It is particularly important that in questions of this type, *any stock given in the question at selling price must first be reduced to the equivalent cost price*. Consequently the question will always give either the basis of valuation or the profit margin (or mark-up on cost) in the particular line of goods.

10. Practical matters to watch

In valuing stock, the following points are of particular importance.

(a) *Purchases.* If an invoice has been passed through the books, i.e. Purchases Account debited and the customer credited, then this item is *included* as part of your stock, even though it may not be on your premises. If, however, the invoice is not passed through your accounts until delivery is effected, then the goods *are not included* in your stock until you actually receive them.

(b) *Sales.* If the goods have been invoiced to the customer, the Sales Account having been credited and the customer debited, then they are *not included* in your stock, even though the goods may still be on your premises awaiting delivery to or collection by the customer.

(c) *Returns inwards.* If you have issued a credit note (C/N) and have passed this through your accounts, then the goods *are included* as part of your stock, even if they are still in transit or, for any other reason, not on your premises. If you have not issued a C/N, then they are *not included* as part of your stock.

(d) *Returns outwards.* If you have received a C/N, and have passed this through your accounts, the goods are *not included* as part of your stock, even though the goods may still be in your possession awaiting actual return to the supplier.

(e) *Goods sent out on a 'sale or return' basis.* These goods are not charged out to the customers, the customers being simply informed of the value of the goods on a 'pro forma invoice'.

If the customer sells the goods he will make a profit and remit to you (the supplier) the price as stated on the pro forma invoice. If he cannot sell them they are simply returned to you, no charge having been made.

Such goods are *always included* as part of your stock in trade, even though they may be on someone else's premises.

Sample question
_____

H. Lockwood took stock on 31 December 19__, and the following information was obtained on that date.

Actual stock on the premises, valued at selling price £5,390. This figure included goods valued at £200 which had been sold on 30 December, but were still in the warehouse pending collection by the buyer.

A credit note had been received from Jones for goods returned at cost price £35; these goods were still in the warehouse on 31 December. Lockwood had issued a credit note to Kippax for goods returned valued at £40 selling price, but these goods were in transit on 31 December. Goods sent out to an agent on a sale or return basis, valued at £250 selling price, had not been taken into account.

Show your calculation of the value of the closing stock on 31 December 19__, which H. Lockwood should use in the preparation of his final accounts, assuming that the average profit margin on which he deals is 25 per cent on cost price.

Answer

(NB 1/4 on cost = 1/5 on selling price.)

Stock on 31 Dec., at selling price		£5,390
Less Profit margin 1/5		1,078
Stock on 31 Dec., at cost price		£4,312
Add Returns inwards		
Selling price	40	
Less Profit 1/5	8	
	Cost price 32	
Goods on sale or return: SP	250	
Less Profit 1/5	50	
	Cost price 200	
		232
		4,544
Deduct Goods sold, not yet delivered	200	
Less Profit 1/5	40	
	Cost price 160	
Returns outwards, pending despatch:	Cost price 35	
		195
Stock at cost price on 31 December 19___		£4,349

NOTE: In the above illustration the detailed workings reducing the figures to cost prices have been shown; in practice, it would be sufficient to show the net cost price figure.

11. Rate of stock turnover

Although the gross profit percentage is important to a business, the number of times this gross profit has been earned is even more important. Assuming that the stock of a business is reasonably constant, this gross profit expressed as a percentage of the stock is earned each time the stock is sold. Assuming that all the stock is sold, then the greater the number of times it is sold, the greater the total gross profit.

We use the expression rate of stock turnover to denote the

number of times the stock has been turned over during the year and this figure will be found by the formula:

$$\text{Rate of stock turnover} = \frac{\text{Cost of sales}}{\text{Average stock at cost price}}$$

Since stock is always valued at cost price, sales must also be reduced to cost price.

Since stocks fluctuate it is usual to use the figure representing the *average stock held*, and this is found by the formula:

$$\text{Average stock held} = \frac{\text{Opening stock + closing stock}}{2}$$

Example

The following figures relate to the accounts of a trader for the year ending 31 December 19__

Opening stock £5,500 Purchases for the year £26,425
Closing stock £8,575 Calculate the rate of stock turnover for the year.

	£
Opening stock	5,500
Purchases	26,425
	31,925
Less Closing stock	8,575
Cost of goods sold	£ 23,350

Average stock held

$$= \frac{£5,500 + £8,575}{2}$$

$$= \frac{£14,075}{2}$$

$$= £7,037.50$$

To find the rate of stock turnover:

Divide the *cost of goods sold* by the *average stock held*, i.e. £23,350 ÷ £7,037.50 = 3.3 times. Thus, the average stock has been 'turned over' 3.3 times during the year. Each time it turns over it makes a profit for the trader. Consequently any action the trader can take to increase the rate of stock turnover will be beneficial.

We can derive more useful information from this rate of stock turnover. For example, how long is the average item in stock?

$$\text{Time in stock} = \frac{12}{3.3} \text{ months} = 3.6 \text{ months};$$

$$\text{or} \quad \frac{52}{3.3} \text{ weeks} = 15.75 \text{ weeks};$$

$$\text{or} \quad \frac{365}{3.3} \text{ days} = 110.6 \text{ days}.$$

Is this a good rate of stock turn? We cannot say unless we know the goods being traded. It might be all right for bicycles, or furniture, or office equipment. It will not do for new laid eggs, newspapers or even ladies fashions.

12. Quantity columns

Figures for quantities can often be shown in the Trading Account to assist the work.

Sample question

In preparing the accounts of a bicycle dealer for the year ended 31 December 19__, the following information is extracted.

Stock 1 Jan. at cost £45 each	100 bicycles
Purchases for the year all at £45 each	400 bicycles
Stock 31 Dec. valued at cost	200 bicycles
The bicycles are sold at £100 each.	

You are required to set out a Trading Account, and from this account to set out answers to the following questions.

(a) How many bicycles were sold during the year?
(b) What were the total sales in £?
(c) What was the cost of the goods sold?
(d) What was the gross profit?
(e) What was the value of the average stock held?
(f) Calculate the rate of stock turnover.
(g) What is the percentage of gross profit on sales?
(h) What is the percentage of gross profit on cost price?
(i) If the retailer had sold the bicycles at £75 each, what would:
    (i) The percentage of gross profit on sales have been?
    (ii) The percentage of gross profit on cost price have been?

Answer

TRADING ACCOUNT FOR THE YEAR ENDED 31 DECEMBER 19__

Opening stock	100	at £45	£4,500	Sales 300 **(a)** at £100	**(b)** £30,000
Purchases	400	at £45	18,000		
	500		22,500		
Less Closing stock	200	at £45	9,000		
Cost of sales	300	at £45	13,500 **(c)**		
Gross profit			16,500 **(d)**		
			£ 30,000		£ 30,000

(e) Value of the average stock held:

$$\frac{£4,500 + £9,000}{2} = £6,750$$

(f) The rate of stock turnover:

$$\frac{\text{Cost of sales}}{\text{Average stock held}} = \frac{13,500}{6,750} = 2, \text{ i.e. twice a year}$$

(g) Gross profit as a percentage of sales:

$$\frac{£16,500}{£30,000} \times \frac{100}{1} = 55 \text{ per cent}$$

(h) Gross profit as a percentage of cost price:

$$\frac{16,500}{13,500} \times \frac{100}{1} = 122.2 \text{ per cent}$$

(sometimes referred to as the mark-up percentage)

(i) If the bicycles had been sold at £75 each:

Total sales would have been 300 at £75	=	£22,500
Less Cost of sales		13,500
Gross profit		£9,000

(*i*) Gross profit as percentage of sales:

$$\frac{£9,000}{£22,500} \times \frac{100}{1} = 40 \text{ per cent}$$

(*ii*) Gross profit as percentage of cost price:

$$\frac{£9,000}{£13,500} \times \frac{100}{1} = 66\frac{2}{3} \text{ per cent}$$

NOTE: When the word *turnover* is used on its own it means *net sales*, i.e. sales *less* returns. In the sample question above, turnover for the year to 31 December, 19__ is £30,000.

Progress test 5

1. What do you understand by the terms FIFO and LIFO?   **(1)**

2. What do you understand by the term WAC?   **(1)**

3. Give reasons why it may be impracticable to take stock on the last day of the financial year.   **(7)**

4. Outline the principles in arriving at the stock valuation:

   (a) when stock is taken *before* the end of the year;
   (b) when stock is taken *after* the end of the year.   **(8)**

5. Outline the importance of the purchases figure in arriving at the valuation of the stock on hand.   **(10)**

6. Why is it most important to record carefully details of stock movements towards the end of the year?   **(7)**

7. How do you find the cost price of the goods sold?   **(11)**

8. What do you understand by the 'rate of stock turnover'?   **(11)**

9. How do you calculate the rate of stock turnover? **(11)**

10. What do you understand by the 'average stock held'? **(11)**

11. How can you calculate the value of the average stock held? **(11)**

Specimen questions

1. Using the following information you are to draw up a simple statement in tabular form showing the value of closing stock at each stage of stock movement:

    (a) first in, first out method; and
    (b) last in, first out method.

January	Stock received	20 units	at £60
February	Stock issued	5 units	
March	Stock received	15 units	at £65
April	Stock issued	25 units	
May	No activity	—	
June	Stock received	5 units	at £70
July	Stock issued	8 units	

Assume there was no previous balance of stock brought forward into January.

    (c) If a business changed from LIFO to FIFO methods of valuation for its closing stock, what would be the effect on its gross profit in that year?

2. Mr. A. Trader has the following transactions in a certain product for six months to 30 June 19__:

January 1	purchases	600 items at £1.00 each
February 1	purchases	200 items at £1.20 each
February 15	sells	200 items at £1.50 each
April 1	purchases	300 items at £1.50 each
April 15	sells	400 items at £2.00 each
June 1	purchases	300 items at £2.00 each
June 15	sells	350 items at £2.50 each

You are required to compute:

(a) the gross profit earned during the period; and

(b) the value of the closing stock at 30 June 19_0 using *each* of the following alternative bases of valuation:

   (i) FIFO;

   (ii) LIFO;

   (iii) weighted average cost.

3. On 15 January the premises of A. Wood were damaged by fire. Last stocktake at year end was £32,900 while sales and purchases for period 1–15 January were £11,500 and £8,300 respectively. All goods subject to a gross profit of 50 per cent on sales. Stock salvaged amounted to £14,000. Prepare a statement giving your estimate of stock destroyed by fire.

4. A trader began stocktaking on 31 May, but it was not completed until 4 June. From the following details draw up a statement to show the value of stock (at cost price), on 31 May.

Value of stock in warehouse on completion of stocktaking £4,710.

Purchases 1–3 June, inclusive £260.

Sales 1–3 June, inclusive £480.

NOTES:

(a) The gross profit on all goods in which the business deals is 33 1/3 per cent of selling price.

(b) The value of stock in the warehouse included goods invoiced and charged to a customer at £75 but held in the warehouse pending delivery instructions.

5. Fenella's Fashions is a boutique run by Jon Stocker. The proprietor was abroad on a skiing holiday on 31 December, which was the year end for the business. In his absence the manageress forgot to take stock on the due date. The stock was counted on 14 January, in the sum of £68,471. Subsequent investigations revealed the following.

(a) Sales in the first fourteen days of the new year were £21,406, and that of this amount £16,720 was achieved during the new year sales when a mark up of 50 per cent on cost was used for pricing. The normal mark up is 100 per cent on cost.

(b) Goods purchased during the first fourteen days of the year cost £5,732 of which only £2,814 worth had been delivered by 14th January, and included in the count.

(c) Stock which cost £846 was considered too outdated for sale and was sold to a rag merchant for £83 on 6 January. This is to be counted as worth £83 on 31 December.

(d) Goods costing £2,400 ordered in November were delivered on 9th January. They are not to be counted as in stock on 31 December.

(e) Sales made in December totalled £42,801, but of this amount goods costing £1,263 were still not despatched as at 14 January. They are the property of the buyers.

(f) A page of the stock sheet for 14 January was overcast by £3,120 and another page was undercast by £416.

(g) Goods costing £1,658 were returned to the suppliers on 12 January.

(h) 260 dresses costing £18 each had been extended on the stock sheet at £1.80 each.

You are required to compute the stock figure as at 31 December. All calculations to the nearest £1.

6. From the details given below, calculate:

   (a) the rate per cent of gross profit on turnover;
   (b) the rate per cent of net profit on turnover;
   (c) the cost of goods sold;
   (d) the rate of turnover of stock (correct to one decimal place).

   Stock — 1 January, £5,382   Returns inwards £2,320
   Stock — 31 December, £8,386 Returns outwards £1,200
   Sales — £79,760   Office expenses £30,976
   Purchases — £35,180

7. R, who is at present employed at a salary of £16,000 per annum, is considering investing his savings in a small shop with

a flat above. What will be the gains and losses? Should R take the shop?

You are asked to prepare a statement on which to base his decision, using the information given below for your calculations.

The price asked for the freehold property, shop fittings and goodwill is £49,600 and for the stock is £22,400 valued at cost. The stock consists of product E which cost £3,200, product F which cost £8,400 and product G which cost £10,800. Debtors and creditors would not be taken over and may be ignored.

The rates of gross profit on products E, F and G, *calculated as percentages of selling prices,* are estimated at 40, 30 and 10 respectively, and the annual stock turnover rates (based on existing stock levels) are expected to be 3 for E, 4 for F and 10 for G.

Annual business expenses other than wages are estimated at £5,600.

If R bought the shop he would work in it full time, and his wife would also give up her present part-time job at £2,800 per annum to help him. R and his wife would give up their present accommodation which they rent at £2,400 per annum and would occupy the flat above the shop.

If R does not buy the shop he can invest his savings at 10 per cent per annum, the degree of risk being about the same.

Ignore taxation and inflation.

6

Subsidiary books and sources of information

1. Sources of information

Book-keeping began with the entry of all transactions into *one book*, the Ledger, which recorded the details of transactions. To simplify the work in the Ledger, while retaining the principle of having a means of referring to the details of any transactions, certain transactions are put into books of their own, thus enabling work to be dealt with by different members of staff. Such books are called *subsidiary books*. The entries are made in chronological order, and hence, they are often called 'day books' or 'Journals'. The common ones are the Purchases Day Book, the Sales Day Book, the Purchases Returns Book, the Sales Returns Book, the Cash Book, the Petty Cash Book and the Journal Proper. Of course, all such records can be computerised, and often today these books of original entry are stored electronically and become available as printouts.

All entries in books of account must be supported by documentary evidence, and these books are written up from the details provided by the following documents.

(a) *Invoice*. This is made out by the seller, usually in triplicate at least, and will be sent:

(*i*) *to the buyer*; the buyer will enter the details in his/her Purchases Book, debiting Purchases Account in total at the end of each month, crediting the account of the seller with the individual amount. The seller becomes a creditor in the buyer's books.

(*ii*) *to the Accounts Dept of the seller*; the seller will debit the item to the account of the buyer, entering the details in the Sales Day Book, the total of which will be credited to the Sales Account at the end of the month. The buyer becomes a debtor in the seller's books.

(*iii*) *to the Sales Dept of the seller*; often after use as a delivery note. It is used to deal with queries.

(b) *Credit note* (C/N). Sent by the seller to the buyer following a complaint.

(*i*) the seller will enter the details in his/her Returns Inwards Book, taking the total to the debit of the Returns Inwards Account at the end of each month; the individual items being credited to the account of the buyer;

(*ii*) the buyer will debit the account of the seller and enter the details in his/her Returns Outwards Book, taking the total to the credit of Returns Outwards Account at the end of each month.

(c) *Debit note or supplementary invoice.* Sent by the seller to the buyer to correct for an undercharge on the original invoice. For all practical purposes this is treated in exactly the same way as an invoice.

(d) *Cheques received* form the basis for entries on the debit side of the Bank Account in the Cash Book, the account of the debtor being credited with the amount of the cheque.

(e) *Cheques paid* form the basis for entries on the credit side of the Bank Account in the Cash Book, the account of the creditor being debited with the amount of the cheque.

> NOTE: With many systems nowadays the Cash Book entries are made at the same time as the cheques are made out.

(f) *Cash received* would be debited in the Cash Account in the Cash Book and credited to the debtor who paid it, or to the Sales Account if it was cash sales. Cash paid would be credited in the Cash Account in the Cash Book and debited to an appropriate account, often a nominal account like Wages Account, Postage Account, etc.

(g) *Petty cash vouchers* cover payments entered on the credit side of the Petty Cash Book, individual expense accounts being debited at the end of each month.

BREAK-DOWN OF ORIGINAL ENTRIES

Function of Day Book	Name given to subsidiary book	Documents from which details are entered
Book to record details of *credit* purchases	Purchases Day Book or Purchases Journal	Incoming invoices and supplementary invoices and debit notes
Book to record details of *credit* sales	Sales Day Book or Sales Journal	Copies of outgoing invoices
Book to record details of purchases returns or returns outwards	Purchases Returns and Allowances Journal or Returns Outwards and Allowances Book	Incoming credit notes
Book to record details of sales returns or returns inwards	Sales Returns and Allowances Journal or Returns Inwards and Allowances Book	Copies of credit notes sent out
Book to record all cash and bank and cash discount transactions	Three-Column Cash Book We may find a Four-Column Cash Book — the extra column being for VAT purposes.	*Debit entries:* (a) Receipts given for cash, or till slips (b) Incoming cheques *Credit entries:* Cheque counterfoils. Receipts for cash paid, or invoices (paid in cash)
Book to deal with small cash payments.	Petty Cash Book	Petty cash vouchers

(h) *The Journal Proper.* Originally the Journal Proper contained details of all transactions. Now it plays the important part of recording the details of any transaction that cannot be recorded in any other subsidiary book.

NOTE: Before any entry is made in the Ledger it must first be recorded in one or other of these subsidiary books. This means that the full details of transactions will be available in chronological order while the bulk of the work in the Ledger will be reduced. We will now be posting totals only from these subsidiary books into the nominal accounts in the Ledger (such as Purchases Account and Sales Account).

For examination purposes you will be required to be able to write up formal day books containing details of transactions. In practice, much of this work has been computerised.

2. Details contained in subsidiary books

The day books or subsidiary books are mainly concerned with showing the details of invoices and other documents relating to transactions. Accordingly, they will show details of:

(a) *prices per article* and the appropriate quantity which should agree with the quantity ordered;

(b) *trade discount* which represents a reduction in the price of goods;

> NOTE: Trade discount need be recorded only in the subsidiary books, since this represents a reduction in the price of goods. It does not appear in a Ledger Account at any time.

(c) *extra charges* made for packing material and/or carriage charged on the goods;

(d) *value added tax.*

3. Value added tax (VAT)

VAT is a tax which a business must *add* to the price it charges for goods and/or services. The standard rate is 17.5 per cent at present, added to the selling price and although businesses are involved in calculating the tax and collecting it from their customers, it is ultimately borne by the consumer. Since VAT rates may change at the whim of the Chancellor a rate of 10 per cent has been used in the examples in this book.

(a) *Business involvement.*

      (*i*) All businesses in the chain of distribution are involved in the calculation and collection of VAT (unless exempt:

see **(c)** (*ii*)), and have to register with Customs & Excise (C & E).

    (*ii*) Businesses with a turnover of less than £36,600 p.a. need not register (*see* **(c)**).

(b) *Input Tax and Output Tax*

    (*i*) A business registers with C & E and adds VAT to its selling prices. This VAT is referred to as *output tax*. The business collects this money from its customers.

    (*ii*) When the business buys goods or incurs expenses which attract VAT it must pay this VAT to its suppliers. VAT included in such purchases is referred to as *input tax*.

    (*iii*) Input tax can be set off against output tax, i.e. the business will pay over to C & E the tax it charges on its sales *less* the tax it has paid to suppliers of goods and services.

    (*iv*) VAT is payable to C & E every three months.

Example

Manufacturer (M) sells 100 articles to wholesaler (W) for £100.

Wholesaler (W) adds a gross profit of 20 per cent and sells goods to retailer (R).

Retailer (R) adds profit of 25 per cent and sells goods to final consumer (C).

VAT calculation		*Tax paid to Customs & Excise for ten articles*		
M sells 100 at £1 each				
to W	£100	M Output tax		£1
plus VAT 10%	10			
	£110			
W sells to R		W Output tax	1.2	
10 at £1 + 20% profit	12	Less Input tax		
plus VAT 10%	1.2	paid to M	1.0	.2
	13.2			
R sells to C 10 at £1.20		R Output tax	1.5	
+ 25% profit	15	Less Input tax		
plus VAT 10%	1.5	paid to W	1.2	.3
Price to consumer	£16.5	Total VAT		
		on ten articles		£1.5

(Equal to the final VAT charge made to the consumer.)

(c) *Relief from VAT*. There are two methods by which relief is given.

(*i*) *Zero rating*, i.e. the rate is 0 per cent. The firm does not have to charge tax to its customers but can reclaim any input tax paid to its suppliers.

(*ii*) *Exemption*.

(1) A firm supplying exempt goods or services does not have to charge any output tax — but is not entitled to reclaim any input tax.

(2) A business with a turnover of less than £36,600 p.a. *need not* register and therefore need not charge VAT on sales. If it does not register, however, it cannot reclaim input tax paid to its suppliers.

(d) *Recording VAT*. Where VAT is charged on invoices by a supplier it is recorded by what is called the 'Normal Method', with tax invoices and tax credit notes recorded in the four day books — the Purchases Day Book, the Sales Day Book, the Purchases Returns Book and the Sales Returns Book. A VAT column (or in computerised systems some system of VAT data capture) collects the input tax and output tax and records it in a VAT Account. Where a retailer (a word which in VAT parlance means anyone who supplies goods or services without using invoices) supplies goods or services the figures are collected using one of the Special Schemes for Retailers. There are 12 different schemes, but the details need not worry us at this point. The Simplex VAT Book, from George Vyner Ltd, Holmfirth, Huddersfield HD7 1BR is the best for these records. Here we need only refer to the 'Normal Method'.

(e) *Purchase Day Book* (PDB). This records in the books of the buyer the individual purchases made. Each supplier will be credited, but at the end of the month the columns for purchases and for VAT are totalled and these totals are debited to the appropriate accounts. Thus the VAT input tax will go to the debit side of the VAT Account since Customs and Excise Department are debtors for this tax (we are entitled to get it back).

(f) *The Sales Day Book* (SDB). In dealing with sales, cash sales will be recorded under the Special Schemes referred to above. Where sales are invoiced the invoices will be entered in the Sales Day Book (*see* Example below).

Example

Sales Day Book of J. Small, a wholesaler, recording the details of sales on credit

SALES DAY BOOK FOLIO 98

Date 19__	Particulars	Ledger Folio	Details	Total	VAT	Total invoice
Sept.7	F.T. Smuts & Son		£	£	£	£
	6 doz vases at £10 per doz		60			
	2 doz pans at £15 per doz		30			
	Assorted crockery at £120		120			
			210			
	Less 33⅓% trade discount	DL72	70	140	14	154
22	F. A. Pickaxe					
	2 boxes crockery at £20 per box		40			
	7 doz cups & saucers at £15 per doz		105			
	20 bowls at £1.25 each		25			
			170			
	Less 33⅓% trade discount	DL54	56.67	113.33	11.33	124.66
				253.33	25.33	278.66
				total taken to the credit of Sales A/c	total taken to the credit of VAT a/c	Individual items in this column are debited to personal accounts

If this represents all the items for the month of September the double entry of the accounts in the Ledger would be completed as follows:

Dr	SALES ACCOUNT			Cr
			SDB	£
		Sept. 30 Sundries	98	253.33

We are now posting a total from a subsidiary book, thus we use the term sundries.

VAT

			SDB	£
		Sept. 30 Sundries	98	25.33

F. T. SMUTS & SON (72)

	SDB	£
Sept. 7 Sales	98	154.00

F. A. PICKAXE (54)

	SDB	£
Sept. 22 Sales	98	124.66

NOTE: (1) Individual items are debited to the personal accounts of the buyers, reflected by corresponding credits in Sales Account and VAT Account. (2) Compare the detail shown in the Sales Day Book with the record necessary in the Ledger. A little thought will show that if we normally add the Sales Day Book every month, then Sales Account will have only twelve entries relating to credit sales, plus, of course, any entries for cash sales. This means that the work in the Ledger is considerably reduced.

Example

Where zero-rated items enter the picture typical entries might be:

Purchases Day Book of J. Small.

FOLIO 73

INVOICE		SUPPLIER		Liable at 10%	Liable at zero rate	Deductible VAT input tax
Date	No.		Total			
19__			£	£		
Sept. 6	25	*D. Flick & Sons*	132	120		12
14	26	*F. Dan & Co.*	22	20		2
27	27	*U. Fly & Co. Ltd*	95	—	95	—
			249	140	95	14

The relevant entries in the Ledger of J. Small would appear as follows. The VAT Account is of course being continued with this further entry.

Dr			VAT		Cr
19__	*PDB*	£	19__	*SDB*	£
Sept. 30 Sundries	73	14	Sept. 30 Sundries	98	25.33

	PURCHASES ACCOUNT		
19__	*PDB*	£	
Sept. 30 Sundries	73	235	

D. Flick & Sons			
	19__	*PDB*	£
	Sept. 6 Purchases	73	132

F. Dan & Co.			
	19__	*PDB*	£
	Sept. 14 Purchases	73	22

U. Fly & Co. Ltd.			
	19__	*PDB*	£
	Sept. 27 Purchases	73	95

(g) VAT and returns. When goods are returned or a credit note is given for an allowance off the invoice price an adjustment must be made for VAT.

In larger organisations Returns Inwards and Returns Outwards Books are kept in a very similar way to Purchase and Sales Day Books (in smaller firms returns are sometimes recorded in red ink but the principle is the same).

In addition to VAT care must be taken to deduct trade discount where this was given on the original transaction.

Example _____

If F. T. Smuts & Son returned on 30 September, 2 doz. vases sold to them on 7 September the credit would be made up as follows:

2 doz. vases at £10 per doz.		20.00
Less Trade discount (33⅓%)		6.67
		13.33
Add VAT		1.33
		14.66

and the entries would be:

RETURNS INWARDS DAY BOOK

Credit Note				Liable at	VAT
		To whom	*Credit note*	*10% cost excl.*	*output tax*
Date	*Number*	*given*	*total*	*VAT*	*credited*
19__ Sept. 30	36	*F.T. Smuts & Son*	14.66	13.33	1.33

To complete these entries three accounts would be affected thus:

RETURNS INWARDS

19__		
Sept. 30 Sundries		13.33

F. T. SMUTS & SON

19__		SDB		19__	
Sept. 7 Sales	98	154.00		Sept. 30 Returns inwards	14.66

VAT a/c

19__		PDB		19__		SDB
Sept. 30 Sundries	73	14.00		Sept. 30 Sundries	98	25.33
do	RIB	1.33				

(h) *Returns Outwards.* If certain of the goods purchased from D. Flick & Son were returned, say one third of the total, on 30 September, the entries would be:

RETURNS OUTWARDS DAY BOOK

	Credit Note Number	From whom received	Total	Liable at 10%	Deductible VAT input tax
Date					
Sept. 30	4	D. Flick & Sons	44	40	4

RETURNS OUTWARDS

		19__	
		Sept. 30 Sundries	40.00

D. FLICK & SONS

19__			19__		PDB	
Sept. 30 Returns	44.00		Sept. Purchases	73	132.00	

VAT a/c

19__			19__			
Sept. 30 Sundries			Sept. 30 Sundries			
	PDB	14.00			SDB	25.33
	RIB	1.33			ROB	4.00
Balance c/d		14.00				
		£ 29.33				£29.33
			19__			
			Oct. 1 Balance b/d			14.00

The balance of £14.00 represents the amount due to the Customs & Excise and in this example a cheque would be paid for that amount.

When it is customary for the business to grant a cash discount the VAT is calculated at 10 per cent on the net amount receivable. If the invoice is for £100 less 5 per cent cash discount then VAT is 10 per cent on £95 not on £100.

VAT ACCOUNT
Period 1 Jan 19__ to 31 March 19__

	Tax deductible			Tax due	
	£			£	
Input tax			Output tax		
January	810		January	982	
February	743		February	793	
March	821		March	856	
		2,374			2,631
			Tax due on imported goods and goods ex warehouse		
			January	43	
			February	26	
			March	64	
					133
Total tax deductible	2,374				
Tax payable (Bank A/c)	390				
	£2,764				£2,764

It must also be remembered that tax is payable on services, e.g. telephone charges. The VAT included in this account is available for set off in exactly the same way as that paid on purchases. Throughout this chapter examples have been kept extremely simple but the above is a specimen of a VAT account as published by HM Customs & Excise. The reader is also reminded of the important part played in VAT Accounts by the twelve Special Schemes for Retailers referred to earlier.

Progress test 6

NOTE: *Students attempting this test and the exercises to this chapter may feel it is difficult, without appropriately ruled paper. Schools and colleges requiring supplies of such paper should approach Formecon Services Ltd who do sell special rulings for Day Books, Ledger, Running Balance Ledger, Petty Cash and similar pages. Their address is: Formecon Services Ltd, Gateway, Crewe, CW1 1YN.*

1. A. Cooke is in business in the grocery trade. Some of his transactions are listed below. You are asked to tabulate a statement showing the subsidiary book into which they would

be entered and naming the accounts which receive immediately, or ultimately, the debit and credit entries.

(a) Paid rent by cheque.
(b) Sold goods to F. Smith on credit.
(c) Bought goods from T. Jones on credit.
(d) Sold goods to A. Room who paid in cash.
(e) Received credit note from M. Lampard.
(f) R. Matthew's cheque which Cooke had paid into bank was returned, marked 'refer to drawer'.
(g) Purchased from Motor Traders Ltd a supply of petrol and oil, for cash.
(h) Withdrew a sum of money from bank to restore the imprest figure on petty cash.

Your answer should take the following form:

Transaction	Subsidiary book	Account debited	Account credited
(a)	Cash Book	Rent	Bank

2. Write up the Purchases Day Book, Sales Day Book and Returns Inwards book from the following transactions of H. L. Bush, furniture manufacturers. VAT is to be taken as at 10% on all items, after Trade Discount (if any) has been deducted.

19__

May 4 Sold on credit to P. Dunn.
      8 fireside chairs at £83 each
      6 bedroom chairs at £45 each
      2 wardrobes at £57 each
      (All subject to 40 per cent trade discount)
   6 Purchased on credit from XF Co. timber value £340
   8 Purchased on credit from Ven Supplies Ltd veneer
      sheets at £215.50
   9 Sold on credit to W. Tait
      2 bedroom suites style 'B' at £198.50 each
      2 bedroom suites style 'A' at £252.50 each
      2 dining-room suites Type 'X' at £310.50 each
      (Trade discount of 40 per cent on all items)

12 Sent credit note to P. Dunn for overcharge of £3 each on the wardrobes sold to him on 4th May

14 Purchased on credit from G. Parker & Co.
   40 yds Rexine at £3.50 per yard
   60 yds simulated leather PVC at £2.60 per yard
   Plastic bindings £30.70
   (Total invoice subject to 45 per cent trade discount)

16 Sold on credit to Better Furnishers Ltd
   5 occasional tables at £45 each
   12 television chairs at £22 each
   6 television tables at £30 each
   4 tea trolleys at £36 each
   4 telephone tables at £35.50 each
   (Trade discount of 40 per cent on all items)

Specimen questions

1. Enter the following transactions of M. Hamilton into the correct books of original entry, post to the Ledger, balance where necessary and extract a Trial Balance of this limited range of accounts on 30 April. Assume VAT at 10 per cent on all transactions.

19__

Apr. 26 Sold to W. Smith: 2 inner spring mattresses at £95.50 each, and 2 divan bases at £40 each. All less 25 per cent trade discount.

27 Bought from Novo & Co. Ltd 12 pillows at £4.60 each. Less 33⅓ per cent trade discount.

29 W. Smith returned 1 inner spring mattress invoiced on 26th April — soiled. Sent him a credit note.

30 Sold to W. Smith: 6 cot mattresses at £6.50 each.

2. (a) Enter the following credit transactions in the appropriate accounts in the Sales and Purchases Ledgers and in the Bank A/c, etc. Balance the accounts at the end of May, and take out a Trial Balance. You do not need to make the entries in the books of original entry.

			List price £	VAT %
May	1	Bought goods from P. Ellison (20 per cent trade discount is allowed)	150	10
	3	Sold goods to G. Brandon	300	10
		Sold goods to R. Strong	200	10
	7	Returned goods to P. Ellison (don't forget the trade discount).	50	10
	8	G. Brandon returned goods	40	10
	10	Settled P. Ellison's account less 2½ per cent cash discount		
	13	Sold goods to R. Strong	200	
	18	Sold goods to G. Brandon	300	10
	24	G. Brandon settled his account by cheque, in full.		
	29	Bought goods from P. Ellison (this transaction subject to 25 per cent trade discount)	200	10

(b) Write up the VAT account in the general ledger.
(*Note:* 10 per cent may not be the rate ruling at the time of examination, but it is selected for its convenience in calculations.)

3. D. Jones, a wholesale dealer in electrical goods, has three departments: (a) Hi Fi; (b) TV; and (c) Sundries. The following is a summary of D. Jones' sales invoices during the period 1 to 7 February 19__:

		Invoice no.	Department	List price less trade discount	VAT	Total invoice price
				£	£	£
Feb.	1	P. Small	261	TV	2,600	260	2,860
	2	L. Goode	262	Hi Fi	1,800	180	1,980
	3	R. Daye	263	TV	1,600	160	1,760
	5	B. May	264	Sundries	320	nil	320
	7	L. Goode	265	TV	900	90	990
		P. Small	266	Hi Fi	3,400	340	3,740

(a) Record the above transactions in a columnar book of original entry and post to the General Ledger in columnar form.

(b) Write up the personal accounts in the appropriate ledger.

7
Cash Book and Petty Cash Book

1. The Four-column Cash Book

The Cash and Bank Accounts are taken out of the Ledger and put into *one* book, thus enabling one person, the cashier, to be responsible for this aspect of the work. The principle of double entry remains unchanged, but now these *two* accounts will be kept in one book with separate columns for each account, lying alongside one another.

(a) This book is further enlarged and converted into a subsidiary book by the inclusion of separate columns for recording the details of *cash discount* (hence the expression 'three-column Cash Book'). Since discount can be given to those who pay us (discount allowed) and can be deducted by us when we pay others (discount received) we have a discount column on each side of the book, but it is a memorandum column in each case — not an account like the Cash Account and the Bank Account.

(b) Since VAT enters into many transactions today it is helpful to have similar memorandum columns for VAT on either side of the Cash Book, although entries will be much more common on the credit side (when we buy small items) than on the debit side.

> NOTE: The difference between a Memorandum Column and an account is that entries in the Cash Account and Bank Account are part of the double entry system and therefore part of the Ledger — whereas Memorandum Columns are for memory purposes only, and have to be taken to Ledger Accounts, such as the Discount Allowed Account (a loss of the business) or Discount Received Account (a profit of the business) or VAT Account (the account of HM Customs and Excise).

It is important to note that the Cash Book has two functions.
(*i*) It is part of the ledger system since it contains the Cash Account and the Bank Account.
(*ii*) It is also a subsidiary book recording the details of cash discount and VAT, and providing convenient totals.

2. Cash Book ruling

In Fig. 7.1 below is an illustration of a crossed cheque which merits careful study. Then Fig. 7.2 shows some entries

Figure 7.1 *A crossed cheque*

NOTES:

1 The cheque is an order to a banker to pay money to a named person.

2 The banker in this case is Barclays, High Street, Caxton, London.

3 They are ordered to pay Symphonia Musicale (Camside) Ltd, £2,096.84. This is written both in words and figures.

4 The cheque is signed by J M England, who is called the drawer of the cheque.

5 20-99-93 is the computer code for the Caxton branch which will have to pay the money.

6 The computer codes at the bottom of the cheque show the cheque number, the branch number and the account number of J M England. Note that before the cheque is processed through the electronic system the bank at which the cheque is paid in will encode the amount of the cheque (£2,096.84) in machine code on the end of this computer code line. The computer can then read all the information it needs to make the entry in the bank's records.

CHANCELLOR Accounting Paper   Four Column Cash Book

Folio No. CB 1

19.. Month	Day	Dr. (Receipts) Details:	Folio No.	VAT £ p	Disc. Allowed £ p	Cash £ p	Bank £ p	19.. Month	Day	Cr. (Payments) Details:	Folio No.	VAT £ p	Disc. Received £ p	Cash £ p	Bank £ p
Jan	1	Opening Balance	J1			50 00	2,320 00	Jan	1	Postage	GL12				5 80
	1	Cash Sales (£115·00)	GL1	11 50		126 50			2	Motor Expenses (£12·27)	GL13	1 23			13 50
	2	A. Palmer	CL1		1 08		42 16		3	Fares	GL4			11 55	
	2	Cash Sales (£214·18)	GL1	21 42		235 60			3	M. Lucas	DL1		4 96		94 28
	3	Cash Sales (£168·73)	GL1	16 87		185 60			4	Bank	C			427 50	
	4	Cash	C				427 50		5	Wages	GL15				72 50
	4	Cash Sales (£479·59)	GL1	47 96		527 55			6	Sundry Expenses (£1·77)	GL18	= 18		1 95	
	5	Rent Received	GL6				50 00		6	Balance	c/d			1,767 85	2,671 08
	5	Commission Received	GL7				17 50									
	5	Cash Sales (£451·23)	GL1	45 12		446 35									
	6	Cash Sales (£533·86)	GL1	53 39		587 25									
			£	196 26	1 08	2,208 85	4,167 85				£	1 41	4 96	2,208 85	2,957 16
					(GL4)	(GL40)							(GL4)	(GL10)	
Jan	7	Balance	b/d			2,208 85	2,617 08								

Figure 7.2 *The Four-column Cash Book.*

Ref. FC5.4 Published and supplied by Formecon Services Ltd., Gateway, Crewe, CW1 1YN. Tel. 0270 500800
© Formecon Services Ltd., 1989

NOTES:

(a) The page is divided down the middle with a four-column ruling on each side. The left-hand side is the debit side, where cash received and cheques received are recorded. The other two columns are not accounts, but only memorandum columns where we collect together some useful information. The right-hand side is the credit side where cash paid and cheques paid (credit the giver) are recorded. Once again the other columns are only memorandum columns.

(b) Whenever you make an entry on the debit side of the Four-Column Cash Book you put (i) the date, (ii) the name of the person or account that is giving the money to the business, (iii) the amount received in the Cash column (if it was cash) or in the Bank column if it was a cheque. Note that if we have a till and take money from customers it doesn't matter whether they pay in cash or by cheque or by credit card vouchers we regard it all as 'cash' for that day and enter the figure as 'cash sales' in the Cash column. VAT can be treated differently in different businesses according to which VAT scheme they choose. In this example VAT has been recorded at 1/11 (the VAT fraction for 10 per cent VAT). The other 10/11 is recorded alongside the words 'cash sales' to show the actual sales made. You might like to check that the VAT is 10 per cent of this sales figure.

(c) Going down the debit side now we have:

(i) the opening balances in the Cash Account and Bank Account coming in from the page above the previous week.

(ii) Each day we have cash sales being recorded (Jan. 1, 2, 3, 4, 5 and 6).

These amounts are the amounts cashed up at closing time from the tills, and recorded in the Cash Account. The VAT element is entered in the VAT column and the amount to go to Sales Account is written in the details column. We shall need it when we post the cash sales to the Sales Account, net of VAT.

(iii) We also received three other items — all cheques — A. Palmer (a debtor) paid us £42.16 after taking discount of £1.08 and we received some rent from a sub-tenant and some commission.

(iv) The only other item is a contra entry for £427.50. Notice that this money is coming into the Bank Account. Where is it coming from? The details column tells us the Cash Account is giving us this money. If we look across to the right-hand side of the Cash Book we shall see that there is an exactly similar entry on that side. This entry says that the Bank Account is receiving the money and it is being given by the Cash Account. So the money is going out of the Cash Box and into the Bank Account. The letter 'c' in the folio column tells us that the double-entry for this entry can be found opposite (contra). This is the only place in double-entry book-keeping where the two halves of a double entry can be seen at the same time, for it is the only place where we have two accounts side by side — the Cash Account and the Bank Account.

(d) Now we must study the credit side (the right-hand side) of the Cash Book. To make an entry on the credit side we put (i) the date (ii) the name of the person or account that is receiving the money we are paying out (iii) the amount paid; either cash out of the Cash Column or if it is a cheque, the cheque goes out of the Bank column. If there is any VAT on the item purchased we record it in the VAT column. It will be part of our input tax. *Note:* Although the full amount including VAT is being paid out of the cash box or the Bank Account, the VAT input tax will be collected and put into the VAT Account. Therefore when we post the figure to Motor Expenses Account and Sundry Expenses Account we will only debit them with the net of VAT figure. It is convenient as we make the Cash Account Book entry to put this net of VAT figure in the details column ready for when we post the Cash Book to the Ledger. If we are taking discount when we pay the bill we record the amount of the discount in the Discount Received column.

(e) Going down the credit side now to study the entries we find we have:

(i) Paid various expenses, postage, motor expenses, fares and sundry expenses. Two of these had VAT on them. Two were paid by cheque and two in cash. These entries will be posted to the Ledger Accounts in due course. They are losses of the business.

(ii) M. Lucas (a creditor) was paid some money we owed him, but we did take a discount of £4.96. We also paid wages of £72.50.

(iii) The other half of the contra entry has already been explained.

At the end of the week (in a busy office we could do it every day) we balance off the Cash Account and the Bank Account and bring down the balances. We can see that the balance in hand is larger than the balances we had on 1 January.

in the Four-column Cash Book. These are explained in the notes on pp. 97–8. Remember as you work through this example that the Four-column Cash Book will have four columns on the debit side printed on one side of the book and the other four columns opposite, on the right-hand side. The Cash Book will therefore be opened out to a double page. This means that the first right-hand page in a new Cash Book has to be left blank and the book starts to be used when we turn the page and have a double page to work on. This double page will have folio number CB1 — Cash Book Page 1. It is quite usual to take out an insurance policy on the cashier. This is called a Fidelity Bond. If the cashier is not faithful, and runs off with the money, the insurance will refund it. However they don't do so until the cashier has successfully been charged with theft.

3. Posting the Cash Book to the Ledger

Get one thing clear in your mind: the Cash Book is really part of the Ledger because it has two accounts in it lying side by side, the Cash Account and the Bank Account. They are only put in a special book because these accounts are vulnerable and are made the responsibility of one person — the cashier. It is convenient to have these two accounts side by side because we often make transfers from Cash Account to Bank Account, and vice versa. With these entries we can see both sides of the double entry, and the letter c (contra) in the folio column shows the double entry is opposite — as explained in the notes below Fig. 7.2.

With the rest of the entries we can see only one half of the double entry, and we need to do the other half of the double entry. The only ones that are done already are the balances carried down on 1 January and marked b/d (brought down).

Posting the debit side of the Cash Book. To make double entries for all the other entries we go to the Appropriate Ledger Account either in the General Ledger, or the Debtors Ledger or the Creditors Ledger. We have to make the entry on the opposite side of each of these accounts. For example, all items debited in the Cash Book have to go to the credit side of the Ledger Accounts. So Sales Account will be credited with all the Sales figures, but note that it is the figures for sales 'Net of VAT' written in the Details column that will be used. The VAT element has been extracted into its special column and the total for the week will be credited to VAT Account (it is the output tax we owe to HM Customs).

Similarly A. Palmer's Account will be credited both with the amount to be paid and the discount allowed, so that his debt is cleared. Rent Received Account and Commission Received Account will similarly be credited. We put GL1 in the folio column against all the Cash Sales items, and Palmer's account number CL1 (Creditors Ledger 1) against Palmer's entry in the Cash Book. Rent Received A/c is GL6 and Commission Received is GL7.

The VAT A/c has to be credited with a total of £196.26, which is entered in the VAT Account, GL9. The folio number is written below the total figure.

The Discount Allowed total of £1.08 is rather special and is explained below (*see* 4).

Posting the credit side of the Cash Book. The double entries for the items on the credit side of the Cash Book are made on the debit side of the various accounts. For example, the Postage, Motor Expenses (net of VAT), Fares, Wages and Sundry Expenses items (net of VAT) will all need to be debited in the respective accounts. These are nominal accounts, the money has been spent and the amounts are recorded as losses of the business; they will be written off the profits at the end of the year. The money paid to M. Lucas will be debited in Lucas's Account and so will the Discount Received, otherwise his account would not be cleared. Note that the small sums of VAT paid will be debited to VAT Account — they are actually input tax which can be reclaimed against the output tax charged on the sales to our customers. These accounts are illustrated in Fig. 7.3. However, before looking at Fig. 7.3 we must just say a word about Discount Allowed and Discount Received.

Posting Discount Allowed and Discount Received. These two totals are rather special. They are the only items that are not posted over to the opposite side. The Discount Allowed (£1.08 on the debit side of the Cash Book) is debited in the Discount Allowed Account, and the Discount Received (£4.96 on the credit side of the Cash book) is credited in Discount Received Account. Just why is explained below, but first look at the accounts on pp. 101–2.

SALES ACCOUNT GL1

		£
	19__	
	Jan. 1 Cash	115.00
	2 "	214.18
	3 "	168.73
	4 "	479.59
	5 "	451.23
	6 "	533.86

A. PALMER ACCOUNT GL1

19__			£	*19__*		£
Jan. 1 Balance	b/d	43.24		Jan. 2 Bank		42.16
				2 Discount Allowed		1.08

RENT RECEIVED ACCOUNT GL6

		£
	19__	
	Jan. 5 Bank	50.00

COMMISSION RECEIVED ACCOUNT GL7

		£
	19__	
	Jan. 5 Bank	17.50

VAT ACCOUNT GL9

19__		£	*19__*		£
Jan. 6 Bank		1.41	Jan. 6 Cash		196.26

DISCOUNT ALLOWED ACCOUNT GL10

	£
19__	
Jan. 2 Sundry discounts	1.08

POSTAGE ACCOUNT GL2

	£
19__	
Jan. 1 Bank	5.80

MOTOR EXPENSES ACCOUNT GL3

	£
19__	
Jan. 2 Bank	12.27

FARES ACCOUNT GL4

	£
19__	
Jan. 3 Cash	11.55

M. LUCAS ACCOUNT DL1

19__		£	19__		£
Jan. 3 Cash		94.28	Jan. 1 Balance	b/d	99.24
3 Discount		4.96			

WAGES ACCOUNT GL5

19__		£
Jan. 5		72.50

SUNDRY EXPENSES ACCOUNT GL8

19__		£
Jan. 6		1.77

DISCOUNT RECEIVED ACCOUNT GL11

			19__		£
			Jan. 6 Sundry Discounts		4.96

Note: For the sake of realism A. Palmer's original debt and M. Lucas's original claim for goods supplied are shown.

4. Why the Discount Allowed and Discount Received do not cross over sides

In double-entry book-keeping we always need a perfect double entry. Consider the double entry for A. Palmer. We have the following entries, in the accounts named:

Bank A/c (Fig. 7.1): A debit entry for £42.16. (The £1.08 does not count — it is only in a memorandum column.)

A. Palmer A/c (Fig. 7.2): A credit entry for £42.16 and another for £1.08. There is only £42.16 debited in the Bank A/c and a total of £43.24 credited in A. Palmer's A/c.

So we have another imperfect double entry. To put it right the £1.08 in the Discount Allowed A/c must be on the debit side, not the credit side. It must not cross over.

Similarly, the payment to M. Lucas has:

Bank A/c: A credit for £94.28.
M. Lucas A/c: Debits for £94.28 and £4.96 = £99.24.

To get a perfect double entry the £4.96 Discount Received must be on the credit side of the Discount Received Account.

5. Contra entries in the Cash Book

Since we are now keeping the Cash and Bank Accounts together in one book using separate columns, it follows that payments of cash into bank and withdrawals of cash from bank will result in a double entry, both halves of which will be visible on the book — but not in the same account. Thus:

> Payment of cash sales into bank. The cash is the giver, and therefore the Cash Account will be credited. The Bank Account is the receiver, and hence the Bank Account is debited. Such an entry is shown in Fig. 7.2. The term contra entry (*contra* = Latin for opposite) is given to such entries where both halves of the double entry can be seen on opposite sides of the book.

> It is possible to have an entry the opposite way, with cash being drawn out of the bank and put in the cashier's safe. In that case the Bank Account is the giver (credit the Bank Account) and the Cash Account is the receiver (debit the Cash Account).

6. Discounts subsequently disallowed

Sometimes a cash discount is deducted in error: due to an oversight the terms of payment may not have been complied with or cash discount may not be applicable to the particular transaction.

(a) In the case of a *discount received*; when we are informed that we are *not entitled* to the discount which we deducted when making a payment:

> (i) *credit* the account of the supplier (we still owe him the discount deducted in error);
> (ii) *debit* Discount Received Account.

(b) If a *debtor deducts discount* to which he is not entitled, we record the amount received by cheque or cash, leaving his account 'open' with a debit balance brought down, and send him a letter informing him that the discount was not allowable.

Figure 7.3   *The Petty Cash Book*

CHANCELLOR Accounting Paper — Petty Cash Book — Folio No. PCB 1

Debits (Receipts) £ p	Month	Day	Details (for both debits and credits)	Petty Cash Voucher or Folio No.	Total £ p	Postage £ p	Fares £ p	Vehicle Expenses £ p	Stationery £ p	Sundry Expenses £ p	VAT Folio No.	VAT £ p	Ledger a/c Folio	Ledger a/c £ p
80 11	Jan	1	Imprest from main CashBook	C61										
		1	Postage stamps	1	2 50	2 50								
		2	Fares to Oxford	2	3 95		3 95							
		2	Petrol	3	12 50			11 36				1 14		
		2	M. Knight & Son	4	8 75								C-L7	8 75
		3	Envelopes	5	2 24				2 04			- 20		
		3	Postage	6	1 96	1 96								
		4	Refreshments (Export byer)	7	4 25					3 86		- 39		
		4	Fares	8	92		92							
		4	String & Sealing Wax	9	2 19					1 99		- 20		
		5	Postage stamps	10	3 80	3 80								
		5	Paper	11	4 18				3 80			- 38		
		6	Postage	12	- 52	- 52								
		6	Petrol	13	13 41			12 19				1 22		
4 65		6	Private telephone calls	GL8										
			Balance c/d		61 07									
84 65					84 65	8 68	4 87	23 55	5 84	5 85		3 53		8 75
						(GL5)	(GL8)	(GL11)	(GL12)	(GL10)		(GL14)		
23 58	Jan	8	Balance b/d	b/d	23 58									
56 42		8	Imprest restored	CB3										

Ref. PCB.5 Published and supplied by Formecon Services Ltd. Gateway, Crewe, CW1 1YN. Tel. 0270 500800   © Formecon Services Ltd. 1989

NOTES:

(a) The page is divided into two halves, but the debit half is very tiny as we only have money coming in once a week, as the imprest is drawn from the cashier. We do just occasionally get other money coming in, for example someone paid £4.65 for private telephone calls in the example above.

(b) All the details are written on the credit side, whether they refer to the debit side or the credit side. If they do refer to a debit entry of course all the credit columns are left clear.

(c) Payments are all credit entries and are entered twice — once in the total column to show the total money spent, and once in the analysis column to show how the money was spent. If there is any VAT element the money was spent. If there is any VAT element in the items purchased the analysis is split between the net-of-vat expense and the VAT element. An entry on the credit side in the total column must cross-tot to the same amount in the analysis columns.

(d) Although the analysis columns enable several items of the same type to be collected together into a single sub-total before being posted to the expense account concerned in the ledger, there are some payments which must be kept separate. Thus M. Knight & Son were paid £8.75 on 2 January and this item can only go in M. Knight's account; it cannot be joined up with any similar item. We therefore analyse it off into a 'Ledger A/cs' column which has a folio column alongside it. Any item in this column can be posted separately to its Ledger Account. Similarly, if we purchase an asset — say a weighing machine for letter post, this would go in an asset account (Office Equipment A/c) and would be analysed off into the Ledger A/cs column.

(e) At the end of the week we rule across the whole credit side and add up the various columns. We rule a double line under these totals, but not in the Total column because there the balance of cash left over has to be inserted and the debit and credit columns are balanced off, as shown.

(f) Note that the headings chosen for the analysis columns are at your own choice, to suit the particular business concerned, but the VAT column and the Ledger A/Cs column have been pre-printed. When the columns are added the analysis column totals must cross-tot to the money spent.

(g) Every payment should have a *petty cash voucher* to vouch for the honesty of the payment made. Ideally, a petty cash voucher should come from outside the business, but if this is not possible an internal petty cash voucher should be made out and signed by a manager to authorise the payment to the employee claiming to have spent the money. Petty cash vouchers are numbered and filed, and kept for six years, since they form part of the VAT records.

Posting the Petty Cash Book. Remember that the Petty Cash Book is really an account — the Petty Cash Account. It shows receipts on the debit side and payments on the credit side. The debit items have to be credited in another account. The Imprest is credited in the Cash Account in the main Cash Book, and the refunded telephone money is credited in Telephone Expense Account (to reduce the telephone bill for the firm or company). The credit items are posted over to the debit side of the various accounts — but we use the total figures only. So postage, fares, etc., will all be debited in the accounts shown, and the folio numbers inserted below each column, as shown.

NOTE: Even if a letter is not sent, the debtor would receive a statement of account at the end of the month because of the existence of the debit balance on his account.

7. Trade and cash discount

The main point of these two discounts can be summarised as follows:

Trade discount		*Cash discount*
1.	Is *unconditional* — you are either entitled to it or you are not.	1. Is *conditional* — you must do something to *earn it*, i.e. settle the account within the time allowed.
2.	Deducted *by the seller* when preparing the invoice and is shown as a deduction on the invoice.	2. Deducted by the *debtor* when settling his account within the time allowed by the 'terms of payment'.
3.	Appears in subsidiary books *only*, a note being made of the rate per cent and the amount deducted, i.e. details of the invoice appear in the subsidiary books.	3. Appears in the Cash Book, being noted in separate columns provided. It appears in the Ledger, Discount Allowed Account being *debited* and Discount Received Account being *credited* with the *totals* of discount columns in the Cash Book.
4.	It must also be deducted from any goods returned.	4. Individual items of discount *must be* entered in the personal accounts of debtors and creditors.

8. Petty Cash Book

All firms have numerous small items of expenditure to meet, and to ease the burden of work and entries in the Cash Book they keep what is known as a Petty Cash Book, based on a system in which one person is made responsible for these small disbursements against documents referred to as **petty cash vouchers**. The petty cashier usually has a fixed sum which is made up each week from the main cash book. This amount is known as the *imprest figure*, and the system is referred to as the *imprest petty cash system*.

The book is a true cash book having a debit side and a credit side, but because the chief activity is spending small amounts on such items as postage, fares, etc. the credit side has any number of analysis columns assigned to suit the particular requirements of the business concerned and to produce totals for items of expenditure, which are then taken at convenient intervals to the *debit* of expense accounts in the General Ledger. A typical ruling for a Petty Cash Book is shown in Fig. 7.3 from the Formecon series of ruled papers referred to earlier (*see* p.89). Note that there is a VAT column for collecting together any elements of VAT input tax included in the price of any items purchased. Study Fig. 7.3 now and the notes below it.

9. Computerisation of accounting systems

We have been concerned with the formal entries in subsidiary books, and for examination purposes this is the accepted method of testing a candidate's knowledge of the *principles involved*.

Whilst the principles remain the same, the advent of the computer has reduced clerical effort and speeded up the process of preparing and recording information in easily retrievable form and, *at the same time*, performing the function of posting/updating the relevant ledger accounts. There are many applications to cope with a wide range of situations, we can only give a simple example.

(a) *Sales*

   (*i*) Sales invoices can be prepared with a computer producing the invoice for transmission to each customer, simultaneously transferring detailed records of prices, quantities, discounts, VAT, etc., into a storage system 'A' which in effect becomes the Sales Day Book.

   (*ii*) At the same time, a storage system 'B' representing the Sales or Debtors Ledger will update individual personal accounts with the value of the invoices going out in this batch.

   (*iii*) At the month end, statements of account showing the

balance due from each customer can be produced by the computer.

   (*iv*) Video display units (VDUs) can also be used if required to produce an instant display of selected information, e.g. in the event of queries regarding prices, quantities, discounts, etc.

(b) *Cash/bank*. Receipts and payments can be processed by a computer which will:

   (*i*) transfer the information into a storage system representing the Cash Account and Bank Account, automatically updating and making the current balances on Cash Account and Bank Account instantly available;

   (*ii*) Transfer the appropriate Dr or Cr to the relevant ledger accounts retained in a separate storage system, automatically updating the balances on those accounts.

(c) *Debtors and creditors — Sales and Purchases Ledgers*. It follows that extracting information in the form of printed lists of debtors and creditors becomes a relatively simple task which can take place as and when required.

Computers therefore provide accurate records of the *details* of individual transactions, i.e. performing the function of Subsidiary Books, whilst simultaneously performing the function of the Ledger, i.e. recording the financial aspect of each transaction only. (*see* 17:2 for computerisation of cash, bank and personal accounts).

Progress test 7

1. How is cash discount recorded in the Ledger? **(3)** and **(4)**

2. How does the Cash Book perform the function of a subsidiary book? **(1)**

3. What are contra entries in the Cash Book? **(3)** and **(5)**

4. How do you deal with discounts disallowed? **(6)**

5. Distinguish between trade and cash discounts. **(7)**

6. What is the function of the Petty Cash Book? **(8)**

7. A typewriter bought for £90 has been entered in the Cash Account. What is the corresponding double entry for this?

8. What effects do cash discounts have on the profit of a business?

9. Name the necessary accounts for cash discount in the Ledger.

Specimen questions

1. Enter the following transactions of C. Richard during May 19__ in his four-column Cash Book. Describe each item in the 'Details' column so as to denote clearly the account in the Ledger to which it would be posted. Balance the Cash Book as on 13 May, and bring down the balances. In every case cash sales includes VAT.

May 1 Cash in hand £29.80; Cash at Bank £3,814.50 (brought down from previous month).

2 Received from R. Jones a cheque for £86.65, in full settlement of his debt of £91.21. Cash sales £427.28, of which VAT is £38.84.

5 Cash Sales £1,326.50, of which VAT is £120.59. Paid into bank £1,000 (contra entry).

6 Paid cash to petty cashier £100.

8 Paid M. Larkin's account by cheque £275.50.

9 Sold for cash goods valued at £386.50, of which £35.14 is VAT.

10 Sent a cheque for £87.75 to E. Boardman, in full settlement of his account for £90.

10 Bought scales for postage £13.25 by cheque, of which VAT was £1.20.

10 R. Usher owed C. Richard £85, and sent him a cheque in full settlement, after deducting 5 per cent discount.

11 Cash sales £1,425.60 of which VAT = £129.60.
Banked £1,500 (contra entry)

11 Bought stock (cash purchases) by cheque for £275, of which VAT is £25.

12 Received and banked a cheque for £85 from J. Eyre in part payment of his account.

12 Richard's bank notified charges amounting to £5.50.

13 Sent a cheque for £256 to R. Botham for rent due to him.

13 Sold an office typewriter for £25 cash to a member of staff. Withdrew £150 from bank for private use.

2. Enter the following transactions of R. Parker during the first week of July 19__ in his four-column Cash Book. Describe each item in the 'Details' column so as to denote clearly the account in the Ledger to which it would be posted. Balance the Cash Book as on 6 July, and bring down the balances.

July 1 Cash in hand £25.60, bank overdraft £98.70 (brought down from previous month).
Received from Helpful Finance PLC a loan of £1,000 and paid the cheque into the bank.
Cash sales £386.50 of which VAT is £35.14.

2 Paid cash to petty cashier £60.00.
Paid electric light account by cheque £85.27.
Cash sales £624.60 (of which VAT is £56.78).
Purchased goods for re-sale by cheque £132.50 (of which £12.05 is VAT).
Sent a cheque for £98.50 to B. Green in full settlement of his account for £103.68.

3 Cash sales £892.56 of which £81.14 is VAT.
Parker owed G. Long £95.00 and sent him a cheque in full settlement, after deducting 5 per cent discount.
Banked £1,000 from cash box.

4 Cash sales £925.68 of which £84.15 is VAT.
Bought office chair for £65.50 of which £5.95 is VAT. Paid by cheque.
Paid M. Clark by cheque £121.65 in settlement of his account for £131.51.

5   Received and banked a cheque for £39 from T. Jones
in full payment of his account of £40.00.
Parker's bank notified charges amounting to £17.36.
Cash sales £1,042.96 of which £94.81 was VAT.
Banked £1,500 from cash box.
Withdrew £200 from bank for private use.

3.   The petty cashier of Miniscula Ltd has an imprest of £100 on
1 May 19__. The following transactions take place in the week
beginning on that date. The Petty Cash Book has analysis
columns for postage, travelling expenses, stationery, vehicle
expenses, sundry expenses and ledger accounts.

May   1   Paid for postage £11.56; fares £1.25; sealing wax £1.15
(VAT £0.10) and fuel for the oil stove £3.86 (of which VAT
was £0.35).
2   Paid for postage £1.95; vehicle expenses £12.94 (of
which VAT was £1.18); sundry expenses £1.85 (VAT
17 pence).
3   Paid T. Roberts A/C £13.56 and sundry expenses £4.95
(VAT included of £0.45). Collected telephone money
for private telephone calls by staff £19.95.
4   Paid petrol £15.26 (of which VAT was £1.39); fares
£1.94; postage £12.76; sandwiches for visitors £3.95.
5   Paid M. Marshall's small account of £5.95 in cash; paid
for office stationery £13.26 (of which VAT was £1.21);
paid fares £1.95; sundry expenses £2.45.

Rule off the book, bring down the balance and restore the
imprest to £100. Mark in all petty cash voucher numbers and
folio numbers as if you had posted the entries to the
Ledger Accounts.

4.   The petty cashier of Microdots Ltd has an imprest of £80 on
1 July 19__. The following transactions take place in the week
beginning on that date. The Petty Cash Book has columns for
analysing postage, travelling expenses, stationery, vehicle
expenses, sundry expenses and Ledger Accounts.

July   1   Paid for postage £6.25; fares £3.30; copying paper
£8.40 (VAT £0.76) and refreshments for visitors £3.25.

2   Paid for postage £1.95; vehicle expenses £14.26 (of which VAT was £1.30); sundry expenses £1.45 (VAT £0.13).

3   Paid M. Cook's A/C £9.25 and sundry expenses £3.78 (VAT included of £0.34). Collected telephone money for private telephone calls by staff £25.79.

4   Paid petrol £11.50 (of which VAT was £1.05); fares £3.86; postage £2.75; purchased spirit lamp for office £13.24 (VAT £1.20).

5   Paid R. Miller's small account of £8.60 in cash; paid for office stationery £9.56 (of which VAT was £0.87); paid fares £1.34; sundry expenses £2.05.

Rule off the book, bring down the balance and restore the imprest to £80. Mark in all petty cash voucher numbers and folio numbers as if you had posted the entries to the Ledger Accounts.

8
Bank Reconciliation Statements

1. Form and purpose

A Bank Reconciliation Statement is a statement made out by a trader when he/she receives a Bank Statement purporting to show that the bank's records and his/her own records are in agreement even though the figures shown may be different. The relationship between a bank and its customer is one of debtor and creditor. Thus, when Mr A pays £1,000 cash into the bank, from the bank's point of view it will *debit* cash account and *credit* the personal account of Mr A, recording the fact that it owes him the £1,000 which he has deposited with it. This is the reason why the same balance (say the £1,000 referred to above) will appear as a credit balance on the Bank Statement sent to a customer (the bank owes the customer £1,000) but as a debit balance on the books of the trader (the trader has an asset, cash at bank £1,000).

Statements of account from a bank will often give a different balance from that shown in the trader's own records.

Example

If Mr A, having paid £1,000 into a current account at the bank on 1 January, issues a cheque for £300 to Mr B on 2 January his record of the bank account will appear:

BANK ACCOUNT

Jan. 1 Capital	£1,000	Jan. 2 Mr B	£300

This clearly indicates a balance of £700, *but* until the cheque is *presented for payment at the bank* the bank will not know of its existence.

Consequently the bank will say that Mr A still has a balance of £1,000 standing to his credit at the bank.

The purpose of a Bank Reconciliation Statement is to explain the difference that exists between the two figures, due to the fact that entries in either the Bank Statement or the trader's own records, or both, are not up to date.

The chief reasons why the bank's records and a trader's records may not agree are:

(a) The bank often pays standing orders and direct debits which the trader either does not know about, or waits to enter into his/her books until the bank's Statement of Account confirms that they have been paid.
(b) The bank takes time to clear cheques paid in by the trader, who has already entered them in the Cash Book before paying them in.
(c) The bank receives credits for the customer's account which it records but the trader does not know about them (for example, interest on gilt-edged securities, payments by home agents to mail-order firms, start-up allowances from the Government, etc.).
(d) A cheque drawn by a trader and sent to a creditor cannot appear on the bank's records until that payee presents it for payment through the Clearing House procedure. A payee may not be able to get to a bank because of illness, holidays, remoteness from a bank, etc.
(e) Both parties can make mistakes.

2. Getting the trader's Cash Book right

In practice, the obvious first step is to bring the Bank Account in the trader's Cash Book as nearly as possible into line with the Bank Statement by entering those items that appear on the statement but which have not been entered in the Cash Book. The result is a revised balance on the trader's Cash Book (Bank column) now the trader is fully informed. This means that the Bank Reconciliation Statement will be concerned only with:

(a) cheques which have not been presented at the bank for payment;

(b) cheques which have not been credited by the bank at the time the statement is collected.

Examinations frequently set questions that require candidates to check the Bank Account entries against a Bank Statement to establish those items which give rise to the difference in the final balances, and then to set out the Bank Reconciliation Statement.

Sample question

Set out a Bank Reconciliation Statement from the following information:

Bank Statement of D. Ando

Date	Particulars		Debit	Credit	Balance
19__			£	£	£
Apr. 1	Balance b/fwd				420
2	A. Petty	(*)	10		410
3	Cash		80		330
12	A. Black			72	402
13	T. Rose		25		377
18	B. Cream			57	434
21	H. Lock		32		402
24	J. Charles			17	419
30	Charges	(*)	3		416

Cash Book of D. Ando

Dr.   BANK ACCOUNT   Cr.

19__		£	19__		£
Apr. 1	Balance b/d	410	Apr. 3	Cash	80
12	A. Black	72	10	T. Rose	25
18	B. Cream	57	19	H. Lock	32
24	J. Charles	17	28	G. Watt (*)	44
30	S. James (*)	29	29	T. Brown (*)	28
			30	Balance c/d	376
		£585			£585
May 1	Balance b/d	376			

NOTE: The items marked (*) are not entered in both the Statement and the Bank Account.

(a) The opening position on 1 April is important. We can see that the accounts were not in agreement at this date. However on 2 April A. Petty presented a cheque for payment at the bank. This brings the balances on both Statement and Account into line and must obviously represent a cheque paid to A. Petty prior to 1 April. This can therefore be omitted from the reconciliation.

(b) On 30 April £3 was charged by the bank. Since this has not yet been entered in the Cash Book, we will have to enter it now.

(c) On 30 April £29 was received and entered in the Cash Book, but this has not yet been credited by the bank. It is in the clearing process.

(d) Two cheques, i.e. £44 and £28 have been paid out, but have not yet been presented at the bank for payment.

The revised Cash Book balance will be as follows

BANK ACCOUNT

19__	£	19__	£
May 1 Balance b/d	376	May 1 Bank charges	3
		1 Balance c/d	373
	£376		£376
19__	£		
May 1 Balance b/d	373		

Answer

BANK RECONCILIATION STATEMENT AT 1 MAY 19__

		£	£
Balance as per Cash Book			373
Deduct cheque not yet credited by bank			
	S. James		29
(Because the bank does not yet believe you have the money)			344
Add cheques not yet presented			
	G. Watts	44	
	T. Brown	28	
(Because the bank thinks you still have this money)			72
Balance as per Bank Statement			£416

3. Bank Reconciliation Statements without corrections to the Cash Book

In real life we always get the Cash Book right first, and then reconcile this revised balance with the Bank Statement. In examinations we are sometimes only given one balance and the reconciliation must be effected in the Bank Reconciliation Statement alone. This is shown in the alternative presentation below.

BANK RECONCILIATION STATEMENT AT 30 APRIL 19__

	£	£
Balance as per Bank Statement		416
Add Cheques not credited by bank: James	29	
Charges not entered in Cash Book	3	
	—	
		32
		448
Deduct Cheques not presented for payment:		
Watts	44	
Brown	28	
		72
Balance as per Cash Book		£376

A good general rule is:

(a) Collect all the items you intend to *add* first.
(b) Collect all the items you intend to *subtract*.
(c) The final statement should have no more than *five* items in the final column.

A useful standpoint to adopt is to say, when moving from the Cash Book to the Bank Statement 'Now what does the Bank think about this item?' When moving from the Bank Statement to the Cash Book one asks 'Now what does the trader think about this item?' For example, in the last example given above the trader thinks he still has £3 even though the bank has actually claimed it as charges. We therefore add back the £3 to arrive at what the trader's Cash Book says.

4. Treatment of overdraft

When the form of presentation summarised in **3** above is

adopted it can prove useful in those questions where the balance on either Bank Account or Statement is reflected by an overdraft, i.e. when you are working from a balance on the Bank Account to an overdraft on the Statement, or vice versa.

Sample question

The Bank Statement of J. Gloom showed a debit balance of £15 on 1 October. On checking with the Cash Book, he found that cheques amounting to £127 had not been presented for payment while cheques amounting to £166 had been debited in the Cash Book but had not been credited by the bank. The bank had also debited his account with £2 for bank charges. Prepare a Bank Reconciliation Statement.

> NOTE: In this question you have no alternative but to start with the overdraft shown on the Bank Statement.

Answer

J. GLOOM — BANK RECONCILIATION STATEMENT AS AT 30 SEPTEMBER 19__

	£	£
Overdraft as per Bank Statement		15
Add Cheques not presented for payment		127
(as these will increase the overdraft)		
		142
Deduct Cheques not credited by bank	166	
Bank charges not entered in Cash Book	2	
		168
Balance as per Cash Book.		£26

> NOTE: The amount we are deducting — £168 — exceeds £142, thus we take the £142 from £168 and the character of the answer changes, in this case, *from an overdraft on the Statement to a debit (or favourable) balance in the Cash Book.*

The chief points to note are:

(a) Cheques paid into an overdrawn account decrease the overdraft.

(b) Cheques drawn out of an overdrawn account increase the overdraft.

(c) Bank charges made for interest etc. on an overdrawn account increase the overdrawn balance.

Progress test 8

1.   What is a Bank Reconciliation Statement?   **(1)**

2.   Why is a Bank Reconciliation Statement necessary?   **(1)**

3.   Explain why a Bank Statement and a Bank Account in the Cash Book could differ.   **(1)**

4.   What are the main points of difference that arise?   **(1)**

5.   How can we have cheques that have not been credited by the bank?   **(1)**

6.   Explain why cheques may not be presented for payment. **(1)**

7.   What items sometimes omitted from the Cash Book do you usually enter in the Cash Book before preparing the Bank Reconciliation Statement?   **(2)**

8.   Explain how you would deal with a bank overdraft on: (a) the Bank Account; and (b) the Bank Statement, when preparing a Bank Reconciliation Statement.   **(4)**

Specimen questions

1.

Bank of Loamshire Statement

Date	Particulars	£	£	Balance
19__				£
Dec. 3	Balance			700
3	0029	50		650
4	Sundries		300	950
5	0031	250		700
6	Sundries		900	1,600
7	S/O insurance	50		1,550
10	Sundries		150	1,700
11	0034	50		1,650
12	0032	400		1,250
	0035	250		1,000
13	Credit transfer			
	P. Rowan		100	1,100

Cash Book Extract

19__		£	19__		£
Dec. 1	Balance	650	Dec. 4	Black & White	170
4	G. Brown	300	5	Wages	250
5	Sales	700	7	W. Green	400
6	R. Smith	200	9	P. Garland	150
10	M. Williams	150	11	Cash	50
			12	Wages	250

Above is your bank statement for the first two weeks in December, and an extract from your Cash Book covering the same period. You are able to ascertain from your cheque book that the cheque sent to Black & White was numbered 0030. The rest follow in order.

You are required to bring up to date and balance the Cash Book, and prepare a Bank Reconciliation Statement to explain any difference in the two balances.

2. On 31 December 19_6 the bank balance appearing in the Cash Book of A.B. Ltd was a debit of £3,375. The cashier successfully reconciled the balance appearing in the firm's bank statement after taking into account the following.

(a) Cheques amounting to £437 paid into the bank on 31 December 19_6 were not entered by the bank until 1 January 19_7.

(b) Bank charges of £16 entered in the Bank Statement on 31 December 19_6 had not been entered in the Cash Book.

(c) A cheque for £37 received from T. Johnson had been credited to B. Johnson, although it was correctly entered in the Cash Book.

(d) A payment by cheque of £343 to D. Faulkner had been entered in the Cash Book as £334. An entry to correct this error was made.

(e) Subscriptions of £20 paid by standing order had not been entered in the Cash Book.

(f) A dividend of £65 paid directly into the Bank Account had not been entered in the Cash Book.

(g) Cheques payable to suppliers and entered in the Cash

Book amounted to £254. At 31 December 19_6 they had not been presented for payment.

Required:

(a) A statement showing the bank balance appearing in the Cash Book of A.B. Ltd after making the necessary corrections.

(b) A copy of the Bank Reconciliation Statement as at 31 December 19_6 prepared by the cashier.

3. Summarised information taken from the cash book of Berry Ltd for June 19_0 shows the following:

CASH BOOK (Bank columns only)

Opening balance	£2,800	Payments	£32,000
Receipts	£30,000	Closing balance c/d	800
	£32,800		£32,800
Opening balance	800		

After examining your records you discover that:

(a) £70 bank charges on the Bank Statement have not been entered in the Cash Book;

(b) a cheque drawn for £95 has been entered as a receipt;

(c) a cheque for £40 received from a creditor has been dishonoured but not recorded;

(d) a cheque drawn for £850 has not been presented;

(e) the opening balance in the Cash Book should have been £3,800;

(f) £2,750 cash paid in to the bank has not been credited to the company's Bank Account at the bank.

(g) the bank has debited a cheque for £85 in error to the company's account;

(h) the Bank Statement shows an overdrawn balance of £485.

You are required to:

(i) show the adjustments in the Cash Book;

(ii) prepare a Bank Reconciliation Statement as at 30 June 19_0.

4. According to his Cash Book, Hastings' bank balance on 31 January was £147. After investigation it was discovered that:

(a) dividends received by the bank on behalf of Hastings, £15, had not been recorded in the Cash Book;

(b) a cheque for £22 had been dishonoured in January, but no mention of this appears in the Cash Book;

(c) bank charges of £7 had not been recorded in the Cash Book;

(d) cheques £434 had been credited in the Cash Book, but had not been presented for payment;

(e) the Bank Statement did not include cheques paid into the bank on 31 January, and debited in the Cash Book on that day £312;

(f) a credit sale amounting to £21 on 28 January had been recorded in Hastings' books as a cash sale (proceeds paid to bank).

You are required to calculate:

(i) the correct Cash Book balance on 31 January;

(ii) the Bank Statement balance on 31 January.

NOTE: all workings must be shown.

5. On 31 December XY's Bank Statement showed an overdraft of £306. On comparing it with the Cash Book the following differences were found.

(a) Bank interest and charges at 31 December, £36 had not been entered in the Cash Book.

(b) A standing charge of £100 for an annual insurance premium paid by the bank on 1 December had not been entered in the Cash Book.

(c) Cheques drawn amounting to £64 had not yet been presented for payment.

Prepare a Bank Reconciliation Statement at 31 December, bringing out the balance in the Cash Book, before any adjustments are made.

6. According to the cash book of Rex Ltd, the company has a credit balance at the bank of £380 on 30 June 19__, but this is *not* borne out by the Bank Statement on the same date. An investigation into the difference yields the following information.

(a) A standing order for a charitable subscription of £40 had been paid by the bank on 29 June but no entry had been made in the Cash Book.

(b) A cheque paid for advertising on 10 June for £179 had been entered in the Cash Book as £197.

(c) Cheques for £1,037 sent to creditors on 30 June were not paid by the bank until 6 July.

(d) Cheques received from customers amounting to £1,680 were paid into the bank on 30 June but were not credited by the bank until 1st July.

(e) On 20 June a cheque for £114 was received from a customer in settlement of an invoice for £120. An entry of £120 had been made in the Cash Book.

Required:

Prepare a statement reconciling the Cash Book balance with the Bank Statement.

9
Bills of Exchange

1. **Definition**

   The Bills of Exchange Act 1882, defines a bill of exchange as:

   'an unconditional order in writing, addressed by one person to another, signed by the person giving it, requiring the person to whom it is addressed to pay on demand or at a fixed or determinable future date a sum certain in money, to or to the order of a specified person or to bearer'.

   Apart from the legal definition given above, it is intended only to give sufficient detail here to enable the entries in books of account to be fully understood.

2. **What is their purpose?**

   Basically bills of exchange can best be understood in the context of normal trade bills, since in this case they are the means of bridging the gap that exists between a *seller* who cannot or does not wish to give credit and a *buyer* who wants possession of the goods *now* but who wishes to pay for them later. It does this by enabling the buyer to accept an undertaking to pay a fixed sum of money at a fixed date in the future.

3. **Parties to a bill**

   Drawer (seller) — the person to whom the money is owing — who draws the bill.

   Drawee (buyer) — the person who owes money, upon whom the bill is drawn.

   Payee — A person named on the bill of exchange as the one to whom the money is to be paid.

4. Acceptance

Bills of Exchange require acceptance if the drawee is to be made liable upon them. Until a bill is accepted the drawer has the primary liability on the bill.

The *drawee* accepts the bill of exchange by writing 'Accepted' and signing his/her name across the face of the bill. Until a bill has been accepted in this way it is known as a 'draft'; after acceptance it is known as an 'acceptance' and the *drawee* becomes the *acceptor* and as such assumes the primary liability on the bill.

5. The seller (drawer) parts with goods and receives *the accepted bill in exchange.* He can:

(a) keep it until it matures (this would tend to defeat the object of the bill);

(b) negotiate the bill — by endorsing it and in so doing use it to pay the sum of money to a third party;

(c) discount it at a bank (selling it for *less* than its face value).

    Q. Why would he sell it for less than its face value?

    A. He anticipates that he will be able to put the sum received to *work* and earn far more than the discount deducted by the bank, i.e. £95 *now* is worth more to him than £100 in, say, two or three months' time.

6. The buyer (drawee) will obtain possession of the goods and anticipates that he will be able to dispose of them for more than the value of the bill and before the bill matures. He will thus make a profit.

7. Banks are in a better position to wait for bills to mature and for the service of putting firms in possession of funds on the one hand, and enabling others to obtain goods on the other hand, the small margin or discount is a legitimate charge for a service that buyers and sellers find extremely valuable.

8. Due date

Once the bill has been accepted, the *drawee* becomes liable on the bill and must honour it on the due date.

Example

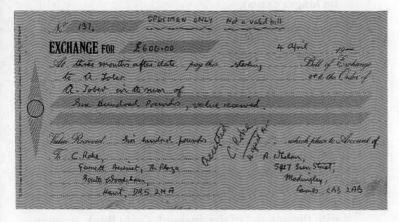

Figure 9.1

In Fig. 9.1, the *due date* will be 4 July 19_ since the *tenor* of the bill is three months (calender months). Note that C. Roke is the *drawee*, who becomes the *acceptor*, and A. Whelan is the *drawer*. A. Toher is the payee in this case, but in many cases the drawer would ask the drawee to 'pay me the sum of' so that the drawer and the payee would be the same person.

9. Accounting aspects

There are two aspects to every bill. To the *creditor* who holds it, it is a *bill receivable* and as such it is an asset. To the *debtor* who accepts it, it is a liability and he will regard it as a *bill payable*.

(a) when the bill is accepted:
  - (*i*) *credit* the debtor from whom it is received (cancelling out his/her debt);
  - (*ii*) *debit* Bills Receivable Account (this will be shown as an asset in the Balance Sheet);

(b) If it is kept until maturity, then when it matures:
  - (*i*) *debit* Bank Account;
  - (*ii*) *credit* Bills Receivable Account;

(c) if the bill is negotiated to a third party in part payment of a debt (the amounts will rarely be exactly the same).
  - (*i*) *debit* the creditor to whom it has been given (cancelling part of the debt), at the discounted value on the day in question.

> (*ii*) *credit* Bills Receivable Account with the full value (the asset no longer exists);

NOTE: A creditor who is prepared to take a Bill in this way in part payment of a debt will clearly only take it at its discounted value on the day it is taken. As we need to clear the whole value of the bill from the Bills Receivable Account, but can only debit the creditor with the discounted value we must debit Discount on Bills Account with the balance. So:

> (*iii*) *debit* Discount on Bills Account with the amount of the discount suffered and *credit* Bills Receivable Account.

(d) If the bill is discounted at a bank:
> (*i*) *debit* Bank Account and *credit* Bills Receivable Account with the full value of the bill;
> (*ii*) *debit* Discount on Bills Account or Bank Charges Account with the amount of the discount. *Credit* Bank Account.

Example

On 1 March, A sells goods to B valued at £500. B accepts a bill of exchange for the amount payable in three months. On 16 March A, being in need of funds, discounts the bill with his bankers at 15 per cent per annum discount. The bill is duly met at maturity. Show the relevant entries in the ledger of A.

NOTE: Calculation of discount. Time from date of discounting to date of maturity = 77 days, i.e. from 17 March to 1 June inclusive.

$$\frac{£500}{1} \times \frac{15}{100} \times \frac{77}{365} = £15.82$$

Ledger of A

B's A/C

Mar.1 Sales	£500	Mar. 1 Bills Receivable	£500

BILLS RECEIVABLE

Mar. 1 B's A/c	£500	Mar.16 Bank	£500

BANK (EXTRACT)

Mar. 16 Bills Receivable	£500	Mar.16 Discount Charges A/c	£15.82

DISCOUNT ON BILLS
OR
BANK CHARGES A/C

Mar.16 Bank	£15.82	(Subsequent transfer to Profit and Loss A/c)

NOTE: Where a firm handles Bills Payable or Bills Receivable it is usual to keep a subsidiary book for each, i.e. a Bills Receivable Book or a Bills Payable Book. Such books are available from Formecon Services Ltd, Gateway, Crewe, CW1 1YN.

10. Rebated bills

The acceptor may pay the bill before maturity, i.e. before the full period has elapsed for which he was allowed credit. In this case he *may* receive interest for the unexpired term, similar to the discount charged by the bank.

When this occurs:

(a) *debit* Bank Account with the actual amount received;
(b) *debit* Discount Charges Account (with the interest or rebate);
(c) *credit* Bills Receivable Account with the full face value of the bill.

11. Dishonoured bills

The *acceptor* is the person who is primarily liable on a bill. By accepting he/she engages to pay it according to the tenor of the bill.

The *drawer* of a bill engages that on due presentment it shall be accepted and paid according to its tenor, and that if it is dishonoured *he/she will compensate the holder* or any *indorser* who is compelled to pay it, provided that the requisite proceedings on dishonour have been duly taken.

The dishonour of a bill is usually 'noted' by a notary public as proof of the dishonour. The charge made for this is called a 'noting charge', which will usually be *claimed* from the defaulting debtor (the acceptor). A more formal procedure is the full 'protesting' of the bill. Foreign bills must be protested by a notary public before they can form the basis of a legal action.

(a) *On dishonour of a bill: debit* the Debtor and *credit* Bills Receivable

Account. (This restores the debt to the debtor and clears the worthless asset from the books.)

(b) *If the bill has been discounted at the bank: debit* the Debtor and *credit* Bank Account (with the full amount of the bill).

(c) *On charging the debtor for noting charges: debit* the Debtor (the Acceptor), *credit* Bank Account (we will have paid the charges to the Notary Public).

12. Retiring a bill

A drawer of a bill that has been dishonoured may (by arrangement) draw a second bill payable at a later date. The old bill that has been dishonoured is then said to be 'retired' or 'renewed'. In such an event, interest would probably be charged for the extended period of credit since this is longer than the period originally agreed.

Example

On 1 January, A. White sells goods to C. Blue valued at £200. Blue accepted a Bill at three months. On 1 February White discounts the bill at his bank receiving £194.

On 1 April, the bill is dishonoured, notarial charges being £16. On 10 April White agrees to draw a new bill at 3 months from 1 April, for the full value including the notarial charges and interest at 16 per cent on £216 for 3 months, correct to the nearest £1.

Show the entries in the ledger of A. White.

Ledger of A. White

C. BLUE

Jan. 1 Sales	£200	Jan. 1	Bills Receivable	£200
Apr. 1 Bank	200	Apr.10	Bills Receivable	225
Bank	16			
Interest Received	9			

BILLS RECEIVABLE

Jan. 1 C. Blue	200	Feb. 1 Bank A/c	200
Apr. 10 C. Blue	225		

BANK A/C

Feb. 1 Bills Receivable A/c	200	Feb. 1 Discount Charges A/c	6
		Apr.1 C.Blue	200
		C. Blue (for noting charges)	16

DISCOUNT CHARGES A/C

Feb. 1 Bank A/c	6

INTEREST RECEIVED A/C

Apr.10 Blue	9

---

13. Trial balances and final accounts

Although bills of exchange are used less these days, examiners often set questions showing bills payable and bills receivable in a Trial Balance or list of balances. It is important to remember that:

(a) Bills receivable are current assets; and
(b) bills payable are current liabilities.

They will therefore appear as such in the Balance Sheet.

Another important point is that even when a bill receivable is discounted with a bank and disappears from our financial records there is still a chance that we shall have to honour it should our customer (who accepted liability on it) dishonour it on the due date. This is called a *contingent liability*. Contingent liabilities must be shown as a note below Balance Sheets — for example:

NOTE: Contingent liabilities exist on bills of exchange to the value of £1,780.

Progress test 9

1. Define a Bill of Exchange. (1)

2. Why is a Bill of Exchange useful and what does it do? (2)

3.   Who are the parties to a bill?   **(3)**

4.   What do you understand by the term 'acceptance'?   **(4)**

5.   How does acceptance alter the position of one party to the bill?   **(4)**

6.   A seller can take one of three steps with a bill. What are these?   **(5)**

7.   What do you understand by dishonour of a bill?   **(11)**

8.   Who is primarily liable on a dishonoured bill?   **(11)**

9.   What do you understand by retiring and renewing a bill. **(12)**

Specimen questions

1.   On 1 January, S. Ltd sells goods to D. Ltd valued at £700. S. Ltd received in payment a three months' bill. On 1 February S. Ltd discounts the bill at a bank for £694. On 1 April, the bill is dishonoured, notarial charges being £10. Show the entries in the ledger of S. Ltd.

2.   On 1 June 19_2, X purchased goods from Y for £860 and sold goods to Z for £570.

On the same date, X drew a bill (No. 1) at three months on Z for £400 and Z accepted it.

On 12 June 19_2, Z drew a bill (No. 2) at three months on Q for £150 which Q accepted.

On 14 June, Z endorsed bill No. 2 over to X and, on 16 June, X endorsed this bill over to Y.

On 20 June, X accepted a bill (No. 3) at three months for £720 drawn by Y in full settlement of his account including interest. On 23 June, Y discounted bill No. 3 at his bank.

On 17 September, Y informed X that Q's acceptance had been dishonoured and X sent a cheque for £150 to Y. The other bills were paid on the due dates.

On 20 September, X received a cheque from Z for half the amount due from him.

Show the entries to record these transactions in the ledger and cash book of X.

3. On 1 January, T. Hull sells goods valued at £1,500 to S. King. Upon inspecting the goods, King finds that damage has occurred to some items which reduces the price by £250. Hull agrees to allow credit for this amount. Hull then draws a bill at three months for the balance which is accepted by King. After one month, Hull decides to discount the bill with his bank at a nominal rate of 5 per cent. However, on maturity the bill is dishonoured. Noting charges amount to £10. Subsequently King settles his debt in cash on 31 May. You are required to show the above transactions as they would appear in the Cash and Ledger Accounts of T. Hull.

10
The Journal

1. Purpose of the Journal
The Journal is the subsidiary book in which we record the *details of any transaction that cannot be recorded in any other subsidiary book.*

(a) Its main purpose is to provide a convenient record of the details of such transactions *in date order.*

(b) To achieve this the Journal states which accounts are affected by the transaction and gives the debit and credit entries that are to be made in the Ledger.

(c) In addition, the Journal explains *why* we are going to *debit* one account and *credit* another. The explanation of the entries to be made in the Ledger is a very important part of a Journal entry and is referred to as the *narration*. A Journal entry is not complete without a narration.

(d) Although it is not strictly necessary we do frequently Journalise important entries so as to have them on record in the books of the business. Thus the original contribution of capital by a proprietor could simply be debited in the Cash A/c or Bank A/c and be credited to Capital Account, but this would be better acknowledged by a formal 'Journal Entry'.

2. Transactions that require Journal entries
The most common Journal entries are:

(a) Opening entries (when a business starts up).

(b) Closing entries (when we work out the Final Accounts of the business).

(c) Bad Debts (*see* Chapter 12).

(d) Dishonoured cheques.
(e) Depreciation (*see* Chapter 13).
(f) Purchases of assets.
(g) Sales of worn-out assets.
(h) The correction of errors (*see* Chapter 14).

Some of these entries are dealt with later in this chapter. Others are dealt with later in the book.

3. Journalising a transaction

To journalise a transaction we decide what the double entry is to be. This may be simple (debit Trading Account; credit Stock Account for example) or it may be more complex, with more than one account to debit, and more than one account to credit.

The form is shown below, with the account to be debited shown first and the account to be credited shown later.

A narration then explains the entry, usually beginning with the word Being ...'

Example

Date	Particulars	Fol.	Debit	Credit
19__ Oct. 17	Bad Debts A/c Dr John W. Steps A/c Being debt written off as bad on bankruptcy of debtor		£ 42	£ 42

(*see* Chapter 12 for treatment of bad debts.)

NOTE: (1) This transaction cannot be entered in any other book of prime entry, i.e. it does not affect Sales, Purchases, Returns Inwards, Returns Outwards, Cash, Bank or Petty Cash. (2) The accounts which are to be debited and credited are clearly stated. (3) The narration explains *why* the debt is being written off.

4. Composite Journal entries

You will often encounter transactions that involve debiting one account and crediting a number of other accounts. Such transactions are recorded in the Journal by means of a composite Journal entry.

Example

On transferring the balances from the Ledger accounts into the final accounts, although the entries may appear in the accounts in detail, the Journal entry can take the following form:

			£	£
Dec. 31	Trading A/c	Dr	19,000	
	To Stock			3,000
	Purchases			9,000
	Wages			7,000
		£	19,000	19,000
	Being transfer of balances at this date			

5. Opening Journal entries

On opening the accounts for the first time, e.g. on the purchase of business, the accounts would be opened in the Ledger by means of a Journal entry as follows:

Example

			£	£
Aug. 17	Stock	Dr	2,500	
	Debtors ABC		50	
	DEF		40	
	Van		3,410	
	Fixtures		4,500	
	Creditors: HIJ			20
	KLM			30
	Vendor (C. Roke)			10,450
		£	10,500	10,500
	Being assets and liabilities acquired from C. Roke this day			

The next step in this transaction would be to record the introduction of capital by the new proprietor, and the subsequent payment of £10,450 to settle the amount owing to the vendor of the business, C. Roke.

Since this involves the receipt of cash into the bank and this payment of funds out of the bank, there is no need to journalise the transactions, since they already appear in the Cash Book.

---

6. Depreciation (*see* **Chapter 13**).

This is charged against profits in the Profit and Loss Account, and obviously will need to be journalised.

> NOTE: In cases where the calculation of the amount of depreciation may be somewhat involved, the narration in the Journal entry shows how the ultimate charge has been arrived at.

Example

			£	£
Dec. 31	Profit and Loss A/c	Dr	550	
	To provision for depreciation on machinery			550
	Being depreciation on machines at 25% per annum, on cost, as follows:			
	M/c No. 1 £1,400 full year. £350			
	M/c No. 2 £1,200 six months. £150			
	M/c No. 3 £800 three months. £50			

---

7. Purchase of assets on credit

When assets are purchased on credit the transaction must be journalised, since it does not fit into any other subsidiary book.

> NOTE: Assets are purchased with the intention of retaining them in the business to be used over a period of time, and the purchase of assets must never be confused with the *normal* purchases of goods that are intended for resale and which are dealt with in the Purchases Day Book.

Example

(a) On the purchase of a motor van on credit from ABC Garages Ltd, the Journal entry would appear:

			£	£
Jan. 9	Motor Van A/c	Dr	4,425	
	To ABC Garages Ltd			4,425
	Being new van purchased on credit this day			

(b) When allowances are given for assets taken in part exchange for new assets purchased the composite Journal form can be used (*see* **4**).

Jan. 15	Motor Van A/c Dr	4,425	
	To Motor Van A/c		500
	ABC Garages Ltd		3,925
	Being new van purchased on credit		
	this day, less an allowance made		
	on the old van number . . .; taken		
	in part exchange		

8. Purchase of fixed assets involving adjustments and Completion Statements

On the acquisition of freehold property the price arrived at, called the *purchase consideration*, often includes adjustments for rents, insurance, rates and repairs, etc., that have either been *paid* or are *owing* by the previous owner of the property.

Problems of this type are often set in examination papers with a view to testing the principles involved and the ability of the candidate to set out a solution in Journal form. Very often the problem is really one of applied common sense, and normally should present little or no difficulty.

Sample question

On 1 January 19__, V. Hugo acquired freehold premises from L. Mann. The purchase consideration was agreed at £72,500, which figure *included* adjustments in respect of the following:

Rates, £440, had been paid to the following 31 March.
Insurance on the property, £120, had been paid to 30 June.
Part of the property was let to a tenant, and rent, £180, was owing to L. Mann for the month of December 19__. It had been agreed that this rent would be collected by the new owner, V. Hugo.

Show, by means of Journal entries, the details of the acquisition in the books of V. Hugo. Final settlement was made by cheque on 7 January. Journalise cash and bank transactions.

NOTE: V. Hugo acquires the benefit of £440 rates prepaid and £120 insurance prepaid; he also takes over the £180 debtors for rent.

These items total £740. This must be deducted from the figure of £72,500 to arrive at the price paid for the property, i.e. £72,500 - £740 = £71,760, since the question tells us that the price of £72,500 *included* adjustments for the items listed.

Answer

The Journal entries in the books of V. Hugo would appear as follows:

Jan. 1	Freehold premises	Dr	71,760	
	Rates	"	440	
	Insurance	"	120	
	Rent	"	180	
	Vendor L. Mann			72,500
			72,500	72,500
	Being premises acquired together with rates prepaid to March 31, insurance prepaid to June 30 and accrued rents due from tenants for the month of December			
Jan. 7	Vendor. L. Mann	Dr	72,500	
	Bank			72,500
	Being cheque in settlement of account on purchase of freehold premises			

9. Sale of worn-out assets

Here the decision about which accounts to debit and which to credit is simple. The rules are:

(a) Remove the asset from the books entirely by crediting the asset account with its book value, whatever that happens to be.

(b) Debit the Cash A/c, or the Bank A/c or the personal account of

the person who took the asset from us, according to whether we received cash, or a cheque, or a promise to pay at some future date.
(c) If there is a difference between the figures it must either be a 'loss on sale of asset' or a 'profit on sale of asset'. What this really means is that in the past we estimated the depreciation wrongly. If we over-depreciated we shall make a 'profit on sale of asset'; if we underestimated depreciation we make a 'loss on sale of asset'.

Example

Peter Brown sells a motor vehicle surplus to requirements for £1,200. Its book value is £800. What will be the Journal Entry? The buyer Ray Motors Ltd pays be cheque.

Answer

Debit Bank A/c £1,200; Credit Motor Vehicles A/c £800 and credit 'Profit on Sale of Motor Vehicle A/c' £400.

10. Dishonoured cheques
When a cheque is dishonoured the rules are:

(a) Restore the debt to the debtor, including any discount allowed, since the original debt has not been settled.
(b) Credit the Bank A/c with the value of the cheque (to remove the funds recorded on our books which never arrived).
(c) Credit Discount Allowed A/c with the amount of any discount, because we are no longer going to suffer this loss. (Of course we might suffer an even bigger one if our debtor really is in financial difficulties.)

Progress test 10

1. What is the Journal?   **(1)**

2. What is a Journal entry?   **(1)**

3. How do we set about journalising a transaction?   **(3)**

4. Give examples of transactions that require journalising. **(2)**

5. What do you understand by a composite Journal entry? **(4)**

6. What is a narration and what does it do? **(1)**

Specimen questions

1. B. Bee has not kept any books. He asks you to introduce a double-entry system starting with the following assets and liabilities on 1 June 19__

Premises	£45,000
Delivery van	£3,500
Stock	£1,800
Debtors	£200
Cash at Bank	£1,400
Cash in hand	£30
Creditors	£320

Draft an opening journal entry for B. Bee. (*Note*: You have to discover the amount of the proprietor's capital — which is the difference between the total of the assets and the total of the liabilities.)

2. Draft the journal entries to record the following (all on 31 December).

(a) The correction of an error in posting whereby R. Brown was debited with £50 instead of P. Brown.
(b) The purchase on credit of a new motor lorry from T. Edmunds (for use in the business).
(c) Commission is earned in cash from the sale of a vehicle displayed on the forecourt.
(d) Bought a typewriter on credit from the Reliance Typewriter Co. at a cost of £60.

3. When completing the accounts of A. Builder for the year ending 31 March 19__ the following details were found.

(a) The trustee in the bankruptcy of A. Customer sent a cheque for £52, which was a first and final payment of £0.65 in the £1 in respect of the amount due on Customer's Account in the Sales Ledger.

(b) Work carried out at the private residence of A. Builder, costing £160, had not been invoiced.

(c) Included in the Purchases Account was £569 and in the Wages Account £631 paid in respect of building an extension to Builder's own offices.

(d) V. Slow paid the balance of £500 owing by him for work done, together with a further £10 in respect of interest on his overdue account.

Draft the entries necessary in the Journal of A. Builder, and sow the effects on the profit for the year.

4. Scott was in business on his own account, and during the year to 31 December 19__

(a) he used goods, valued at £69 selling price for private purposes;

(b) he purchased a motor van for £1,340, and a further £48 for tax and insurance paid in advance; he received an allowance of £350 on an old van taken in part exchange and paid the balance by cheque (the old van stood in Scott's books at £380);

(c) a cheque for £100 received from Smith, a customer, in settlement of the latter's account for that sum was dishonoured and returned by the bank; Scott is of the opinion that nothing can be recovered from Smith;

(d) on 1 July he lent £100, privately and free of interest, to a senior employee; he later decided that the loan should be shown in the books as a business asset; the money paid being regarded as extra capital contributed. The money was to be repaid as a deduction from the employee's new year bonus.

These matters were all carried out, but no entries were made in the books. Give the Journal entries in Scott's books to record these matters.

5.   (a) On 1 November 19__ Property Ltd purchased freehold premises, part of which was let at a rent of £240 a month, and paid (including the deposit) a total of £65,658, made up as follows:

	£	£
Purchase price		65,000
Add Water rate proportion for five months to 31 March 19__	325	
Rent due from tenant for September and October (now to be collected by purchaser)	480	
		805
		65,805
Less Business rates, proportion for the month of October		147
		£65,658

No personal accounts were opened. Show the entries in the Journal of Property Ltd. The money paid is to be journalised.

   (b)   On 31 December 19__ Poulton, a trader, paid £174 to a firm of builders. £54 was for repairs to Poulton's private house and £120 represented repairs to his business premises. It was agreed that the landlord of the business premises should bear £40 of the cost of repairs and that this amount should be deducted from the quarter's rent of £100 due on 31 December. On that date Poulton paid the amount due to the landlord. Show the entries in Poulton's Journal.

No personal account is to be opened for the landlord and cash is to be journalised.   (*RSA*)

6.   You are required to state precisely and briefly the circumstances which could have given rise to each of the following journal entries:

			£	£
(a)	F. Brown's Account	Dr	11,000	
	Sales Account			10,000
	VAT Account			1,000
(b)	Manufacturing Wages Account	Dr	14,000	
	Bank			9,300
	PAYE Account			2,900
	National Insurance Account			1,800
(c)	Trading Account	Dr	41,000	
	Profit and Loss Account			41,000
(d)	Bills Receivable Account	Dr	2,000	
	N and Co. Limited Account			2,000

11
Nominal accounts and adjustments

1. Treatment

All nominal accounts are transferred to Trading or Profit and Loss Account at the end of the financial period, when these 'Final Accounts' are prepared. Adjustments arise when it is necessary to adjust any of the figures to achieve the aims of all good book-keepers. These are:

(a) That the profits shall take account of every penny earned in the financial year, and every penny expended in earning the incomes received.

(b) That the Balance Sheet shall give a 'true and fair view' of the assets and liabilities of the business at 23.59 hours on the last day of the financial year.

Since we are concerned with finding *true* figures for gross and net profits, we must only transfer *those amounts which relate to the period with which we are dealing*.

We must therefore bring into account:

- (*i*) *all* items of *expense* for the current year whether we have actually paid them or not; and
- (*ii*) *all* items of *income* for the current year whether we have actually received them or not.

This invariably involves adjustments to nominal accounts at the end of the financial period to allow for:

- (*i*) expenses incurred but not yet paid;
- (*ii*) expenses paid which relate to the following period;
- (*iii*) income due but not yet received;
- (*iv*) income received which is not income of the present year but is received in advance for next year's efforts.

Example

Expenses owing. If a firm rents premises at an *annual rental* of £3,600, i.e. £300 per month, at the end of one year on 31 December, the firm has actually paid £3,300 rent up to the month of November. The Rent Account in the Ledger after the final accounts for the year ended 31 December 19__, have been prepared will be as follows.

RENT ACCOUNT

19__		£	19__		£
Jan. 1 — Nov. 30	Bank	£3,300	Dec. 31 Profit and		
Dec. 31 Balance c/d		300		Loss A/c	£3,600
		£3,600			£3,600
			19__		£
			Jan. 1 Balance b/d		300

Consider the following questions.

(a) What does this balance of £300 represent? Rent owing by the firm.
(b) On which side of the account has the balance been brought down? Credit side.
(c) What are all credit balances remaining on accounts in the Ledger? Liabilities of the business.
(d) Where should we show this balance of £300? In the Balance Sheet.
(e) How will we show it? As a current liability. (Can you explain why?)

The charge to the Profit and Loss Account must be the *full* amount of the rent for the year. Therefore we must *debit* Profit and Loss with £3,600 and *credit* Rent Account.

This means that the *two* sides of the Rent Account do not agree, and to balance the account we insert the 'difference' on the *debit* side, carrying down a *credit* balance to start the next financial period.

This credit balance will be shown in the Balance Sheet as a *current liability*.

NOTE: *Accruals basis* Dealing with the Final Accounts in this way by taking account of any adjustments required, is called keeping accounts on an **'accruals basis'**. We take account not only of what has been received and paid, but what has accrued due at the time of calculating the profits.

2. Effect of balance brought down on the next payment

When an *expense account* has a *credit balance* with which to start the new financial period it represents expenses owing, i.e. a creditor for expenses. The first payment made in the next financial period will obviously be a payment to discharge this liability that relates to the preceding financial period.

3. A profit for the year, not yet received

We have seen that an expense of the business in arrears has to be viewed as if it had been paid (£3,600 Rent in the last example, leaving a liability of £300 for rent due to be paid next year).

Consider the same £300 from the point of view of the property company waiting to receive its rent. Its Rent Receivable Account is as shown below:

RENT RECEIVED ACCOUNT

19__		£	19__		£
Dec. 31	Profit & Loss A/c	1,964,750	Jan. –	(Many entries to	
			Dec.	a total value of	1,627,000
			Dec. 31	Balance c/d	337,750
		£1,964,750			£1,964,750
19__		£			
Jan. 1	Balance b/d	337,750			

NOTES:
(*a*) The firm has many properties on its books, and a lot of tenants are overdue — to the tune of £337,750. Among these is the £300 owed by our example above.

(*b*) The balance carried down this time is a debit balance — Rent Receivable due. This will appear on the Balance Sheet as an asset. By doing the adjustment we achieve our two aims: (*a*) the correct profit for the year is arrived at (*b*) the Balance Sheet shows the true position of the business, it has £337,750 of debts due from tenants.

4. Accrued expenses

A firm may end its financial year on 31 December, but 31 December may fall on a Wednesday. If the firm makes up wages to the preceding Saturday, then at the date of the final accounts and Balance Sheet, wages must be *owing* to the employees for the four days Sunday, Monday, Tuesday and Wednesday.

To ensure that the full amount of wages and/or salaries is charged against profits in the final accounts, the amount owing must be carefully estimated and adjusted in the Wages and/or Salaries Account.

Sample question

A firm's financial year ends on 31 December. On 31 December 19__, the debit balance brought down on the Wages and Salaries Account was £37,046, but this did not include £733 wages and salaries due to employees at 31 December.

Show the Wages and Salaries Account after the final accounts have been prepared on 31 December 19__.

Answer

Dr		WAGES AND SALARIES ACCOUNT		Cr
19__		£	19__	£
Dec. 31 Balance b/d		37,046	Dec. 31 Profit and Loss	
31 Balance c/d		733	A/c	37,779
		£37,779		£37,779
			19__	£
			Jan. 1 Balance b/d	733

This balance of £733 will be shown as a current liability in the Balance Sheet on 31 December 19__. With the first payment of wages and salaries in the following January, this amount will be discharged.

5. Payments in advance (or prepayments)

If the financial year ends on 31 December and a policy of insurance is taken out on 1 July, then at the end of December in the year in which the policy is taken out only half the amount of the premium has been used up, and we are still covered by insurance for the first six months of the following financial year.

Example

Tims starts business on 1 April 19__, and prepares his final accounts on 31 March 19__. On 1 July he paid an annual insurance premium of £300 by cheque covering his premises and stock for twelve months from that date.

Show the Insurance Account with the transfer to Profit and Loss Account at the end of the year.

INSURANCE ACCOUNT

19__		£	19__		£
July 1	Bank	300.00	Mar. 31	Profit and Loss A/c	225.00
			31	Balance c/d	75.00
		£300.00			£300.00
19__		£			
Apr. 1	Balance	75.00			

Why only £225 to Profit and Loss Account? From 1 July to 31 March = 9 months — thus he has 'used up' only three-quarters of the insurance premium already paid. What does the £75 represent? An asset? Why?

On 1 April in the following year he will start, having already paid £75 during the previous year, and this provides him with insurance cover until 30 June, since on 1 July another *annual* premium will become payable.

6. Income received in advance

Where income is received in advance it is not properly a profit of the current year, but part of next year's profit. Many firms and companies, such as British Rail receiving season ticket money and insurance companies taking premiums on an annual basis need to do adjustments for these incomes received in advance.

Consider the insurer referred to in the last example (5 above). Their customer Tims has paid £75 in advance for next year's cover, and so have thousands of others. The Insurance Co's Premiums Received A/c might appear as shown below.

PREMIUMS RECEIVED ACCOUNT

19__		£	19__		£
Dec. 31	Premiums earned (to Profit and Loss A/c)	19,780,000	Jan. 1–	Sundry premiums	
			Dec. 31	of various sorts	24,294,726
	Balance c/d	4,514,726			
		£24,294,726			£24,294,726
			19__		£
			Jan. 1	Balance b/d	4,514,726

Clearly, the balance is a liability, Premiums Received in Advance. The Insurance Co. owes all these customers cover against various risks for some part of the coming year.

7. Nominal accounts with debit and credit balances

Examinations frequently include questions which involve balances on both sides of a nominal account.

Sample question

A trader sub-lets part of his business premises to two tenants — Green and Brown. At 31 December 19__ Green owed £260 rent for the month of December, and Brown had paid a month's rent, £200 for the month of January 19__ in advance.

During the following year the trader received £3,640 from Green representing rent for the fourteen months to 31 January 19__, and £2,000 from Brown, representing rent for the ten months to 30 November 19__.

The trader makes up his accounts annually at 31 December. Show the Rent Receivable Account in the trader's Ledger for the year 19__. No personal accounts are kept for Green and Brown.

(RSA)

Answer

Dr		RENT RECEIVABLE ACCOUNT			Cr
19__		£	19__		£
Jan. 1	Balance b/d	260	Jan. 1	Balance b/d	200
Dec. 31	Profit and		Jan. to Dec.	Bank	
	Loss A/c	5,520		(Green)	3,640
	(12 x £260 +		Jan. to Dec.	Bank	
	12 x £200)			(Brown)	2,000
31	Balance c/d	260	Dec. 31	Balance c/d	200
		£6,040			£6,040
19__		£	19__		£
Jan. 1	Balance b/d	200	Jan. 1	Balance b/d	260
	(Asset in Balance Sheet.			(Liability in the Balance Sheet.	
	Amount owing to the			Amount paid in advance by	
	trader by Brown.)			Green.)	

8. Treatment in the Profit and Loss Account

In examinations you may be required to deal with the adjustments in the Ledger Accounts or in the Trading and Profit and Loss Accounts. Usually in the case of the final accounts the adjustments are given by way of footnotes to a Trial Balance or list of balances, and you are required to act upon the instructions given in the question and incorporate the adjustments in the final accounts.

You will have no difficulty if you keep our two points in mind:

(a) The amount that appears in the 'Final Accounts' must be the full amount of the loss suffered or the profit achieved under the heading you are dealing with — not a penny more, and not a penny less.

(b) Since the adjustments are 'footnotes' drawn up after the Trial Balance has been taken out they have not yet been dealt with in the ledger. They must therefore appear twice — once in the Final Accounts and once in the Balance Sheet. You have already learned to do this with Closing Stock, but it has to be done with all adjustments.

Sample question _____

From the following Trial Balance and the notes appended below, prepare the Trading and Profit and Loss Accounts for the year ended 31 December 19__, and a Balance Sheet as at the date.

TRIAL BALANCE OF A. JONES AT 31 DECEMBER 19__

	Dr £	Cr. £
Capital A. Jones		56,500
Sales		65,500
Purchases	23,500	
Salaries	11,200	
Rent	2,150	
Insurance	530	
Drawings	12,500	
Fixed assets	56,000	
Bank	5,450	
Stock at 1 January	11,520	
Debtors	1,250	
Creditors		2,100
	£124,100	124,100

(a) Stock on hand at 31 December, £4,900.
(b) Salaries owing at 31 December, £300.
(c) Rent paid in advance at 31 December, £200.
(d) Insurance paid in advance at 31 December, £90.
(e) During December Jones took £100 in goods at selling price for his own use. This has not been recorded in the books.

Answer

A. JONES — TRADING AND PROFIT AND LOSS ACCOUNT FOR THE YEAR ENDED 31 DECEMBER 19__

	£			£
Opening stock			Sales	65,500
Jan. 1	11,520		Drawings (Goods for	
Purchases	23,500		own consumption)	100
	35,020			65,600
Less Closing stock	4,900			
Cost of stock sold	30,120			
Gross Profit c/d	35,480			
	£65,600			£65,600

	£			£
Rent	2,150		Gross profit b/d	35,480
Less Rent pre-				
paid (c)	200			
		1,950		
Insurance	530			
Less Insurance				
prepaid (d)	90			
		440		
Salaries and wages	11,200			
Add Salaries				
owing (b)	300			
		11,500		
Total		13,890		
Net profit to Capital Account		21,590		
		£35,480		£35,480

BALANCE SHEET AS AT 31 DECEMBER 19_

	£		£	£	£
Fixed assets	56,000	Capital A/c Jan. 1			56,500
		Add Net profit		21,590	
		Less Drawings	12,500		
		+ Drawings in kind	100		
				12,600	
					8,990
					65,490
Current assets:		Current liabilities:			
Stock (*a*)	4,900	Creditors		2,100	
Debtors	1,250	Salaries due (*b*)		300	
Bank	5,450				2,400
Rent prepaid (*c*)	200				
Insurance prepaid (*d*)	90				
		11,890			
		£67,890			£67,890

NOTE: The items given as footnotes have been dealt with twice.

		Debit effect	*Credit effect*
(*a*)	Stock at Dec. 31:	Asset in the Balance Sheet	In the Trading Account
(*b*)	Salaries owing:	In Profit and Loss Account	Liability in the Balance Sheet
(*c*)	Rent prepaid:	Asset in the Balance Sheet	In the Profit and Loss Account (deducted from rent paid)
(*d*)	Insurance prepaid:	Asset in the Balance Sheet	In the Profit and Loss Account (deducted from insurance paid)
(*e*)	Goods taken from stock:	Increase the figure for drawings, which is deducted from capital in the Balance Sheet	In the Trading Account; by increasing the figure for sales

9. Points to note

With *nominal accounts*, it is only necessary to note:

(a) the *side* on which the balance has been brought down; and
(b) the *name* of the account concerned in order to deduce what it must represent.

Remember that debit balances represent assets and credit balances represent liabilities.

Progress test 11

1.   A credit balance brought down on Wages Account represents a liability; explain how this can arise.   **(4)**

2.   A debit balance brought down on Insurance Account represents an asset. How and why?   **(5)**

3.   A credit balance brought down on Rent Account equals what?   **(1)**

Specimen questions

1.   The balances on certain accounts of Foster Hardware Co. as at 1 April 19_1 were:

Rent and rates payable:	£
accruals	2,200
prepayments	1,940

Rent receivable:	
prepayments	625

During the financial year, the business:
paid rent by cheque,   £5,200;
paid rates by cheque,   £3,050;
received cheque for rent of sub-let premises £960.

Closing balance as at 31 March 19_2 were:

Rent and rates payable:	£
accruals	2,370
prepayments	1,880

Rent receivable:	
prepayments	680

You are required to post to and balance the appropriate accounts for the year ended 31 March 19_2, deriving the transfer entries to Profit and Loss Account, where applicable.

2. On 31 May 19_3 R. Gee's Balance Sheet showed the following:

Items in advance		*Items outstanding*	
	£		£
Insurance	20	Stationery	30
		Salaries	700
		Rates	300

During the year ended 31 May 19_4 the following payments were made by cheque:

	£
Insurance	240
Stationery	370
Salaries	20,000
Rates	2,700

On 31 May 19_4 the Balance Sheet showed the following:

Items in advance	£	*Items outstanding*	£
Insurance	40	Stationery	10
Rates	600	Salaries	800

Prepare the ledger accounts for each of the above items for the year ended 31 May 19_4 showing clearly the amount charged to Profit and Loss Account in each case.

3. (a) L.J. owns a number of properties which he rents to tenants. He keeps the following accounts:
  (i)   Freehold Properties Account;
  (ii) Rents Received Account;
  (iii) Property Expenses Account.
  On 1 July 19_1 the properties showed a book value of £214,000, rent was owing £356, repairs outstanding were £2,700 rates prepaid amounted to £900.

Open the three accounts named above and enter the opening balances.

From the information on page 156 relating to the half year ended 31 December 19_1 make the entries which would arise in these accounts during the half year.

Balance the accounts as at 31 December 19_1 assuming that L.J. prepares his final accounts at that date.

Aug. 10 Sold property, book value £52,000 for £62,600.

Sept. 14 Paid £3,596 for repairs and extensions to property, £1,500 of this amount to be capitalised as improvements.

Sept. 30 Rents received for quarter ended at this date £16,520.

Sept. 30 Paid insurances on property for one year to 30 September 19_2, £624.

Oct. 15 Purchased an additional property for £32,850.

Nov. 20 Paid half year's rates on properties to 31 March 19_2, £3,140.

Dec. 31 Rents received for quarter ended at this date £17,525. Rents owing at 31 December 19_1 £375.

4. From the following Trial Balance of Alexander Mackay, a wholesale trader, prepare Trading and Profit and Loss Account for the year ending 31 March 19_6 and Balance Sheet as at that date.

	£	£
Capital		98,000
Stock, 1 April 19_5	46,580	
Purchases	285,000	
Sales		362,000
Bank overdraft		14,320
Personal drawings	5,500	
Wages (Trading A/c)	26,000	
Rates and insurance	6,250	
Heat and light	840	
Salaries	18,750	
Motor expenses	5,260	
Office expenses	1,440	
Bank charges	1,400	
Discounts allowed	2,650	
Discount received		2,200
Office furniture and fittings	4,200	
Motor vans	7,400	
Loan to business		50,000
Loan interest	3,000	
Freehold buildings	75,000	
Debtors	71,000	
Creditors		34,000
Cash in hand	250	
	£560,520	£560,520

(a) Stock at 31 March 19_6 £53,450.
(b) Included in the heat and light item is the sum of £80 for electricity for Mackay's private residence.
(c) Insurance premiums paid in advance amounted to £500 at 31 March 19_6.
(d) A bill for petrol and oil, £120, was unpaid at the 31 March 19_6.   (*RSA*)

5. A. Kemp owns a small restaurant and the following balances appeared in his books at 30 June 19_5:

	£		£
Revenue received from restaurant	51,750	Rates and Insurances	420
		Heat and Light	1,300
Stocks (1 July 19_4):		General Expenses	1,180
Food and drinks	120	Trade creditors	700
China, glass and cutlery	584	Cash in hand and	
Purchases:		balance at bank	463
Food and drinks	8,169	Loan from bank as at	
China, glass and cutlery	172	1 July 19_4	3,000
Kitchen equipment	826	Furniture and fittings	24,560
Wages: kitchen	11,040	Proprietor's drawings	12,500
restaurant	6,000		

From the above list of balances, calculate the capital of the business and prepare A. Kemp's Trading and Profit and Loss Account for the year ended 30 June 19_5 and a Balance Sheet as at that date taking into account the following:

On 30 June 19_5:

(a) stocks of food and drinks were valued at £160 and of china, glass and cutlery at £580;
(b) a full year's interest at 12 per cent per annum on the bank loan was due but had not been paid.

NOTE: All wages are to appear in the Trading Account and losses of china glass etc. are to be treated as depreciation in the Profit and Loss Account.

12

Bad debts and provision for bad debts

1. Bad debts

When we supply customers on credit terms they receive the goods or services supplied and pay later, according to the terms agreed. Normal business credit is 'cash 30 days', but since this means 30 days from the rendering of a monthly 'statement of account' the actual credit period may be anywhere between one month and two months. *Credit control* is usually exercised. Some common rules for good credit control are:

(a) Specify a limit on the size of orders which must not be exceeded without special authority.
(b) Never pass an order to the Dispatch Department without checking the credit situation — the new order may carry the debtor over the limit allowed.
(c) When an account becomes overdue, stop all further orders and ring (and write) for an explanation, and requesting payment.
(d) Follow-up any failure to pay after requesting with a solicitor's letter and a threat of legal action. Debtors pay the person who is pressing them.

When a debt becomes irrecoverable it is written off as bad. For this purpose we open a *Bad Debts Account*.

(a) *When the debt is written off: debit* Bad Debts Account; *credit* the Debtor (Personal Account).
(b) At the end of the financial year the *total* of the Bad Debts Account *will be transferred to the Profit and Loss Account: debit* Profit and Loss Account; *credit* Bad Debts Account.

Sample question

On 10 December 19__, A. Wenn, a debtor for £80 in the books of J. Rowlands, is adjudicated bankrupt and a final dividend of 75p in the £ is received by cheque, the remaining balance being written off.

Show the entries in the Ledger Accounts of J. Rowland, assuming that debts already written off at 1 December amount to £37 and show the subsequent transfer to the final accounts at 31 December 19__.

Answer

A. WENN

Dr				Cr
19__		19__		
Dec. 1 Balance b/d	£80	Dec. 10 Bank		£60
		10 Bad Debts A/c		20
	£80			£80

BANK ACCOUNT (EXTRACT)

Dec. 10 A. Wenn	£60

BAD DEBTS ACCOUNT

Dec. 1 Balance b/d	£37	Dec. 31 Profit and	
10 A. Wenn	20	Loss A/c	£57
	£57		£57

PROFIT AND LOSS ACCOUNT (EXTRACT)

Bad debts	£57

NOTE: (1) Examinations frequently require candidates to show entries in the accounts in this fashion, and you should clearly indicate that the account is not a complete one by the use of the word 'extract' as in the above example. (2) Students sometimes have difficulty in deciding what to show in answer to a question, and what not to show. A careful reading of the question will normally overcome this difficulty, but a golden rule to follow is that unless the question specifically tells you *not* to show certain accounts, you should show the entries that would be made in them in the form of an extract as in the above example.

2.   Bad debts recovered

When a debt previously written off as bad is subsequently paid the debt must first be reinstated in the personal account, if it is still on the books and then the receipt of cash is recorded through the personal account. In this way the personal account contains an accurate record of the transaction.

If, as is more likely, some time has elapsed and the debtor has ceased to trade and the account is no longer in our ledger it is usual to ignore the personal record and to treat the cash recovered as a 'Bad Debt Recovered'. Such a recovery will usually include interest, and possibly legal charges recovered as well.

Example

On 3 January 19__, a cheque for £47 is received from R. Coke. The £47 represents a debt of £30 with interest of £9, and legal charges of £8. Coke's account has previously been written off as bad.

The entries in the Ledger to deal with this transaction will be as follows:

BAD DEBTS RECOVERED ACCOUNT

		19__	£
		Jan. 3 Bank	30

INTEREST RECEIVABLE

		19__	£
		Jan. 3 Bank	9

LEGAL CHARGES

		19__	£
		Jan. 3 Bank	8

BANK

19__	£		
Jan. 3 Bad Debt Recovered etc.	47		

3.   Provision for bad and doubtful debts

When a debt is irrecoverable we write it off to a Bad Debts Account, which finds its way ultimately to the debit of Profit and Loss, being written off as a loss or expense. As the size of the business grows, the number of personal accounts will increase, thus the incidence of bad debts will increase also. At the end of any given year we shall have a certain number of debts on our books, which are being passed on to the new year for collection. The question is 'Are all these debts good?' The answer must be that some of them will inevitably prove to be bad. We have thus committed two errors:

(a) Our Final Accounts for the year just ended do not carry all the losses for the year, for some hidden bad debts have been passed on as if they were good.
(b) Our Balance Sheet does not present a 'true and fair view' for it shows a number of debtors, some of which are bad, as if all were good.

To put these matters right we make a reasonable **Provision for Bad Debts**. A provision is a part of the profits of a business which is held back from the proprietor, to cover an eventuality that may arise in the future, such as a bad debt, a tax assessment or some similar event. Suppose we believe 8 per cent of our debtors normally prove to be bad. The correct procedure at year end is as follows:

(a) Scrutinise the debts. If any are bad, write them off at once, and the resulting Bad Debts figure will be debited in the Profit and Loss A/c.
(b) All the rest of the debts are now deemed to be good, but we know that 8 per cent of them may yet prove to be bad. Therefore:

> (*i*) Debit Profit and Loss Account with the appropriate amount (say 8 per cent of total debts of £1,500 = £120). The Profit and loss Account is now carrying the full burden of bad debts for the year
>
> (*ii*) Since we cannot credit any particular debtor (we do not know who will fall on hard times), we credit Bad Debts Provision Account.

PROFIT AND LOSS ACCOUNT (EXTRACT)

19__		£
Dec. 31 Bad Debts		173
31 Provision for Bad Debts		120

BAD DEBTS ACCOUNT

19__	£	19__	£
Jun. 5 Smith	102	Dec. 31 Profit & Loss	173
Oct. 7 Jones	71		
	£173		£173

BAD DEBTS PROVISION ACCOUNT

		19__	£
		Dec. 31 Profit & Loss	120

The entry on the Balance Sheet in the Current Assets section will read:

Debtors	1,500	
Less Provision	120	
Net debtors		1,380

The Balance Sheet now presents a 'true and fair view' of the value of the debtors.

4. Bad Debts Provisions at the end of the financial year

There are two ways of treating Bad Debts Provision Account at the end of the year. Sometimes the Bad Debts Provision is regarded as being kept independently of the actual Bad Debts Account. Consequently, the actual bad debts will still be debited to the Profit and Loss Account, and the treatment of the Provision will be as follows:

(a) The provision will rarely be the same from year to year, because it is a percentage of the debtors outstanding at the end of the year. We may need to increase the provision or to decrease it.
(b) *To increase: debit* Profit and Loss; *credit* Bad Debts Provision with the amount of the increase.
(c) *To reduce: debit* Bad Debts Provision; *credit* Profit and Loss with the amount by which it is to be reduced. This brings back that part of the Provision which is no longer required into the profits of the business.

More realistically, the actual bad debts are written off against the provision created to meet this particular loss; the resulting transfer to the Profit and loss Account represents the amount necessary to re-establish the Provision at the necessary figure for the coming year.

Sample question

Having some doubts about some of the debtors in his Ledger, Mr T. Gibbs decided at the end of the last financial year to create a Bad Debts provision of £320.

During the following year debts amounting to £215 were written off as bad, and on 31 December the balances on the personal accounts for sundry debtors amounted to £5,800.

T. Gibbs decided to maintain the Provision for Bad Debts at a figure equal to 5 per cent of total debtors.

Show the entries in the Bad Debts Account and in the Provision for Bad Debts Account, assuming that the bad debts are written off against the provision.

Answer

LEDGER OF T. GIBBS
Bad Debts

Jan. – Dec. Sundry		Dec. 31 Bad Debts	
Debtors	£215	Provision	£215

NOTE: The items on the debit side would have been written off as the debts became irrecoverable, actual amounts being entered as they were written off against the personal accounts.

BAD DEBTS PROVISION

Dec. 31 Bad Debts	£215	Jan. 1 Balance b/d	£320
31 Balance c/d	290	Dec. 31 Profit and Loss	185
	£505		£505
		Jan. 1 Balance b/d	290

NOTE: The balance on this provision must be 5 per cent of £5,800, i.e. £290; thus after debiting the actual bad debts to this account the transfer from Profit and loss Account must be such an amount as will leave £290 to be brought down as the balance in the Provision for Bad Debts Account. Since there are some funds still in the Account (£320 - £215 = £105) the amount required is a further £185 to be provided out of profits.

It is an interesting thought — to whom is the balance of £290 owed? It is clearly a liability. Answer: to the proprietor — it includes some of his profits tucked away in this Provision Account to meet any chance of bad debts in the opening months of the new financial year.

Progress test 12

1. What do you understand by the term 'provision'? **(3)**

2. Give two reasons why the proprietor of a business should create a Provision for Bad Debts? **(3)**

3. What are the entries in the Ledger on creating a Bad Debts Provision? **(3)**

4. Explain the entries necessary to increase a Bad Debts Provision. **(4)**

5. Explain the entries necessary to reduce a Bad Debts Provision. **(4)**

6. How does the Bad Debts Provision appear in the Balance Sheet? **(3)**

7. What do you understand by the term 'Net Debtors'? **(3)**

8. Explain the *two* methods available for the transfer of bad debts at the end of the financial year. **(4)**

Specimen questions

1. At the commencement of his financial year on 1 June 19__, Mr T. Rainbow created a Provision for Bad Debts of £500.

    In the following twelve months he wrote off bad debts as follows:

		£
July 9	S. Black	110
Aug. 14	F. Brown	280
Aug. 20	W. Gray	100
Nov. 9	D. White	40
Mar. 11	E. Green	18

On 31 May, when his financial year ended, his sundry debtors totalled £8,400 and he decided that the Provision for Bad Debts now required was 5 per cent of sundry debtors.

You are asked to show the entries in the appropriate nominal account(s); the personal accounts are *not* required.

2. On 1 July 19__, a firm's Provision for Bad Debts Account showed a balance of £175. During the following year ended 30 June 19__, the firm's bad debts amounted to £185 and £30 had been received for a debt previously written off.

At the end of the year it was decided to carry forward a provision of 5 per cent on the firm's debtors which amounted to £4,000.

You are required to draft the Provision for Bad Debts Account, as it would appear after the appropriate entry had been made in the Profit and loss Account. Assume that all entries are made via the Provision for Bad Debts Account. (*RSA*)

3. Among others, the following accounts appeared in the books of W. Tonge at 1 January 19_4:

		£
Debtors	A. Silkin	50
	H. Symons	120

During the year 19_4 each of these debtors became bankrupt and although nothing could be recovered from Silkin, a dividend of 70p in the £ was received in relation to Symons on 8 July 19_4. The balances then remaining on the accounts were written off as bad. Tonge's financial year ended on 31 December 19_4. Show how these items were recorded in Tonge's books as at that date. Unexpectedly on 31 May 19_5 a cheque was received from H. Symons for £36. What entries should be made to record in Tonge's books the bad debt recovered?

4. The following items appear in Smith's Trial Balance dated 31 December 19_4:

	Dr	Cr
	£	£
Bad Debts Provision (1 January 19_4)		240
Bad debts	220	
Trade debtors	2,600	

It is Smith's policy to keep the Bad Debts Provision equal to 8 per cent of the trade debtors.

You are required:

(a) to show the entries in Smith's Accounts for the year ended 31 December 19_4 to deal with the above matters; assuming bad debts are cleared to the Provision for Bad Debts Account.

(b) to show an extract from Smith's Balance Sheet at 31 December 19_4 for these matters.

13

Depreciation and amortisation

1. Entries in the accounts

The fixed assets of a business lose value or are said to *depreciate* over the length of time during which they have been used in the business.

This loss in value is chargeable against profits made during the working life of the asset concerned, and is called **depreciation**.

Debit Depreciation Account *credit* the Asset Account (thus reducing its value). Eventually all the depreciation collected together in the Depreciation Account will be cleared to Profit and Loss Account.

2. Amortisation

In the case of leasehold premises, the principle is the same, but the term *amortisation* is used, since the lease is dying away with each passing year. (mort = death)

If a lease on premises is purchased for £16,000 and the length of the lease is ten years, then one-tenth, or £1,600, will be written off each year.

3. Methods of calculating depreciation

(a) *Fixed instalment or straight-line method.* The working life of the asset is estimated. The scrap value is estimated, and is deducted from the cost price, and the *net figure* obtained is divided by the number of years of working life, to arrive at the annual charge for depreciation. (This method is often called *the equal instalment method* as the charge for each year is usually the same.)

Example

A jig costing £1,650 is estimated to have a working life of eight years, at the end of which time its scrap value will be £50.

$$\text{Annual depreciation} = £\ \frac{1,650 - 50}{8} = \frac{1,600}{8} = £200 \text{ per annum.}$$

(b) *Percentage on the diminishing balance.* Most assets lose a larger proportion of their value during the first year of their life than they do in the second year, and more in the second year than in the third year and so on.

To account for this, a percentage is taken, based on the balance *brought down* on the asset account.

Example

A jig costing £2,000 is to be depreciated by 20 per cent per annum on the diminishing balance. The amount of depreciation for the first *two* years will be as follows.

	£
Cost price, year 1	2,000
Depreciation, 20%	400
Balance b/d	1,600
Depreciation, 20%	320
Balance b/d	£1,280

Depreciation for the *two* years is therefore £400 + £320 = £720.

One advantage of the 'diminishing balance method' is that with many assets repair bills rise year by year as the asset gets older. Since the diminishing depreciation year by year offsets the rising repair bills the charge against the profits is evened out over the years.

(c) *Revaluation.* The asset may be revalued at the end of the financial year. The current market value could be taken as the basis for the Balance Sheet valuation, thus Depreciation will be the loss in value since the last valuation.

Example

A van bought for £1,570 may only have a market value of £570 twelve months later, thus depreciation for the first year would be £1,000 using this basis.

Revaluation can result in a profit for the year rather than a loss; as in farming, where a herd may rise in value rather than fall in value.

4. Treatment of depreciation in the Asset Account

For first examinations depreciation is usually taken to the credit of the Asset Account, such account showing the written-down balance which appears in the Balance Sheet.

Sample question

A motor van which cost £4,000 is to be depreciated at the rate of 25 per cent per annum on the diminishing balance.

Assuming that the motor van was purchased on 1 January 19__, show the entries to record this in the Asset Account, and show how the asset would appear in the Balance Sheet.

Answer

MOTOR VAN

19_1	£	19_1	£
Jan. 1 Bank	4,000	Dec. 31 Depreciation	
		Account	1,000
		Balance c/d	3,000
	£4,000		£4,000
19_2	£	19_2	£
Jan. 1 Balance b/d	3,000	Dec. 31 Depreciation	
		Account	750
		Balance c/d	2,250
	£3,000		£3,000
19_3	£		
Jan. 1 Balance b/d	2,250		

BALANCE SHEET (EXTRACT)

Year 1

	£	£
Motor Van		
(at cost)	4,000	
Less Depreciation	1,000	
		3,000

Year 2

	£	£
Motor Van	3,000	
Less Depreciation	750	
		2,250

5. Treatment of depreciation in a separate Provision Account

It is often more informative to show the asset in the Balance Sheet at cost, less the aggregate amount of depreciation written off to date on the Balance Sheet. In the case of limited companies the Companies Acts lay down that this is the method which must be employed. To enable the cost price of the asset to be readily available for the Balance Sheet, the original cost of the asset is left on the Asset Account unchanged, and the depreciation is recorded in a separate Provision Account, which is shown as a deduction from the cost price of the asset in the Balance Sheet.

Example

Using the same information as in the example shown in 4 above, but now recording depreciation in a separate Provision Account, the relevant accounts and Balance Sheet would appear as follows.

NOTE: The asset account remains at cost price throughout.

MOTOR VAN

19__	£	(If there are no other
Jan. 1 Bank	4,000	additions, this debit balance
		will remain the same)

PROVISION FOR DEPRECIATION ON MOTOR VAN

	£		£
Year 1		*Year 1*	
Dec. 31 Balance c/d	£1,000	Dec. 31	£1,000
Year 2	£	*Year 2*	£
Dec. 31 Balance c/d	1,750	Jan. 1 Balance b/d	1,000
		Dec. 31	750
	£1,750		£1,750
		Year 3	£
		Jan. 1 Balance b/d	1,750

BALANCE SHEET (EXTRACT) AT 31 DECEMBER

Year 1	£	£
Motor van		
(at cost)	4,000	
Less Deprecia-		
tion (to date)	1,000	
		3,000
Year 2		
Motor van		
(at cost)	4,000	
Less Deprecia-		
tion (to date)	1,750	
		2,250

6. Depreciation and sale of assets

At the end of its working life the book value of an asset will rarely be the same as the scrap value or trade-in value received on disposal of the asset. The result may be a profit (or loss) on sale of the asset. The basic book-keeping requirement is that the book value of the asset must be cleared from the books at the time of disposal. When depreciation is shown in a separate Provision Account, care must be taken when an asset is subsequently sold to ensure that the *written down value* of this asset is calculated so that the correct profit or loss on sale can be ascertained. The entries in the Ledger Account are as follows.

(a) *Open a Sale of Asset Account; debit* Sale of Asset with the cost price; *credit* the Asset Account.

(b) *Transfer the appropriate amount of depreciation* from the Depreciation Provision to the Sale of Asset Account; *debit* Provision for Depreciation; *credit* Sale of Asset Account.

(c) *The Sale of Asset Account will now disclose the written-down value*, and any cash received is recorded in the Sale of Asset Account; *debit* Bank; *credit* Sale of Asset Account.

(d) *the balance remaining on the Sale of Asset Account* will represent a profit or loss on the sale which can be transferred to Profit and Loss Account, or held in a separate account pending the completion of the final accounts.

Sample question

A company was incorporated on 1 January 19_1, and on that date purchased two machines, each costing £1,000.

Depreciation is provided at the rate of 20 per cent per annum by the straight-line method. Each year the amount so provided is credited to an account called 'Provision for Depreciation', and the balance on this account is deducted in the Balance Sheet from the original cost of the asset.

On 31 December 19_3, three full years after purchase, one machine was sold for £420 and on the same day was replaced by a new machine which cost £1,200.

You are asked to give all the accounts necessary to record these matters, including transfers to the Profit and Loss Account for each of the three years and to show the balances carried down on 1 January 19_4.

(RSA)

Answer

MACHINERY ACCOUNT

Dr				Cr
19_2	£	19_2		£
Jan. 1 Bank	2,000	Dec. 31 Balance c/d		2,000
19_3	£	19_3		£
Jan. 1 Balance b/d	2,000	Dec. 31 Sale of Asset		
Dec. 31 Bank	1,200	A/c	1,000
		Balance c/d	2,200
	£3,200		£3,200
19_4	£			
Jan. 1 Balance b/d	2,200			

PROVISION FOR DEPRECIATION ACCOUNT

19_1	£	19_1	£
Dec. 31 Balance c/d	400	Dec. 31 Deprecation A/c	400
19_2	£	19_2	£
Dec. 31 Balance c/d	800	Jan. 1 Balance b/d	400
		Dec. 31 Depreciation A/c	400
	£800		£800
19_3	£	19_3	£
Dec. 31 Sale of Asset A/c	600	Jan. 1 Balance b/d	800
Balance c/d	600	Dec. 31 Depreciation A/c	400
	£1,200		£1,200
		19_4	£
		Jan. 1 Balance b/d	600

SALE OF ASSET ACCOUNT

19_3	£	19_3	£
Dec. 31 Machinery A/c	1,000	Dec. 31 Provision for Deprecia-tion A/c	600
Profit & Loss A/c	20	Bank	420
	£1,020		£1,020

PROFIT AND LOSS ACCOUNT
(EXTRACTS YEAR BY YEAR)

19_1	£		£
Provision for depre-ciation	400		
19_2			
Provision for depre-ciation	400		
19_3		19_3	
Provision for depre-ciation	400	Profit on sale of asset	20

Progress test 13

1. What are the entries for depreciation in the accounts? **(1)**

2. Explain the terms *depreciation* and *amortisation*. **(1) and (2)**

3. Explain the revaluation method of calculating depreciation. **(3)**

4. Explain the fixed instalment method of calculating depreciation. **(3)**

5. Explain the diminishing-balance method of calculating depreciation. **(3)**

6. How is depreciation shown in the Balance Sheet? **(4)**

7. Explain why depreciation is sometimes shown in a separate Provision Account. **(5)**

8. What do you understand by a 'Sale of Asset Account' and when is such an account *usually* employed? **(6)**

Specimen questions

1. On 1 January 19__ A. Lever purchases a machine for £2,800. He believes it will have a useful life of 10 years and will fetch £400 for its scrap value in ten years' time. Show the Machinery Account for the first 3 years.

2. On 1 July 19_1 A. Peters buys a motor vehicle for £8,900. The firm's policy is to keep motor vehicles for only 3 years, depreciating them on the straight-line method. It is estimated that the car will fetch £4,400 after 3 years. Show the Motor Vehicle Account for the three years, assuming it is traded in for a new £10,000 vehicle on 31 Dec. 19_3 at the expected figure, the balance being paid by cheque.

3. A machine purchased for £17,295 is depreciated at 25 per

cent per annum on the diminishing balance method
(calculations to the nearest £1). Show the Machinery Account
for the first two years.

4. A farmer has a herd of cattle valued on his books at £28,800
on 1 January 19_1. On 31 December the herd is revalued at
£24,350. Show the Herd A/c for the year.

5. On 1 January 19_1, a company purchased four machines for
£2,000 each. The balance on Machinery Account has been
carried down at cost and the annual charge for depreciation,
calculated at the rate of 10 per cent per annum on cost, has
been credited to a Provision for Depreciation Account. On 1
January 19_2, one of the machines was sold for £1,722,
(payment received by cheque) and on the same day two
additional machines were purchased at a cost of £2,400 each.
On 1 January 19_3, another of the original machines was sold
for £1,625 but was not replaced. The buyer paid by cheque.

You are required to show

(a) the Machinery Account, the Provision for Depreciation
Account for the three years and the Sale of Asset
Account;
(b) how the machinery would appear in the Balance Sheet
at 31 December 19_3. *(RSA)*

6. The balances on certain accounts of Foster Hardware Co. as
at 1 April 19_1 were:

Vehicles (at cost) £10,540;
provision for depreciation of vehicles £4,720.

During the financial year, the business traded in a vehicle:
original cost £4,710;
accumulated depreciation £3,080; part exchange allowance
£1,100;
paid balance of price of new vehicle by cheque £5,280.

The closing balances as at 31 March 19_2 were:

vehicles (at cost) (to be derived);
provision for depreciation of vehicles £3,890.

You are required to post to and balance the appropriate accounts for the year ended 31 March 19_2, deriving the transfer entries to Profit and loss Account where applicable.

(ACCA)

7.   Emir operates a parcel delivery service. He uses three vans and, because of the high mileage, his policy is to trade them in within three years. As at 1 May 19_1 his records showed that:

- (a) van 1 was bought during the year to Apr. 19_0 at a cost of £2,700;
- (b) van 2 was bought during the year to Apr. 19_1 at a cost of £3,000;
- (c) van 3 was bought on 1 May 19_1 at a cost of £6,000.

Emir uses the straight-line method of depreciation, and in calculating depreciation he does not allow for any possible scrap value. A full year's depreciation is charged in the year of purchase, on the last day of the year.

During the year to 30 April 19_2 the following transactions occurred.

- (a) Van 1 was traded in for £1,200 against a new van, Van 4, and its total cost amounted to £5,400.
- (b) Van 3 was involved in an accident and it was a complete write-off. The insurance company allowed Emir £4,000 in compensation.
- (c) He replaced Van 3 with Van 5 which cost £9,000, paid for out of the business bank account.

You are required to:

- (a) write up the following accounts for the year to 30 April 19-2:
  - (i) Van Account;
  - (ii) Van Depreciation Account;
  - (iii) Van Disposals Account; and
- (b) show how the vans would be presented on the Balance Sheet at 30 April 19-2.

(AAT)

14
Correction of errors

1. The wide variety of errors

Errors can occur in numerous ways, and the student must always fall back upon a sound knowledge of double entry to discover what the error is, and how to correct it. Some of the commoner errors are illustrated in this chapter, but students must expect to meet errors in real-life accountancy situations which they have not encountered before. The only real rules are:

(a) Discover what has happened and the impact this has had on the existing pattern of double entries;

(b) Decide what the true pattern of double entries should have been;

(c) Make corrective entries in the Ledger Accounts, through a Journal Entry, to solve the problem.

Some errors are discovered as a result of a Trial Balance failing to agree. Other errors do not show up on a Trial Balance, as is explained below. Sometimes we cannot discover the error, or cannot afford the time to look for it. In such situations we open up a Suspense Account, as explained below.

2. Errors that do not affect the agreement of the Trial Balance

Some errors will not be disclosed by the disagreement or lack of balance in a Trial Balance. These errors usually fall into one or other of the following categories.

(a) Compensating errors, as when a £50 understatement in one account is compensated by a £50 overstatement in another account.

(b) Errors of principle, arising from a lack of understanding of the principles of accounts. For example, if a purchase of an asset is entered in Purchases Account, instead of the Asset Account.

(c) Errors of omission, when items have been left out of the Ledger altogether, as when an invoice is mislaid.

(d) Errors of commission (something has been done wrongly), as where a sale to P. Smith is entered in P. Smythe's Account.

Therefore, even if a Trial Balance does agree we cannot be absolutely sure an error is not hidden away within it. We say a Trial Balance that agrees is *prima facie* (at a first view) correct.

In each case the correction of the error is made by passing a Journal entry through the books, and posting it to the Ledger.

NOTE: The correction of the error must still follow the double entry principle, unless it is a single-sided error, as explained below.

Sample question

Show by means of Journal entries how the following errors should be corrected in the books of C. Careless, after his Final Accounts have been completed.

(a) Fixtures and fittings purchased for £300 had been debited to the Purchases Account.

(b) Goods sold on credit to G. Watson for £50 had been debited to the account of G. Weston.

(c) After preparation of the Final Accounts it was found that depreciation of £100 on machinery had been entirely omitted.

(d) Careless's final stock had been undervalued by £200.

Answer

Note the alternative form of Journal ruling, sometimes used.

Furniture & Fittings Dr	£300		Correction of error of principle; fittings incorrectly debited to Purchases A/c	
Capital A/c		£300		
G. Watson Dr	50		Correction of compensating error; amount incorrectly charged to G. Weston.	
G. Weston		50		
Capital A/c Dr	100		Correction of error of omission; depreciation of machinery.	
Machinery		100		
Stock Dr	200		Correction of error of commission; undervaluation of the closing stock	
Capital A/c		200		

NOTE: With regard to entries 1, 3 and 4 since the Final Accounts have been completed and the profits have been presumably credited to Capital A/c, these late alterations to the profit must be corrected in that account. (*See* below.)

3. Correcting profit

Questions frequently require a net profit figure to be corrected in addition to the correction of the errors made in the accounts.

Sample question

Taking the details as given in the question above, assuming that C. Careless had found a net profit of £19,750 on the basis of his accounts *before* making the corrections, set out the calculation of the true net profit.

Answer

	£	£
Net profit on the basis of incorrect figures		19,750
Add Reduction in the value of purchases	300	
Increase in value of closing stock	200	
		500
		20,250
Less Depreciation on machinery,		
not provided for		100
True net profit		£20,150

4. Suspense Account to correct errors that affect the Trial Balance

A number of errors may be made which are disclosed by the fact that the Trial Balance does not agree.

Pending the finding and subsequent correction of these errors, the amount by which the Trial Balance does not agree can be inserted on the side of the Trial Balance which is the smaller of the two sides, and this 'difference' entered on an account called a Suspense Account. Of course it will be a single-sided entry only.

When the errors are discovered they are corrected by double entry through the Suspense Account. Thus when *all* the errors have been discovered and corrected the balance on the Suspense Account is eliminated.

Sample question

TRIAL BALANCE AS AT 31 MARCH 19__

	Dr	Cr	
	Detailed items		
	£	£	
	91,075	91,069	Totals disagree.
Suspense Account		6	'Difference' on books.
	£91,075	91,075	

NOTE: The Suspense Account in this case will be opened with a credit balance, since we need £6 on the credit side to make the Trial Balance agree.

Suppose the following errors were discovered in the next month.

(a) A cheque for £22 received for rent due from a tenant had been posted in the Cash Book, but the double entry had not been completed. Error found on 9 April.
(b) The account of a debtor for £16 had been written off as bad, but the entry had been made in the personal account only. Error found on 17 April.

Show the Suspense Account *after* the correction of the errors.

Answer

SUSPENSE ACCOUNT

Apr. 9 Rent Receivable	£22	Mar. 31 Difference in Books	£6
		Apr. 17 Bad Debts	16
	£22		£22

NOTE: The double entry will be completed by: (1) crediting Rent Receivable with £22, and (2) debiting Bad Debts with £16.

The original difference was in fact made up by the difference between *two* figures; it would thus have been useless trying to spot just £6.

Single-sided errors. Some errors do not require a double entry to correct them. For example, if a Debtor's balance of £35 is extracted to the Trial Balance as £55 and as a result causes £20 to appear on a Suspense Account, its discovery will not need any correction in the Debtor's Account (it is already correct). A single-sided Journal entry will remove the Suspense Account balance and the narration will explain what happened.

5. Errors involving the Suspense Account and subsidiary books

Very often examination questions, instead of giving the original difference in the books, simply list the errors that have been made and require them to be corrected.

Many of the errors, but not all of them, may require a Suspense Account; those that do not will simply involve correction by transfer from one account to another. Any balance remaining on the Suspense Account will then represent the original amount by which the Trial Balance disagreed.

Sample question _____

The following errors were discovered in the books of A. Slack on 31 December. The difference on the Trial Balance had been entered in a Suspense Account, and on correction of the errors the Suspense Account was eliminated.

(*i*) The total of the Purchases Day Book had been undercast by £100.

(*ii*) The discount column on the debit side of the Cash Book had been posted to the credit of Discount Received Account, £20.

(*iii*) £76 for motor repairs had been taken to the Motor Vans Account.

(*iv*) A cheque received from F. Bunn £39 had been debited in the Cash Book, but the double entry had not been completed.

(*v*) The Returns Outwards Book had been overcast by £50.

(a) Show by means of Journal entries how these errors would be corrected in the books of A. Slack.

(b) Show the Suspense Account, bringing out the original difference in the books.

(c) A provisional set of Final Accounts to 31 December had been prepared on the basis of the incorrect figures. The net profit disclosed by these accounts was £34,320. Show your calculation of the correct net profit for the year.

Answer

(a) *Journal entries*

(i) Purchases A/c Dr	£100		Correction for Purchases Book undercast for the month of . . .
Suspense A/c		£100	
(ii) Discount Dr Allowed A/c	20		Correction for discount allowed taken in error to the credit of Discount Received A/c.
Discount Dr Received A/c	20		
Suspense A/c		40	
(iii) Motor Dr Repairs A/c	76		Transfer of amount incorrectly posted to Motor Vans A/c.
Motor Vans A/c		76	
(iv) Suspense A/c Dr	39		Completion of double entry for a cheque omitted from the personal account.
F. Bunn		39	
(v) Returns Outwards A/c Dr	50		Correction for overcast in the Returns Outwards Book for the month of . . .
Suspense A/c		50	

NOTE: In the case of entry *(ii)* above discount on the debit side of the Cash Book is reflected by individual items taken to the *credit* of personal accounts. If the total of the discount allowed column is taken to the credit of Discount Received Account *we will have two credits and no debit!* The effect on the Trial Balance will be to double the amount invoved. Remember that an item on the wrong side of a Trial Balance causes a difference in the totals of twice the amount of the item.

(b) *Suspense Account*

SUSPENSE ACCOUNT

Dec. 31 Difference on			Dec. 31 Purchases (*i*)	£100
Book	£151		31 Discount	
			allowed (*ii*)	20
31 F. Bunn (*iv*)	39		31 Discount	
			received (*ii*)	20
			31 Returns	
			outwards (*v*)	50
	£190			£190

(c) *Corrected net profit*

		£
Net profit as per the accounts		34,320
Deduct:		
Returns outwards overstated	£50	
Discount overcredited	40	
Purchases undercast	100	
Motor repairs omitted	76	
		266
Correct net profit		£34,054

6. Separate effect of errors on Trial Balance and profit

You may be set questions that require you to state the effect of *each* error on the Trial Balance before setting out the Suspense Account. You may also be required to tabulate a statement showing the effect of *each* error on the profit given in the accounts.

In such cases you must discipline your thinking, so that you are always considering the effect of the error in terms of what the difference on the Trial Balance will be by virtue of the error. You will find it helpful to prepare a small tabulated statement headed as follows:

Debit side in excess	Credit side in excess	Effect on profit already found	
		+	−

Sample question ───────────────────────────────

The Trial Balance of a trading company failed to balance on 31 March 19__. The difference had been entered in a Suspense Account, and Final Accounts for the year ended 31 March 19__, and a Balance Sheet had been prepared on the basis of the figures shown in the Trial Balance. The net profit arrived at was £43,750.

The following errors were subsequently discovered, and on correction the Trial Balance agreed.

(a) Discounts, shown as £80 on the credit side of the three-column Cash Book, had been posted to the debit of Discount Allowed Account. Error found on 4 April.

(b) A payment of £72 for repairs to motor vans had been debited to Motor Vans Account. Error found on 6 April.

(c) The bank overdraft of £172 had been entered in the Trial Balance as £162. Error found on 7 April.

(d) Premises were let to a sub-tenant from 1 March. The sub-tenant paid £720 on 1 March, representing three months' rent in advance. This had been entered in the Cash Book, but no other entry had been made. Error found on 12 April.

(e) Goods (selling price £75, cost price £55) were returned by a customer on 31 March. No entry had been made in the books, and the goods had not been included in the closing stock. Error found on 13 April.

(f) P. Duff's debit balance of £39 had been omitted from the debtors in the Trial Balance. Error found on 14 April.

You are required:

(i) to tabulate an answer showing the effect of *each* of the above errors on the Trial Balance and on the net profit;

(ii) to show the Suspense Account, bringing out the original difference on the books; and

(iii) to produce a statement showing the correct net profit *after* adjustment of the errors.

Answer

(i) TABULATED STATEMENT

	Debit side in excess	Credit side in excess	Effect of correction on net profit +	Effect of correction on net profit −
	£	£	£	£
(a)	160		160	
(b)	no effect	no effect		72
(c)	10		no effect	no effect
(d)	720		240	
(e)	no effect	no effect	55	75
(f)		39	no effect	no effect
			£455	£147

(ii) SUSPENSE ACCOUNT

19__	£	19_	£
Apr. 4 Discount		Mar. 31 Difference on	
Allowed	80	Books	851
4 Discount		Apr. 14 P. Duff	39
Received	80		
7 Bank overdraft	10		
13 Rent receivable	720		
	£890		£890

(iii) STATEMENT OF ADJUSTED PROFIT

	£	£
Net profit as per the a/c		43,750
Add Discounts	160	
Rent receivable	240	
Stock	55	
		455
		44,205
Deduct Returns inwards	75	
Van repairs	72	
		147
Adjusted net profit		£44,058

(iv) STATEMENT OF ADJUSTED PROFIT
(Alternative method)

Van repairs	£72	Net profit b/d	£43,750
Returns inwards	75	Discounts	160
Adjusted net profit		Rent receivable	240
to Capital Account	44,058	Closing stock	55
	£44,205		£44,205

Progress test 14

1.   Does the Trial Balance prove that the books are absolutely correct?   **(2)**

2.   What types of errors will the Trial Balance not disclose?   **(2)**

3.   How would you normally correct errors not disclosed by the Trial Balance?   **(2)**

4.   What is a Suspense Account, and when is it used?   **(4)**

5.   When would a Suspense Account be opened with : (*a*) a debit balance; (*b*) a credit balance?   **(4)**

6.   Explain the effect on : (*a*) the Trial Balance, and (*b*) net profit, of *overcasting*:

   (i)   the Purchases Day book;
   (ii)   the Sales Day book;
   (iii)   the Returns Outwards Book;
   (iv)   the Returns Inwards Book.   **(6)**

7.   Explain the effect on: (*a*) the Trial Balance, and (*b*) net profit, of *undercasting*:

   (i)   the Purchases Day book;
   (ii)   the Sales Day book;
   (iii)   the Returns Outwards Book;

(iv) the Returns Inwards Book. **(6)**

8. What is the effect on the Trial Balance of posting the total of the 'discount allowed' column in the Cash Book, to the *credit* of the Discount Received Account? **(5)**

9. What is the effect on the Trial Balance of posting the total of the 'discount received' column in the Cash Book, to the *debit* of the Discount Received Account? **(5)**

Specimen questions

1. A book-keeper extracts a Trial Balance which fails to agree. He places the difference in a Suspense Account and then finds the following errors.

    (a) The Sales Day Book had been overcast by £10.
    (b) £130 had been credited to Apperton Bros. instead of £100.
    (c) The balance on Blenkinsopp's Account of £35 in the Sales Ledger had been extracted in error as £55.
    (d) £5 discount allowed to Cantrell & Co. had been debited to their account.

Show the Suspense Account after the above errors had been adjusted, bringing out the original difference on the books, and giving the necessary Journal entries.

2. By means of Journal entries, correct the following errors.

    (a) A vehicle had been sold for £250, this being the written-down value. Cash Account had been *debited* and Sales Account *credited*.
    (b) Goods taken by the proprietor for personal use at sale price £220, had been omitted from the books.
    (c) The Sales Day Book had been overcast by £20.
    (d) A cheque for £40 received from B. Brown had not been credited to his account.

3. The Profit and Loss Account of a business for the year ended

30 September showed a net profit of £32,980. This differed so much from the expected profit that a check of the accounts was ordered and the following errors were discovered.

(a) the cost of a new van £5,620 had been debited to Purchase Account.

(b) The charge in the Profit and Loss Account for rent £4,680 included £936, the rent for the quarter ended 31 December, paid in advance.

(c) Drawings of £1,000 in July had been debited to Returns Inwards Account.

(d) In the closing stock on 30 September, twenty-five articles had been priced at £5.50 each instead of £0.55 each.

(e) Goods valued at £316.50 were sold on credit to C. Doyle in September, but no entry had been made in the books.

Show either as a statement or in the form of an account, your calculation of the true net profit for the year.

4. The Treasurer of the Lion Sports Club discovered the following errors at 31 March 19_2.

(a) Hill's subscription of £10 had been credited to High's account.

(b) The purchase of bar equipment for £250 was included in bar purchases.

(c) Wages Account debit entry £350 had been brought down as £530.

(d) Subscriptions Account credit balance £10,796, had been brought down as £10,976.

(e) £50 for rent received was debited to Rent Account and credited to Bank Account.

(f) A donation of £210 in cash had been entered in the books as £110.

(g) A creditor was demanding payment of £75 for bar purchases which he had supplied. No details of this transaction could be found in the books although the barman accepts that the goods had been received.

Give the journal entries to correct the above transactions, stating clearly the type of book-keeping error that has occurred.

(AAT)

5. On 30 November, L. Howard drew up the following Trial Balance:

	Dr £	Cr £
Capital		28,400
Drawings	12,764	
Stock (1 July)	8,417	
Purchases	27,994	
Sales		83,704
Trade debtors	2,858	
Trade creditors		5,066
Business expenses	14,947	
Fixtures and fittings	5,457	
Suspense Account		267
Premises	45,000	
	£117,437	£117,437

The Suspense Account was included as the Trial Balance did not balance.

During the month of December, the following errors were discovered. These errors accounted for the 'difference'.

(a) Goods invoiced to L. Rust at £139 and correctly entered in the Sales Book had been posted to Rust's account as £193.

(b) A purchases of goods from F. Williams £121 had been entered on the wrong side of his account.

(c) Business expenses paid by cheque and correctly entered in the cash book as £130 had been posted to the Business Expenses Account as £120.

(d) A purchase of fittings by cheque £158 had been entered in Fixtures and Fittings Account as £185.

(e) Goods £46 had been invoiced to Howard (the proprietor) and entered in the Sales Account but no other entry had been made.

Re-write the Trial Balance as it should have been if the errors had not been made.

Write up the Suspense Account as it would appear after the errors have been corrected and balance it as at 31 December.

(*RSA*)

15
Manufacturing Accounts

1. Purpose of Manufacturing Accounts

The Manufacturing Account is a prelude to the Trading Account, being prepared by those firms engaged in a manufacturing process. The essential feature of such firms is that they do not buy finished goods merely to trade in them at a profit. Instead they buy appropriate raw materials, manufacture them into finished goods and pass these finished goods to the Sales Department for sale. The purpose of the Manufacturing Account is twofold:

(a) to find the cost of the goods manufactured;
(b) to ascertain the amount of any profit on the manufacturing process, if that is possible.

2. Cost of manufacturing

This is obtained by taking into account *all* those items of expense which relate to the manufacturing process. For convenience of comparison and analysis the items making up the total cost are separated in the Manufacturing Account as follows.

(a) *Prime cost*. This is expenditure directly related to the manufacturing process and includes:
    (i) cost of raw materials used;
    (ii) direct labour costs;

(*iii*) power used in manufacturing;

(*iv*) other direct expenditure.

Such costs are often called direct costs, because they are embodied directly in the product. They are also called variable costs because they vary with output (i.e. if we make twice as many tables we need twice as much wood, etc.)

The cost of raw materials used will be found by :

(*i*) taking opening stock of raw materials;

(*ii*) adding purchases of raw materials;

(*iii*) deducting closing stock of raw materials.

(b) *The cost of manufactured goods.* This is found by taking the Prime Costs found in the Prime Cost system and adding to them the *factory overheads.* these relate to expenditure incurred in running the factory , e.g.:

(*i*) rent and rates;

(*ii*) upkeep of factory buildings;

(*iii*) depreciation on machinery;

(*iv*) supervisory salaries, etc.;

We shall also need to make an adjustment for work-in-progress. (*See* **5** and **6** below.)

3. Method of presentation

Since the Manufacturing Account is mainly concerned with the costs of manufacture, and these expenses will be transferred in from the various nominal accounts where they have accumulated throughout the year, nearly all the figures will be debits to the Manufacturing Account.

The order of presentation is most important, since in most examinations you will be required to disclose specific figures and to name them. It is usual to show the Account in two sections, a Prime Cost Section and Cost of Manufactured Goods Section. The total of the Prime Cost Section will be carried down into the Cost of Manufactured Goods Section, and the final total of this section will then be transferred to the Trading Account (*see* **4** below).

Example

MANUFACTURING ACCOUNT FOR THE YEAR ENDED 31 DECEMBER 19__

Prime Cost Section

	£			£
Raw materials		Prime costs		
Opening stock	22,100	of manufacture		
Purchases	38,500		(c/d)	98,600
	60,600			
Less Closing Stock	3,300			
Cost of materials used:	57,300			
Manufacturing wages	37,050			
Power	4,250			
	£98,600			£98,600

Cost of Manufactured Goods Section

		£		£
Prime costs b/d		98,600	Manufacturing cost	
Factory overheads:			transferred to	
Machinery			Trading A/c	140,450
depreciation	12,000			
Machinery				
maintenance	4,500			
Factory rent				
and expenses	12,500			
Supervision				
salaries	12,850			
	41,850			
	£140,450			£140,450

4. Transfer to Trading Account

It is usual to regard the factory as quite distinct from the warehouse. In the example above the total factory cost is transferred to the Trading Account, which account remains to perform its usual function of finding the actual profit made on selling the finished goods. The transfer can be made at the actual factory cost, as shown, or sometimes the transfer is made at a 'loaded' price in order to obtain a separate profit on the manufacturing process. Such a 'loaded' price would normally be the price at which the finished goods could be obtained *if purchased elsewhere* at wholesale prices. Such a price is called a *market price*. If no such price can be found to act as a guide, the 'loaded' price will be a notional one to give what is deemed to be a 'fair' profit on manufacture.

The Trading Account of the same business might appear as follows:

TRADING ACCOUNT FOR THE YEAR ENDED
31 DECEMBER 19__

	£		£
Opening stock of		Sales	328,000
finished goods	18,250		
Manufacturing cost			
transferred	140,450		
	158,700		
Less Closing stock of			
finished goods	16,700		
Cost of goods sold	142,000		
Gross Profit			
(to P & L A/c)	186,000		
	£328,000		£328,000

5. Work in progress

In addition to having stocks of raw materials and finished goods most businesses will also have *stocks of partly finished goods in the factory* at the end of the financial year. Work-in-progress is work which has entered the manufacturing processes but has not been completed when the financial year ends on the last day of the year. It is important that this item should be brought into the Manufacturing Account as an adjustment to the figures. Usually it is valued at cost of materials and labour plus an extra charge to cover factory expenses.

6. Adjusting for work-in-progress

The adjustment for opening and closing stock of work-in-progress cannot be dealt with against one particular item, and is therefore dealt with as affecting the whole account. The usual method is to adjust the Cost of Manufactured Goods (£140,450 on the example given above) by the amount of work-in-progress at the start of the year (which has of course gone forward into production in the first few days of the year) and also by the amount of work-in-progress at the end of the year. This has of course been held back for completion next year. The result gives an alteration to the Cost of Manufactured Goods Section as follows; assuming work-in-progress at start £4,800 and at the end £3,250.

		£
Expenditure as above		140,450
Add Work-in-progress 1 Jan	4,800	
Less Work-in-progress 31 Dec	3,250	
		+1,550
		£142,000

(a) If the opening work-in-progress is *greater* than the closing figure the difference is *added* — more has gone on into production at the start of the year than was held back at the end.

(b) If the opening work-in-progress is *less* than the closing figure the difference is *deducted* — more held back at the end than went on at the start.

The sample question which follows embodies the following features which are met in Manufacturing Accounts questions.

(a) Three lots of stock (a Stock of Raw Materials used in the Prime Cost Section, a Stock of Work-in-Progress used in the Cost of Manufactured Goods Section and a Stock of Finished Goods, used in the Trading Account).

(b) A value for the finished goods, as manufactured, to bring out the Manufacturing Profit.

Sample question

Prepare a Manufacturing, Trading and Profit and Loss Account for the year 19__ from the following figures taken from the books of G.O.A. Head:

	£
Sales	445,600
Materials:	
Stock 1 Jan.	13,216
Purchases	88,942
Stock 31 Dec.	12,964
Manufacturing wages	82,860
Work-in-progress at factory cost:	
1 Jan.	4,748
31 Dec.	6,894
Factory expenses	3,656
Office expenses	11,450
Depreciation:	
Plant and machinery	16,500
Delivery vans	4,250
Stock of finished goods:	
1 Jan.	15,064
31 Dec.	17,138
Value of finished goods completed	
during the year	281,800
Factory power	3,670
Advertising	11,034
Van running expenses	2,426
Salesmen's commission	24,630
Maintenance of machinery	12,160
Light and heat (3/4 factory)	4,800*
Rent, rates and insurance (¾ factory)	16,400*
Salaries (£16,000 factory)	40,000*

* In allocating items of expense such as these the amount to be charged to the factory is given, and by implication the *remainder* will be taken in the usual way to the Profit and Loss Account.

Answer

MANUFACTURING, TRADING AND PROFIT AND LOSS ACCOUNT
31 DECEMBER 19__

Prime Cost Section

	£		£
Materials consumed:		Prime costs	175,724
Stock 1 Jan	13,216		
Purchases	88,942		
	102,158		
Less Closing Stock	12,964		
Cost of raw materials used	89,194		
Manufacturing wages	82,860		
Power	3,670		
	£175,724		£175,724

Cost of Manufactured Goods Section

		£		£
Prime costs b/d		175,724	Transfer to Trading A/c	
Factory overhead expenses:			at market value	281,800
Rent, rates, insurance	12,300			
Light and heat	3,600			
Salaries	16,000			
Sundries	3,656			
Machinery maintenance	12,160			
Machinery depreciation	16,500			
		64,216		
		239,940		
Work in progress 1 Jan	4,748			
Less Work in progress				
31 Dec.	6,894	– 2,146		
Cost of manufacture		237,794		
Manufacturing profit		44,006		
		£281,800		£281,800

Stock of finished goods 1 Jan		15,064	Sales	445,600
Market value of goods transferred from Manufacturing Account		281,800		
		296,864		
Less Stock of finished goods 31 Dec.		17,138		
Cost of goods sold		279,726		
Gross profit on trading		165,874		
		£445,600		£445,600
Administration expenses:				
Rent, rates and insurance	4,100		Manufacturing profit	44,006
Light and heating	1,200		Gross profit	165,726
Salaries	24,000			209,732
Office expenses	11,450			
		40,750		
Selling and distributive expenses:				
Advertising	11,034			
Salesmen's commission	24,630			
Delivery van expenses	2,426			
Delivery van depreciation	4,250			
		42,340		
Total expenses		83,090		
Net profit		126,642		
		£209,732		£209,732

Progress test 15

1.   What is meant by the term 'manufacturing'?   **(1)**

2.   What does a Manufacturing Account attempt to do?   **(1)**

3.   What is a prime cost?   **(2)**

4.   Detail the items entering into the cost of manufacture of a large business.   **(2)**

5. What is meant by 'work-in-progress'? **(5)**

6. In which of the final accounts would the following items appear?

(a) Stock of raw materials
(b) Work in progress.
(c) Stock of finished goods. **(6)**

Specimen questions

1. T. Segrave manufactures components for marine engines. He prepares Manufacturing and Trading Accounts, charging the Trading Account with the manufactured goods at market price.

You are required to:

(a) prepare his Manufacturing and Trading Accounts and begin the Profit and Loss Account;
(b) show the prime cost of manufactured goods.

STOCKS AT 1 JAN 19_4

	£		£
Raw materials	23,000	Purchases of raw	
Work in progress	17,500	materials	120,000
Finished goods	24,500	Sales of finished goods	363,000
		Returns inwards	1,500
		Production wages	36,900
		Supervision wages	11,250
		Factory power (Prime)	3,750
STOCKS AT 31 DEC. 19_4		Depreciation of	
	£	machinery	12,500
Raw materials	21,700	Salaries of stock clerks	22,200
Work in progress	22,500	(*Trading Account*)	
Finished goods	23,000	Warehouse wages	12,750
		Warehouse rent and	
		rates	4,800

Market price of manufactured goods is estimated at £218,000.

2. From the following details extracted from S. Turner's books prepare:

(i) a Manufacturing Account;
(ii) a Trading Account;
(iii) a Profit and Loss Account;

for the year ended 31 December 19__.

	£	£
Stocks (1 Jan. 19__) – raw materials	21,841	
– finished goods	25,697	
– work in progress	11,524	
Purchases of raw materials		73,843
Sales of finished goods		459,756
Manufacturing expenses		5,914
Factory power, light and heat (overhead)		4,893
Office power, light and heat		896
Rates ($\frac{4}{5}$ factory, $\frac{1}{5}$ offices)		10,555
Insurance $\frac{4}{5}$ factory, $\frac{1}{5}$ offices)		2,370
Carriage on raw materials		597
Carriage on Sales		1,389
Wages:		
Factory		94,748
Office		31,980
Salesmen		22,435
Salaries:		
Factory		14,800
Administration		22,200
Commission to salesmen		4,714
Advertising		12,500
Depreciation:		
Machinery		8,150
Furniture and fittings		1,486
Stocks (31 December 19__)		
Raw materials		11,698
Finished goods		15,186
Work in progress		9,255

From your accounts state:

(a) the cost of raw materials used;
(b) the prime cost of goods manufactured;

(c) the total cost of goods manufactured;
(d) the manufacturing profit;
(e) the gross profit;
(f) the net profit.

NOTE: The goods manufactured are to be transferred to the Trading Account at a notional value of £300,000.

3. S. Wave is engaged in manufacturing components for television sets and at 30 September 19__, the following balances are extracted from his books of accounts.

	£		£
S. Wave Capital	42,252	Power, lighting and	
Freehold property	140,000	heating:	
Plant and machinery:		Factory(Prime cost)	4,926
Cost	25,000	Office	1,189
Provision for		Rates:	
depreciation	5,430	Factory	2,592
Opening stocks:		Office	2,128
Materials	5,952	Drawings	20,500
Finished products	16,818	Insurance:	
Work in progress	9,850	Factory	1,259
Debtors	15,785	Office	421
Creditors	4,795	General office expenses	2,651
Purchases		General factory expenses	3,715
(Raw Materials)	85,451	Carriage inwards	848
Factory wages	48,268	Carriage outwards	1,180
Office salaries	16,619	Bank balance	28,611
Sales	381,286		

With the help of the following information and instructions prepare a Manufacturing, Trading and Profit and Loss Account for the year ending 30 September 19__, and a Balance Sheet as at that date:

Market value of goods manufactured £265,000; stocks, 30 September 19__, raw materials £6,219, finished products £15,216; work in progress £11,715; insurance paid in advance, factory £50, office £25; power, heating and lighting (accrued), factory £152, office £54; plant and machinery to be depreciated at the rate of 15 per cent per annum on cost.   (*CIMA*)

4. A. Jones owns and manages a manufacturing business. The following balances have been extracted from his books at 31 March 19_2:

	Dr £	Cr £
Administration expenses	18,795	
Advertising	11,500	
Bank and cash in hand	15,675	
Capital at 1 April 19_1		106,390
Debtors and creditors	11,500	10,750
Drawings	17,500	
Factory direct wages	38,500	
Factory indirect wages	22,000	
Factory power (prime cost)	4,500	
Office furniture and fittings	12,300	
Heat and light	2,000	
Plant and equipment	34,600	
Plant Hire (Manufacturing overhead)	500	
Provision for bad debts		400
Provision for depreciation at 1 April 19_1:		
Furniture and fittings		3,690
Plant and equipment		17,300
Raw material purchases	28,500	
Rent and rates	2,500	
Sales		303,680
Selling and distribution expenses	28,300	
Stocks at cost at 1 April 19_1		
Raw materials	21,000	
Work in progress	12,000	
Finished goods	23,000	
Freehold warehouse	137,540	
	£442,210	£442,210

The following additional information has also been obtained:

(a) Expenditure on heat and light, and rent and rates is to be apportioned between the factory and the office in the ratio of 9 to 1, and 3 to 2 respectively.

(b) Accruals at 31 March 19_2 were:

Factory power	£200
Rent and rates	£500

Neither of these items had been included in the list of balances shown above.

There was also a prepayment of £100 for salesmen's car insurance included in the item 'selling expenses'.

(c) Stocks at 31 March 19_2 were valued at cost as follows:

raw materials	£18,000
work in progress	£13,800
finished goods	£15,700

(d) Depreciation is charged on plant and equipment at 50 per cent per annum using the reducing balance method, and at 10 per cent per annum on furniture and fittings using the straight-line method of depreciation.

(e) The provision for bad debts is to be made equal to 5 per cent of debtors outstanding at 31 March 19_2.

(f) The goods manufactured are transferred to Trading Account at a valuation of £200,000.

You are required to prepare Jones' Manufacturing, Trading and Profit and Loss Account for the year to 31 March 19_2, and a Balance Sheet as at that date.　　　　　(*AAT*)

16
Departmental Accounts

1. Analysed Day Books

Many business concerns are divided into separate departments, and even in the case of a small undertaking it is often found convenient to separate the activities into a number of departments in which specialists can be employed to direct the running of that section of the business.

(a) A dealer may sell radio and television receivers, video machines, hi-fi and compact disc players.

(b) Rather than deal with the business as one unit, the accounting records may be separated to deal with each department, thus enabling final accounts to be produced for each department.

(c) This entails keeping separate records of Purchases, Sales, Stock, Cash, Bank and sometimes Personal Accounts, plus, of course, records of goods returned inwards and outwards by each department.

(d) This work is made easier by the addition of separate columns in the subsidiary books, which analyse the details of transactions into separate departments.

Example

In the case of a radio dealer, his Purchase Day Book might appear as follows:

Date	Details	Invoice	Total	Radios and TV	Videos and CD	Records and tapes

(e) Alternatively, departments can simply be classified as Dept, A, B, C, etc.

(f) Whichever method is adopted, it is obvious that separate figures for the Trading Account will be readily available, and comparisons between departmental results can easily be made.

2. Presentation of final accounts

The usual method of presenting the final accounts is to set out the Trading and Profit and Loss Accounts, using separate columns for each department, with an additional column to record the total for all departments.

In the case of a business with *two* departments, the accounts would appear as follows:

TRADING AND PROFIT AND LOSS ACCOUNTS FOR THE YEAR
ENDED . . . .

	Dept A	*Dept B*	*Total*		*Dept A*	*Dept B*	*Total*

When the Trading Account is set out on a departmental basis it follows that the Profit and Loss Account should also contain separate columns to deal with the allocation of the overhead expenses.

3. Overhead expenses and the Profit and Loss Account

Since the Profit and Loss Account will now have separate columns, we must consider the methods by which the overhead expenses can be allocated to the departments.

The *two* most common methods which you will encounter in examination problems are as follows.

(a) *To apportion the expenses between the departments in proportion to the area* (i.e. floor space) taken up by the department concerned.

Example

Dept A occupies 1,000 m² and Dept B 500 m², thus the ratio of the area taken up by the departments is:

$$A : B :: 2 : 1$$

Insurance of £450 and rates of £1,200 will therefore be allocated as follows:

	Dept A	Dept B	Total
	£	£	£
Insurance	300	150	450
Rates	800	400	1200

(b) *To apportion the expenses in proportion to the turnover (sales) of each department.*

Example

Sales: Dept A £25,000; Dept B £10,000; thus the ratio of departmental sales is:

$$A : B :: 5 : 2$$

Insurance of £700 and rates of £2,100 will therefore be allocated as follows:

	Dept A	Dept B	Total
Insurance	500	200	700
Rates	1,500	600	2,100

In practice, some expenses are analysed separately, and in examinations you may be given separate figures for some items of expense, e.g. salaries of department managers, commission, advertising, etc.

4. Expenses requiring adjustment

An important point to bear in mind is that since expenses in the Profit and Loss Account have now to be allocated to departments, *any item requiring adjustment must be adjusted before allocation to the departments concerned,* to ensure that the correct amount is charged in the accounts.

Example

Assume that in the list of balances, rates appear as £650 but a footnote states that £150 rates have been prepaid.

Then if rates are allocated three-fifths to Dept X and two-fifths to Dept Y, the Profit and Loss Account should appear as follows:

		Dept X	*Dept Y*	*Total*
		£	£	£
Rates	650			
Less Rates prepaid	150	300	200	500

(a) For this reason, many students find it helpful to *complete the total column first, allocating the items afterwards.*

(b) The total column provides a means of checking the accuracy of the final allocation of expenses.

Sample question

J.S.B. runs a business which has two departments. The following balances were extracted from his books on 30 June 19__ :

	Dept A	*Dept B*		
	£	£		£
Opening stock at 1 Jan.	12,000	13,000	Commission payable	1,500
Purchases	24,520	36,544	Salaries	15,100
Sales	86,030	89,070	Advertising	2,500
Closing Stock	12,100	13,300	Rates	1,450
Wages	22,800	21,200	Insurance	400
Returns in	1,030	4,070	Repairs	800
Returns out	520	544	Lighting and heating	2,000

You are required to set out departmental Trading and Profit and Loss Accounts for the six months ended 30 June 19__, after taking into account the following information:

    (a) (*i*) Salaries of £400 are due but have not yet been paid.
        (*ii*) Rates £250 have been paid in advance.
        (*iii*) Insurance £80 is prepaid.
    (b) Commission, salaries and advertising are to be charged to the departments in proportion to net turnover (sales — returns in); all other expenses are to be apportioned ¼ to Dept A and ¾ to Dept B.

Answer

TRADING AND PROFIT AND LOSS ACCOUNTS
FOR THE SIX MONTHS ENDED 30 JUNE 19_

	Dept A	Dept B	Total		Dept A	Dept B	Total
Opening stock	12,000	13,000	25,000	Sales	86,030	89,070	
Purchases	24,520	36,544		*Less* Returns			
Less Returns				In	1,030	4,070	
Out	520	544		Net turnover	85,000	85,000	170,000
	24,000	36,000	60,000				
	36,000	49,000	85,000				
Less Closing							
stock	12,100	13,300	25,400				
Cost of stock							
sold	23,900	35,700	59,600				
Wages	22,800	21,200	44,000				
Cost of sales	46,700	56,900	103,600				
Gross profit c/d	38,300	28,100	66,400				
	£85,000	£85,000	£170,000		£85,000	£85,000	£170,000
	£	£	£		£	£	£
Commission	750	750	1,500	Gross profit			
Salaries 15,100				b/d	38,300	28,100	66,400
Add Salaries							
due 400							
	7,750	7,750	15,500				
Advertising	1,250	1,250	2,500				
Rates 1450							
Less Rates							
prepaid 250							
	300	900	1200				
Insurance 400							
Less Insurance							
prepaid 80							
	80	240	320				
Repairs	200	600	800				
Light and heat	500	1,500	2,000				
Total	10,830	12,990	23,820				
Net profit	27,470	15,110	42,580				
	£38,300	£28,100	£66,400		£38,300	£28,100	£66,400

Progress test 16

1. What are Analysed Day Books? **(1)**

2. What do you understand by Departmental Accounts? **(2)**

3. Name the two common methods of apportioning overhead expenses. **(3)**

4. What are the important points to remember when overhead expenses are paid in advance? **(4)**

5. Why are Departmental Accounts essential when managers are paid a commission on profit? **(4)**

Specimen questions

1. A. Wright owns a business which has two departments, A and B. He wishes to present his Trading Account in columnar forms so as to show clearly separate gross profits for each department as well as for the business as a whole.

The following balances appeared in his books for the year ended 31 December, 19_2:

	Dept A £	Dept B £	Total £
Stock (1 Jan, 19_2)	5,800	6,400	12,200
Purchases	40,000	50,000	90,000
Sales	150,000	100,000	250,000
Wages of shop assistants			21,800
Rent, rates and insurance			4,320
Stationery and office expenses			1,260
Motor vehicle expenses and depreciation			3,240
Carriage on purchases			1,440
Light and heat			1,270

Required:

A columnar Trading Account as specified above and Profit and Loss Account for the year ended 31 December 19_2, taking into consideration the following.

(a) Carriage on purchases which is to be apportioned to the separate departments in proportion to purchases, and wages to be allocated on the same basis as sales.

(b) Stock on 31 December 19_2, was: Dept A £9,000; Dept B £6,000.

(c) An amount owing for insurances, £120, has not been recorded in the books.

(d) The provision for bad debts which is shown in the books as £300 is to be increased to £400.

Columnar form is not required for the Profit and Loss Account as the net profit is required only for the business as a whole.

2. Ironmakers Ltd manufacture two products, A and B, in separate sections of their factory. The following information is available for the year ended 31 December 19_3:

	Product A £	Product B £
Stock of raw material 1 Jan. 19_3	6,800	5,670
Purchase of raw material during year ended 31 Dec. 19_3	40,000	37,000
Stock of raw material 31 Dec. 19_3	8,950	7,700
Work in progress 1 Jan. 19_3	4,360	5,400
Work in progress 31 Dec. 19_3	5,410	7,370
Direct wages	37,350	35,880
Manufacturing expenses (variable)	12,700	13,000
Wages outstanding 31 Dec. 19_3	3,150	2,120
	£	
Factory salaries	34,000	
Factory fixed overhead expenses	33,000	

Plant and machinery have already been written down to scrap value.

The factory expenses are divided between A and B in the ratio of 2:1.

The factory salaries are divided between A and B in the ratio of 3:1.

During the year 1,000 product A, and 9,000 product B were produced. Goods are despatched to wholesalers immediately on completion.

Product A sells at £300, product B at £23.50 each.

(a) Prepare a columnar Manufacturing Account for the year ended 31 December 19_3, showing the cost of production for each article, and the total cost of production.

(b) Calculate the manufacturing profit as a percentage of the cost of production for each article.

3. John Dobson is the proprietor of a retail business which has two main departments which sell respectively hardware and electrical goods. He had previously prepared his annual accounts in such a way that the relative profitability of the two departments was not ascertainable, but now he wishes to attempt to identify the profit attributable to each in order that he may pay a bonus to the more successful of the departmental managers. At 30 September 19_5, the balances in the books of the business were as follows.

	£	£
Capital		84,000
Sales:		
Hardware		259,000
Electrical		129,500
Purchases:		
Hardware	128,000	
Electrical	64,000	
Stocks at 1 Oct. 19_4:		
Hardware	10,320	
Electrical	12,135	
c/f	214,455	472,500

	b/f	214,455	472,500
Salaries and Wages (Profit & Loss)			
Hardware		30,565	
Electrical		45,440	
Advertising		5,616	
Discounts Allowed:			
Hardware		1,360	
Electrical		1,200	
Drawings		23,000	
Premises (cost)		48,000	
Shopfittings and Equipment:			
Hardware		18,000	
Electrical		17,000	
(at cost less depreciation)			
Debtors and Creditors		10,200	5,319
Bank		25,600	
Rent and rates		4,580	
Canteen Charges		5,872	
Heating and Lighting		2,880	
Insurance of Stock		1,980	
General Administrative Salaries			
and Expenses		22,071	
		£477,819	£477,819

NOTES:

(i) At 30 September 19_5, the following amounts were owing:

	£
Wages:	
Hardware	250
Electrical	170
Heating and lighting	210

(ii) The general administration expenses and the rent and rates included prepayments of £33 and £80 respectively.

(iii) Stocks at 30 September 19_5 were:

	£
Hardware	12,800
Electrical	12,450

(iv) Depreciation is to be provided on shop fittings and equipment at 10 per cent of the written down value.

(v) The managers of the hardware and electrical departments are to be paid a commission of 5 per cent of the net profit (prior to the commission payment) of the respective departments. (Calculations correct to the nearest £1.)

(vi) In apportioning the various expenses between the two departments due regard is to be had to the following information:

	Hardware	*Electrical*
Number of workers	3	5
Average stock levels	12,500	10,000
Floor area (m2)	4,000	2,000

The general administration salaries and expenses are primarily incurred in relation to the processing of purchase and sales invoices.

Required:

(a) Prepare the departmental and total Trading and Profit and Loss Accounts for the year ended 30 September 19_5, and a Balance Sheet at that date.

(b) Prepare a schedule showing the basis on which you have apportioned the various expenses between the two departments.

(c) Mr Dobson considers that the profit performance of the electrical department is far from satisfactory. What are the main issues he should investigate before judging the manager incompetent?

17
Self-balancing Ledgers

1. Subdivision of the Ledger

Although in a small business the Ledger is a single book, containing all the personal, nominal and real accounts, in large firms it is necessary to sub-divide it into several books for ease of working. Computerised systems are also adept at breaking down accounting transactions to assist control by management. The chief subdivisions are:

(a) *Sales Ledger or Debtors Ledger*. This contains the personal accounts of debtors for goods sold in the normal course of business. It is common for a *credit limit* to be indicated on the Debtors Account. Such limit will be determined by a credit control function in the firm 'and represents the maximum credit allowed'. These accounts will be drawn up from:

 (*i*) second copies of outgoing invoices
 (*ii*) second copies of outgoing credit notes
 (*iii*) incoming cheques or remittance advice notes.

 NOTE: the Debtors' and Creditors' Ledgers are often subdivided into alphabetical sections, e.g. we might have four Debtors' Ledgers: A–F, G–L, M–R and S–Z.

(b) *Purchases Ledger or Creditors Ledger*. This contains the personal accounts of creditors for goods purchased in the normal course of business. These accounts will be written up from:

 (*i*) incoming invoices;
 (*ii*) incoming credit notes; and
 (*iii*) outgoing cheques, or remittance advice notes.

(c) *General or Nominal Ledger*. This contains all the remaining accounts; the real accounts (assets of the business) the nominal accounts (losses of the business and profits of the business), the

Final Accounts and the private accounts of the proprietor or proprietors. However, these may be separated off into **(d)** below.

(d) *Private Ledger.* Recording the personal accounts of the proprietor, e.g. Capital Account, Drawings Account and the Final Accounts. Only authorised persons have access to this ledger.

2.   Traditional ledgers and computerised ledger accounts

Traditionally all ledger accounts had debit and credit sides like the one illustrated below, which is an account of L.Kent in the Debtors Ledger of F. Surrey, a wholesaler.

L.KENT

Dr		£			Cr £
19__		£	19__		£
Feb. 1	Balance b/d	80	Feb. 7	Returns	
3	Sales	60		inwards	12
3	Containers	2	7	Containers	2
13	Sales	120	23	Bank	76
			23	Discount allowed	4
			27	L. Kent (contra)	80
			28	Balance c/d	88
		£262			£262
19__		£	19__		£
Mar. 1	Balance b/d	88			

Most of these entries are simple enough. Kent was a debtor at the start of the month, bought more goods on 3 Feb and on 13 Feb; returned some goods and some containers on 7 Feb, and paid the balance owing on 1 Feb on 23 Feb. One entry on 27 Feb requires some explanation. Because the ledger has been sub-divided, with the debtors split away from the creditors, any debtor who also happens to supply us with goods (in other words has an account also in our Creditors Ledger) will finish up with both a debtor's balance to pay, and a creditor's balance to receive. Such accounts are said to be 'contra accounts' (they are the opposite of one another). At the end of the month they will be contra'd off against one another, in such a way that the larger one (in this case the debt) will be reduced by the amount of the smaller balance (in this case £80 in the Purchases Ledger). Surrey's purchase from Kent has been 'set-off' against Kent's purchases from Surrey. The result is a balance of £88 only on L. Kent's Account in the Debtors Ledger, when Kent's account is finally balanced off.

Computerised Running Balance Accounts. If the traditional account is replaced by a computerised system it is usual to run it as a running balance account, the computer recalculating the balance on every entry, as shown in the account of L. Kent below. Computerised Debtors and Creditors Ledgers give immediate information about balances owing, debtors exceeding credit limits, etc.

Sales ledger			Credit limit £300 L. Kent	
Date	Particulars	Debit	Credit	Balance
19_		£	£	£
Feb. 1	Balance b/fwd			80
3	Sales	60		140
3	Containers	2		142
7	Returns inwards		12	130
7	Containers		2	128
13	Sales	120		248
23	Bank		76	172
23	Discount allowed		4	168
27	L. Kent (Purchases Ledger) contra		80	88

3. Self-balancing Ledgers

The principle of self-balancing ledgers is that a particular ledger, or part of a ledger (such as the A–E Debtors Ledger) which is the responsibility of a particular individual, is made self-checking by the addition of one further account in the book, the entries of which are reversed. This extra account may be given various names, such as Total Account, Control Account or Adjustment Account.

Consider a typical month's entries in the A–E Sales Ledger. We shall have:

(a) Numerous opening balances on the debit side of the debtors' accounts.

(b) A very few opening balances on the credit side where one or two debtors are temporarily creditors (usually because of returns made after settling their accounts).

(c) Numerous debit entries in the month on various debtors' accounts as they were supplied with goods or services.

(d) Numerous credit entries on various debtors' accounts as they

    (*i*) paid for the previous month's supplies or

    (*ii*) returned goods or were given allowances.

(e) Finally we shall have balances owing on all the accounts, carried down as debit balances for the new month. However, in a very few cases we may have debtors ending up as creditors, because we do in fact owe them a small balance at the end of the month.

If you now imagine that this section of the ledger is being kept by one person, perhaps as a set of ledger cards, and all the postings from the Sales Day Book, or the Sales Returns Book, or the Cash Book, or the Journal Proper are being entered by this one individual it should be easy to check the accuracy of this person's work by drawing up a Control Account. We could make this account simply imitate the section of the ledger concerned with the figures on the same side (i.e. the usual side for debtors' entries). Such a Control Account is shown below. Study it and the notes below it.

Example

A–E SALES LEDGER CONTROL ACCOUNT

19__		£	19__		£
Mar. 1	Balances b/d	13,729	Mar. 1	Balances b/d	138
31	Sales	89,255	31	Returns	656
31	Balance c/d	184	31	Bank	56,254
			31	Discount Allowed	824
			31	Bad debts	136
			31	Purchases Ledger Contra entry	426
			31	Balance c/d	44,734
		£103,168			£103,168
19__		£	19__		£
Apr. 1	Balance b/d	44,734	Apr. 1	Balance b/d	184

NOTES:

(a) The source of the data to be used in this Control Account is the total figures for the month obtained from some original source. For example the Sales Figure above would be the total of the Sales Day Book, and the Returns Figure would be the total of the Sales Returns Book.

(b) Some figures would not be as readily available — for example we would have to extract figures for the A–E Sales Ledger for Bank and Discount Allowed from the Cash Book — a fairly easy activity. Similarly the 'Bad Debts' figure would be analysed out of the Journal Proper, by going through the few 'bad debts' entries made during the month.

(c) How does this sort of Total Account make the A–E Ledger self-balancing? Of course it will not, but if we imagine this account as shown above is headed:

A–E Sales Ledger Control Account (as in the General Ledger)

and it then appears in the General Ledger, representing the whole of the A–E Sales Ledger on one single page, an exactly equal and opposite account can appear in the back of the A–E Sales Ledger tray, as shown below.

Look at this entry now, and read the notes below it.

A–E SALES LEDGER CONTROL ACCOUNT
(as in the A–E Sales Ledger)

19__		£	19__		£
Mar. 1	Balances b/d	138	Mar. 1	Balances b/d	13,729
31	Returns	656	31	Sales	89,255
31	Bank	56,254	31	Balance c/d	184
31	Disc Allowed	824			
31	Bad debts	136			
31	Purchases Ledger				
	Contra Entry	426			
31	Balance c/d	44,734			
		£103,168			£103,168
19__		£	19__		£
Apr. 1	Balance b/d	184	Apr. 1	Balance b/d	44,734

NOTES:

(a) Since this account is a total account which exactly balances all the individual items posted into the A–E Sales Accounts it must make the book self-balancing.

(b) The final credit balance of £44,734 balances up with all the debtors' balances (on the debit side) scattered around the accounts.

(c) The small debit balance of £184 balances up with the one or two debtors who finish up as creditors, because for some reason we owe them money at the end of the month — usually because after they paid for something they returned it for some reason.

(d) At the end of any month the book-keeper whose book balances simply phones the accountant and says 'The A–E Sales Ledger balances' and he/she says 'Well done, and thanks for letting me know. No need to say what the figures are, the accountant knows because he/she has the whole ledger on a single page in the General Ledger.

Sample question _____
C. Lincoln keeps his books so that a Purchases Ledger Control Account and a Sales Ledger Control Account are shown in his General Ledger and balanced at the end of each month. From the following details, show how these accounts would appear in the General Ledger for the month of October 19__.

Oct.	1	*Dr* balances in Sales Ledger	£13,693
	1	*Dr* balances in Purchases Ledger	116
	1	*Cr* balances in Sales Ledger	£295
	1	Cr balances in Purchases Ledger	11,966
Oct.	31	Sales	19,945
	31	Purchases	17,046
	31	Sales returns and allowances	367
	31	Purchases returns and allowances	200
	31	Cash received from customers	20,461
	31	Cash paid to suppliers	15,318
	31	Discount Received	112
	31	Discount Allowed	359
	31	Bad debt written off	41
	31	Sales Ledger debit balance transferred to Purchases Ledger	78
	31	Debit balances in Purchases Ledger	102
	31	Credit balances in Sales Ledger	121

(RSA)

Answer

SALES LEDGER (DEBTORS LEDGER) CONTROL ACCOUNT

19__			19__		
Oct. 1 Balance b/d		£13,693	Oct. 1 Balance b/d		£295
31 Sales		19,945	31 Returns in		367
31 Balance c/d		121	31 Cash		20,461
			31 Discount		
			allowed		359
			31 Bad debts		41
			Purchases		
			Ledger contra		78
			31 Balance c/d		12,158
		£33,759			£33,759
Nov. 1 Balance b/d		12,158	Nov.1 Balance b/d		121

PURCHASES LEDGER (CREDITORS LEDGER) CONTROL ACCOUNT

19__			19__		
Oct. 1 Balance b/d		£116	Oct. 1 Balance b/d		£11,966
31 Returns out		200	31 Purchases		17,046
31 Cash		15,318	31 Balance c/d		102
31 Discount					
received		112			
31 Sales Ledger					
contra		78			
31 Balance c/d		13,290			
		£29,114			£29,114
Nov.1 Balance b/d		102	Nov. 1 Balance b/d		13,290

NOTES:

(a) Since these accounts in the General Ledger will exactly imitate the whole of the ordinary Sales Ledger and Purchases Ledger you will decide where each item goes by saying 'Where would this entry go in an ordinary debtor's account (or creditor's account)'.

(b) At the end of the month, remember that a debit balance (to finish up on the debit side after balancing) must be entered on the credit side before balancing. Similarly, the credit balance of £121 on the Sales Ledger is put on the debit side before balancing so it can be brought down to the credit side after balancing.

Progress test 17

1. Name the main subdivisions of the Ledger. **(1)**

2. Give another name for the Sales Ledger. **(1)**

3. Give another name for the Creditors' Ledger. **(1)**

4. What accounts would you expect to find in the Purchases Ledger? **(1)**

5. What accounts would you expect to find in the Sales Ledger? **(1)**

6. Outline the main advantages to be derived from the use of computerised Debtors' and Creditors' Ledgers. **(2)**

7. Explain how it is possible for us to have *two* accounts for the same person. **(2)**

8. What is a 'running balance' account? **(2)**

9. Explain what you understand by the term 'set off'. **(2)**

10. What accounts would you expect to find in the General Ledger? **(1)**

11. What action is usually taken on the Sales and Purchases Ledgers at the end of each month? **(2, 4)**

12. Name the sources of information for writing up Control Accounts. **(3)**

13. If we have *two* personal accounts, explain the effect on the Control Accounts at the month end. **(3)**

14. What can be the effect on the Sales Ledger Control of a personal account for a debtor which has a credit balance at the month end? **(3)**

15. What do the balances on Control Accounts represent? **(3)**

Specimen questions

1. Using the following figures prepare the Sales and Purchases Ledger Control Accounts for the month of January:

		£
Sales Ledger balances at 1 Jan.,	Dr	41,210
	Cr	321
Purchases Ledger balances at 1 Jan.	Dr	161
	Cr	37,621
Receipts from credit customers		32,632
Payments to trade creditors		29,625
Credit sales		36,719
Purchases on credit		21,776
Debtors' cheques dishonoured		315
Discounts received		1,416
Discount allowed		1,521
Returns inwards		782
Returns outwards		421
Bad debts written off		558
Sales Ledger debits transferred to Purchases Ledger		120

2. The following balances have been extracted from the accounts of Z Ltd for the year ending 31 December, 19_3.

	£
Sales Ledger debtor balances, 1 Jan. 19_3	16,500
Purchases Ledger creditor balances, 1 Jan. 19_3	15,224
Payments to suppliers	41,250
Sales	60,236
Purchases	43,425
Returns inwards	936
Returns outwards	335
Bad debts written off in 19_3	250
Credit received from suppliers for overcharge	34
Credit balances on Sales Ledger at 31 December 19_3	120
Sales receipts	56,250

You are required to prepare the Sales Ledger and Purchase

Ledger Control Accounts showing the balance of debtors and creditors respectively for the year ending 31 December 19_3.

3. The Purchases and Sales Ledgers of B. Box Ltd contain the following at 1 March:

	Dr	Cr
	£	£
Purchases Ledger	41	7,631
Sales Ledger	8,932	70

The following totals for March were obtained from the sources indicated:

CASH BOOK

	£		£
Debit side Sales Ledger	7,175	Discount	271
Credit side Purchases Ledger	6,121	Discount	159

Purchases	Sales	Returns	Returns
Book £5,793	Book £6,987	Inwards	Outwards
		Book £113	Book £211

At 31 March debit balances brought down for the new month in the Purchases Ledger amounted to £23 and credit balances brought down for the new month in the Sales Ledger amounted to £48. You are required to prepare and balance the Control Accounts in the General Ledger for the month of March.

(NCTEC ONC)

4. The ABC Company maintains a Debtors Control Account in its general ledger, and keeps the individual account for each customer in a subsidiary debtors ledger. There are 230 accounts in the debtors ledger. At 1 Jan. the balances on the first six accounts were as follows: B. Archer £290; J. Atwood £456; S. Banks £nil; R. Boole £187; F. Bragg £74; T. Charles £371. The total of the balances outstanding in the debtors ledger at 1 Jan. (including the above) was £25,418.

Transactions during January were:

	Sales £	Returns inwards £	Bad debts £	Cheques and cash received £	Cash discounts allowed £
B. Archer	140	20	—	265	10
J. Attwood	291	18	—	103	5
S. Banks	—	—	—	300	—
R. Boole	—	—	187	—	—
F. Bragg	—	—	—	74	—
T. Charles	518	41	—	320	15
All other accounts	14,660	720	470	14,111	470
	£15,609	£799	£657	£15,173	£500

The cheque received from S. Banks for £300 was payment for a debt which had been written off last year.

A cheque from F. Bragg received and banked in the sum of £50 was returned by the bank marked 'refer to drawer'. It must be written back.

You are required to:

Head up accounts for the Debtors Control, and the first six accounts in the Debtors Ledger, with a further account to represent all the other customers accounts; enter the above transactions, balance all accounts and check that the ledger agrees with the Control Account. (*AAT*)

More difficult final accounts

1. The range of final accounts activities

The student of accountancy must be able to prepare the full range of final accounts, which involves understanding the books of:

(a) small scale businesses run by sole traders.
(b) partnerships.
(c) private limited companies.
(d) clubs and non-profit making organisations.
(e) businesses which only keep the most rudimentary accounts, often described as 'single-entry' book-keeping.
(f) public limited companies.

Assuming that the student has already mastered the simplest type of 'final accounts' exercise dealt with in the earlier chapters of this book, we will consider the more difficult type of sole trader exercise (i.e. those with a number of adjustments) in this chapter. The following chapters then deal with all the other types of Final Accounts.

2. A difficult sole trader exercise

The following example is designed to illustrate most of the adjustments which you are likely to encounter in examinations at this stage. Follow it through carefully. The adjustments have been specially cross-referenced to assist you. Do read the question through carefully; the adjustments have been worded in the various ways you will encounter in the examination room. Please note that the long list of balances has been printed in two columns, but they are not intended to be debit balances in one column and credit balances in the other. The layout is purely to save space.

Sample question _____

The following balances were extracted from the books of T. Brown, a wholesaler. From these figures and the notes which accompany them, prepare the Trading and Profit and Loss Accounts for the year ended 31 December 19__, and a Balance Sheet as at that date.

	£		£
Capital Account		Balance at bank (Dr)	12,583
T. Brown	82,655	Cash in hand	120
Drawings	18,000	Light and heat	2,472
Trade debtors	4,500	Rates paid	2,248
Trade creditors	3,500	Freehold premises	
Sales	121,324	(cost)	57,635
Sales returns	361	Fixtures (cost)	11,520
Purchases	27,472	Vehicles (cost)	11,600
Purchases returns	547	Stationery	1,156
Wages (warehouse)	33,200	Postage and telephone	
Salaries	21,500	expenses	1,200
Discount allowed	1,248	Insurance	1,060
Discount received	426	Bad debts provision	1,200
Provision for depreciation:		Bad debts written off	1,072
Fixtures	4,290	Vehicle expenses	3,386
Vehicles	4,800	Stock 1 Jan. 19__	16,584
		Loan (15 per cent)	11,000
		Interest on loan	825

(a) Rates are to be apportioned three-quarters to warehouse. £64 rates are prepaid.

(b) Three-quarters of the charge for light and heat relates to the warehouse.

(c) Stock on 31 December 19__ was valued at £15,210.

(d) Depreciate fixtures at 5 per cent on cost; and vehicles at 20 per cent on reducing balance.

(e) Only half year's interest on the loan had been paid.

(f) Insurance unexpired amounts to £72.

(g) The Provision for Bad Debts is to be adjusted to £1,500.

(h) An invoice for goods purchased during December, £100, has been omitted from the books.

(i) During December Brown took £400 of goods at selling price for his own use, and this has not been recorded in the books.

Answer

Before you read through and check the solution you may find it useful, as revision, to set out the above balances in the form of a Trial Balance; the totals of the Trial Balance should come to £229,742.

The golden rule to remember in the preparation of final accounts is that items in the Trial Balance are only dealt with *once*, but that adjustments need to be dealt with *twice*. This is because the effect of an adjustment is to leave some balance either a debit or a credit balance, on an account somewhere, and this balance will therefore appear on the Balance Sheet either as an asset or a liability.

The thinking behind each adjustment is as follows:

(a) The amount to be written off in the Final Accounts for rates is only £2,184, leaving a balance of £64 on the Rates Account — a prepayment.

(b) We need to put ¾ in the Trading Account and ¼ in the Profit and Loss Account, but there is no balance outstanding.

(c) This goes to the Trading Account and also appears as a current asset on the Balance Sheet.

(d) These will appear in the Profit and Loss Account and will increase the respective Provision for Depreciation Accounts (and thus reduce the value of these assets on the books).

(e) Loan interest charged must be increased by £825 to £1,650, and the £825 will appear as a current liability — interest due — on the Balance Sheet.

(f) Insurance charged must be reduced by £72, this balance appearing as a current asset — insurance prepaid.

(g) The provision must be increased by writing off £300 in the Profit and Loss Account. The bigger provision will reduce the value of the debtors on the Balance Sheet.

(h) The Purchases Account must be increased by £100 and the Trade Creditors figure increased to £3,600.

(i) The £400 must be added to the Sales figure, and drawings must be increased by £400 — this is 'drawings in kind'.

The Final Accounts will therefore appear as shown below:

T. BROWN
TRADING AND PROFIT AND LOSS ACCOUNTS
FOR YEAR ENDED 31 DECEMBER 19__

	£	£			£
Opening stock Jan. 1		16,584	Sales		121,324
Purchases (+ £100) (h)	27,572		+ Invoice (h)		400
Less Returns Out	547				121,724
		27,025	*Less* Sales Returns		361
Total Stock available		43,609	Net turnover		121,363
Less Closing Stock		15,210			
Cost of Stock sold		28,399			
Direct expenses:					
Wages		33,200			
Rates ($^3/_4$ x 2,248-64) (a)		1,638			
Light and heat ($^3/_4$ x 2,472)		1,854			
		65,091			
Gross profit c/d		56,272			
		£121,363			£121,363
Administrative expenses:			Gross profit b/d		56,272
Rates			Discount received		426
($^1/_4$ x 2,248 - 64) (a)		546			56,698
Insurance	1,060				
Less Insurance					
prepaid (f)	72				
		988			
Light and heat					
($^1/_4$ x 2,472) (b)		618			
Salaries		21,500			
Stationery		1,156			
Postage and telephone		1,200			
Depreciation of fixtures (d)		576			
Selling and distributive expenses:		26,584			
Vehicle expenses	3,386				
Vehicle depreciation (d)	1,360				
Discount allowed	1,248				
Bad debts	1,072				
Bad debts provision (g)	300				
		7,366			
Financial charges:					
Loan interest paid	825				
Add Due	825				
		1,650			
		35,600			
Net profit to Capital Account		21,098			
		£56,698			£56,698

BALANCE SHEET AS AT 31 DECEMBER 19__

	£	£	£		£	£	£
Fixed assets:				T. Brown,			
Freehold premises (cost)			57,635	Capital A/c			
Fixtures (cost)		11,520		Balance 1 Jan.			82,655
Less Depreciation to				*Add* Net profit		21,098	
date (d)		4,866					
			6,654	*Less* Drawings			
				plus goods (i)		18,400	
Vehicles (cost)		11,600					2,698
Less Depreciation to							85,353
date (d)		6,160		Long term liability			
			5,440	loan (15%)			11,000
			69,729	Current liabilities:			
Current assets:	£	£		Trade creditors		3,500	
Stock (c)		15,210		*Add* Invoice (h)		100	
Debtors	4,500					3,600	
Less Bad debts				Accrued expenses			
Provision (g)	1,500			Interest due (e)		825	
		3,000					4,425
Rates prepaid (a)		64					
Insurance prepaid (f)		72					
Balance at bank		12,583					
Cash in hand		120					
			31,049				
			£100,778				£100,778

---

3. Vertical style final accounts

Changes have taken place in the United Kingdom in the presentation of final accounts in that it is now common to present them in single column or vertical form. The advantage of the system is that there is more space to display them than in the normal account form, but although accountants have adopted the layout very widely, it is actually more difficult for the layman to understand. It has not been widely adopted in Europe where the alternative, more logical presentation is to present the Final Accounts across a double page in the annual report, with the centre of the double page becoming the centre of the accounts, with plenty of room on either side to display the debit side and the credit side across a full page.

Adopting the vertical style format the accounts would appear as follows:

T. BROWN
TRADING AND PROFIT AND LOSS ACCOUNTS
FOR THE YEAR ENDED 31 DECEMBER 19__

	£	£	£
Sales			121,324
Add invoice			400
			121,724
Less Sales Returns			361
			121,363
Less Cost of Sales:			
Opening Stock		16,584	
Add Purchases	27,472		
Add Invoice (h)	100		
	27,572		
Less Returns Out	547		
		27,025	
Total stock available		43,609	
Less Closing stock		15,210	
		28,399	
Add Direct Expenses:			
Wages		33,200	
Rates ($^3/_4$ x £2,248 - £64) (a)		1,638	
Light and Heat ($^3/_4$ x £2,472)		1,854	
Cost of Sales			65,091
Gross profit			56,272
Add Discount Received			426
			56,698
Less Administrative Expenses			
Rates ($^1/_4$ x £2,248 - £64)		546	
Insurance	1060		
Less prepaid	72	988	
Light and Heat ($^1/_4$ x £2,742) (b)		618	
Salaries		21,500	
Stationery		1,156	
Postage and telephone		1,200	
Depreciation on fixtures		576	
		26,584	
Less Selling Expenses			30,114
Vehicle expenses		3,386	
Vehicle depreciation (d)		1,360	
Discount allowed		1,248	
Bad debts		1,072	
Bad debts provision		300	
Less Financial charges			7,366
Loan interest paid		825	22,748
Loan interest due		825	
			1,650
Net profit to Capital Account			£21,098

BALANCE SHEET AS AT 31 DECEMBER 19__

Fixed assets:	£	£	£
	At cost	*Less* Depreciation to date	Net value
Freehold Premises	57,635	—	57,635
Fixtures	11,520	4,866	6,654
Vehicles	11,600	6,160	5,440
	80,755	11,026	69,729

Current assets:			
Stock		15,210	
Debtors	4,500		
Less Provision	1,500		
		3,000	
Rates prepaid (a)		64	
Insurance prepaid (f)		72	
Balance at bank		12,583	
Cash in hand		120	
		31,049	

Less Current Liabilities			
Trade creditors	3,500		
Add invoice (h)	100		
	3,600		
Accrued expenses:			
Interest due	825		
		4,425	
		Net Current Assets	26,624
		Net Assets	£96,353

Financed by:			
Capital (at start)			82,655
Add Net profit		21,098	
Less Drawings	18,000		
Plus drawings in kind	400		
		18,400	
			2,698
	Net worth to the proprietor		85,353
Long-term Liabilities			
Loan			11,000
			£96,353

NOTES:

(a) The current liabilities are deducted from the current assets to bring out the net working capital (labelled as 'net current assets' above). This reveals the excess of current assets available if all short-term debts were paid.

(b) The term 'Financed by:' shows how the net assets in the top half were financed by the capital employed in the business.

(c) Sometimes the Capital etc. is shown first and the assets below. In that case the words 'Financed by' are replaced by the words 'Represented by:' because the funds provided by the proprietor etc. are represented in real life by the fixed assets and net current assets owned by the business.

Progress test 18

1. What are the entries needed to adjust the accounts for rates paid in advance? **(2)**

2. Explain the term 'provision for depreciation'. **(2)**

3. Explain the term 'provision for bad debts'. **(2)**

4. How do motor vehicles appear on a Balance Sheet? **(2)**

5. Explain the advantages and disadvantages of the vertical style of Final Accounts. **(3)**

Specimen questions

1. On 1 January 19__, W. Ord started business as a wholesale confectioner. The following were among the balances extracted from his books on 31 December. From this information prepare

Ord's Trading and Profit and Loss Accounts for the year ended 31 December 19_, and a Balance Sheet at that date.

	£		£
Purchases	43,377	Bad Debts	679
Sales	126,475	Insurance and Rates	826
Returns Inwards	242	Heat and Light	430
Returns Outwards	268	Interest Paid	1,021
Carriage on purchases	347	Discounts Allowed	337
Advertising	2,110	Discounts Received	210
Motor Van Expenses	755	Bank Loan	10,365
Driver's Wages (P&L A/c)	5,052	Rent of Premises sub-let	1,100
Freehold Premises	85,000	Plant and Machinery	5,800
Fixtures and Fittings	12,580	Motor Vehicles	11,725
Debtors	460	Mortgage on Premises	30,000
Creditors	3,250	Capital	28,332
Drawings	12,560	Bank balance	16,358
		Cash in hand	341

(a) Stock in hand at 31 December £11,898.

(b) Provide £105 for bad debts.

(c) A van which cost £4,800 is to be depreciated by 15 per cent on cost.

(d) A half year's interest, £780 is due on the loan.

(e) A demand for £560 rates for the half year to 31st March had been received but not paid. An appropriate amount is to be included for the current year.

(f) The figure for advertising includes £110 for next year.

(g) £126 is owing to Crossways Garage Ltd for maintenance and repair of the motor van.

(h) A partial repayment of the loan £2,000 is due on 31 December and has not been paid. The outstanding loan is to be reduced and the amount shown as a current liability.

(i) Depreciate Fixture and Fittings by 10% and Plant and Machinery by $12\frac{1}{2}\%$.

2. The following balances were extracted from the books of T. Branch, a wholesaler, at 31 December 19__. Prepare the

Trading and Profit and Loss Accounts for the year ended December 31, 19__ and a Balance Sheet at that date.

	£		£
Capital A/c	86,900	Office Salaries	21,500
Drawings	16,000	Lighting and Heating	1,472
Trade debtors	4,520	Rates	1,248
Trade creditors	2,422	Freehold Premises	76,500
Stock Jan. 1	17,334	Fixtures and Fittings	10,440
Purchases	29,472	Vehicles	9,600
Sales	152,232	Stationery	1,156
Returns Inwards	2,361	Sundry Expenses	1,164
Returns Outwards	547	Postage and Telephone	436
Balance at bank	27,641	Insurance	560
Cash in hand	1,142	Bad Debts Provision	125
Discount Allowed	1,248	Bad debts written off	72
Discount Received	426	Vehicle Expenses	1,386
Warehouse Wages	43,200	Mortgage	30,000
		Interest on mortgage	4,200

In preparing the accounts, provide for the following:

(a) Stock at 31 December was valued at £11,516.

(b) Lighting and Heating, and Rates are to be apportioned three-quarters to warehouse, one-quarter to office.

(c) Depreciate fixtures and fittings by 10 per cent and vehicles by 20 per cent.

(d) Rates prepaid amount to £164.

(e) Insurance unexpired amounts to £100.

(f) The provision for bad debts at the end of the year is to be made equal to 10 per cent of the trade debtors.

3. The following balances were extracted from the books of T. Branch, a wholesaler, at 31 December 19__. Prepare the Trading and Profit and Loss Accounts for the year ended 31 December, and a Balance Sheet at that date. Present your accounts in vertical style, with the Balance Sheet showing the net current assets and the net assets, and how these net assets were financed.

	£		£
Capital A/c	98,465	Office Salaries	31,275
Drawings	24,000	Lighting and Heating	2,460
Trade debtors	4,560	Rates	996
Trade creditors	5,250	Freehold Premises (cost)	74,650
Stock Jan.1	16,124	Fixtures and Fittings (cost)	12,600
Purchases	39,718	Vehicles (cost)	17,500
Sales	184,929	Stationery	1,245
Returns Inwards	1,929	Sundry Expenses	379
Returns Outwards	718	Postage and Telephone	1,450
Balance at bank	23,495	Insurance	840
Cash in hand	386	Bad Debts Provision	530
Discount Allowed	1,425	Bad Debts written off	477
Discount Received	836	Vehicle Expenses	2,358
Warehouse Wages	19,256	Plant and Machinery	
Provision for deprec-		(cost)	35,000
iation (a) Plant etc.	14,000	Carriage In	1,250
(b) Fixtures etc.	6,300	Carriage Out	1,655
(c) Vehicles	7,000	Goodwill	3,000

In preparing the accounts, provide for the following.

(a) Stock at 31 December was valued at £19,596.
(b) Lighting and Heating, and Rates are to be apportioned after adjustment three-quarters to warehouse, one-quarter to office.
(c) Depreciate fixtures and fittings by 10 per cent of original cost, vehicles by 20 per cent and Plant and Machinery by 20 per cent.
(d) Rates prepaid amount to £84.
(e) Insurance unexpired amounts to £210.
(f) The provision for bad debts at the end of the year is to be made equal to 8 per cent of the outstanding debtors, after one debt of £60 has been written off in the 'end of year' review.
(g) A lighting bill for £240 has just arrived and is to be included.
(h) £1,500 of the Goodwill is to be written off and charged to Drawings Account.

19
Partnership final accounts

1. Definition

Two or more persons joining together in business with a view of profit constitute a partnership. Partnerships are usually governed by a deed of partnership, and this document will show:

(a) how profits and losses are to be shared;

(b) how much capital each partner is to contribute to the business;

(c) whether any interest is to be *given* on the capital contributed, and if so, at what rate;

(d) whether any partner is entitled to a salary or a commission;

(e) Any restrictions on drawings; e.g.
  (i) a monthly limit may be set by agreement, or
  (ii) interest may be charged on drawings made by the partners, in which case the rate of interest must be agreed upon;

(f) the procedure to be followed on the death or retirement of a partner, etc.

2. Partnership Act 1890

When a partnership *does not have an agreement*, either express or implied, then the provisions of this Act apply.
Section 24 of the Act lays down that:

(a) profits and losses are to be shared equally;

(b) any *loan* made to the business by a partner is to carry interest at the rate of 5 per cent per annum;

(c) no partner is entitled to a salary;

(d) no partner is entitled to interest on capital.

NOTE: You will be expected to apply the above conditions when the question states that there is no agreement or that the partnership is one governed by the Act of 1890.

3. Accounting aspects

The main changes affecting the book-keeping process can be summarised as follows.

(a) The Profit and Loss Account will now have a separate section called the Appropriation Account.

    (*i*) Net profit found in the Profit and Loss Account will be carried down into this new section.

    (*ii*) This net profit will be allocated between the partners in their profit-sharing ratios *after other appropriations* out of profits have been made.

(b) Each partner will have a Capital Account, a Current Account, and a Drawings Account.

    (*i*) The Capital Account will normally remain constant, i.e. you will *not now take profit* to the Capital Account.

    (*ii*) The Current Account will be used to record any profits, losses, drawings, salary, interest, etc., attributable to each partner.

(c) The balances on Capital and Current Accounts will appear *separately* in the Balance Sheet. The Drawings Account will be cleared into the Current Account (for each partner).

4. Interest on drawings

Where partners are allowed to earn interest on their capital it seems appropriate that any drawings should be charged interest. If the partnership deed requires this the calculations are:

(a) *Calculations:* interest is calculated *from* the date the amount is withdrawn *to* the end of the financial year.

Example

_____

If the year ends on 31 December, interest being calculated at 15 per cent per annum, then if A draws £2,000 on 1 April and £3,000 on 1 July, the total interest would be £450, made up as follows:

	£
15% on £2,000 for $\frac{3}{4}$ year	225
plus 15% on £3,000 for $\frac{1}{2}$ year	225
	£ 450

_____

(b) *Book-keeping entries: debit* partner's Drawings Account; *credit* Profit and Loss Appropriation Account. In this way the extra 'drawings' charged to the partner for interest becomes a source of extra profit to be shared among all the partners.

5.   Guaranteed share of profit

Sometimes the amount of a partner's share of profit is guaranteed by the other partners. When such a partner's share of profit amounts to *less* than the amount guaranteed:

(a) *debit* Appropriation Account with the guaranteed amount; *credit* the partner's Current Account;

(b) the *remaining profits* will then be shared among the other partners in the ratios in which they share profits and losses *as among themselves*.

6.   Accounting entries at the end of financial year

These can be summarised as follows.

(a) Net profit: Transfer to Appropriation Account by *debiting* Profit and Loss A/c and *crediting* Appropriation Account.

(b) Writing off Goodwill or other capital expense. If any partnership decision has called for some use of profits before the final division takes place this will be dealt with first. *Debit* Appropriation Account, *credit* Goodwill Account (or other fictitious or intangible Asset Account).

(c) If any partner has made a loan to the firm the interest on this loan is given before the balance of the profits is shared: *debit* Appropriation Account; *credit* Current Account of the partner concerned.

(d) Salary: *debit* Appropriation Account, *credit* Current Account of *each* partner entitled to a salary.

(e) Interest on capital: *debit* Appropriation Account, *credit* Current Account.

(f) Interest on drawings: *credit* Appropriation Account, *debit* Current Account of *each* partner.

(g) Share of profit: *debit* Appropriation Account, *credit* Current Account of *each* partner.

(h) Share of loss: *credit* Appropriation Account, *debit* Current Account of *each* partner.

NOTE: Drawings will be transferred direct to each partner's Current Account: *debit* Current Account; *credit* Drawings Account (of *each* partner, to clear the Drawing Account in each case).

Sample question

Bull and Bear start a business as solicitors on 1 April 19_. Each partner brings in £15,000 as capital, but Bull makes an additional advance of £10,000 to the business. The profit for the year to the following 31 March was £38,500. During the course of the year Bull has drawn £12,400 and Bear £8,156.

Assuming that Section 24 of the Partnership Act 1890, is to apply, and that the 5 per cent rate of interest is to apply, draw up:

(a) the Appropriation Account at the end of the year;
(b) the relevant personal accounts of the partners for the year;
(c) the details that would appear in the Balance Sheet at 31 March 19_1.

Answer

APPROPRIATION ACCOUNT FOR THE YEAR ENDED 31 MARCH 19__.

	£	£		£
Interest on loan: Bull		500	Net profit(from P & L A/c)	38,500
Share of profit:				
Bull $\frac{1}{2}$	19,000			
Bear $\frac{1}{2}$	19,000			
		38,000		
		£38,500		£38,500

LOAN ACCOUNT — BULL

	Apr. 1 Bank	£10,000

CAPITAL ACCOUNTS

		Bull	Bear
	Apr. 1 Bank	£15,000	£15,000

CURRENT ACCOUNTS

	Bull	Bear			Bull	Bear
	£	£			£	£
Mar. 31 Drawings	12,400	8,156	Mar. 31 Interest on		500	—
31 Balance c/d	7,100	10,844	loan			
			31 Share of			
			profit		19,000	19,000
	£19,500	19,000			£19,500	19,000
			Apr. 1 Balance b/d		7,100	10,844

DRAWINGS ACCOUNTS

	Bull	Bear		Bull	Bear
	£	£		£	£
Sundry Accounts			Mar. 31 Current		
drawn at			A/c	12,400	8,156
various times	12,400	8,156			
	£12,400	8,156		£12,400	8,156

EXTRACT OF BALANCE SHEET AS AT 31 MARCH 19_1

	£	£
Capital Accounts		
Bull	15,000	
Bear	15,000	
		30,000
Loan A/c: Bull		10,000
Current Accounts		
Bull	7,100	
Bear	10,844	
		17,944

Example

During the second year of operations Bull and Bear admit Bear's son Teddy to the firm. He brought in £6,000 as capital. An agreement is drawn up which provides that Bull receives a commission of 5 per cent of the profits after paying Loan Interest. Teddy is allowed a salary of £6,000; interest is allowed on capital and on opening balances of Current Accounts and charged on drawings at 12½ per cent per annum. Interest on the loan was now to be given at 14 per cent per annum. All calculations correct to the nearest £1.

Profits after paying loan interest, commission, salary and interest on capital and opening Current Account balances are shared equally for the first £30,000, any profits above £30,000 to be shared in the ratios 4:4:1 respectively. This ensures that the ratio between Bull and Bear is the same as before. (*Note:* In the exercise Bear takes £1 less profit due to rounding difficulties in the calculation.)

Profits for the year before any adjustments above were £72,000 and the drawings were £13,600 *each* for Bull and Bear and £12,400 for Teddy. It can be assumed that funds were drawn out regularly throughout the year (in other words interest on drawings will be calculated as if they had all been drawn for 6 months).

APPROPRIATION ACCOUNT FOR THE YEAR ENDED
31 MARCH 19_2

	£		£	£
Interest on loan: Bull	1,400	Net profit		72,000
Commission 5%		Interest on drawings:		
on £70,600 Bull	3,530	Bull	850	
Salary Teddy	6,000	Bear	850	
Interest on capital: £		Teddy	775	
Bull	1,875			2,475
Bear	1,875			
Teddy	750			
	4,500			
Interest on Current A/c				
opening balances £				
Bull (£7,100)	888			
Bear (£10,844)	1,356			
	2,244			
Share of profit:				
First £30,000				
Bull	10,000			
Bear	10,000			
Teddy	10,000			
	30,000			
Residue of				
profits: £26,801				
Bull $\frac{4}{9}$	11,912			
Bear $\frac{4}{9}$	11,911			
Teddy $\frac{1}{9}$	2,978			
	26,801			
	£74,475			£74,475

CAPITAL ACCOUNTS

	Bull	Bear	Teddy
Apr. 1 Balance	£15,000	15,000	—
Bank			£5,000

CURRENT ACCOUNTS

19_	Bull	Bear	Teddy	19_	Bull	Bear	Teddy
Mar. 31				Apr. 1	7,100	10,844	—
Drawings				Balance			
A/cs	14,450	14,450	13,175	Mar. 31			
Balance c/d	22,255	21,536	6,553	Interest on			
				loan	1,400	—	—
				Commission	3,530	—	—
				Salary	—	—	6,000
				Interest on			
				capital	1,875	1,875	750
				Interest on			
				Current A/c	888	1,356	—
				Share of			
				profits	10,000	10,000	10,000
				Share of			
				residue	11,912	11,911	2,978
	£36,705	35,986	19,728		£36,705	35,986	19,728
				Apr. 1 Balance			
				b/d	22,255	21,536	6,553

DRAWINGS ACCOUNTS

19_	Bull	Bear	Teddy		Bull	Bear	Teddy
Apr.—Mar.							
Sundry							
amounts				Mar. 31 Current			
drawn	13,600	13,600	12,400	Account	14,450	14,450	13,175
Interest	850	850	775				
	£14,450	14,450	13,175		14,450	14,450	13,175

EXTRACT OF BALANCE SHEET AS AT 31 MARCH 19_2

	£	£	Capital Accounts	£	£
			Bull	15,000	
			Bear	15,000	
			Teddy	6,000	
					36,000
			Loan Account		
			Bull		10,000
			Current Accounts		
			Bull	22,255	
			Bear	21,536	
			Teddy	6,553	
					50,344

7. Debit balance on current account

Occasionally a partner overdraws his/her Current Account by taking out more than his/her fair share of profit. In such an eventuality a debit balance will arise on the partner's Current Account at the end of the period. This debit balance represents an amount due to the business from the partner, and it is usual to show this figure in the Balance Sheet as a separate item among the current assets. In practice, however, the partner will repay the debt as soon as the amount has been ascertained (provided he/she has funds available).

(a) If the partner concerned is not in a position to repay the debt it may be deducted from his/her capital. In examinations you will normally adopt this method only if the question specifically tells you to do so.

(b) Sometimes the debit balance is deducted from the total credit balances shown in the Balance Sheet on the current accounts of the other partners so that a net figure of *all* the current accounts is shown. This is simply a method of presentation in the Balance Sheet and must not be confused with a transfer to other Current Accounts.

Progress test 19

1. What are the main items usually incorporated into a deed of partnership? **(1)**

2. What are the main provisions of section 24 of the Partnership Act of 1890? **(2)**

3. What are the main changes in the final accounts of partnership when compared with those of a sole trader? **(3)**

4. What are the main items usually dealt with in the Appropriation Account? **(3)** and **(6)**

5. How do you calculate interest on drawings and how do you record it in books of account? **(4)**

6. How is a debit balance on a partner's Current Account usually dealt with? **(7)**

Specimen questions

1. Brown, Fawcett and Southlands are in partnership sharing profits and losses equally.

During the year ended 31 December, the net trading profit of the firm was £47,302 and the partners' drawings and interest were:

	Drawings	Interest on Drawings
	£	£
Brown	12,000	620
Fawcett	11,900	570
Southlands	13,000	450

Interest is allowed on partners' capital at the rate of 10 per cent per annum. Fawcett is entitled to a salary of £9,000 per annum as Sales Manager. The partners had agreed that Brown should withdraw £1,000 from his capital at 1 July, and that Southlands should contribute a similar amount as at that date, and this had in fact been done.

The balances on the partners' accounts at 1 January, were:

	Capital Accounts (all credit balances) £	Current Accounts £
Brown	9,000	1,600 credit balance
Fawcett	8,000	400 debit balance
Southlands	7,000	300 debit balance

Prepare the partnership Profit and Loss Appropriation Account and the partners' Capital and Current Accounts for the year ended 31 December, 19__.

2. Andrews and Banfield are in partnership. On 30th June 19_3, their capital accounts are: Andrews £15,000; Banfield £10,000. Their deed of partnership provides that after the net profit for any year has been ascertained, the balance available will be applied as follows.

(a) Banfield is to receive a commission of 10 per cent of the net trading profit, calculated before charging interest on capital, for managing the business.

(b) Each partner is to be credited with interest on capital at 12 per cent per annum. This also applies to initial balances on Current Accounts, the partner either receiving or paying interest.

(c) Profits or losses are to be shared A:B::2:1.

(d) No interest is to be charged on drawings.

On 1 July 19_2 Current Account balances were: Andrews Dr £1,200 Banfield Cr £1,500. During the year to 30th June 19_3 drawings in cash were: Andrews £12,400; Banfield £22,000. In addition Andrews took goods from stock £700 and Banfield £900. Repairs to Banfield's car, £755 which has been charged to the Profit and Loss Account, are to be transferred to his Current Account. The net trading profit for the year ended 30 June 19_3 was £45,225 (before adjusting for repairs to Banfield's car).

Show:

(i) the Profit and loss Appropriation Account for the year ended 30 June 19_3; and

(ii) the Current Accounts of the partners for the year ended 30 June 19_3.

3. Rathlin and Lambay were partners sharing profits and losses in the ratio of 3:2. The following Trial Balance was extracted from their books on 31 December 19__.

	£	£
Capital A/c 1 Jan.:		
Rathlin		28,000
Lambay		14,000
Drawings:		
Rathlin	16,800	
Lambay	14,400	
Office equipment (cost £1,700)	1,360	
Stock 1 Jan. 19__	21,000	
Trade debtors and creditors	16,328	12,750
Purchases and sales	102,000	206,000
Freehold property at cost	48,500	
Wages and salaries	25,454	
Rates	1,300	
General expenses	9,832	
Balance at bank	5,803	
Discounts allowed and received	4,153	1,630
Rents received		4,550
	£266,930	266,930

You are given the following additional information.

(a) Stock in trade at 31 December, £23,500.
(b) Wages and salaries outstanding at 31 December, £306.
(c) Rates paid in advance at 31 December, £325.
(d) Rent received includes £350 for the following January.
(e) Depreciation on office equipment to be provided at 10 per cent per annum on cost.
(f) Interest on capital is to be credited at the rate of 15 per cent per annum.
(g) Interest on drawings is to be charged as follows: Rathlin £840; Lambay £720.

(h)   Two fifths of wages and salaries is to be charged to the Trading Account.

(i)   Lambay is entitled to a salary of £5,000 as a first charge against the profits.

(j)   Current Account balances were clear on 1 January 19__ .

You are required to prepare a Trading and Profit and Loss Account, an Appropriation Account and Current Accounts for the partners for the year and a Balance Sheet as at 31 December 19__ .

4.   The following Trial Balance was extracted from the books of the partnership of Myers and Young who share profits and losses: Myers three-fifths and Young two-fifths. They are dentists, and do not have either a Trading Account or a Profit and Loss Account. Instead they have a Revenue Account, followed by an Appropriation Account and a Balance Sheet. You are required to draw up these accounts, together with the partners' Capital Accounts, Current Accounts and Drawing Accounts for the year ended 31 December 19__ , bearing in mind the following facts:

(a)   Capital Accounts earn interest at 10 per cent on the balances at the start of the year.

(b)   Current Accounts in credit at 1 January earn interest on the balance at 10 per cent, but those in debit pay interest at 10 per cent.

(c)   Drawings Accounts pay interest at 10 per cent per annum, assuming that drawings are steady throughout the year and therefore will pay on average 6 months' interest.

(d)   The balance on the Goodwill Account is to be reduced by 50 per cent as a first charge against the profits in the Appropriation Account.

(e)   £109 of the debts are believed to be bad.

(f)   Young earns a salary of £5,000 as a prior charge against the profits.

TRIAL BALANCE AT 31 DECEMBER 19__

	Dr £	Cr £
Stock of dental materials at 1 January	2,650	
Fees received		159,360
Rent from ground floor tenant		5,640
Light and heat	1,600	
Telephone	1,766	
Secretarial wages	8,650	
Dental assistants salaries	22,756	
Insurance	3,842	
Dental technicians' services	18,420	
General expenses	3,460	
Premises	65,680	
Dental equipment	56,255	
Office equipment	3,850	
Capital A/c Myers 1 Jan.		60,000
Young 1 Jan.		30,000
Current A/c Myers 1 Jan.		5,000
Young 1 Jan.	4,200	
Drawings Myers	22,000	
Young	16,000	
Cash at Bank	15,944	
Cash in hand	326	
Purchases of dental materials in year	12,601	
Goodwill	10,000	
Debtors	2,500	
Creditors		12,500
	£272,500	272,500

NOTE: The closing stock of dental materials was valued at £2,545. Dental equipment and office equipment are to be depreciated by 10 per cent (calculations to the nearest £1).

20
The accounts of clubs and non-profit making organisations

1. Types of accounts

Many organisations exist to supply a service to their members and not for the purpose of trading with a view to making a profit.

In place of the Trading and Profit and Loss Account found in the trading concern, such associations produce the following accounts for the information of their members:

(a) a Receipts and Payments Account;
(b) an Income and Expenditure Account, usually accompanied by a Balance Sheet.

2. Receipts and Payments Account

This is simply the analysed Cash Book of a club. The essential features are as follows.

(a) The account is drawn up at the end of the club's financial year for presentation to the members at the Annual General Meeting.
(b) The Cash Book is analysed at the end of the year to collect together the various items of expenditure; and the various classes of receipts. If an analytical Cash Book has been used these figures will be collated as the year draws to a close . (One such analysed Cash Book is the Accounts Book for Club Treasurers, sold by George Vyner Ltd, Holmfirth, Huddersfield, HD7 1BR.)
(c) The analysed results are presented in Cash Book form.
(d) The balance at the beginning and the end of the period represents the amount of cash in hand and at bank, or the bank overdraft.
(e) All receipts and all payments are included, i.e. no distinction is made between capital and revenue items.

A typical Receipts and Payment Account is shown in Fig. 20.1 on p.251.

3.   Limitations of Receipts and Payments Account
When the Receipts and Payments Account alone is available:

(a)   There is no record of assets or liabilities, either at the start or the end of the year.

(b)   The members cannot see whether the year's receipts were sufficient to finance the year's activities.

(c)   If there are assets, there is no indication of depreciation during the year, since we only have a 'Cash and Bank' record.

4.   Income and Expenditure Account
This is a more sophisticated presentation of the affairs of a club. The account overcomes many of the weaknesses of the Receipts and Payments Account, and is the equivalent of a Profit and Loss Account prepared by a trading business.

(a)   Expenses are debited and income is credited.

(b)   Capital items are *excluded*.

(c)   *All* revenue items relating to the period are *included* whether *actually paid or not*, or whether *actually received or not*. In other words, figures are adjusted as with ordinary Final Accounts.

(d)   Revenue items relating to preceding or succeeding periods are *excluded*.

(e)   The balance on the account represents the excess of income over expenditure or vice versa. It is usually referred to as either a *surplus* or a *deficit*.

5.   Accumulated Fund
Many associations own assets of various kinds, and the funds that made the purchase of these assets possible are represented on the Balance Sheet by a capital fund, usually referred to as the Accumulated Fund, which takes the place of the Capital Account found in a trading concern.

(a)   Any surplus at the end of the year is *added* to this fund.

(b)   Any deficit at the end of the year is *deducted* from it.

(c)   When necessary, the amount of this fund at the beginning of

RECEIPTS and PAYMENTS A/c
Annual General Meeting
Year ending 31st March _____ 19.... _____

Receipts				Payments		
	£	p			£	p
Opening Balances at Start of Year:				Col. 1 Equipment	62	50
Cash in Hand	3	54		Col. 2 Refreshment Purchases	250	00
Cash at Bank	86	45		Col. 3 Trip to France	719	25
Col. 1 Subscriptions	142	50		Col. 4 Xmas Parties	56	60
Col. 2 Donations	5	50		Col. 5 Funeral Expenses	5	25
Col. 3 Refreshment Sales	286	45		Col. 6 O.A.P. Charity Donation	10	00
Col. 4 Trip to France	735	60		Col. 7 —		
Col. 5 Xmas Parties	48	24		Col. 8 Miscellaneous	3	64
Col. 6 —						
Col. 7 —				Closing Balances at end of year:		
Col. 8 Miscellaneous	1	84		Cash in Hand	4	62
				Cash at Bank	198	36
	£ 1310	12			£ 1310	12

Auditors' names
and Signatures: _____

Treasurer's Name
and Signature: _____

Notes:
  (i) The Cash of £4.62 is available at the meeting – also the Bank Statement for inspection by members wishing to see it.
  (ii) On refreshments, it appears that very little profit was made but as the purchases also covered entertainment to visiting teams this is not surprising.
  (iii) A stock of refreshments valued at £26 is available (at the start of the year stocks were only £4). Other assets include camping equipment valued at £350, stored on the premises.
  (iv) Creditors. A debt for repairing windows broken in the recent burglary is outstanding £7·25.
  (v) There are no debtors.

Figure 20.1 *Receipts and Payments Account of a club*

the period can be found in the same way as one finds capital, i.e. by taking the excess of assets over external liabilities.

6. Separate fund-raising activities
Many clubs from time to time take part in activities designed to improve their financial position, e.g. they may run dances, parties, whist drives, or in some cases even provide refreshments to members on a profit-making basis.

(a) *In the case of permanent activities,* e.g. a bar or refreshment counter, it is usual to prepare a separate Trading Account to cover this activity.
>   (i) Any profit will be debited to the Trading Account and credited to the Income and Expenditure Account.
>   (ii) If a loss should arise, this will be debited to the Income and Expenditure Account.

(b) *In all other cases* the usual procedure is to set off any expenses against the income, or vice versa.
>   (i) *When a profit is made:* expenses will be *deducted* from income on the *credit* side of the Income and Expenditure Account.
>   (ii) *If a loss is sustained:* income will be *deducted* from expenditure on the *debit* side of the Income and Expenditure Account

Example
(*extract from credit side of Income and Expenditure Account*)

Sales of refreshments		£2,400	
Less Cost of sales:			
Stock Jan. 1	£210		
Purchases	1,720		
	1,930		
Less Closing stock	265		
		1,665	
Profit on sale of refreshments			£735

(c) *Closing stock.* Care must be taken to include the closing stock in the Balance Sheet at the end of the period. This will also be the case with payments in advance and accrued expenses, which will appear on the Balance Sheet either as current assets or current liabilities.

Sample question

Below is a summary of the amounts received and paid by the Upend Social Club for the year to 31 December 19__:

	£		£
Subscriptions received	160	Caretaker's wages	208
Donations	12	Electricity	68
Loan from local council	300	Repairs to premises	24
Sale of dance tickets	191	Purchase of new	
Proceeds of summer fete	325	equipment	350
Rent paid	125	Incidental expenses	47
Secretary's honorarium	52	Dance expenses	100

The following information is also available.

(a) Balance of cash 1 January, £25.

(b) The rent paid is in respect of the *five* quarters to the following 31 March.

(c) The electricity of £68 includes £19 for the previous year; there is also an amount of £22 due at 31 December but not yet paid.

(d) A bill for £25 repairs to premises was due, but has not been paid.

(e) The incidental expenses include £3 relating to the previous year.

(f) Subscriptions received include £15 paid in advance for the following year. In the previous year £20 was received for the current year's subscriptions. Any subscriptions unpaid at 31 December were disregarded, it being assumed that membership had lapsed.

(g) At 1 January the Club owned equipment valued at £400 and had £150 on deposit at the National Savings Bank.

(h) At 31 December the deposit at the National Savings Bank was £154, £4 interest having been added for the year.

(i) The equipment is to be depreciated by £40.

You are required:

(i) to find the Accumulated Fund at 1 January 19__;

(ii) to set out the Receipts and Payments Account of the Club for the year to 31 December 19__;

(iii) to prepare the Income and Expenditure Account for the year ended 31 December 19__ and a Balance Sheet as at that date.

Answer

(i)   *Finding Accumulated Fund at 1 January.*

Assets:

Equipment		£400
National Savings Bank deposit		150
Cash in hand		25
		575
Less Liabilities:		
Subscriptions paid in advance	£20	
Electricity due not paid	19	
Incidental expenses owing	3	
		42
Accumulated Fund 1 January		£533

(ii)   *Receipts and Payments Account*

UPEND SOCIAL CLUB — RECEIPTS AND PAYMENTS ACCOUNT
FOR THE YEAR ENDED 31 DECEMBER 19__

Dr			Cr
Balance Jan. 1 b/d	£25	Rent	£125
Subscriptions	160	Secretary's honorarium	52
Donations	12	Caretaker's wages	208
Loan from council	300	Electricity	68
Proceeds of fete	325	Repairs to premises	24
Sale of dance tickets	191	New equipment	350
		Incidental expenses	47
		Dance expenses	100
		Balance Dec. 31 c/d	39
	£1,013		£1,013

Balance Jan. 1 b/d	39	*Note:* this will appear as an asset in the Balance Sheet.

(iii) Income and Expenditure Account

INCOME AND EXPENDITURE ACCOUNT
FOR THE YEAR ENDED 31 DECEMBER 19__

Rent	£125			Subscriptions	£160	
Less Rent prepaid	25			*Add* Subscription		
		100		received early	20	
Secretary's honorarium		52				180
Caretaker's wages		208				
Electricity paid	68			*Less* Subscriptions in		
Add Amount due				advance	15	
for this year	22					165
	90			Donations		12
				Proceeds of fete		325
Less paid for				Interest on National		
previous year	19			Savings Bank		4
		71		Sale of dance tickets	191	
Repairs to premises	24			*Less* Cost of dance	100	
Add Amount due				Profit on dance		91
not paid	25					
		49				
Incidental expenses	47					
Less Paid for last						
year	3					
		44				
Depreciation of						
equipment		40				
		564				
Excess of income over						
expenditure		33				
		£597				£597

(iv) Balance Sheet

UPEND SOCIAL CLUB — BALANCE SHEET AS AT 31 DECEMBER 19__

Fixed assets:				Accumulated Fund:		
Equipment Jan. 1	£400			Balance Jan. 1	£533	
Additions this year	350			*Add* Excess of income		
	750			over expenditure	33	
Less Depreciation	40					566
		710		Long-term liabilities:		
				Loan from local		
				council		300
Current assets:				Current liabilities:		
National Savings				Electricity due	22	
Bank deposit A/c	154			Repairs due	25	
Cash in hand	39			Subscriptions in		
Rent prepaid	25			advance	15	
		218				62
		£928				£928

7. Legacies and donations

(a) *Legacies* are normally treated as capital, being added to the Accumulated Fund.

(b) *Donations* may vary, large amounts being capitalised and added to the Accumulated Fund; small donations are simply treated as income, hence the £12 in the above example was treated as income, being taken to the credit of the Income and Expenditure Account.

8. Life membership

Life Membership fees should theoretically be credited to the Income and Expenditure Account over the period of life of the member concerned. Since this is practically impossible, two methods are used to deal with fees received on account of life membership subscriptions.

(a) To take credit for a certain percentage each year, e.g. 10 per cent, so that complete credit is taken over ten years.

NOTE: Any amount not credited to income is shown as a *liability* in the Balance Sheet.

(b) When the amount is relatively small and a regular flow of members take advantage of this facility each year, then credit is taken *in full* in the year of receipt.

Example ─────────────────────────────────────

The XYZ Golf Club accepts life members at £50 a time. The rules of the club provide that 10 per cent of the fee is taken into income each year.

During the year to 31 December 19.., five members paid £50 each to become *the first life members* of the club.

The liabilities side of the Balance Sheet would appear:

	£	£
Life subscriptions	250	
Less Transferred to income	25	
		225

───

Progress test 20

1. What is a Receipts and Payments Account?   **(2)**

2. What is an Income and Expenditure Account?   **(4)**

3. In what ways are the two accounts similar?   **(2)** and **(4)**

4. In what ways are the two accounts different?   **(3)** and **(4)**

5. What do you understand by 'Accumulated Fund'?   **(5)**

6. How do you find the Accumulated Fund?   **(5)**

7. How are separate fund-raising activities dealt with in the accounts of non-trading associations?   **(6)**

8. How are legacies and donations dealt with in the accounts?   **(7)**

9. What methods can be adopted to deal with life membership subscriptions? **(8)**

Specimen questions

1. On 1 April 19_1, the assets of the Acme Youth Centre were:
Cash in hand and balance at bank £46; Furniture and fittings £150; Games equipment £64; Tools and hobbies equipment £41; Subscriptions in arrear £3; Insurance prepaid £25. There were no liabilities.

For the year ended 31 March 19_2, the treasurer produced the following summary of receipts and payments:

Receipts	£	Payments	£
Subscriptions	52	Light and heat	27
Donations	50	Expenses of annual fete	31
Sale of tickets for annual		New tools	9
fete	59	New games equipment	6
Sale of dance tickets	67	Expenses of dances	27
		Cleaners' wages	52
		Printing and stationery	5
		Repairs and renewals	14
		Insurance	44

Prepare an Income and Expenditure Account for the year ended 31 March 19_2, and a Balance Sheet as at that date taking into account the following adjustments.

(a) Subscriptions received included the amount in arrear for the previous year. £2 was outstanding for the current year.
(b) Repairs and renewals outstanding £3.
(c) Annual insurance premiums £44 were paid to 30 June 19_2.
(d) 10 per cent depreciation is to be written off the balance at 31 March 19_2, of furniture and fittings, games equipment, and tools and hobbies equipment.

2. The following is a summary of the amounts received and spent by the Northshire Club from the date of commencement on 1 January 19__, to 31 December 19__:

	£		£
Subscriptions received	525	Rates paid	80
Receipts from sale of		Telephone paid	32
refreshments	4,283	Telephone received	40
Loan from A. Local		Printing and stationery	
on Jan. 1, 19__	53,000	paid	16
Loan from bank	1,000	Bank interest and charges	
Land and building		paid	29
at cost	52,500	General expenses paid	117
Purchase of refresh-		Electricity paid	108
ments	3,692		
Purchase of furniture and		Repaid to A. Local on	
equipment	800	Dec. 31, 19__	500
Wages paid	520		

(Continues in next column)

NOTE:
(a) All the receipts and payments were through the bank.
(b) There was a bill for £236 owing for refreshments at 31 December 19__.
(c) The stock of refreshments on hand at 31 December 19__ was valued at £140.
(d) The rates paid up to 31 December 19__ included £16 paid in advance.
(e) Interest accrued but not yet paid to A. Local amounted to £150.

Prepare:
   (*i*) the Receipts and Payments Account for the year ending 31 December 19__;
  (*ii*) the Income and Expenditure Account for the year ending 31 December 19__; and
 (*iii*) the Balance Sheet at that date.

3. Below is the Receipts and Payments Account of the Freelance Social Club for the year ended 30 June 19_6.

	£		£
Balances 1 July 19_5	230	Bar licence fees	200
Bar takings	42,905	Cleaners' wages	434
Sale of refreshments	5,540	Refreshments	3,289
Sale of dance tickets	2,188	Secretarial expenses	2,369
Sale of equipment	1,240	General expenses	1,209
Subscriptions	412	Payments to creditors for bar supplies	19,303
		Investment in building society	11,600
		Barman's wages	4,950
		New equipment	2,800
		Rates	352
		Dance expenses	1,270
		Balance 30 June 19_6	4,739
	£52,515		£52,515

	£
Balance	4,739

Other assets and liabilities of the club at 1 July 19_5 were:

	£
Premises at cost	40,500
Equipment	2,540
Creditors for bar supplies	227
Subscription in advance	48
Stock of bar supplies	950

(a) All the equipment was sold during the year and replaced. Depreciation of 10 per cent to be provided on balance at end of year.

(b) Stocks of bar supplies at 30 June 19_6, were valued at £835.

(c) Subscriptions of £412 include £35 in respect of the following year. Outstanding subscriptions at 30 June 19_6, were £28.

(d) Creditors for bar supplies at 30 June 19_6 were £196.
(e) The building society notified the club that interest of
£100 had been credited to the investment account at 30
June 19_6.

Prepare a Bar Trading Account and Income and
Expenditure account for year to 30 June 19_6 and a Balance
Sheet at that date.

4. The Green Bank Sports Club produces the following account
for the year ended 31 March 19_1.

Receipts	£	*Payments*	£
Balance b/f Apr. 19_0:		Clubhouse redecorations	580
Cash in hand	196	Ground maintenance	1,310
Bank current		Bar steward's salary	5,800
account	5,250	Insurances	240
Members' subscriptions:		General expenses	1,100
Ordinary	1,575	Building society	
Life	800	investment account	1,500
Annual dinner ticket		Secretary's honorarium	200
sales	560	Annual dinner expenses	610
Bar takings	36,790	New furniture & fittings	1,870
		Bar purchases	23,100
		Rent of clubhouse	5,520
		Balances c/f 31 Mar. 19_1:	
		Bank current account	3,102
		Cash in hand	239
	£45,171		£45,171

	£
Balances: Bank	3,102
Cash	239

The following additional information has been given.

(a) Ordinary membership subscriptions received in
advance at 31 March 19_0, £200. The subscriptions
received during the year to 31 March 19_1 included
£150 in advance for the following year.

(b) Life membership subscriptions are £100 and are apportioned to revenue over a ten year period. Life membership subscriptions totalling £1,100 were received during the first year of the scheme.

(c) The building society investment account balance at 31 March 19_0 was £2,676. During the year to 31 March 19_1 interest of £278 was credited to the account.

(d) All the furniture and fittings in the club's accounts at 31 March 19_0 were bought at a total cost of £8,000. It is the club's policy to provide depreciation annually on fixed assets at 10 per cent of the cost of such assets held at the relevant year end. (Careful: 10% had already been deducted last year).

(e) Other assets and liabilities of the club were:

At 31 March	19_0 £	19_1 £
Bar stocks	1,860	2,110
Insurances prepaid	70	40
Rent accrued due	130	140
Bar purchases creditors	370	460

Required:

(i) the Bar Trading and Profit and Loss Account for the year ended 31 March 19_1;

(ii) the club's Income and Expenditure Account for the year ended 31 March 19_1 and a Balance Sheet at that date.

21

Limited liability companies: Final Accounts and Balance sheet

1. The nature of company Final Accounts

The Final Accounts of companies are no different initially from the Final Accounts of sole traders or partners. A manufacturing company will start with a Manufacturing Account, and proceed to a Trading Account and Profit and Loss Account. A trading company will have a Trading Account and a Profit and Loss Account, which may or may not be run into one another as a Trading and Profit and Loss Account. It is only when we come to the sharing of the profits among the shareholders that changes are needed and, as with Partnership Accounts, the Appropriation Account is used to effect this distribution, though rather differently from the way profits are shared in a partnership. We cannot really understand company Final Accounts unless we know what companies are, how they operate, what abuses follow from the company format and hence the need for Parliamentary control. We must therefore start with a preliminary discussion of the company format.

2. The company format

A company is an association of investors (the members) who wish to participate in some activity (the *objects* of the company as stated in the **Memorandum of Association**) and to that end have been **registered** at Companies House in a formal manner. There are other types of companies (chartered companies granted a Royal Charter) and companies created by private Act of Parliament (statutory companies) but the vast majority of companies are registered companies under the Companies Acts of 1985–9.

The chief purpose of being registered as a company is to secure for the shareholders (members) *limited liability*. This means that they are not liable for the debts of the business personally, but only to the extent that they have contributed capital. As many companies are only £100 companies or even less this means that anyone who supplies goods to a company (the creditors) can only look to the registered capital for payment. One recent takeover bid was launched by a £2 company. As its bid for another company was for £2,300 million (the directors proposing to borrow this sum) it shows what strange arrangements the company format makes possible.

As the creditors can only look to the authorised capital for payment of their bills they are in a vulnerable situation and Parliament has decreed that all limited companies must have names that end in the word 'Limited' or 'Public Limited Company' (PLC) — or the Welsh equivalent. This is a warning to those invited to supply companies with goods or services that they are dealing with a limited company. Public Limited Companies must now have a capital of at least £50,000. Even so, a company trading in £millions may have creditors well in excess of this figure.

To protect creditors there are a number of controls inserted into the Companies Acts, but a full discussion of these is not possible here.

Another important feature of the company format is that the ordinary members (shareholders) cannot play any part in the running of the company which is run by a Board of Directors. As the board is the only body that can recommend a dividend the ordinary shareholders cannot force a distribution of the profits unless they own collectively more than 50 per cent of the voting shares. Undistributed profits still belong to the shareholders but cannot be drawn out, except by selling the shares on the Stock Exchange when the accumulated profits may mean the shares are 'above par' — i.e. worth more than their face value.

The format of a company is an involved subject and we must leave it here. We will proceed to consider how the profits are shared in the Appropriation Account (sometimes called the Appropriation Section of the Profit and Loss Account).

3. Appropriation Account

The Appropriation Account is very similar to the Appropriation Account of a partnership. It is often presented in vertical style, but this is only a form of publication (explained later — *see* Chapter 33) and in the actual accounts of the company will be in the usual form with debit and credit sides. It helps to look at a typical Appropriation Account and discuss its features.

Example _____

Triumvirate Ltd, made profits in the year 19_8 of £183,267. At 31 December 19_8 the balance on the Appropriation Account of undistributed profit from 1 January was £27,301. The directors recommended as follows:

- that a reserve of £60,000 be set aside for Corporation Tax
- that £25,000 be put in Plant Replacement Reserve and £25,000 in Computer Renewals Reserve
- that a full dividend be paid on the 10 per cent Preference Shares of £50,000, and a dividend of 32 per cent on the Ordinary Shares of £100,000
- £40,000 will be placed in General Reserve Account and any balance left, in the Appropriation Account

The Appropriation Account of Triumvirate Ltd would look as follows. One of the reserve accounts has been shown as well, so that the reader can see how these accounts would look after these transfers have been made. A few imaginary figures have been inserted to make the account realistic.

APPROPRIATION ACCOUNT: TRIUMVIRATE LTD

19_8		£	19_8		£
31 Dec.	Corporation Tax		1 Jan.	Balance	27,301
	Reserve	60,000	31 Dec.	Net Profit	183,267
	Plant Replacement				210,568
	Reserve	25,000			
	Computer Renewals				
	Reserve	25,000			
	General Reserve	40,000			
	Preference Share				
	Dividend	5,000			
	Ordinary Share				
	Dividend	32,000			
		187,000			
	Balance c/d	23,568			
		£210,568			£210,568

			19_9		£
			1 Jan.	Balance b/d	23,568

NOTES:

(a) Unlike partnerships the full profits are rarely shared up among the shareholders and consequently a balance at the start of any year usually exists in the Appropriation Account. The profit for the year is added to this.

(b) The various decisions made by the directors are then debited to the account, and then credited to a Nominal Account named for them, so that any appropriate action can be taken. A typical account is shown below, the Corporation Tax Reserve A/c.

(c) All such reserves will appear on the Balance Sheet (*see* below).

(d) Note that Preference Shareholders get a fixed rate of dividend specified in their share issue document (in this case 10 per cent), but are not entitled to any further share of the profits or reserves, all of which belong to the ordinary shareholders. This is explained more fully later.

CORPORATION TAX RESERVE A/C

19_9		£	19_9		£
3 Jan.	Inland Revenue	48,421	1 Jan.	Balance b/d	67,500
31 Dec.	Balance c/d	79,079	1 Jan.	Appropriation A/c	60,000
		£127,500			£127,500
			19_9		
			1 Jan.	Balance b/d	79,079

NOTES:

(a) Accounts like this receive sums from the Appropriation Account on the liabilities side. The reason for this is that all the balances on these accounts really belong to the ordinary shareholders (because they are profits that have not been distributed). The shareholders cannot have them because the directors have decided that they shall be used for other purposes — in this case, to pay the Corporation Tax.

(b) Eventually, as these accounts are used for the purpose intended, they will be debited as the profits in reserve are paid away to the Inland Revenue or the shareholders, or to buy new plant, computers, etc.

4. The Balance Sheet of a limited company

The Balance Sheet of a limited company is similar in many ways to other Balance Sheets in that it has the assets set against the liabilities and the two sides should balance. However, limited companies are controlled by the Companies Acts 1985–9. The 1985 Act sets out in Schedule 4 two alternative presentations of the Balance Sheet which companies are to use. One of these presentations is in continuous style, which means it is a Balance Sheet in vertical style. The other is in horizontal style, with the assets first (i.e. on the left-hand side) and the liabilities second (i.e on the right). We therefore have the Balance Sheet in the correct European style in the way shown on p.269. This is the same style as used with sole traders and partnerships.

Some important features of company Final Accounts are as follows:

Fixed Assets. Fixed assets are divided into three classes: intangible assets, tangible assets and investments.

(a) *Intangible assets* are assets which cannot be touched — there is nothing real about them. We have already discussed 'Goodwill' as an intangible asset. Other intangible assets are trade marks, patents, licences, etc.

(b) *Tangible assets* are the real assets we are familiar with — buildings, cars, etc.

(c) *Investments* are divided into two classes, one of which is regarded as a fixed asset. These are investments in subsidiary companies (companies where we have 51 per cent of the voting shares) and related companies (where we have a substantial, but not a controlling interest). All such shares could be sold off, but if we did sell them we would lose control of the subsidiary or our influence with the related company, and it is therefore better to regard them as fixed assets. They used to be called *trade investments*, since they were investments in companies in the same trade as ourselves.

Current assets. These are the usual current assets, stocks, debtors, etc., but we must add *investments*. This is the second class of investments, which are not kept for the purposes of control, but as a way of holding spare cash so that it earns interest. If we have profits put away in Plant Replacement Reserves or the General Reserve Account it is unwise to leave the money represented by these profits loose in the cash system. If we invest the surplus funds either on the money market or in stocks and shares they will earn some income for the future. Any banker will be happy to arrange this. Investments of this sort should be separated into quoted investments and unquoted investments. The Act requires that the directors should place a value on the investments alongside their original cost as shown on the Investment Account. With quoted investments the value will be that on the Stock Exchange at Balance Sheet date. Unquoted investments will be at the directors' valuation (which must give a 'true and fair view' of the value).

Liabilities. Important points include:

(a) *Authorised share capital*. A detailed note must be made showing the number and classes of shares which the company has authority to issue to the public.

(b) *Issued share capital*. That part of the authorised share capital which the company has issued, again distinguishing between the different classes and types of shares, showing the number issued and the amount called up or paid up on the shares.

(c) *Reserves, aggregate amount classifies under suitable sub-headings*, i.e. Capital Reserves, Plant Replacement Reserve, General Reserve etc. The final balance on the Appropriation Account is also a reserve. Reserves may be defined as profits of the business which have not been distributed but are held back to meet some specific or general need that will (or may) arise in the future. A Capital Reserve is a special case: it is a capital profit (not a revenue profit) and may not be distributed to shareholders (except in the form of bonus shares).

BALANCE SHEET OF TRIUMVIRATE LTD. AS AT 31 DECEMBER 19_8

	£	£
Fixed assets		
Intangibles – Patent Rights		12,000
Tangibles – Land and Buildings	140,000	
Plant and Machinery	44,500	
Fixtures and Fittings	19,742	204,242
Current assets		
Stock	49,460	
Debtors	5,984	
Investments	132,186	
Cash at bank	27,250	
Cash in hand	240	215,120
		£431,362

	£	£
Preference Shareholders' Interest in the Co.	*Authorised*	*Issued*
Preference shares of £1 fully paid	50,000	50,000
Ordinary Shareholders' Interest in the Co.		*Authorised and issued*
Ordinary Shares of £1 fully paid		100,000
Plant Replacement Reserve	17,000	
+ additions	25,000	42,000
Computer Renewal Reserve (new)		25,000
General Reserve	32,000	
+ additions	40,000	72,000
Balance on Appropriation A/c		23,568
Ordinary Shareholders' interest (equity)		262,568
Corporation Tax Reserve		79,079
Current liabilities		
Creditors	2,715	
Preference Dividend due	5,000	
Ordinary Dividend due	32,000	39,715
		£431,362

(d) *Long-term liabilities.* Details of any long-term loans, bank loans, debentures, etc., together with a note of any charge created on assets to secure this liability.

(e) *Current liabilities.* Trade creditors, accrued expenses, bank overdraft and dividends declared or proposed but not yet paid.

5. Characteristics of company Balance Sheets

(a) *Equity of a company.* The most important feature in the Balance Sheet of a limited company is the treatment of the equity or the net worth of the business. The word 'equity' refers to those shares which share equally in the profits of the business i.e. the ordinary shares. As these shareholders also run the risks of losses made by the company they are often taken to be 'risk' shares and equity shares are often spoken of as risky. Since the preference shareholders run less risk than the ordinary shareholders, having both a prior right to dividends and (usually) a prior right to repayment they do not come into the field of equity. The ordinary shareholders have a right not only to the ultimate return of their capital but also to share in the reserves ploughed back over the years.

(b) *Reserves and provisions.*

(i) A *reserve* is a profit that has been set aside from the distribution of profits and retained to work in the business.

There are two types of reserves. Revenue reserves are profits of the business which have been earned in the normal way according to the 'objects' clause in the Memorandum of Association. They may at any time in future be transferred back into the Appropriation Account and used to distribute as dividends. Revenue reserves include General Reserves.

Capital reserves are profits which have accrued to the business in ways outside the 'objects' clause of the business. Some common examples are Profits prior to Incorporation (where a company takes over a business and runs it profitably but cannot count the profits as revenue profits because it has not received its birth certificate (Certificate of Incorporation)); Share Premium Account (where shares are issued above par); Capital Redemption Reserve Fund (where a company reduces its share capital by buying its own shares out of profits. In such a case the creditors — who look to the capital for reimbursement if the company gets into difficulties — are disadvantaged. Such companies must maintain a Capital Redemption Reserve Fund to meet the claims of creditors in the event of dissolution of the company).

Such reserves may not be distributed to the shareholders as dividends, but they can be issued as bonus shares — which turns the reserve into long-term equity capital.

(ii) A provision is different from a reserve. Whereas a reserve is an appropriation of profit (debited in the Appropriation Account), a provision is a charge against the profit. It is debited in the Profit and Loss Account at the time of working out the net profit, and set aside to meet known or envisaged future expenses — i.e. Provisions for Bad Debts, Provisions for Depreciation, etc. In making a provision we debit Profit and Loss Account and credit the Provision Account, for example Provision for Depreciation Account.

(c) *Long-term liabilities.*

(i) Any long-term loan must be shown under this heading in the Balance Sheet, and in the case of companies the loans which usually figure under this heading are termed *Debentures*.

(ii) In the normal course of events Debentures are usually redeemable and are normally secured by the creation of a charge on either one particular asset of the company, e.g. land and buildings, in which case the charge is referred to as a *fixed charge*, or they may be secured by a charge on *all the assets* of the company, in which case the charge is referred to as a *floating charge*. Such a charge floats over the assets and only crystallises into a firm control if some event (such as the non-payment of the Debenture interest) alerts the Debenture trustee to the fact that the company is in financial difficulties.

(iii) All Debentures carry a *rate of interest* which *must be paid* whether on not the company makes a profit.

(d) *Current liabilities.* As well as sundry creditors, some provisions are included under this heading. A *provision* is an amount set aside to provide for a liability or for the cost of replacing an asset. It is an estimate of a loss that will shortly have to be suffered.

6. Goodwill

Goodwill is shown on a Balance Sheet only when a payment has actually been made for it.

The value of the goodwill of a company with a quotation on the Stock Exchange is arrived at by taking the difference between the aggregate market value of the shares and the net worth of the company as disclosed by the Balance Sheet of the company concerned.

Example

If Company A has a total issued capital of 400,000 shares of 25p each at present quoted 40p each, then the market or Stock Exchange values the undertaking at 400,000 x 40p namely £160,000.

(a) If the Balance Sheet of the same company shows a net worth of £120,000 (arrived at by taking the issued capital and the reserves together), then the goodwill of the company is valued at £40,000, i.e. £160,000 minus £120,00.

(b) If Company B buys Company A for the market value of £160,000 and decides to show that company's assets and liabilities in its own Balance Sheet, it will show assets of £120,000 and goodwill as £40,000.

7. Patents

Patents are the *exclusive rights* to use certain formulae, such as the manufacture of nylon yarn, or the exclusive right to produce an article of a particular type for which a patent has been granted.

The patent granted to a manufacturer lasts for twenty years.

8. Trade marks

Manufacturers spend much time and effort in advertising a commodity under a trade mark or brand name. The intention is to encourage the public to ask for the commodity by its brand name or trade mark, and to discourage the manufacture of cheap imitations. Such a name becomes synonymous with quality and service, and to protect the trade name a manufacturer will have the name or trade mark registered. This can often have a value, and as such will be shown as a fixed asset.

9. Investments

These must always be classified as follows:

(a) *Trade investments*, that is, investments in companies operating in a similar trade. Sometimes these investments are in companies which are effectively controlled by the company possessing the shares, in which case the company controlled is referred to as a *subsidiary* company. The company holding the shares is referred as the *holding company*.

(b) *Listed investments*, that is, those investments in companies whose shares are listed on the Stock Exchanges. They must be disclosed separately in the Balance Sheet of the company holding the investment, and a note must be made of the market value of the shares at the date of the Balance Sheet.

(c) *Unlisted investments*, that is, those investments in companies whose shares are not listed on Stock Exchanges, e.g. shares in private companies. They must be shown separately in the Balance Sheet, and if the directors believe their value to be more, or less, than the book value the directors' valuation must be shown alongside the book value, or given as a 'Note to the accounts'.

10. Current assets

Always adopt one order for current assets. The following is suggested as a common form.

Stock in trade	These two are sometimes shown
Work in progress	together.
Debtors and prepayments.	
Balance at bank and cash in hand.	

11. Preliminary and issue expenses

(sometimes called *formation expenses*). The formation of a company is an expensive operation, costs being incurred in solicitors' fees and in stamp duty on the authorised share capital and preliminary documents. The expenditure helps to bring the company into existence, and in a sense creates an asset. As the asset is one of doubtful value, the normal practice is to write it off over a period of three to five years or earlier, sometimes even in the year itself.

12. Vertical presentation of a company's Balance Sheet

The Balance Sheet illustrated on p.269 was presented in correct horizontal form. The Balance Sheet of a limited liability company is illustrated below in vertical style. The assets have been shown first in the order of permanence, (i.e. with the most

XYZ LTD. BALANCE SHEET AS AT 31 MARCH 19_2

	Cost	Deprecia-tion to date	Net book value	Compara-tive figures 19_1
Fixed assets:	£'000	£'000	£'000	£'000
Goodwill	25	5	20	
Freehold property	200	–	200	
Leasehold property	60	20	40	
Plant and machinery	196	76	120	
	481	101	380	

Trade investments listed or quoted:			
10,000 Ordinary Shares			
in AB Ltd, at cost			10
(Market value £10,560)			

Current assets:			
Stock and work in progress	78		
Debtors	65		
Balance at Bank	33		
		176	

Less:			
Current liabilities:			
Trade creditors	30		
Accrued expenses	8		
Current taxation	24		
Proposed dividend	15		
		77	
Net current assets (working capital)			99
Net assets (capital employed)			£489

Financed by:		
Authorised share capital		
2,000,000 Ordinary Shares of 25p each	500	
100,000 8% Preference Shares of 50p each	50	
	£550	

(*Continued on p. 275*)

Issued capital:
  Preference Shareholders' Interest in the company
  100,000 8% Preference Shares of 50p each fully paid   50
  Ordinary Shareholders' Interest in the Company
  1,000,000 Ordinary shares of 25p each fully paid   250
  Share premium account   20
  General reserve   25
  Profit and Loss Account   14
  Ordinary shareholders' interest (the equity)   309
                                                              359

Deferred taxation   30
                                                              389

10% Debenture 19__/19__
  (secured by floating charge on all assets)   100
                                                             £489

permanent items first). The words 'financed by' then lead on to shown how the finances were provided. This order can be reversed by showing share capital and reserves first, followed by fixed assets and working capital. In such an event it is stated that share capital is *represented by* fixed assets, etc.

It is very important that students really understand a company Balance Sheet presented in vertical style and the following points are worth mentioning and should be followed on the Balance Sheet illustrated.

(a) The 'Fixed Assets' should start with the intangible assets (Goodwill, etc.) and then the real assets, and should be shown at cost, less the depreciation to date, to finish with the net book value.
(b) The investments held in subsidiaries and related companies should then be shown. The Act calls these 'trade investments' or 'assets which are neither fixed nor current' (because we can sell them, but if we do we lose control of the company, so we cannot sell them like a current asset — for example an investment held just to earn income from some funds which otherwise would lie idle.).
(c) We could show the current assets next and then add up all the assets, but it is more usual to show the current assets *less* current liabilities. This shows the net current assets or working capital. The working capital is the current assets available to work the business (i.e. use the fixed assets) *after all current liabilities have been paid*.

(d) We now add up the assets (strictly speaking the 'net assets') — because the current liabilities are deducted from the assets. This is the full value of the business, and is termed the 'capital employed'. It is the total value of the assets purchased with the capital made available by the shareholders, debenture holders, etc.

We now have the words 'Financed by' to explain how the purchase of these assets were financed.

(e) We now show the Authorised Capital.

(f) It is important to realise that the Preference Shareholders although they have preference in taking their agreed rate of dividend if the company has been trading profitably, do not share in the reserves of the company (because reserves are accumulated profits that belong to the ordinary shareholders alone).

Progress test 21

1. Name the groupings on the assets side of the Balance Sheet. (4)

2. Distinguish between a reserve and a provision. (5)

3. Distinguish between a revenue reserve and a capital reserve. (5)

4. What do you understand by long-term liabilities? (5)

5. Explain briefly what you understand by goodwill, patents and trade marks. (6–8)

6. Describe the usual make-up of preliminary expenses. (11)

7. Explain the term 'net current assets'. (12)

8. Explain the term 'net assets'. (12)

9. Explain the differences between the preference shareholders' interest in a company and the ordinary shareholders' interest in the company. (12)

Specimen questions

1. The following Trial Balance was extracted from the books of
Kerry Ltd, as at 31 December 19__.

TRIAL BALANCE

	£	£
Authorised and issued share capital		
60,000 Ordinary shares of £1 each		60,000
Share Premium Account		20,000
Sales		181,700
Purchases	59,840	
Stock in trade 1 Jan. 19__	7,120	
Freehold properties at cost	76,500	
Provision for bad debts as at Jan. 1, 19__		180
Bad debts	1,340	
General Expenses	10,458	
Wages (Profit & Loss A/c)	27,494	
Debtors	10,440	
Creditors		8,963
Rates and Insurances	2,680	
Motor Delivery Expenses	2,950	
Motor Vehicles at cost	15,600	
Provision for Depreciation of Motor		
Vehicles as at 1 Jan. 19__		3,360
Directors' Fees (Profit and Loss A/c)	11,000	
Balance at bank	23,921	
Appropriation Account 1 January		1,140
Plant and Machinery	20,000	
Plant Depreciation to date		5,000
Fixtures and Fittings	13,200	
Depreciation on Fixtures and Fittings		2,200
	£282,543	£282,543

You are given the following information.

(a) Stock in trade 31 December 19__, £7,547.
(b) Rates and insurance paid in advance at 31 December
     19__, £60.
(c) The provision for bad debts is to be increased to £260.

(d) Provision is to be made for depreciation on the cost of the motor vehicles at the rate of 20 per cent per annum, and at 10% on Plant and Machinery and Fixtures and Fittings.

(e) The directors propose to recommend a dividend of 20 per cent on the nominal value of the share capital. They also propose to put £20,000 into a Corporation Tax Reserve A/c and £25,000 into a General Reserve A/c.

You are required to prepare a Trading and Profit and Loss Account for 19___ and an Appropriation Account and Balance Sheet as at 31 December 19___.

2. Chairs Ltd have an authorised capital of £120,000 divided into 20,000 8 per cent Preference Shares of £1 each, and £100,000 Ordinary Shares of £1 each. The company commenced trading on 1 January 19_3.

The following balances were extracted from the books on 31 December 19_3.

Preference capital (fully paid)	20,000
Ordinary capital (fully paid)	80,000
Debentures issued	10,000
Profit for year ended 31 Dec. 19_3	113,570
Premises at cost	88,000
Machinery at cost	80,000
Fixtures and fittings at cost	6,000
Provisions for depreciation:	
Machinery	6,000
Fixtures and fittings	600
Provision for doubtful debts	300
Stock	27,000
Debtors	6,300
Bank	26,000
Cash	2,070
Trade creditors	4,900

The directors decided to transfer £30,000 to General Reserve A/c, to create a Reserve for Corporation Tax of £38,000, to pay the Preference Dividend and to recommend a dividend of 20 per cent on the issued ordinary shares.

Prepare the Appropriation Account of the company for the year ended 31 December 19_3, and a Balance Sheet as at that date.

3. The following Trial Balance was extracted from the books of Ohm Ltd as on 31 December 19__ :

	£	£
Share capital authorised and issued		
80,000 Ordinary Shares of £1 each		80,000
Share premium		8,000
Freehold land and buildings	92,000	
Fixtures and fittings at cost	6,300	
Bad debts	460	
Rates	2,610	
Discounts allowed and received	598	419
Appropriation Account balance		
at 1 Jan. 19__		2,678
Rent paid and received	6,600	2,941
Purchases and purchases returns	64,596	1,422
Salaries	29,480	
Directors' remuneration	12,000	
General expenses	11,444	
Sales returns and Sales	2,940	197,345
Stock at 1 Jan. 19__	11,495	
Provision for bad debts as at		
1 Jan. 19__		298
Interim dividend on Ordinary Shares		
paid on 1 July 19__ (Appropriation A/c)	4,000	
Provision for depreciation of fixtures		
and fittings as at 1 Jan. 19__		630
Bought Ledger balances		6,498
Sales Ledger balances	8,920	
Balance at bank	46,788	
	£300,231	£300,231

You are given the following information:

Stock in trade at 31 December 19__ was valued at £12,482.

The rent payable for December 19__ was owing. The sum payable per annum was £7,200.

The provision for bad debts is to be reduced to £240.

Provision for a final dividend of 20p per share is to be made.

The directors propose to transfer £22,500 to general reserve, and to set up a Reserve for Corporation Tax of £30,000.

Rate paid in advance at 31 December 19__ amounted to £48.

Fixtures and fittings are to be depreciated at 10 per cent on cost.

You are asked to prepare a Trading and Profit and Loss Account for the year 19__, the Appropriation Account and a Balance Sheet at 31 December 19__. The Balance Sheet is to be in vertical style and bring out the Net Current Assets and Net Assets.

4.   At 31 March 19_6 JKL Ltd, had an authorised share capital of £40,000, divided into 20,000 8 per cent Preference Shares of £1 each, of which 10,000 had been issued and fully paid, and 20,000 Ordinary Shares of £1 each, which had all been issued and fully paid. The other balances were:

	£
Stock on hand 1 April, 19_5	12,200
Cash in hand	50
Bank overdraft	12,310
Purchases	66,280
Sales	199,120
Warehouse wages	45,350
Office salaries	14,550
Transport expenses	1,410
Rent and rates	2,480
General expenses	12,250
Discounts received	1,190
Bad debts provision 1 April, 19_5	220
Interest on bank overdraft	430
Land and buildings at cost	51,500
Machinery at cost as at 1 April, 19_5	23,950

Machinery purchased during year	2,400
Machinery sold during year — proceeds	1,100
Debtors	6,510
Creditors	5,190
Goodwill at cost	5,000

Accumulated provision for depreciation on machinery 1 April, 19_5	2,670
Directors remuneration	12,660
Appropriation Account 1 April, 19_5	2,620
Share Premium Account	3,000
Preference dividend paid for half year to 30 September 19_5	400

Prepare Trading and Profit and Loss Account for the year ended 31 March 19_6 and an Appropriation Account and Balance Sheet as at that date, taking into account the following information:

(a) The Balance Sheet is to be in vertical style and to bring out the net current assets and the net assets.

(b) A dividend is due on the Preference Shares for the half year ended 31 March 19_6.

(c) The directors propose a dividend of 20 per cent on the Ordinary Shares for the year. They also propose to set up a reserve for Corporation Tax of £20,000 and General Reserve of £15,000.

(d) Depreciation on machinery is to be charged at the rate of 10 per cent on cost for the year. A full year's depreciation is charged on new machinery during the year of purchase and no depreciation is charged on machinery sold during the year of sale.

(e) The machine sold for £1,100 during the year had cost £2,000 when purchased on 15 June 19_2.

(f) General expenses of £75 were owing at the end of the year.

(g) Bad debts provision to be adjusted to £340.

(h) Stock on hand 31 March 19_6 was £17,150.

(i) The goodwill is to be completely written off.

22

Single-entry accounting or incomplete records

1. Incomplete records

Although most businesses keep detailed records, if only for income tax purposes, there are some records that fall short of a complete double-entry system as we, by now, understand it. In some cases very little information is recorded and in others the system only just falls short of a complete double-entry record.

Any system which is not a complete double-entry system we refer to as a 'single-entry' system. For examination purposes we can conveniently classify the problems set on single-entry into *two* types.

(a) Those where few records have been kept, which will require us to *find the net profit* by reference to the net worth of the business, the net worth being calculated from information given in the question.

(b) Those where some records have been kept from which we are *required to reconstruct accounts to produce a normal set of final accounts* at the end of the period.

2. Profit as an increase in net worth

At 'Dawn on Day 1' of a new business suppose the proprietor has various assets totalling £32,000 and one liability (a Bank Loan of £10,000). The net worth of the business to the owner of the business is therefore £32,000–£10,000 = £22,000. This is his/her opening capital. Suppose he/she does not keep any real books of account but at the end of the year has assets worth £56,000 and three liabilities (the Bank Loan – now £9,000 – a mortgage of £20,000 and a creditor £480). What is the net worth of the business to the proprietor now? Clearly it is £56,000 – £29,480 = £26,520. There appears to be an increase in net worth as follows:

	£
Capital at end of year	26,520
Capital at start of year	22,000
Apparent increase in net worth	£4,520

We could call this increase in net worth the *apparent profit*.

3.   Other influences on the net worth

This increase in net worth could have been affected by other things. For example, the proprietor is alive and well, and therefore has enjoyed the fruits of the consumer society. In other words some degree of 'drawings' has been taking place. Had these drawings not been drawn the net worth would have increased more than it did. If we find that the drawings were £150 a week for 52 weeks that is £7,800. The apparent profit must be increased from £4,520 to £12,320.

Suppose the proprietor now tells you that he/she received a legacy from a maiden aunt of £2,500 in the year and that this was injected into the business as extra capital. Clearly some of the revised profit of £12,320 was not due to profits, but to this extra capital introduced. Therefore the true profit is £12,320 − £2,500 =£9,820.

This would be the figure for tax purposes at the end of the year.

4.   Statements of Affairs

It is usual in the simplest kind of 'single entry' calculation to be told what assets and liabilities are available at the beginning of the year, and at the end of the year, and from these figures to draw up two Statements of Affairs. A Statement of Affairs is just like a Balance Sheet, but as there are no accounts we cannot talk about 'balances'; the figures we have discovered are valuations at the start and end of the year.

Sample question ────────────────────────────────
Peter Smith, who does not keep proper records of his business transactions, is able to give you the undermentioned details of his business:

	Jan. 1	Dec. 31
Balance at bank	1,100	
Debtors	500	800
Stock	1,600	4,800
Machinery	2,400	11,200
Creditors	1,700	400
Loan from J. Tidy		2,500
Bank overdraft		1,250
Motor vehicles		5,280

During the year he had withdrawn £100 per week in cash and £40 per week in goods for his own use. You are required to ascertain his correct net profit for the year ended 31 December 19__ bearing in mind that a win on the football pools enabled him to inject £1,000 of extra capital during the year.

The Statements of Affairs are as follows. In each case the net worth has to be inserted as a balancing figure to make the two sides balance.

STATEMENT OF AFFAIRS AS AT 1 JANUARY 19__

Fixed assets		£	*Capital*	£
Machinery		2,400	(net worth)	3,900
Current assets			*Current liabilities*	
Stock	1,600		Creditors	1,700
Debtors	500			
Bank balance	1,100			
		3,200		
		£5,600		£5,600

STATEMENT OF AFFAIRS AS AT 31 DECEMBER 19__

Fixed assets		£	*Capital*		£
Machinery		11,200	(net worth)		17,930
Motor vehicles		5,280	*Long-term liabilities*		
		16,480	Loan (J. Tidy)		2,500
Current assets			*Current liabilities*		
Stock	4,800		Creditors	400	
Debtors	800		Bank overdraft	1,250	
		5,600			1,650
		£22,080			£22,080

STATEMENT OF NET PROFIT FOR THE YEAR TO
31 DECEMBER 19__

	£
Capital at end of year	17,930
Capital at start of year	3,900
Increase in net worth	14,030
Add drawings in cash	
52 x £100	5,200
Add drawings in kind	
52 x £40	2,080
	21,310
Less extra capital contributed	1,000
	£20,310

---

5.   Reconstruction of accounts from incomplete records

Given sufficient information, it is possible for complete
records to be reconstructed by applying the principles of double
entry to the information available. Questions on such types of
'single-entry' can be very varied, and this tends to add to the
pleasure of solving them. The ingenuity of examiners in setting
some of the questions has done much to keep students on their
toes as far as this part of their studies is concerned.

(a) No set of simple rules can be given as a short cut to the
understanding of the principles involved. Unless you have:
  (i) understood the principles of double entry; and
  (ii) can readily recognise that an account should have a debit
      or a credit balance;

you would be strongly advised to revise the earlier parts of this
book.

(b) Some points can be stressed for general guidance in tackling
problems, but you will need to adapt them to meet the
requirements of the particular question you may be working.
  (i) *You must have a figure for the opening balance on the Capital
      Account.* Find this figure if it is not given to you in the
      question. To do this you draw up a simple Statement of
      Affairs at the start of the year, as described above.

Note that since this opening Statement of Affairs is the
effective start of the year for the business whose incomplete

records you are trying to sort out, every item in it must go on to feature in the Final Accounts you prepare. Thus the Opening Stock will come in the Trading Account and the assets listed will come into the Final Balance Sheet etc., while the net worth (capital) at the start will be part of the final calculation of capital at the end of the year.

(ii) *Reconstruct those accounts that are necessary to enable you to find the figures not given in the question.* This usually involves reconstructing debtors and creditors in order to find sales and purchases, but it may be necessary to find cash received and paid or even to find the closing balances on these accounts.

(iii) *Reconstruct any nominal accounts* necessary to find the correct charge to be made in the Profit and Loss Account.

(iv) *Take care with drawings*; remember to adjust the figure for sales, if the proprietor has taken goods at selling price for his own use.

6.   Reconstruction of Control or Total Accounts

Sample question _____

Jones has not kept a complete set of records, but is able to give you the following information on 31 December 19__

	£
Amounts owing to Jones on 1 January	2,540
Amounts owing to Jones on 31 December	3,532
Debts written off during the year	475
Goods returned by customers	327
Cheques received and paid into bank	36,037

You are required to find his sales for the year by reconstructing a Total Debtors or Sales Ledger Control Account.

Answer _____

TOTAL DEBTORS ACCOUNT
OR SALES LEDGER CONTROL ACCOUNT

	£		£
Jan. 1 Balance b/d	2,540	Dec. 31 Bad Debts	475
∴ Sales	37,831	Returns in	327
		Bank	36,037
		Balance c/d	3,532
	£40,371		£40,371
Jan. 1 Balance b/d	3,532		

(a) The information supplied is used to build up a Total Account which represents in full the Sales Ledger over the course of the whole year.
(b) The only figure we do not have is the sales figure.
(c) The opening balances will of course be on the debit side (of a great many debtors' accounts). The bad debts, returns in and cheques raised will all be on the credit side of a great many accounts.
(d) The final balances will finish up on the debit side, but must be inserted on the credit side so that they can be 'brought down'.
(e) The 'sales figure' can therefore be worked out by taking £2,540 from £40,371. It is £37,831.

Sample question

A.M Scammell did not keep a complete set of double-entry records, but was able to provide you with the following information on 31 December 19__.

	Jan. 1	Dec. 31
Trade debtors	£1,628	£1,860
Rates paid in advance	–	50
Trade creditors	1,860	924
Rent owing to landlord	–	250
Expenses accrued	120	150
Stock in trade	12,160	12,465
Machinery	24,500	25,050

Scammell pays all cash received into the bank and makes all payments by cheque, and the following figures are available as summarising the details shown on statements of account from his bank.

	£		£
Balance at bank		Payments to creditors	17,016
1 January	5,262	Wages	22,667
Loan from A.B.C.	1,000	Rent	1,750
Cash sales	46,656	Rates	1,250
Cheques received from		Expenses (various)	14,626
debtors	28,162	New machinery	3,000
		Personal drawings	12,080
		Balance at bank	
		31 December c/d	8,691
	£81,080		£81,080
Balance b/d	8,691		

Further details which came to light showed that the debtors' figure includes debtors for £420 who went bankrupt and nothing is expected to be received from them. Discount of £315 had been allowed on the receipts from debtors, and discount of £654 had been deducted from the payments made to the creditors.

You are required to prepare Trading and Profit and Loss Accounts for the year ended 31 December 19__, and a Balance Sheet as at that date. Show sufficient of your calculations to demonstrate how you arrived at the figures in your answer.

Answer

Step 1 Find the opening capital at 1 January

	£	£
Assets:		
Bank	5,262	
Debtors	1,628	
Stock	12,160	
Machinery	24,500	
		43,550
Less Liabilities:		
Creditors	1,860	
Accrued expenses	120	
		1,980
∴ Capital 1 January		£41,570

All these figures will find their place somewhere in the Final Accounts we are preparing. The capital figure we will use in the Balance Sheet, which should then balance.

Step 2 Reconstruct the various accounts with adjustments

TOTAL DEBTORS (TO FIND THE CREDIT SALES)

	£		£
Jan. 1 Balance b/d	1,628	Dec. 31 Cheques	28,162
∴ Credit Sales	29,129	Discounts allowed	315
		Bad debts	420
		Balance c/d	1,860
	£30,757		£30,757
Jan. 1 Balance b/d	1,860		

The full sales figure will therefore be:

	£
Credit sales	29,129
Cash sales	46,656
∴ Total Sales	£75,785

TOTAL CREDITORS (TO FIND PURCHASES)

Dec. 31 Bank	£17,016	Jan. 1 Balance b/d	£1,860
Discount		Dec. 31 Purchases ∴	16,734
Received	654		
Balance c/d	924		
	£18,594		£18,594
		Jan. 1 Balance b/d	924

RATES ACCOUNT

Dec. 31 Bank	£1,250	Dec. 31 Profit and Loss	
		A/c	£1,200
		Balance c/d	50
	£1,250		£1,250
Jan. 1 Balance b/d	50		

RENT ACCOUNT

Dec. 31 Bank	£1,750	Dec. 31 Profit and Loss	
31 Balance c/d	250	A/c	£2,000
	£2,000		£2,000
		Jan. 1 Balance b/d	250

EXPENSES ACCOUNT

Dec. 31 Bank	£14,626	Jan. 1 Balance b/d	£120
31 Balance c/d	150	Dec. 31 Profit and Loss	
		A/c	14,656
	£14,776		£14,776
		Jan. 1 Balance b/d	150

MACHINERY ACCOUNT

Jan. 1 Balance b/d	£24,500	Dec. 31 Profit and Loss	
Dec. 31 Bank	3,000	A/c	£2,450
		(Depreciation)	
		Balance c/d	25,050
	£27,500		£27,500
Jan. 1 Balance b/d	25,050		

TRADING AND PROFIT AND LOSS ACCOUNTS FOR THE YEAR ENDED 31 DECEMBER 19__

	£		£
Opening stock 1 Jan.	12,160	Sales: Cash	46,656
Purchases	16,734	Credit	29,129
	28,894		75,785
Less Closing stock	12,465		
	16,429		
Gross profit c/d	59,356		
	£75,785		£75,785

Administrative expenses:			Gross profit b/d	59,356
Rent	2,000		Discount received	654
Rates	1,200			
Expenses	14,656			60,010
		17,856		
Selling and distribution expenses:				
Wages	22,667			
Discount allowed	315			
Bad debts	420			
		23,402		
Depreciation: machinery		2,450		
		43,708		
Net profit to capital		16,302		
		£60,010		£60,010

A.M. SCAMMELL
BALANCE SHEET AS AT 31 DECEMBER 19__

Fixed assets:		£			£
Machinery		24,500	Capital Jan. 1		41,570
Plus additions during			*Add* Net profit	16,302	
the year		3,000	*Less* Drawings	12,080	
		27,500			4,222
Less Depreciation		2,450	Long-term liabilities:		45,792
		25,050	Loan A/c A.B.C.		1,000
Current assets:			Current liabilities:		
Stock	12,465		Trade creditors	924	
Debtors	1,860		Rent due	250	
Balance at bank	8,691		Expenses accrued	150	
Rates prepaid	50				1,324
		23,066			
		£48,116			£48,116

In this example the working is verified by the balancing of the Balance Sheet at 31 December, but even in cases where you are not required to produce a Balance Sheet, you could still check the figure for net profit by preparing a Statement of Affairs at the beginning and end of the period.

Progress test 22

1. What do you understand by the expression 'net worth'? **(2)**

2. What is the relationship between net profit and capital? **(2)**

3. How would you treat drawings when finding net profit? **(3)**

4. What effect does new capital have on the profits? **(3)**

5. What are the main steps involved in reconstructing accounts from incomplete records? **(5)**

6. What use is made of control accounts in preparing accounts from incomplete records? **(6)**

7. What do you understand by the expression 'single-entry'? **(1)**

8. How would you set about finding the capital at the beginning and end of a period? **(2)**

Specimen questions

1. The following is a summary of the bank account of Copeman, a retail trader, for the year 19__:

	£		£
Balance 1 Jan.	11,448	Payments to trade	
Shop takings banked	84,722	creditors	28,364
		Rent and rates	4,488
		Drawings	15,816
		Balance 31 Dec.	47,502
	£96,170		£96,170
Balance 1 Jan.	47,502		

You are given the following additional information:

	1 Jan.	31 Dec.
	£	£
Furniture	11,000	12,000
Stock in trade	5,260	4,380
Trade debtors	2,900	3,270
Trade creditors	3,750	3,946

During the year furniture worth £1,000, wages amounting to £11,300 and £1,220 general expenses were paid in cash out of shop takings. All the remaining shop takings were paid into the bank, and all other payments were made by cheque.

You are required to prepare a Trading and Profit and Loss Account for the year and a Balance Sheet at 31 December 19__, bearing in mind that Copeman intends to depreciate Furniture by 10 per cent on the year end value and to create a Provision for Bad Debts of 10 per cent of the value of debtors on 31 December.

2. Smithson's bank account for 19__ is summarised as follows:

	£		£
Balance 1 Jan.	14,500	Paid to trade creditors	33,100
Received from		Paid to creditors for	
customers	77,100	expenses	11,900
Paid in from own		Cheque from	
Girobank A/c	2,500	customer returned	150
		Fixed assets	1,500
		Personal drawings	22,000
		Balance 31 Dec.	25,450
	£94,100		£94,100
Balance 1 Jan.	25,450		

You are given the following information:

	1 Jan.	*31 Dec.*
	£	£
Debtors for goods sold	2,520	3,490
Creditors for goods purchased	1,840	4,910
Creditors for expenses	1,105	1,120
Stock in Trade	11,120	14,090
Fixed Assets	16,000	17,500

The cheque for £150 received from a customer must be treated as a bad debt.

You are asked to prepare a Trading and Profit and Loss Account for 19__ together with a Balance Sheet at 31 Dec. 19__, bearing in mind that fixed assets at the end of the year are to be depreciated by 10 per cent.

Your answer should include clear details of any calculation you find it necessary to make.

3. F.L. Winter did not keep proper books of account. The following information related to his business for the year ended 31 December 19__.

ASSETS AND LIABILITIES AT 1 DECEMBER 19__

Cash in hand and balance at bank £3,541; Sundry trade debtors £194; Stock £4,989: Furniture and fittings £7,250; Motor van £3,600; Sundry trade creditors £1,240.

CASH BOOK SUMMARY FOR THE YEAR ENDED
31 DECEMBER 19__

Receipts	£	Payments	£
Cash sales	46,943	Payments to trade	
Receipts from trade		creditors	15,988
debtors	21,236	Drawings	12,700
		Rent, rates and insurance	2,540
		Light and heat	642
		Motor van expenses	1,226
		Repairs and renewals	2,017
		New shop fittings	1,550
		Refunds to customers on	
		cash sales	473
		General expenses	2,984

Prepare Winter's Trading and Profit and Loss Account for the year ended 31 December 19__, and a Balance Sheet as at that date, taking the following into account.

On 31 December 19__:

(a) stock was valued at cost £3,910, sundry trade debtors were £136, and sundry trade creditors £1,570;
(b) light and heat outstanding was £114;
(c) Rates and insurance prepaid were £364;
(d) 10 per cent depreciation is to be written off the balance of furniture and fittings at 31 December 19__, and 20 per cent off the value of the motor van at 1 January 19__.

4. Tom Smith is a sole trader in the building trade. He has asked you to prepare his accounts for the year ended 31 March 19_1. The accounting records consist of the following:

TOM SMITH: BALANCE SHEET AS AT 31 MARCH 19_0

	£			£
Fixed assets (written down value):		Capital		19,880
Equipment & loose		Loan (Mrs Smith 10%		
tools	4,540	interest)		1,260
Garage	3,150	Current liabilities:		
Office Equipment	120	Trade		
Motor Van	5,430	creditors	1,451	
	13,240	Accrued expenses:		
Current assets:		Telephone	114	
Stock & work in		Electricity	128	
progress	3,480			1,693
Debtors	2,753			
Van insurance				
prepaid	110			
Bank	3,140			
Cash in till	110			
	9,593			
	£22,833			£22,833

SUMMARY OF BANK STATEMENTS FOR YEAR ENDED 31 MARCH 19_1

Lodgements	£	Payments	£
Opening balance	3,140	Materials purchased	7,891
Cash banked	29,656	Telephone	423
Cheques from		Printing and stationery	239
debtors	7,295	Holiday to Blackpool	860
		Van expenses	1,564
		Rent (five quarters to	
		30 June 19_1)	2,240
		Rates (18 months to	
		30 Sept. 19_1)	930
		Van insurance	
		(Year to 31 Dec. 19_1)	252
		Electricity	454
		Plant hire	1,801
		Sundries	2,370
		Bank charges	127
		Cash taken for private	
		use	11,208
		Balance c/d	9,732
	£40,091		£40,091
Balance b/d	9,732		

Mr Smith keeps a list of payments made out of cash received from debtors. This cash is kept in a till until it is banked.

	£
Paid to creditors for materials	2,473
Repairs to equipment	125
Postage	231
Petrol for van	683
Plant hire	836
Cash withdrawn	2,560
	£6,908

(a) Balances at 31 March 19_1:

	£
Cash in till	120
Stock & work in progress	4,847
Debtors	3,024
Trade creditors	562
Accruals:	
Telephone	127
Electricity	241

(b) Mr Smith expects all his fixed assets to have four years of further life from now on, and to be depreciated by 20 per cent per annum as a consequence, starting with the current year.

(c) Mr Smith received £25 a week for six weeks during the year from a mutual sickness benefit scheme. This cash was put in the till with money received from debtors. (Treat as extra capital contributed.)

Prepare a Trading and Profit and Loss Account for the year ended and a Balance Sheet as at 31 March 19_1.

23
Purchase of a business

1. Acquisition

'Buying a business' is a common expression, but it is not always clearly defined. Sometimes a purchaser may acquire a few assets only. In some cases, he/she may acquire all the assets with the exception of cash and leave the vendor to discharge the liabilities of the business. In other cases the purchaser may take over all the assets and accept responsibility for the existing liabilities.

Whatever the arrangements the following points are important:

(a) What is the actual purchase price payable to the vendor?
(b) What will the purchaser actually get for this price?

Obviously there will be some assets, but the purchaser may not agree to value them at the valuation placed on them by the seller, but may *revalue* them at what he/she holds to be the correct value.

Against these assets the purchaser may be taking on certain liabilities. It is not usually possible to alter the value of liabilities, the third parties concerned expecting to be paid in full, but in certain circumstances it might be possible. The difference between the assets and liabilities gives us the net asset position.

Taking an imaginary example:

	£
Assets (at value to the purchaser for the new business)	70,000
Less Liabilities taken over	12,500
Net assets	£57,500

If the purchase price is greater than £57,500 then something has been paid for Goodwill (an intangible asset).

(c) If the purchase price is lower than the net value of the assets the purchaser has gained the advantage of a *capital reserve*.

2. Entries in the books of the purchaser

(a) *Debit* a Business Purchase Account and *credit* vendor *with the agreed purchase consideration*.

(b) *Debit* each asset and *credit* Business Purchase Account *with the agreed valuation of each asset acquired*.

(c) *Debit* Business Purchase Account and *credit* each liability with *the agreed value of liabilities taken over*.

(d) *Transfer any balance on the Business Purchase Account*: either *debit* Goodwill Account and *credit* Business Purchase Account; or *debit* Business Purchase Account and *credit* Capital Reserve Account.

(e) *On settlement of the vendor's account*: *debit* Vendor. *Credit* Bank.

Sample question _____

A. Starter, who agreed to take over the existing business of I. Giveup for £46,000 excluding the cash balance, as from 1 January 19__, paid him a cheque for this amount on 15 January 19__.

The Balance Sheet at the date of the acquisition of the business is shown below in abridged form:

	£		£
Premises	39,000	Capital Account	
Stock	4,640	I. Giveup	44,800
Debtors	2,700	Creditors	1,600
Cash	60		
	£46,400		£46,400

Starter decides to re-value the premises to £60,000; to value the stock at £4,000 and to open up a provision for Bad Debts Account of £270. He will bring in £50,000 capital on 1 January to provide the funds for the purchase of the business and a small balance of cash at bank.

Show the necessary calculations and entries recording the purchase in the books of A. Starter and his Balance Sheet as at 15 January 19__.

Calculations:
Assets at agreed valuations:

		£
Premises		60,000
Stock		4,000
Debtors	£2,700	
Less provision	270	
		2,430
		66,430
Less		
Creditors		1,600
Net assets		64,830

For these net assets of £64,830 Starter only paid £46,000, which means that he had gained the advantage of a capital reserve of £18,830.

A capital reserve is a capital profit of the business (not a revenue profit — which would be taxable). Such a capital profit would only be taken into account as a profit at some future time when the business was re-sold, or when the proprietor died.

Answer _____

BUSINESS PURCHASE ACCOUNT

19__		£	19__		£
Jan. 1	Vendor (I. Giveup)	46.000	Jan. 1	Premises	60,000
1	Creditors	1,600		Stock	4,000
1	Provn. for Bad Debts	270		Debtors	2,700
1	Capital Reserve	18,830			
		£66,700			£66,700

VENDOR (I. GIVEUP)

19__		£	19__		£
Jan 15	Bank A/c	46,000	Jan 1	Purchase of business	46,000

PREMISES ACCOUNT

19__		£
Jan. 1	Purchase of Business	60,000

STOCK ACCOUNT

19__		£
Jan. 1	Purchase of Business	4,000

SUNDRY DEBTORS (each with his/her own account)

19__	£
Jan. 1 Purchase of Business	2,700

BAD DEBTS PROVISION ACCOUNT

	19__	£
	Jan. 1 Purchase of Business	270.00

BANK ACCOUNT

19__	£	19__	£
Jan. 1 Capital A/c	50,000	Jan. 15 Vendor A/c	46,000

SUNDRY CREDITORS (each with his/her own account)

	19__	£
	Jan. 1 Purchase of Business	1,600

CAPITAL RESERVE ACCOUNT

	19__	£
	Jan. 1 Purchase of Business	18,830

A.STARTER
BALANCE SHEET AS AT 15 January 19__

	£			£
Fixed assets			Capital A/c Starter	50,000
Premises		60,000	Capital Reserve A/c	18,830
Current assets				68,830
Stock	4,000			
Debtors	2,700			
Less provision	270			
	2,430		*Current liabilities*	
Bank	4,000		Creditors	1,600
		10,430		
		£70,430		£70,430

3. Company taking over an existing business

As long as cash is paid for the acquisition of a business, there is no difference at all between the entries necessary when a company takes over an existing business and those when an individual does so.

The company acquiring the business may not have sufficient cash with which to pay the vendor, so that the vendor agrees to retain some interest in the business by accepting shares in part payment of the purchase consideration.

4. Acquisitions involving shares

When shares are given in part payment for a business the entries are as before, except that the vendor will now be paid partly in cash and partly by the issue of shares. The shares are credited to the Share Capital Account and debited to the account of the vendor.

Example

If in the previous example I. Giveup had accepted £26,000 cash plus shares to the value of £20,000, then the accounts would appear as follows in the books of A. Starter Ltd:

VENDOR (I. GIVEUP)

	£		£
Jan. 15 Bank	26,000	Jan. 1 Business Purchase A/c	46,000
Share capital	20,000		
	£46,000		£46,000

SHARE CAPITAL ACCOUNT (A. STARTER LTD)

	£		£
Jan. 15 Balance c/d	50,000	Jan. 1 Bank (A. Starter Ltd)	30,000
		15 Vendor (I.Giveup)	20,000
	£50,000		£50,000
		Jan. 16 Balance b/d	50,000

5. Converting a sole trader's business into a limited company

There are certain situations which amount to the same thing as a 'purchase of a business'. For example, if a sole trader or a partnership decides to change its business format and become a limited company the proprietor or proprietors effectively sell the business to themselves in their new capacities as directors. When the business of sole trader is converted into a limited company the accounting procedure is exactly the same as that for a company acquiring a business for shares only.

(a) Initial entries in the books of the company acquiring the business are the same as those for any other business purchase.

(b) The whole of the indebtedness to the vendor (now the chairperson or managing director) is settled by the transfer of shares, i.e. no cash passes.

6. Converting a partnership into a limited company

As a business develops it is quite usual for a partnership to be converted into a limited company. A few years ago all large organisations were built up in this way. Nowadays, however, many enterprises are initially organised as limited companies, often purchased 'off the shelf' from company registration agents.

When a change is made the partners receive shares in the company in exchange for the balances standing to the credit of their respective Capital and Current Accounts in the former partnership.

Sample question

A. Middleman and B. Merchant, who have been in business as partners for many years, decide to form a limited company to be known as M & M Ltd.

The company is formed as from 1 August 19__, on which date the summarised Balance Sheet of the partnership was as follows.

	£		£
Premises	42,500	Capital Accounts:	
Stock	8,400	Middleman	24,000
Debtors	5,300	Merchant	16,000
Cash at bank	1,300	Current Accounts	
Cash in hand	500	Middleman	8,000
		Merchant	7,500
		Creditors	2,500
	£58,000		£58,000

No revaluation of assets takes place and the partners accept Ordinary Shares at par in exchange for their interest in the old partnership.

Show the entries in the books of the company and also the relevant entries in the books of the old partnership.

Answer

The 'purchase price' of the company is £58,000 – £2,500 = £55,500. Of this price Middleman will become a shareholder for £24,000 + £8,000 = £32,000 and Merchant for £16,000 + £7,500 = £23,500.

(a) *In the books of the company.*

BUSINESS PURCHASE ACCOUNT

19__		£	19__		£
Aug 1	Vendor (Middleman		Aug. 1	Premises	42,500
	and Merchant)	55,500		Stock	8,400
	Creditors	2,500		Debtors	5,300
				Cash at Bank	1,300
				Cash in hand	500
		£58,000			£58,000

VENDORS' ACCOUNT

19__		£	19__		£
Aug 1	Share Capital A/c		Aug 1	Purchase of	
	Middleman	32,000		Business A/c	55,500
	Merchant	23,500			
		£55,500			£55,500

ORDINARY SHARE CAPITAL ACCOUNT

		19__		£
		Aug. 1	Vendor's A/c	55,500

(b) *In the books of the partnership.*

When a partnership is closed down all the assets are transferred to a
Realisation Account and are sold for what they will fetch, which offer
results in either a Profit on Realisation or a Loss on Realisation (*see* 29:10).
In this case they are being passed on at the same price to M & M Ltd, who
become debtors for this amount.

REALISATION ACCOUNT

19__		£	19__		£
Aug. 1	Premises	42,500	Aug. 1	Creditors	2,500
	Stock	8,400		M & M Ltd	55,500
	Debtors	5,300			
	Cash at bank	1,300			
	Cash in hand	500			
		£58,000			£58,000

M & M Ltd then pay the debt with the shares they issue and these shares
are transferred to the partners to repay their original capital, and the

balances of accumulated profits that have collected in their Current Accounts.

M & M LTD

19__		£	19__		£
Aug. 1	Realisation A/c	55,500	Aug 1	Shares in M & M Ltd	55,500

SHARES IN M & M LTD

19__		£	19__		£
Aug. 1	M & M Ltd	55,500	Aug. 1	Capital A/c	
				Middleman	32,000
				Merchant	23,500
		£55,500			£55,500

CAPITAL ACCOUNTS

	£ Middleman	£ Merchant		£ Middleman	£ Merchant
Aug. 1 Shares in M & M Ltd	32,000	23,500	Aug. 1 Balance	24,000	16,000
			Aug. 1 Current A/cs transferred	8,000	7,500
	32,000	23,500		32,000	23,500

All accounts are therefore closed and the business has ceased to trade as a partnership.

---

7. Company acquiring another company

Everybody has heard of a 'take-over bid'. In accounting terms this operation simply consists of one company taking over the control of another company, or obtaining the business of another company by paying for the business with its own shares.

(a) The terms of the take-over may vary considerably, e.g. a company may offer one of its own shares plus 50p in cash in exchange for each share in the company being taken over, or three of its own shares for every two shares in the other company.

(b) These terms only affect the arithmetic of the transaction.

(c) The agreed value of the shares in all cases will be debited to the account of the vendor (the company being taken over), the Share Capital Account of the company acquiring the business being credited.

8.   Entries to close the books of the company taken over
The following procedure will be adopted to close the books.

(a)   *Open a Sundry Shareholders' Account.* Transfer to this account all balances on Share Capital, Reserves and Profit and Loss Account. *Credit* Sundry Shareholders; *debit* Share Capital, etc.

(b)   *Open a Realisation Account. Debit* Realisation Account; *credit* Asset Account (with all assets taken over). *Credit* Realisation Account; *debit* liabilities (with all liabilities taken over).

(c)   *Open a Shares in X Ltd* [name of company acquiring the business] *Account. Debit* Shares in X Ltd Account; *credit* Realisation Account (with the value of shares received).

(d)   *If cash forms part of the purchase consideration: debit* bank; *credit* Realisation Account (with cash received).

(e)   *Transfer balance on Realisation Account to Sundry Shareholders' Account:*

- (i) if a profit: *debit* Realisation Account; *credit* Sundry Shareholders' Account;
- (ii) if a loss; *credit* Realisation Account; *debit* Sundry Shareholders' Account.

(f)   *Any cash remaining after paying any expenses: debit* Sundry Shareholders' Account; *credit* bank.

(g)   *The balance on Sundry Shareholders' Account should now equal the balance on the Shares in X Ltd. Debit* Sundry Shareholders' Account; *credit* Shares in X Ltd Account.

Sample question _____
After closing the accounts, the abridged Balance Sheet of A. Smallfellow Ltd on 12 June 19__, was as follows:

	£		£
Assets	29,000	Share capital	20,000
		Capital reserve	4,000
		Profit and Loss A/c	5,000
	£29,000		£29,000

The business was acquired by B. Longfellow Ltd as from the date of the Balance Sheet in exchange for 40,000 Ordinary Shares of £1 each issued at par.

Show the entries in the books of A. Smallfellow Ltd to record the liquidation of the company and the settlement of the shareholders' indebtedness.

Answer

Books of A. Smallfellow Ltd:

REALISATION ACCOUNT

	£		£
June 1 Assets	29,000	June 1 Shares in	40,000
Sundry shareholders		Longfellow Ltd	
(profit on realisation)	11,000		
	£40,000		£40,000

SHARES IN LONGFELLOW LTD

	£		£
June 1 Realisation A/c	40,000	June 1 Sundry shareholders	£40,000

SUNDRY SHAREHOLDERS

	£		£
		June 1 Share Capital A/c	20,000
June 1 Shares in		Capital reserves	4,000
Longfellow Ltd	40,000	Profit and Loss A/c	5,000
		Realisation A/c	11,000
	£40,000		£40,000

Progress test 23

1. What is meant by the expression 'purchasing a business' ?   **(1)**

2. Why are assets normally revalued when a business is purchased?   **(1)**

3. What is the difference between the net assets and the purchase price of a business?   **(1)**

4. How is settlement effected when a sole trader turns his/her business into a limited company?   **(5)**

5. What do you understand by the expression 'take-over bid'?   **(7)**

6. What new accounts are opened in the books of the business being taken over when the business is acquired for shares in the purchasing company? **(8)**

7. How is the balance on Realisation Account dealt with? **(8)**

Specimen questions

1. R. Haines decides to purchase the business of L. Rushkin on 1 January. He has £100,000 at the bank and borrows an additional amount of £20,000 from the Sound Finance Company to provide working capital.

L. Rushkin's Balance Sheet at 1 January was:

	£		£
Balance at bank	856	Creditors	1,500
Stock	12,400	Capital	80,776
Debtors	1,020		
Fixtures	12,000		
Premises	56,000		
	£82,276		£82,276

It was agreed that R. Haines should take over all the assets, except the balance at bank, and all liabilities, and that an amount equal to 10 per cent of the debtors should be allowed for doubtful debts.

R. Haines agreed to pay L. Rushkin an additional amount for the goodwill of his business on the basis of two years' purchase of the average profits for the last five years. These profits were £11,100; £11,255; £13,480; £13,580 and £15,245.

Having concluded the bargain on these terms with Rushkin, Haines then decided that the following assets should be revalued for the purposes of his own books,

Premises	67,000
Fixtures	7,600

the goodwill figure being adjusted in his books to take account of the changes. Rushkin did not know, or need to know, about this decision.

The transaction was completed on 1 January and R. Haines paid L.Rushkin by cheque.

REQUIRED:

(1) Show the accounts in the ledger of R.Haines and his Balance Sheet on 1 January immediately after the transaction.

(2) What do you understand by 'goodwill'?

2. A. Nelson arranged to dispose of his business to a limited company, and for that purpose he formed A. Nelson Ltd with an authorised share capital of £100,000 divided into 80,000 Ordinary Shares of £1 each and 20,000 12 per cent Preference Shares of £1 each.

The Balance Sheet of his business at 31 December 19_0 was:

	£		£
Freehold factory	47,575	Capital Account	82,500
Plant and machinery	25,291	Creditors	2,410
Debtors	8,262	Overdraft at bank	14,203
Stock	17,985		
	£99,113		£99,113

The Helpful Bank PLC would take up the 20,000 Preference Shares at par and this money would be used to repay the bank overdraft and all the creditors so that they need not be considered in changing the form of the business.

The factory was to be revalued to £55,000 and the plant and machinery reduced in value to £20,000. Stock will also be reduced to £13,351. The purchase price of the business was agreed to be £62,500, payable £2,500 in cash and £60,000 in Ordinary Shares valued at par. The remaining 20,000 Ordinary Shares will be taken up at par by Venture Capital Ltd, in cash, to provide working capital. The difference between the purchase price and the book value of the assets is to be treated as a Capital Reserve and called Reserve on Formation.

All these matters were put into effect on 1 January 19_1.

Show how these transactions would appear in the Journal and Cash Book of the Company, and draw up a Balance Sheet at the commencement of trading on 1 January 19_1.

3. The Balance Sheet of Slemish, a retail trader, at 31 December 19_1, was as follows:

BALANCE SHEET

	£		£
Freehold properties	46,000	Capital	50,800
Furniture and fittings	5,200	Creditors	17,100
Stock in trade	21,400	Bank overdraft	4,700
	£72,600		£72,600

On 31 December 19_1 Tiveragh Ltd was incorporated, and on 1 Jan. 19_2 took over all the assets (but not the liabilities) of Slemish at a price of £80,000, which was paid in cash on 31 March 19_2. It was agreed that the freehold property was worth £48,000 and that the stock and fixtures and fittings were worth the above Balance Sheet valuations. On 1 January 19_2 Tiveragh Ltd issued 100,000 shares of £1 each at par; all were applied for and paid in full.

During 19_2:		On 31 Dec. 19_2:	
	£		£
Sales in cash	162,740	Stock in trade	19,760
Purchases in cash	74,120	Creditors for purchases	6,290
Expenses	22,410	Creditors for expenses	780
		Debtors for sales	8,170

All cash received from customers was paid into bank, and all expenses were paid by cheque. You are asked to prepare:

(a) a summary of the company's Bank Account for 19_2; and

(b) A Trading and Profit and Loss Account for 19_2 and a Balance Sheet as on 31 December 19_2 (ignore depreciation). The Goodwill Account is to be written off out of profits on 31 December 19_2. A General Reserve Account of £20,000 is to be created and a Reserve for Corporation Tax of £25,000. A dividend of 15 per cent will be paid on the shares.

4. Field and Hill were in partnership sharing profits in the ratio of 2:1. On 31 December 19_4 their Balance Sheet was as follows.

	£	£		£	£
Freehold property (cost)		60,000	Capital A/cs:		
Motor vehicles (cost)	4,600		Field	34,000	
Less Depreciation			Hill	17,000	
to date	3,100				51,000
		1,500	Current A/cs:		
Stock		4,800	Field	3,285	
Debtors		8,700	Hill	1,715	
Bank		1,600			5,000
			15% Loan A/c: Field		15,000
			Creditors		5,600
		£76,600			£76,600

On 1 January 19_5 the partners agreed to form a company, Fence Ltd, to take over the freehold property and stock (only) at an inclusive price of £78,000. The partners would deal with all other matters.

The purchase consideration was to be satisfied by the issue by Fence Ltd of 78,000 Ordinary Shares of £1 each fully paid. You are required to show the following (calculations to the nearest £1).

(a) The Realisation Account of the partnership and the Capital Accounts of Field and Hill. Apart from matters mentioned above, Hill takes the car at an agreed valuation of £1,900 and the debtors realised £8,000. The creditors were paid in full, and Field's loan was repaid with £15,000 in shares. The other shares in the company were taken by the partners in their profit sharing ratios.

(b) The Balance Sheet of Fence Ltd on 1 January 19_5 after the acquisition, the freehold property having been revalued at £70,000 and the stock at £5,000, the balance being recognised as goodwill.

24
Joint ventures

1. Definition

A joint venture is simply a venture undertaken jointly by two or more persons with a view to gaining a profit.

(a) It differs from a partnership in that it is of a more temporary character.

(b) Nowadays joint ventures are often concerned with one isolated transaction, such as buying up bankrupt stocks or engaging in similar operations.

2. Main characteristics

Because of their temporary nature, no separate books are kept to record the transactions, each venturer keeping a record of his/her part of the enterprise in normal accounting records.

(a) The profit-sharing ratios must be clearly defined.

(b) The capital, activities and scope of the venture must be laid down, e.g. sometimes one venturer does the buying and the other the selling, but often *both* make a capital contribution.

(c) Sometimes one venturer is allowed credit for the use of his/her office, or for services provided, but this must be agreed to by all parties.

3. Accounting procedure

Each venturer opens an account to record all matters which concern the particular venture. This account is called '*Joint Venture with XYZ* [the name of the other party to the venture]'.

(a) *If cash is paid out: debit* Joint Venture Account; *credit* Cash.

(b) *If cash is received from sales or even from the other party: debit* Cash; credit Joint Venture Account.

(c) *Any charges agreed upon, e.g. commission: debit* Joint Venture Account; *credit* the account of the person who is to receive the commission, etc.

(d) *At the close of the venture, or end of the year, whichever is earlier:*the joint accounts of *each* venturer are combined together in a Memorandum Joint Venture Account, on which the profit or loss of the venture is ascertained (*Note*: A Memorandum Account is not part of the double entry books, but is purely a memorandum of what has occurred so that the profit or loss can be found, and shared.)

(e) *The profit having been found,* each venturer must *debit* Joint Venture Account with his/her share of the profit and *credit* Profit and Loss Account with the same amount.

(f) *In the event of a loss,* each venturer must *credit* Joint Venture Account with his/her share of the loss and *debit* Profit and Loss Account with the same amount.

(g) *When all these entries have been made,* the balances remaining on the various Joint Venture Accounts show the indebtedness of one venturer to another.

If, as is usual in most examinations, there are only *two* venturers, cash will be paid by one venturer to the other and the joint venture comes to a close.

Sample question

On learning that the Liquidator of XYZ Ltd was about to invite tenders for the stock in trade of that old-established fashion house, A. Slick and B. Sharp decided to undertake a joint venture to buy up the goods.

The stock which had a book value of £65,000, was obtained by the joint venturers at a discount of 50 per cent. Payment was made on 1 February 19__, when B. Sharp sent a cheque for £10,000 to A. Slick to help him pay for the goods.

Profits were to be shared equally, and each partner was entitled to a commission of 5 per cent on the selling price of the goods which he sold. In addition, A. Slick was to receive an office allowance of £100 and B. Sharp was allowed to charge £550 for the wages of his employees who had been engaged on handling the goods.

The following expenditure was incurred by the venturers up to 31 July 19__.

A. *Slick*. 1 March. Carriage £250. Insurance £450.
B. *Sharp*. 31 July. Rent of warehouse £600.

On 1 April, A. Slick received £14,000 and B. Sharp £10,000 for goods sold, while on 14 July they received £8,000 and £9,000 respectively.

A. Slick agreed to take the residue of the stock valued at £500 for his own use on 31 July, when the venture was closed.

Show the accounts necessary to record the above transactions and also the final settlement between the parties on 31 July 19__.

Answer

In the books of A. Slick

JOINT VENTURE WITH B. SHARP

19__		£	19__		£
Feb. 1	Bank (XYZ Ltd)	32,500	Feb. 1	Bank (B. Sharp)	10,000
Mar. 1	Bank (carriage)	250	Apr. 1	Bank (sales)	14,000
1	Bank (insurance)	450	July 14	Bank (sales)	8,000
Apr. 1	Commission 5%	700	31	Purchases Account	500
July 14	Commission 5%	400	31	Balance c/d	1,900
31	Office allowance	100			
		£34,400			£34,400
July 31	Balance b/d	1,900	July 31	Bank (B. Sharp)	4,400
31	Profit on joint ventures A/c	2,500			
		£4,400			£4,400

BANK ACCOUNT

19__		£	19__		£
Feb. 1	Joint venture with B. Sharp	10,000	Feb. 1	Joint venture with Sharp (purchases)	32,500
Apr. 1	Joint venture with B. Sharp (sales)	14,000	Mar. 1	Joint venture with Sharp (carriage)	250
July 31	Joint venture with B. Sharp (sales)	8,000	1	Joint venture with Sharp (insurance)	450
31	B. Sharp (cheque received	4,400	July 31	Balance c/d	3,200
		£36,400			£36,400
Aug. 1	Balance b/d	3,200			

COMMISSION ACCOUNT

	Apr. 1	Joint venture with Sharp	£700
	July 14	Joint venture with Sharp	400

OFFICE EXPENSES ACCOUNT

	July 31	Joint venture with Sharp	£100

PURCHASES ACCOUNT

July	Joint venture	£500
	with Sharp	

PROFIT ON JOINT VENTURES ACCOUNT

	July 31 Joint venture with Sharp £2,500

In the books of B. Sharp

JOINT VENTURE WITH A. SLICK

19__		£	19__		£
Feb. 1	Bank (A. Slick)	10,000	Apr. 1	Bank (sales)	10,000
Apr. 1	Commission	500	July 14	Bank (sales)	9,000
July 14	Commission	450			
31	Bank (warehouse rent)	600			
31	Wages	550			
31	Balance c/d	6,900			
		£19,000			£19,000
July 31	Profit on joint ventures		July 31	Balance b/d	6,900
	A/c	2,500			
31	Bank (A. Slick)	4,400			
		£6,900			£6,900

BANK ACCOUNT

19__		£	19__		£
Apr. 1	Joint venture with Slick		Feb. 1	A. Slick	10,000
	(sales)	10,000	July 31	Joint venture with Slick	
July 14	Joint venture with Slick			(warehouse rent)	600
	(sales)	9,000	31	A. Slick (cheque	
				forwarded)	4,400
			31	Balance c/d	4,000
		£19,000			£19,000
Aug. 1	Balance b/d	4,000			

COMMISSION ACCOUNT

	Apr. 1 Joint venture with Slick	£500
	July 14 Joint venture with Slick	450

WAGES ACCOUNT

	July 31 Joint venture with Slick	£550

PROFIT ON JOINT VENTURES ACCOUNT

	July 31 Joint venture with Slick	£2,500

In the books of A. Slick and B. Sharp

MEMORANDUM JOINT VENTURE ACCOUNT
(In fashion goods from XYZ Ltd)

Sharp:	£	£	*Sales:*	£	£
Warehouse rent	600		Sharp	10,000	
Wages	550			9,000	
Commission 5%	950				19,000
		2,100	Slick	14,000	
Slick:				8,000	
Purchases	32,500				22,000
Carriage	250		Slick: Goods taken over		500
Insurance	450				
Office allowance	100				
Commission 5%	1,100				
		34,400			
Net profit c/d		5,000			
		£41,500			£41,500
Share of profit:			Net profit b/d		5,000
A. Slick		2,500			
B. Sharp		2,500			
		£5,000			£5,000

NOTE:

The cheque of £10,000 from B. Sharp to A. Slick is eliminated altogether in the Memorandum Joint Venture Account.

The benefit derived from the venture by each venturer is as follows:

	A. Slick £	B. Sharp £
Profit	2,500	2,500
Commission	1,100	950
Office allowance	100	–
Wages of own employees	–	550
	3,700	4,000

	A. Slick £	B. Sharp £
Represented by:		
Stock of goods	500	
Cash at Bank	3,200	4,000
	3,700	4,000

4. Stock of goods

When a Joint Venture Account is prepared before the whole of the stock is disposed of (for example to enable any profit so far to be taken into account by the venturers at the end of a financial year) an adjustment must be made for the value of the stock still on hand. The figure agreed upon for the valuation of the stock is credited to the Joint Venture Account and debited to a Suspense Account. A Suspense Account is an account used to carry an item over from one trading period to another, or from one Trial Balance period to the next. In this case it might be called Joint Venture in Suspense Account.

It must be emphasised that this procedure is not often adopted, as the usual practice is to prepare accounts only upon the completion of the joint venture.

Alternatively, if the venture is brought to a close before all the stock has been disposed of, one of the parties to the venture can take the stock over at an agreed valuation.

Progress test 24

1. What is a joint venture?   **(1)**

2. How does it differ from a partnership?   **(1)**

3. What are the main characteristics of joint ventures? **(2)**

4. What is the function of the 'Memorandum Joint Venture Account' and when is it prepared? **(3)**

5. Can a venturer make a charge for his own services? **(2)**

6. What entries are made if one party sends cash to the other.
(*a*) In the books of the receiver?
(*b*) In the books of the person remitting the cash? **(3)**

7. If a profit is made on the venture, what entries are made in the books? **(3)**

8. What is the procedure if a stock of goods remains on hand **(4)**

Specimen questions

1. B. Prize and J. Matt enter into a joint venture for the purchase of a cargo of timber for £87,500 from K. Accle. Each is to receive 5 per cent commission on any sales he makes, the final profit to be shared equally. On 1 February B. Prize accepts a bill of exchange at thirty days for £87,500, drawn by K. Accle, who discounts it with his banker for £86,493 bearing his own charges. J. Matt pays warehousing £280, carriage £150 and saw-mill costs £429. B. Prize pays carriage costs of £494 and insurance of £120.

	SALES	
	£	£
	B.Prize	*J. Matt*
February	21,600	22,700
March	31,900	43,100

As insufficient timber has been sold by 3 March, B. Prize is unable to meet the bill. He agrees, however, to accept a further bill at thirty days for the amount due plus £45 for charges and £1,007 interest incurred by K. Accle. The second bill is met on the due date, and B. Prize and J. Matt then settle their indebtedness. A small amount of unsold timber is taken by Matt at an agreed valuation of £2,500.

You are required to show:

(a) the Ledger accounts of J. Matt and the results of the joint venture;

(b) the Journal entries of the transactions, including cash, in the books of K. Accle.

2. Powell and Johns entered into a joint speculation to buy and sell second-hand motor vehicles. It was agreed that profits and losses should be shared equally.

Any vehicles unsold at the end of each quarter were to be taken over by the party buying them, at their trade list price.

During the three months ended 31 March 19__, the following transactions took place.

19__

Jan.	5	Powell bought two cars for £1,240 and paid garage rent £30.
Feb.	6	Johns sold one of these cars for £1,420.
	8	Powell sold the other for £150.
Mar.	10	Johns bought a further four cars for £3,380 and paid £60 for cleaning and repairing them.
	15	Powell sold two of these cars for £5,250 and paid commission and advertising £66.
	31	Powell's travelling and hotel expenses were £240 for the quarter while Johns had paid out £160 for similar expenses. The trade list price of the two unsold cars was £1,800.

Prepare an account giving the result of the joint venture as a whole and show how the foregoing transactions should be recorded in each party's books, settlement between them being effected by cheque on 30 April 19__.

3. On 1 July 19_1 Antony and Crespel entered a joint venture to trade in second-hand textile machinery. Crespel receives a commission of 5 per cent on all sales satisfactorily completed. All remaining profits and losses are to be shared as to Antony 75 per cent and Crespel 25 per cent. The following transactions took place.

July 1   Antony purchased a machine for £14,500, paid in full. He incurred expenditure of £525 refurbishing the machine in July.

Aug. 1   Antony purchased another machine for £920. There were carriage costs of £22 met by Crespel whose van transported the machine.

Aug. 12   Crespel bought a machine for £1,500 for which he received £2,500 from a customer on 15 September. The machine was returned on 18 September as defective and an allowance of £2,300 was paid by Crespel to the customer. The machine was unsold at 30 September and it was agreed that Crespel would take it at a valuation of £1,000.

Aug. 20   The machine purchased in July was sold by Antony for £17,500. Delivery costs of £1,525 were paid and borne by the customer.

Aug. 21   The machine purchased by Antony for £920 was sold by Crespel for £1,200.

Sept. 3   The purchaser of the machine sold on 21 August informed Crespel that it was faulty and would be returned to Crespel, who refunded the cost of £1,200 to the customer. A claim for damages was agreed at £150 to cover return carriage and associated costs. Crespel sold the machine for scrap and it realised £100 which was paid to the customer in part settlement of his damages claim. The balance of the damages claim, £50, was paid by Antony direct to the customer when he visited him on business.

Sept. 30   The venture came to an end and final settlement was effected.

You are required to prepare:

(a) the Joint Venture Accounts in the books of Antony and Crespel;

(b) a Memorandum Joint Venture Account.

25
Consignments

1. Definition

Consignment Accounts are concerned with goods sent to an agent who will sell the goods on behalf of his/her principal. In many cases the goods are consigned to an agent abroad, although today United Kingdom businesses do act as agents for foreign principals.

(a) To distinguish the goods from the normal sales they are always described as 'goods on consignment'.

(b) The principal is called the *consignor*, since he/she sends the goods to the agent, and the agent is the *consignee*, to whom the goods are consigned.

(c) Goods are *not sold* to the agent, and he/she accepts no resposibility for payment unless and until they are *sold*.

(d) Any stock of goods held by the agent is therefore counted as a stock of goods belonging to the consignor, and will be shown as such in the consignor's Balance Sheet.

2. Pro forma invoice

Since the goods are not sold to the agent, a pro forma invoice is used when the goods are sent to him (pro forma means 'for form's sake').

(a) This document does not make a charge, but communicates information.

(b) It will inform the agent of the price at which it is hoped it will be possible to sell the goods.

3. Agent's commission
The agent usually receives remuneration in the form of a commission.

(a) This takes the form of a flat rate based on a percentage of the gross sales figure.

(b) When the agent accepts responsibility for any *bad debts* resulting from sales made on credit it is usual to give him/her an additional commission called *del credere* commission. This will take the form of an increase in the flat rate calculated on sales, but for the purpose of the accounts it is usual to show the item separately. *Del credere* means 'in the belief that' the buyer is solvent. The agent is prepared to take the reponsibility for any possible bad debts because he/she knows the buyer to be reliable.

4. Entries in the books of the consignor

(a) *Open two accounts:*
  (i) 'Goods sent on Consignment A/c'.
  (ii) 'Consignment to So & So' (the consignee).

(b) *When goods are despatched: debit* Consignment to So & So; *credit* Goods on Consignment Account.

  NOTE: The amount taken to these accounts should be the *cost price*.

Example
On 12 February 19__ Iced Cold Refrigerators Ltd sent on consignment fifty refrigerators costing £60 each to A.W. Siwel of Trinidad, West Indies. The entries in the consignor's books will be a s follows.

GOODS SENT ON CONSIGNMENT
Feb. 12 Consignment to
A.W. Siwel   £3,000

CONSIGNMENT TO A.W. SIWEL, TRINIDAD
Feb. 12 Goods sent on
consignment   £3,000

NOTE: The 'Goods sent on Consignment Account' will ultimately be closed by transfer to the Trading Account where the amount involved will be *deducted* from the purchases figure.

5.   Completion of consignment

If the goods are sold on satisfactory terms there will be four additional matters to record in the books of the consignor.

(a) Expenditure incurred by the consignor.
(b) Expenditure incurred by the consignee (the agent), such as landing charges and import duties, etc.
(c) The sale of goods by the agent.
(d) The commission earned by the agent.

This information must be entered in the 'Consignment to So & So Account' in order to find the profit or loss on the consignment.

6.   Sources of information – the account sales

The expenditure incurred by the consignor will be found in the Cash Book.

The expenditure incurred and income earned by the agent is, however, given to the consignor on a document called an *account sales*. This document sets out the gross proceeds of sales obtained by the agent and the expenditure incurred and charges made by him/her shown as deductions from the gross sales figure.

The balance represents the amount due to the consignor, and is usually remitted with the account sales itself. On receipt of this document the full details of the consigment can then be entered in the books of the consignor.

An example of an 'Account Sales' is shown below.

Account sales of fifty refrigerators ex MV *Bonnie Lass* sold for the account of Iced Cold Refrigerators Ltd.		
ICR		£
541/545 50 Refrigerators at £90 each		4,500
Deduct:		
Landing charges	£120	
Port dues	60	
Import duties	200	
Commission 5%	225	
Del credere commission	135	
		740
Sight draft enclosed for . . .		£3,760
E & OE	*A.W Siwel*	
	Trinidad, West Indies. 30 April 19__	

7. Further entries in the consignor's books

In addition to recording the actual despatch of goods, the following entries will be made.

(a) *Expenditure incurred by the consignor: debit* Consignment Account; *credit* Bank Account.

(b) *Expenditure incurred by the agent: debit* Consignment Account; *credit* the personal account of the agent.

(c) *Proceeds from the sale of goods: credit* Consignment Account; *debit* the personal account of the agent.

(d) *Agent's commission: debit* Consignment Account; *credit* the personal account of the agent.

(e) *Cash remitted by the agent: debit* Bank Account; *credit* the personal account of the agent.

(f) *Transfer the balance on the Consignment Account.*

    (i) If a profit: *debit* Consignment Account; *credit* Profit and Loss Account.

    (ii) If a loss; *credit* Consignment Account; *debit* Profit and Loss Account.

NOTE: Sometimes the profit is first taken to a Profit and Loss on Consignment Account.

Example

Referring to the consignment to A.W Siwel, Iced Cold Refrigerators Ltd paid on 20 February freight and shipping charges of £160 and insurance £70. They also received the account sales featured earlier from A.W Siwel on 12 May.

The accounts on the books of Iced Cold Refrigerators Ltd would appear as follows:

CONSIGNMENT TO A.W. SIWEL, TRINIDAD

19__		£	19__		£
Feb. 12	Goods on consignment outwards	3,000	Apr. 30	A.W. Siwel (agent) Proceeds of sale	4,500
20	Bank: freight	160			
	Bank: Insurance	70			
Apr. 30	A.W. Siwel:				
	Landing Charges	120			
	Port dues	60			
	Import duties	200			
	Commission 5%	225			
	Del credere 3%	135			
		3,970			
May 12	Profit and loss on consignment	530			
		£4,500			£4,500

A.W. SIWEL (AGENT)

19__		£	19__		£
Apr. 30	Consignment A/c Proceeds of sale	4,500	Apr. 30	Consignment A/c	
				Landing charges	120
				Port dues	60
				Import duties	200
				Commission 5%	225
				Del credere 3%	135
			May 12	Bank	3,760
		£4,500			£4,500

PROFIT AND LOSS ON CONSIGNMENT ACCOUNT

		£
	May 12 Consignment to A.W. Siwel	530

8. Treatment of unsold stock

In practice, all the stock consigned to the agent may not have been sold by the end of the financial year or within the period required by the principal (the consignor).

The agent will usually render an account sales for that part of the consignment which has been disposed of, leaving a stock of goods held by him/her.

(a) The account sales will show certain expenses which have been incurred and which relate to the *whole consignment*.

(b) Any commission deducted by the agent will, however, relate only to that part of the consignment so far disposed of.

(c) The unsold stock must be brought down as a *debit balance* on the consignment account.

9. Valuation of unsold stock

In valuing the unsold stock two considerations must be taken into account:

(a) the original cost price of the goods;

(b) the expenditure incurred on the goods up to the moment of stocktaking.

Unless detailed records have been kept, it is necessary in both cases to take a proportion of the two elements of cost to arrive at the value of the stock held by the agent.

In each case the fraction taken is the proportion which the unsold stock bears to the total stock sent out on consignment.

Example
_____

Referring to the consignment to A.W. Siwel; if when A. Siwel submitted an account sales on 30 April only *half* of the goods had been sold, the entries in the books of Iced Cold Refrigerators Ltd would appear as follows:

CONSIGNMENT TO A.W. SIWEL

		£	£			£	£
Feb. 12	Goods on consignment outwards		3,000	Apr. 30 A. Siwel (sales)			2,250
20	Bank: Freight	*160		May 12 Stock c/d			
20	Bank: Insurance	* 70		$\frac{1}{2}$ of cost		1,500	
Apr. 30	A. Siwel:			$\frac{1}{2}$ of expenses		305	
	Landing charges	*120		(i.e. all the items marked *)			1,805
	Port dues	* 60		($\frac{1}{2}$ of 610 = £305)			
	Import duties	*200					
			610				
	Commission 5%		$112\frac{1}{2}$				
	Del credere 3%		$67\frac{1}{2}$				
			3,790				
May 12	Profit and loss on consignment		265				
			£4,055				£4,055
May 13	Balance (stock) b/d		1,805				

10. Entries in the books of the consignee (agent)

The consignee (agent) may keep a record for his/her own convenience of the receipt of the goods, *but as they do not belong to the agent* there is no need to include them in his/her accounts.

The agent will, however, keep a *personal account of the consignor* (the principal), and the entries made can be summarised as follows.

(a) On paying expenses: *debit* consignor; *credit* bank.

(b) On selling the goods: *credit* consignor; *debit* bank (or customer, if the goods were sold on credit).

(c) Commission: *debit* consignor; *credit* Commission Receivable Account.

(d) Remittances to consignor: *debit* consignor; *credit* bank.

NOTE: If a bill of exchange is drawn against the consignment: *debit* consignor; *credit* Bills Payable Account.

Example

The personal account of Iced Cold Refrigerators Ltd in the books of A. Siwel would appear as follows:

(a) *If all the goods had been sold as in the first example:*

ICED COLD REFRIGERATORS LTD

		£			£
Feb. 28	Bank		Mar. 21	Cash (proceeds of	
	Landing charges	120		sales)	4,500
	Port dues	60			
	Import duties	200			
Apr. 30	Commission 5%	225			
	Del credere	135			
	Bank	3,760			
		£4,500			£4,500

(b) *If half the goods had been sold as in the second example:*

ICED COLD REFRIGERATORS LTD

	£		£
Feb. 28 Bank		Mar. 21 Cash (proceeds of	
Landing charges	120.00	sale)	2,250.00
Port dues	60.00		
Import duties	200.00		
Apr. 30 Commission 5%	112.50		
Del credere	67.50		
Bank	1,690.00		
	£2,250.00		£2,250.00

Progress test 25

1. How does a transaction dealing with goods on consignment differ from a normal sale or return transaction? **(1)**

2. What is a pro forma invoice? **(2)**

3. What form does the agent's remuneration take? **(3)**

4. What is del credere commission? **(3)**

5. How is the stock of goods sent out on consignment treated in the books of the consignor? **(4)**

6. What is an 'account sales' and what does it do? **(6)**

7. How is the unsold stock dealt with in the books of the consignor? **(8)**

8. How is the unsold stock valued? **(9)**

9. What accounts are usually kept by the consignee (the agent)? **(10)**

10. Does the agent have to record the receipt of goods? **(10)**

Specimen questions

1. On 31 December 19_0 Potts and Co. of Winchester consigned forty bales of cotton goods to A. Blanc and Co. Ltd of Mombasa, per *Zanzibar Castle*. Potts and Co. paid £5,800 for the cotton goods, and they also paid £140 for carriage to the docks, freight at £18 per bale and marine insurance of £86. On arrival in Mombasa the goods attracted dock dues of £160. A. Blanc and Co. Ltd paid these and other charges of £130. Commission was 6 per cent to Blanc on the selling price of the goods sold and *del credere* commission of $2\frac{1}{2}$ per cent. On 31 March 19_1, A. Blanc and Co. Ltd sold half the goods, which realised a total of £8,400. In settlement of the net proceeds of the goods sold to that date Blanc sent an account sales showing the gross proceeds, all the expenses incurred to date and claiming both commissions. The sight draft was forwarded to Potts and Co. on 31 March 19_1. Show (*a*) the account sales and (*b*) the necessary entries in the Ledger of Potts and Co, to show the transactions and the profit or loss on this consignment to 31 March 19__.

2. On 1 February, India Products Ltd consigned to their agent, Comfihomes Co. Ltd, fifty carpets at a pro-forma value of £140 each. The agents were to receive 10 per cent on actual sales plus 2½ per cent *del credere* commission, and to be reimbursed for any charges incurred. The carpets cost India Products Ltd £28 each, plus freight £860 and insurance £240 for the whole consignment. On 20 March, Comfihomes rendered an account sales showing that thirty carpets had been sold for £8,280 and deducting landing charges £72, inward carriage from the port £84 and their commission. On 21 March the consignors drew a bill at thirty days for the amount shown on the Account Sales which was accepted by Comfihomes and discounted on 25 March for £7,010.

You are asked to show (*a*) the Account Sales, which claims all the expenses and commission to date set against the gross invoice and (*b*) the accounts in the consignor's books at 31 March showing the profit so far on this consignment. (Calculations correct to the nearest £1.)

3. On 1 July 19__, Smithson of London sent 100 cases of goods to Jackson, of Melbourne, Australia, on consignment terms. Smithson paid £800 per case for these goods, and it was agreed that he should bear all the expenses of the consignment. He paid freight and insurance amounting to £2,400.

On 31 December 19__ Smithson received an account sales from Jackson showing that 60 cases had been sold for £124,000. Jackson had paid duty and landing charges on the whole consignment amounting to £2,200. His selling expenses were £700 and he was entitled to a commission of 5 per cent on the gross value of the goods sold and a *del credere* commission of 3 per cent. Jackson enclosed with the account sales a remittance for the amount due from him to Smithson.

You are required to set out:

(a) the Account Sales;

(b) The Ledger Accounts in the consignor's books showing the profit to date on the consignment.

26
Royalties

1. Nature

Royalties represent sums relating usually to *output* of one kind or another or a sum relating to the use of an asset, e.g. so much per tonne on the output of ore from a mine, or so much per book sold by a publisher.

2. If paid

It represents a charge (*debit*) against the *Revenue Account* — or in the case of a manufacturing concern, a charge against the *Manufacturing Account*.

3. If received

It represents income and as such will be *credited* to the Revenue Account.

4. Categories

Questions usually require the treatment to be shown in the accounts of the firm paying the royalty and may be categorised into the following groups:

(a) Straightforward royalties with few problems;
(b) royalties with a minimum rent and the right to recoup shortworkings;
(c) royalties with sub-royalties (which involve both Royalties Payable and Receivable in the same books of account).

5. Straightforward case

(a) When the royalty becomes due: *debit* Royalty Account; *credit* landlord (or patentee or lessee).

(b) When the royalty is paid: *debit* landlord; *credit* bank.
(c) At the end of financial period: *credit* Royalty Account; *debit* Manufacturing Account, or Revenue Account.

Example

A landlord grants a lease to the Pald Mining Company under the terms of which a royalty of £5 per tonne is payable on the output.

The output during the first *three* years was as follows: year 1: 10,000 tonnes; year 2: 20,000 tonnes; year 3: 24,000 tonnes.

The financial year ends on 31 December and all sums due are paid on that date each year. Show the accounting entries to record the above in the books of the company.

Answer

ROYALTY ACCOUNT

Year 1	£	*Year 1*	£
Dec. 31 Landlord	50,000	Dec. 31 Manufac-	
		turing A/c	50,000
		or	
		(Mineworking A/c)	
		or (Product A/c)	
Year 2	£	*Year 2*	£
Dec. 31 Landlord	100,000	Dec. 31 as above	100,000
Year 3	£	*Year 3*	£
Dec. 31 Landlord	120,000	Dec. 31 as above	120,000

LANDLORD

Year 1	£	*Year 1*	£
Dec. 31 Bank	50,000	Dec. 31 Royalty	50,000
Year 2	£	*Year 2*	£
Dec. 31 Bank	100,000	Dec. 31 Royalty	100,000
Year 3	£	*Year 3*	£
Dec. 31 Bank	120,000	Dec. 31 Royalty	120,000

6. Royalties with minimum rent and right to recoup shortworkings

Sinking a mine to work mineral deposits is often a lengthy

process and the landowner may not be prepared to wait for a reward until ore extraction actually begins. To offer a reward to the person from whom the mine has been leased (or rented) while at the same time avoiding hardships to the producer, agreements are sometimes made to guarantee the landlord (or lessor) a minimum rent. Such a rent becomes payable even if no ore is extracted.

Such agreements often contain a provision that if the *rent due* (calculated on the tonnage produced) does not reach the minimum amount, the minimum will be payable but the difference or deficiency may be carried forward and deducted from the payment of future royalties.

These agreements are referred to as a *right to recoup shortworkings*, and usually this right only extends over a limited period (often five years).

PROCEDURE:

(a) Where the royalty is *less* than the minimum rent:
  (i) Always debit the Royalty Account with the true charge for the actual tonnage extended. This will later be transferred to Production Account.
  (ii) Always credit the landlord with the minimum rent.
  (iii) Always debit Shortworkings Account with the amount of the shortworkings. Until such time as the right to recoup shortworkings expires Shortworkings Account is an asset — and appears as a Current Asset on the Balance Sheet. When the right to recoup expires the amount left on the Shortworkings Account becomes a loss and must be written off.
  (iv) When the landlord is paid debit landlord and credit Bank Account.

(b) *When the royalty* exceeds *the minimum rent*:
  (i) *debit* Royalty and *credit* landlord. If there is already a *debit* balance on the Shortworkings Account this will be followed by:
  (ii) *debit* landlord (to the extent of shortworkings, but limited so as to leave an amount equal to the minimum rent);
  (iii) *credit* Shortworkings Recoverable Account.

NOTE: When the right to recoup shortworkings expires: (1) *debit*

Shortworkings Irrecoverable Account (ultimately this will be transferred to Profit and Loss Account); (2) *credit* Shortworkings Recoverable Account.

(c) *General points to note.*

(i) Once the shortworkings balance has been eliminated, the landlord will receive in any one year (until another deficient year arises), the full royalty.

(ii) When the time limit for recouping shortworkings has expired, simply treat royalties for subsequent years as if no right to recoup exists. The shortworkings irrecoverable are at once written off to Profit and Loss Account.

(iii) Shortworkings Recoverable Account should never have a *credit* balance (unless there is an exceptional agreement, e.g. to anticipate shortworkings in future years).

Example

A landlord grants a lease to the Pald Mining Co. A royalty of £5 per tonne is payable with a minimum rent of £80,000 per annum. Shortworkings are recoupable during the year following the year of deficiency only.

The financial year ends on 31 December and output was as follows:

Year 1, 10,000 tonnes; year 2, 20,000 tonnes; year 3, 24,000 tonnes.

Answer

ROYALTY ACCOUNT

	£		£
Year 1 Landlord	50,000	Year 1 Manufacturing A/c	50,000
Year 2 Landlord	100,000	Year 2 Manufacturing A/c	100,000
Year 3 Landlord	120,000	Year 3 Manufacturing A/c	120,000

LANDLORD

	£		£
Year 1 Bank	80,000	Year 1 Royalty and Shortworkings	80,000
	£		£
Year 2 Shortworkings (recouped)	20,000	Year 2 Royalty	100,000
Year 2 Bank	80,000		
	£100,000		£100,000
Year 3 Bank	£120,000	Year 3 Royalty	£120,000

SHORTWORKINGS RECOVERABLE ACCOUNT

	£		£
Year 1 Landlord	50,000	Year 1 Balance c/f	50,000
Year 2 Balance b/f	50,000	Year 2 Landlord	20,000
		Year 2 Shortworkings irrecoverable	30,000
	£50,000		£50,000

SHORTWORKINGS IRRECOVERABLE

	£		£
Year 2 Shortworkings	30,000	Year 2 P & L A/c	30,000

7. Sub-royalties

If a right to sub-let (sub-lease) exists then the entries in the books of the lessee in respect of royalties receivable are the reverse of those entries for royalties payable. Should the sub-letting be at a higher rate than that payable by the lessee to his landlord, then such an excess must be treated as a profit to be credited to Profit and Loss Account. Otherwise the amount receivable from sub-letting is credited to the Manufacturing Account — or Production Account — against the royalty payable by the lessee, since the latter accounts to the landlord *for the royalty on the whole output, i.e. the output of all firms engaged in the process.*

Open separate accounts for royalty payable and royalty receivable, the net royalty payable being transferred to the debit of the Manufacturing Account.

If the right to recoup exists then a Shortworkings Allowable Account can be introduced to cope with the sub-letting.

Progress test 26

1. What is a royalty? **(1)**

2. Explain what is meant by a minimum rent. **(4)** and **(6)**

3. What is a sub-royalty? **(7)**

4. What are shortworkings? **(6)**

5. Outline the accounting procedure adopted when royalty is *less* than the minimum rent. (6)

6. Outline the accounting procedure adopted when royalty *exceeds* the minimum rent. (6)

7. Explain the treatment of a balance on Shortworkings Account when the time limit for recouping shortworkings has expired. (6)

8. Under what conditions is it possible for a *credit* balance to exist on a Shortworkings Recoverable Account? (6)

9. When royalties have been paid how would you treat them in final accounts? (2)

10. If royalties are received how would they be treated in final accounts? (3)

Specimen questions

1. Butcher owned the patent of a safety lock. He granted Quill & Co. a licence for seven years to manufacture and sell the lock on the following terms.

   (a) Quill & Co. to pay to Butcher a royalty of 25p for each lock sold with a minimum annual payment of £2,500. Accounts to be settled annually on 31 December.
   (b) If in any year the royalties calculated on locks sold amounted to less than £2,500, Quill & Co. to have the right to deduct the deficiency from the royalties payable in excess of that sum in the two following years.

   The number of locks sold was as follows:

Year ended 31 December 19_4	8,000
Year ended 31 December 19_5	9,000
Year ended 31 December 19_6	11,000
Year ended 31 December 19_7	18,000

Show the ledger accounts necessary to record the above royalty transactions in the books of Quill & Co which are closed annually on 31 December.

2. Shipton, who had patented an automatic door closer, granted Doors Ltd a licence for ten years to manufacture and sell the closer on the following terms.

(a) Doors Ltd to pay a royalty of £1 for every closer sold with a minimum payment of £500 per annum. Calculations to be made annually as on 31 December and payment to be made on 31 January.

(b) If, for any year, the royalties calculated on closers sold amount to less than £500, Doors Ltd may set off the deficiency against royalties payable in excess of that sum in the next two years.

With effect from the end of the second year the agreement was varied and a minimum annual payment of £400 was substituted for £500, the other terms of the agreement remaining unchanged.

The numbers of closers sold were:

Year ended 31 December 19_2	200
Year ended 31 December 19_3	400
Year ended 31 December 19_4	600
Year ended 31 December 19_5	500

You are required to show the ledger accounts recording the above transactions in respect of royalties in the books of Doors Ltd which are closed annually on 31 December.

3. On 1 January 19_1, CVN Ltd, patentees of a new type of electric razor, granted to SRB Ltd a licence to manufacture and sell razors.

By the terms of the licence SRB Ltd was to pay a royalty of £1 per razor sold, subject to a minimum payment of £16,000 per annum, to be paid annually on 31 December. Should the royalties, calculated on the number of razors sold, be less than

£16,000 in any year, the deficiency could be set off against royalties in excess of £16,000 in either of the next two succeeding years.

The number of razors sold was as follows:

19_1	12,000
19_2	14,400
19_3	19,200

Payments to CVN Ltd were made punctually on the due dates. The annual accounts of SRB Ltd are made up to 31 December in each year. You are required to show the entries in the ledger of SRB Ltd.

4.   The Gwennap Manufacturing Co. Ltd has a licence to manufacture hair-dryers from Weissblau GmbH of Stuttgart. This gives Gwennap the sole manufacturing rights for the dryer in the United Kingdom in return for a royalty of £1 per unit on all such dryers made in the country.

With the approval of Weissblau, Gwennap grants a sub-licence to Wendron Ltd on 1 April 19_1 at a royalty of £1,25 per unit *sold*. This agreement specifies a minimum payment of £5,000 in each year, with a right to recoup any shortworkings from royalties due in excess of £5,000 per annum in the two trading years immediately following that in which the shortworkings arise.

The relevant sales and output figures for the years ending 3 March are:

	Output in units		Sales in units
	Gwennap	Wendron	Wendron
19_2	10,500	2,000	1,600
19_3	14,000	6,000	4,400
19_4	15,000	10,000	5,600
19_5	12,000	3,000	6,400

You are required to prepare:

(a) the Royalties Payable to Weissblau Account in the books of Gwennap;
(b) the Royalties Payable Account in the books of Wendron;
(c) the Shortworkings Account in the books of Wendron.

5. I. Wright is an author whose income is derived mainly from royalties based on the number of his books sold. He also receives fees for articles and features which he writes for magazines and periodicals. Two of his books have been reproduced in instalments by a newspaper which pays serialisation fees to his publisher who then pays Wright a proportion of these fees. He also derives some income from publicity activities and from lecturing. He carries out his writing activities in a purpose-equipped study room at his home. His accounting year ended on 31 May 19_2, for which the following information is available:

	£
Royalties received (including £900 advance royalties)	23,650
Fees received for articles published	8,000
Serialisation fees received	5,400
Fees received for publicity activities	2,734
Fees received for lecturing	250

EXPENSES:

Rates £440; heating and lighting £916; postage £414; stationery £659; telephone charges £762; secretarial expenses £6,866; travelling expenses £3,427; photocopying expenses £640; fees paid to artist for book illustrations £715; insurance £308; subscriptions £296; miscellaneous expenses £691.

Other information:

Drawings £21,547; office equipment at 1 June 19_1 £1,650 (cost price £2,200); office furniture at 1 June 19_1 £480 (cost price £600); bank balance at 31 May 19_2 £2,265; cash balance at 31 May 19_2 £28; Capital Account at 1 June 19_1 £2,070.

The following matters are to be taken into account.

(a) When invoices are received which include combined business and private expenses, it is Wright's practice to pay them out of the business bank account and to make the necessary transfers at the end of the accounting year, when he treats the private expenses as further drawings.

(b) Rates of £480 for the half year to 30 September 19_2 have not been paid. One-quarter of the total rates is attributable to his study.

(c) Electricity of £60 for the quarter ended 31 May 19_2 has not been paid. One-quarter of the total heating and lighting charges is attributable to his study room.

(d) Items of stationery unused at 31 May 19_2 amount to £123.

(e) A telephone invoice has been received, but not yet paid, as follows:

	£
Telephone rental: 3 months 1 June to 31 August 19_2	24
Telephone calls: 3 months 1 February to 31 April 19_2	270
	£294

An estimated one-third of all the telephone charges for the year are deemed to cover private purposes not connected with Wright's authorship.

(f) Insurance premiums of £72 have been prepaid. One half of the total insurance charge has been incurred for private purposes.

(g) Depreciation is to be provided on the original cost of fixed assets, office equipment at 25 per cent, office furniture at 20 per cent. There were no additions to fixed assets during the current year.

(h) Advance royalties are a fixed fee paid by publishers to authors when the contract is signed and/or when the draft manuscript is delivered to them. They are deducted from royalties later, but if the contract proves abortive they are returnable. They should be shown in a note to the Balance Sheet as a 'Contingent Liability £900'. A contingent liability is one that will only take effect if some unfortunate contingency arises to prevent completion of the book.

(i) Publicity fees include a total amount of £456, being reimbursement of travelling expenses, £370, and of miscellaneous expenses, £86, incurred by Wright in carrying out these activities. Reduce the fees by £456 and the expenses concerned by the amounts shown.

Prepare the Profit and Loss account for Wright for the year ended 31 May 19_2 and his Balance Sheet at that date.

27
Cash flow statements

NOTE: In this chapter we introduce the notation £1K for £1,000 and/or £000s for columns of figures.

1. Importance of cash

Although acquiring assets and incurring liabilities play a prominent part in accounting, cash itself is still very important. The amounts received, paid out and left to help run the business are of great significance. Many businesses fail because they have insufficient cash to meet their commitments. Other businesses cannot increase sales because cash is not available for the extra expenditure needed in such an operation.

2. Cash flow

Every trading transaction ultimately generates or absorbs cash.

(a) Sales of £1,000 must eventually result in an inflow of cash of £1,000. Should the sale be on credit a debtor of £1,000 will first be created but when the debtor eventually settles, cash of £1,000 is received. Should there be a reduction from the £1,000 for any reason, e.g. returns, allowances, bad debts or discounts allowed, these reductions should be made from the sale; in this way the net sales should always be exactly the same as the cash eventually received.

(b) Purchases of £600 will result in an outflow of cash of £600 or a liability in the form of a creditor might first be created. The creditor will ultimately be paid when an outflow of cash takes place. Should there be any deductions for returns, allowances or discounts received, these should be deducted so that net purchases exactly equal cash paid.

(c) Expenses follow the same pattern. Cash paid must eventually be the same as the expense itself (depreciation is a different matter — *see* 10), so that expenses of £100 must involve an outflow of cash of £100.

The main purpose of a cash flow statement is to help us to understand what funds have become available to a business and how they have been used.

3. Net profit as a measure of net cash inflow

If the foregoing three examples are brought together it can be seen that there will be extra cash (or a net cash inflow) of £300 e.g.:

Amount of cash from sales	£1,000
Less Purchase and expenses	700
	£300

Looked at in another way, this figure is the net profit resulting from the transactions:

Sales	£1,000
Less Purchases	600
Gross profit	400
Less Expenses	100
Net profit	£300

Hence it can be stated that net profit is a measure of net cash inflow. If we have made a profit we should have had an inflow of cash of an amount equivalent to the net profit.

4. Proprietor's drawings

The equation that net profit equals a similar inflow of cash assumes that nothing was taken out of the business by the owner. If cash is taken out as drawings, an outflow of cash occurs. Thus drawings of £180 in the above example, would mean that only £120 would be left as the profit retained. Other movements of cash could have had the same effect. For example if we spend some of the cash generated by profitable activities on new equipment the funds will not be available in the system; they will have been used to expand the business.

5. Cash flow statements

A simple cash flow statement gives the cash at the commencement of the period, the amount received and paid during the period and the balance at the end.

If the business in question had £2,000 to start with, the cash flow statement would be:

Cash at start	£2,000
Add Net profit	300
	2,300
Less Drawings	180
Cash at end	£2,120

As it is the retained profit, which will increase the cash during the period, an alternative way of presenting the cash flow statement would be:

Cash at start	£2,000
Add Retained profit	120
Cash at end	£2,120

6. Effect of delaying settlement

Net profit is always treated as an inflow of cash, whether or not all the transactions giving rise to the profit have been settled for cash. Profit which does not give rise to an increase in cash flow is reflected as either an increase in other assets, particularly stock or debtors, or as a decrease in liabilities.

Rather than attempt to break down the profit according to its effect on cash and other assets, these other assets and liabilities are adjusted.

7. Debtors

Profit may be reflected as an *increase* in debtors and such an increase may be viewed as:

(a) a decrease in receipt of cash, or
(b) an investment of the cash due to be received in 'debtors'.

(a) is easy to follow, but **(b)** is only evident if we look at profits.

If profit has been viewed as a net cash inflow, there must have been an outflow of cash to allow for the increase in debtors. The granting of credit to a debtor is a voluntary decision by us to invest some of our cash in their business, for a limited period. Of course if they do not pay it can quickly become an involuntary decision to prolong the use of our funds in their business.

Using the same figures but assuming that there was a debtor of £100 at the end of the period, cash would be lower by this figure, and the cash flow would be:

Cash at start	£2,000
Add retained profit	120
	2,120
Less outflow for debtor	100
Cash at end	£2,020

NOTE: The £100 is the increase in the 'debtors' during the period, i.e. from 'nil' to £100.

8.   Creditors

An increase in creditors is equivalent to an inflow of cash, because purchases exceed the cash paid to suppliers. This time it is the creditor who has voluntarily decided to invest some of his funds in our business. We are using the creditor's capital.

Putting it another way, if a liability is created, cash should have been received to give rise to that liability.

Using the same figures, if a creditor of £80 had not been paid at the end of the period, cash would be £2,100 made up as follows:

Cash at start	£2,000
Add retained profit	120
Increase in creditors	80
	2,200
Less increase in debtors	100
Cash at end	£2,100

NOTE: The expression *'increase in creditors'* has been used. A decrease or payment of creditors would result in an outflow of cash.

9.   Variation of levels of stock-in-trade

Any increase (or decrease) in the value of stock is reflected by a corresponding decrease (or increase) in profit, and an adjustment is necessary in the cash flow statement to account for the effect on profit of these differences.

When an *increase* in stock occurs it is considered that an outflow of cash was necessary to acquire the increase.

A *decrease* in stock results in (an equivalent amount of) cash coming into the business.

If in the previous example, closing stock had been £200, but the net profit was the same, purchases would be £800 and cash at the end £1,900. The cash flow statement would be:

Cash at start		£2,000
Add retained profit		120
increase in creditors		80
		2,200
Less increase in debtors	100	
increase in stock	200	300
Cash at end		£1,900

10.   Depreciation and net profit

If we pay out money as an expense of the business the expense appears as a deduction from profits in the Profit and Loss Account. However, deductions for depreciation reduce the net profit without any movement of cash having occurred. So if the net profit is the chief source of funds to the business and it has been reduced by depreciation we must add this reduction back to find the total funds available.

The cash inflow shown by net profit is understated when depreciation has been charged. It will therefore be necessary to adjust the figure of profit by *adding* the depreciation charge. The cash that has flowed into the business is nothing to do with the depreciation itself, it has come from the firm's profitable activities. It is just that the reduction in profits due to depreciation which we have made to arrive at the true profit figure has not reduced the cash available to the business. This cash is still available in the system.

11. Losses on sales of fixed assets

When an asset on our books is sold at less than its book value it means that our estimates of depreciation over the years have been under-estimates. The loss appears on the Profit and Loss Account and reduces the profit, although no actual cash has flowed out. Therefore, as with depreciation (in **10** above) we must add back this figure to net profit to get the 'cash available to the business'.

12. Profits on sales of fixed assets

When an asset is sold at more than its book value it means we have over- depreciated in past years. This means that our profits in earlier years were understated because of excessive depreciation and the Inland Revenue requires us to add back this amount to the current year's profit figure. As no money has usually come in (the adjustment being part of some other transaction, and only made to clear the old asset off our books) we must deduct this amount from the net profit to find the correct 'funds becoming available'. This part of the net profit did not become available in cash form. It became available as part of a new capital asset (*see* **13** below).

13. Capital movements

Any movement of capital assets into or out of the business is going to represent either a decrease of funds or an increase in funds. We may list:

(a) When fixed assets or goodwill are acquired they involve an outflow of cash.

(b) Conversely a sale of fixed assets during the period would be an inflow of cash equal to the proceeds of the sale.

(c) Money borrowed on loan during the period would be regarded as an inflow of cash.

(d) The repayment of a loan during the period would be regarded as an outflow of cash.

(e) New capital introduced by the proprietor would be an inflow of cash.

(f) Capital withdrawn by the proprietor, and ordinary 'drawings in expectation of profits made' represents a loss of funds (i.e. an application of funds).

14. Examples of cash flow statements

Consider the following Balance Sheets.

Example 1

BALANCE SHEET OF A. GREEN AT 31 DECEMBER 19_5

Fixed assets		£K	Capital		£K
At cost		25	At start		20
Less Depreciation		9	*Add* Net profit	16	
		16	*Less* Drawings	6	
Current assets					10
Stock	13				30
Debtors	9		Loan A/c		–
Bank	8		Current Liabilities		
		30	Creditors		16
		£46			£46

BALANCE SHEET OF A. GREEN AT 31 DECEMBER 19_6

Fixed assets		£K	Capital		£K
At cost		43	At start		30
Less Depreciation		12	*Add* Net profit	15	
		31	*Less* Drawings	9	
Current assets					6
Stock	18				36
Debtors	14		Loan		10
Bank	1		Current liabilities		
		33	Creditors		18
		£64			£64

Required: a statement of Sources and Application of Funds, for the year 19_6.

The answer may be shown either as a single statement or presented on two sides of an account, as follows.

(a) Using a tabulated presentation we can produce the following.

	£K
(i) The *main source* of funds is the net profit of	15

To this must be added the depreciation charge for the year, because although this figure is deducted from the net profit no outlay of cash occurred, and the money for this depreciation is still available. If the figure for depreciation is not given, it can, in the absence of any asset sales, be

c/f 15

b/f   15

found by deducting the opening provision for depreciation from the closing figure.

In this example £12K is the closing figure and £9K the opening figure, giving a difference of — 3

The adjusted 'profit' figure is therefore — 18

So £18K of funds becomes available from profits in the year.

(ii) Look at *other sources* of funds. As there was no loan in 19_5 but £10K in 19_6, the new loan is a source of funds — 10

Current liabilities have increased from £16K to £18K thus creating a source of funds of — 2

This is the result of the generosity of our creditors. Total of all sources of funds is therefore — £30K

£K

(iii) How were these funds used? Firstly, drawings took — 9

The acquisition of fixed assets during the year is represented by the difference between the 19_5 figure of £25K and the 19_6 figure of £43K, namely — 18

Current assets: stock has increased from £13K to £18K — 5

Debtors have increased from £9K to £14K, an application of funds of — 5

£37K

Applications exceed sources by £7K, suggesting a decrease in cash or bank of the same amount, and a glance at the question will confirm the decrease in the bank balance from £8K to £1K, i.e. £7K.

(b) Using the orthodox account method of presentation we would show:

SOURCES AND APPLICATION OF FUNDS FOR THE YEAR TO 31 DEC. 19_6

Sources			*Applications*	
		£K		*£K*
Net profit	15		Drawings	9
Add Depreciation	3		Fixed assets acquired	18
		18	Increase in stock	5
Proceeds of new loan		10	Increase in debtors	5
Increase in creditors		2		
		30		37
Add decrease in bank		7		
		£37		£37

Example 2

Involving the sale of an asset.

From the following abridged Balance Sheets of Henry Bloggs prepare a Statement of Sources and Application of Funds for the year ended 31 December 19_5.

	31 Dec. 19_4 £K		31 Dec. 19_5 £K
Capital	157		219
Premises	12		80
Machinery (at cost) 163		163	
Less Depreciation 42		47	
	121		116
Bank	24		23
	£157		£219

During the year:

(a) Bloggs introduced £68K from his private resources which was used to acquire new premises;

(b) machinery which cost £15K and on which depreciation of £6K had been provided was sold for £7K;

(c) Bloggs withdrew £8K for his personal use.

Answer

First step: find the profit. This we do by the increased net worth method.

	£K
Net worth at end of year (capital)	219
Net worth at start of year (capital)	157
Apparent increase in net worth	62
But drawings taken (add back)	8
	70
Less Extra capital from private funds	68
Net profit	£2K

(NOTE: This is a very small profit, and as Bloggs drew £8K he really lived on his capital during the year to the tune of £6K.)

Second step: calculate the depreciation.
The charge for depreciation may be found by reconstructing the

Provision for Deprecation Account. Three items are known: opening balance, £42K; closing balance, £47K; accumulated depreciation on asset sold, £6K. Thus the charge for the year is found by completing the equation:

PROVISION FOR DEPRECIATION ACCOUNT

	£K		£K
Asset A/c transfer		Balance b/f	42
sale	6	∴ Depreciation for the	
Balance c/d	47	year is	11
	£53K		£53K
		Balance b/d	47

To find the over- or under- provision for depreciation, the Sale of Asset a/c can be reconstructed as follows:

SALE OF ASSET ACCOUNT

	£K		£K
Asset a/c transfer		Provision for Depreciation	
cost	15	A/c	6
		Bank (proceeds of sale)	7
		Under-provision of	
		depreciation	2
	£15K		£15K

It would appear that no assets have been acquired during the year since the figure for machinery of £163K is the same at the end as at the beginning of the year. However we are informed that machines which cost £15K were sold during the year. It must therefore follow that machinery costing £15K was bought during the year. Among the inflow cash must be included the proceeds from the sale of machinery £7K.

STATEMENT OF SOURCES AND APPLICATION OF FUNDS
31 DEC. 19_5

Sources:	£K	£K
Net profit as calculated	2	
Add Depreciation	11	
Add Loss on sale of asset (or under-provision of depreciation)	2	
		15
Capital introduced		68
Proceeds of sale of machinery		7
Total Sources		£90K
Applications:		
Drawings	8	
Premises	68	
New machinery acquired	15	
		£91K
Excess of applications over sources of funds becoming available		$\frac{K}{1}$
Financed by:		
Decrease in liquid resources (bank)		1

---

15. Working capital

Working capital consists of current assets less current liabilities. (*See* Chapter 28.) In cash flow statements cash or bank is *not* included, the changes in cash or bank being reserved to the last line of the cash flow statement so working capital is then defined as stock and debtors less creditors.

16. Alternative method of presentation

Very often working capital is substituted for stock, debtors and creditors. A simple rule is:

(a) an increase in working capital is an *application*. It means we have increased assets relative to liabilities.
(b) a decrease in working capital is a *source* of funds. It means we have increased the use of our creditors' funds relative to assets.

Using this formula, Example 1 (A. Green's books) can be presented in the following form:

Calculation of working capital:

	31 Dec. 19_5	31 Dec. 19_6
	£K	£K
Stock	13	18
Debtors	9	14
	22	32
Less Creditors	16	18
	£6K	£14K

An increase of £8K.

Sources:	£K	£K
Net profit (as adjusted)	18	
Proceeds of new loan	10	
		28
Applications:		
Drawings	9	
Fixed assets acquired	18	
Increase in working capital	8	
		35
Decrease in cash		£7K

17. Working Capital Flow Statements

In some respects working capital is the most important factor in a business. Its adequacy ensures the continuing success of the enterprise and often bankruptcies and insolvencies have been attributed to the lack of it. Viewed as the cycle of current assets from cash to stock, to debtors and back to cash, it can be regarded as cash going through the process of working the fixed assets of the business.

Creditors have some claim on the cash of the business so cash required for the payment of creditors should be included in the calculation of the working capital available — hence the deduction of creditors from current assets to find working capital (often called 'net working capital').

When the business is in a state of equilibrium, fixed assets remain constant and so do the means of financing them, i.e. by loans, etc. Any additional activity in the business involves only the magnitude of the working capital, hence a funds flow statement is required to show how the cash has been obtained to finance the extra working capital, or if there is a decrease, to show how the cash thus resulting has been utilised.

When any new funds are available to the business, the statement shows how much of the new funds went to fixed capital and how much to working capital.

As a Working Funds Statement the figures would appear as follows:

	£K	£K
Sources of Funds:		
Internally generated, profit (as adjusted)	18	
Externally generated, proceeds of new loan	10	
		28
Application of Funds:		
Drawings	9	
Acquisition of fixed assets	18	
		27
		£1K

Actual increase in working capital		
from £6K to £14K		£8K
Amount available from above	1K	
Decrease in cash	7K	
Financing of working capital thus achieved		£8K

18. Points to remember

(a) An application of funds arises from:
   (i) an *increase* in debtors or stock;
  (ii) an increase in *working* capital;
 (iii) an increase in *assets or goodwill*;
  (iv) a *decrease* in creditors;
   (v) *any loan repaid*;
  (vi) drawings by the proprietor or dividends paid to shareholders;
 (vii) withdrawal of capital;
(viii) an adjustment to profits which have been increased by a 'profit on sale of an asset'.

(b) A source of funds arises from:
  (i) a *decrease* in debtors or stock;
 (ii) a decrease in working capital;

(iii) an *increase* in creditors;
(iv) any sums borrowed;
(v) any new capital introduced;
(vi) any *sale of assets*;
(vii) an adjustment to profits which have been reduced by a charge for depreciation.

Progress test 27

1. What is the main purpose of a cash flow statement? (2)

2. Why is net profit treated as an inflow of cash? (3)

3. What is the effect on cash flow of an increase in each of the following items: (*a*) debtors; (*b*) creditors; (*c*) stock? (7–9)

4. How is the annual charge for depreciation dealt with in the cash flow statement? (10)

5. How are loans to a business dealt with (*a*) when first made, and (*b*) when repaid? (13)

6. When an asset is sold, how are the following dealt with?
(a) Profit on sale.
(b) Loss on sale.
(c) Proceeds of sale. (11–13)

7. In what respects does a Working Capital Flow Statement differ from a cash flow statement? (17)

Specimen questions

1. The Chichester Sailing School was very active in the 19_6 season but finance to extend its business was not easy to find.
The Balance Sheets for 19_5 and 19_6 were:

	30.9._5	30.9._6		30.9._5	30.9._6
	£	£		£	£
Sailing dinghies	20,000	40,000	Capital	8,500	14,000
Less: Depreciation	15,000	20,000	Creditors	4,000	5,000
	5,000	20,000	Bank overdraft		4,500
Stock	1,000	2,000			
Debtors	500	1,500			
Bank	6,000	–			
	£12,500	23,500		£12,500	23,500

The operating figures summarised for 19_6 were:

School fees and sales		26,500
Wages	10,000	
General overheads	6,000	
Depreciation	5,000	
		21,000
Net profit		£5,500

Draw up a Sources and Applications Statement to show how a bank balance of £6,000 at the start has been converted into an overdraft at the end of 19_6 of £4,500.

2. Balance Sheets of E. Hatt, a grocer, at 31 May 19_4 and 31 May 19_5 are reproduced below, together with a summary of Mr Hatt's Capital Account for the year ended 31 May 19_5.

E. HATT
BALANCE SHEETS AT 31 MAY

	19_4	19_5		19_4	19_5
	£	£		£	£
Fixed assets			Capital	54,000	55,000
(at cost)	50,000	65,000	Creditors	25,000	35,000
Less:					
Depreciation	20,000	25,000			
	30,000	40,000			
Stock	20,000	35,000			
Debtors	14,000	11,000			
Bank	15,000	4,000			
	£79,000	90,000		£79,000	90,000

CAPITAL ACCOUNT FOR THE YEAR ENDED 31 MAY 19_5

	£
Opening balance	54,000
Add: Net profit for year	25,000
	79,000
Less: Drawings	24,000
	£55,000

Prepare a Cash Flow Statement for the year.

3. H. Pool's summarised Balance Sheets at 31 May 19_1 and 19_2 are as follows.

		19_1		*19_2*
Fixed assets:	£	£	£	£
Motor vehicles, at cost	10,500		18,500	
Less Depreciation	3,900		6,300	
		6,600		12,200
Furniture, at cost	1,500		1,500	
Less Depreciation	900		1,050	
		600		450
		7,200		12,650
Current assets:				
Stocks	12,100		14,600	
Debtors	800		2,000	
Bank	9,000		–	
	21,900		16,600	
Less Current liabilities:				
Creditors	3,600		4,000	
Bank overdraft	–		7,600	
	3,600		11,600	
		18,300		5,000
		£25,500		£17,650

Financed by:		
Capital	15,000	15,500
Net profit for the year	9,000	12,150
Less Drawings	8,500	10,000
	500	2,150
	15,500	17,650
Loan	10,000	–
	£25,500	£17,650

During the year to 31 May 19_2 Pool received £600 in cash for the sale of a motor vehicle which had originally cost £2,000, and had been depreciated by £1,500 at 1 June 19_1.

You are required to prepare a Source and Application of Funds Statement for the year to 31 May 19_2.

4. The Balance Sheets of Miss Phoebe, a spinner by trade, as on 31 December were as follows.

	19_5 £	19_5 £	19_4 £	19_4 £
Capital Account				
Balance at beginning of year	15,000		12,000	
Net profit for the year	27,000		11,000	
	42,000		23,000	
Less: Drawings	15,000		8,000	
		27,000		15,000
Loan — W. Shadbolt		12,000		25,000
Trade creditors		10,000		9,000
Bank overdraft		8,600		–
		£57,600		£49,000
Freehold land at cost		27,000		20,000
Spinning machines:				
Cost	1,500		1,000	
Accumulated depreciation	900		600	
		600		400
Property at Tower Green		–		2,000
Stock		12,000		8,000
Trade debtors		18,000		12,000
Balance at bank		–		6,600
		£57,600		£49,000

The only fixed asset disposed of during the year was the property at Tower Green which realised £5,000; the surplus on disposal is included in the net profit for the year.

Prepare a statement which explains in a meaningful way the reasons for the change in the balance at bank during the year.

28
Cash budgets and accounting ratios

(The notation £K for £000 has again been used in this chapter.)

1. The purpose of cash budgets

The purpose of cash budgets is to enable businesses to know the cash expected to be available at certain dates in the immediate future. They thus help management in planning financial commitments, and are prepared by estimating the total inflow of cash compared with the total outflow.

There is a similarity with Funds Flow Statements in that both deal with cash inflow and cash outflow. Budgeting, however, is concerned with projected or future estimates of cash flow.

2. Basis on which figures are computed

While complete certainty is impossible, projected future cash flows are based on:

(a) the expected activity of business;
(b) the usual cycle of cash receipts and payments;
(c) the expectation that commitments will be settled in the time agreed.

With these three factors taken into account a reasonably accurate budget can be prepared.

3. Expected activity of the business

(a) *Sales*. A forecast of sales is normally based on the previous year. It may be slightly increased or decreased according to economic circumstances.

(b) *Purchases.* These bear a certain relationship to sales, i.e. 60 per cent or 50 per cent of sales, etc.

(c) *Expenses* are divided into fixed and variable. Fixed expenses are easily determined from existing contracts, e.g. rent. Variable expenses are often a certain percentage of sales, e.g. 2 per cent or 10 per cent.

4. Usual cycle of cash receipts and payments

Once the income and expenditure have been agreed there is normally a recognised time lag before settlement is effected. Sales may be made on two months' credit terms. Purchases may be acquired on one month's credit terms. Expenses may be settled immediately or within a week.

Capital items of both receipts in the form of loans and payments in the form of acquisition of assets, are included in the cash budget at the appropriate time.

Past experience is a guide as to whether or not the terms of sales or purchases have been complied with. It is important that if the past suggests that debtors are taking longer to settle than the time allowed this factor must be accepted in the calculations.

Example

The month by month forecast of profitability of Expansion Limited for the five months August to December is given below.

				£K	
	Aug.	*Sept.*	*Oct.*	*Nov.*	*Dec.*
Materials consumed	70	80	95	110	140
Wages	32	36	36	40	44
Depreciation	6	6	6	6	6
Factory expenses	8	8	8	8	8
Rent	4	4	4	4	4
Salaries and office expenses	30	30	30	30	30
Advertising and publicity	20	20	15	10	5
Sales commission	7	8	9	11	13
	177	192	203	219	250
Sales	170	190	220	270	320
Profit (Loss)	(7)	(2)	17	51	70
Raw material stock (end-month)	70	80	85	90	90

The following additional information is given.

(a) On average payment is made to suppliers one month after delivery.
(b) There is a lag in payment of wages of a quarter month.
(c) Factory expenses are paid during the month incurred.
(d) Rent is paid quarterly on the last day of March, June, September and December.
(e) Salaries and office expenses are paid in the month in which they arise.
(f) Advertising and publicity expenditure is paid monthly but two months' credit is taken.
(g) Sales commission is paid one month in arrear.
(h) On average debtors take two months' credit.
(i) The cash balance at bank on 1 October is £50K.
(j) In December £50K will be paid for machinery.
(k) A dividend and tax thereon amounting to £10K will be paid in November.

You are required to prepare a cash budget for each of the three months to 31 December. The notes below the solution will help you.

Answer

Cash budget for period 1 October to 31 December 19__.

	Oct. £K	Nov. £K	Dec. £K
Receipts:			
Balance at bank			
Beginning of month	50	28	2
Proceeds from sales (debtors)	170	190	220
	220	218	222
Payments:			
Suppliers (for purchases)	90	100	115
Wages	36	39	43
Factory expenses	8	8	8
Salaries and office expenses	30	30	30
Advertising and publicity	20	20	15
Sales commission	8	9	11
Rent			12
Dividend and tax		10	
Acquisition of machinery			50
	£192	£216	£284
Balance at bank at end of month	£28	£2	
Overdraft at end of month			£62

(a) Proceeds of sales (debtors) is figure for two months earlier, i.e. December cash for October sales.

(b) Payment to suppliers for purchases is the figure for one month earlier. Purchases, however, need to be calculated by making adjustments for opening and closing stocks as below.

	Sept.	Oct.	Nov.
	£K	£K	£K
Material consumed	80	95	110
Add Closing stock	80	85	90
	160	180	200
Less Opening stocks	70	80	85
Purchases for month	£90	£100	£115

(c) Wages:

	Oct.	Nov.	Dec.
	£K	£K	£K
¾ of current month	27	30	33
¼ of previous month	9	9	10
Payment during month	£36	£39	£43

5. Special points to watch

(a) Some items have a regular time interval between expenditure and payment or between income and receipt of cash.

(b) Certain items, such as rent, have payments only at stated intervals and do not necessarily occur every time the cash budget is prepared.

(c) Depreciation is shown on the Revenue Account but omitted altogether from the cash budget. Acquisition of assets is shown in the cash budget during the relevant period of payment.

(d) If only cost of sales is shown in the revenue account an adjustment involving opening and closing stock is made to find the figure of purchases. It is then an easy calculation to ascertain the amount payable to suppliers.

(e) Dividends, taxation, etc., must be shown in the period they are expected to be paid.

(f) In real life it may be possible to practice *cash flow smoothing*. This is done by postponing avoidable cash payments at times of cash shortage (for example the purchase of capital equipment) until a time when cash is more plentiful. Similarly a loan to be repaid could be arranged so that payments coincide with cash surplus times rather than regular monthly payments, when cash might, or might not, be available.

6. Accounting ratios

Figures of themselves mean little; only their relationships with other features of the accounts have any significance. A profit of £100 means nothing unless the period is shown. Is it a year? Is it a week? Or is it an hour? Similarly to state that a business has liquid resources of cash of £10,000 is of little significance until the size of the business and its current liabilities are known. With no liabilities the amount would be more than adequate. If current liabilities were £100,000 and there were no debtors or stocks the amount would be quite inadequate. By expressing the relationship of current assets to current liabilities as a ratio, a clearer picture emerges. The ratio, so calculated, is a meaningful figure for management purposes. Often ratios are grouped under three main types:

(a) Revenue Account ratios (those to do with the Trading Account and Profit and Loss Account)
(b) Balance Sheet ratios
(c) financial ratios

The purpose of accounting ratios is to show the relationship of figures in the final accounts with each other in simple fractions or percentages. Such an exercise assists in the interpretation and understanding of financial statements. It is useful in suggesting trends and in particular makes easier comparisons possible, both with earlier years and with other businesses.

7. Revenue Account ratios

Certain ratios can be found from the Trading and Profit and Loss Account (or Accounts) and can throw up interesting features of any business. We will use the simple example of 'Tasty Sweets' below to bring out those points.

TRADING AND PROFIT AND LOSS ACCOUNT
FOR YEAR ENDING 31 DECEMBER 19_9

19_9		£	19_9	£
Opening Stock		5,250	Sales	139,500
Purchases	42,160		*Less* Returns	1,500
Less Returns	410		Net turnover	138,000
Net Purchases		41,750		
Total stock available		47,000		
Less Closing Stock		4,500		
Cost of stock sold		42,500		
Gross Profit		95,500		
		£138,000		£138,000
Mortgage interest		5,250	Gross Profit	95,500
Light and Heat		2,350	Rent Received	2,500
Telephone Expenses		1,460	Discount Received	350
Salaries		27,640		98,350
Insurance paid		420		
Interest paid		350		
Business rates		4,875		
Motor Vehicle Expenses		2,536		
Packaging and Selling Expenses		4,419		
		49,300		
Net Profit		49,050		
		£98,350		£98,350

(a) *Gross profit percentage and stock turnover.* These two ratios are found from the Trading Account. Their formulae are:

$$\text{Gross profit percentage} = \frac{\text{gross profit}}{\text{turnover}} \times 100$$

$$\text{Rate of stock turnover} = \frac{\text{cost of sales}}{\text{average stock at cost price}}$$

Gross profit percentage

$$\text{Gross profit percentage} = \frac{\text{gross profit}}{\text{turnover}} \times 100$$

Substituting the figures from the Trading Account we have:

$$\text{Gross profit percentage} = \frac{£95,500}{£138,000} \times 100$$

$$= \frac{9,550}{138} \%$$

$$= \underline{\underline{69.2\%}}$$

Comments on this percentage. Gross profit percentage should always be quite a high figure because we have to cover a great many overhead expenses with this gross profit. One of the commonest causes of failure in business is not taking a big enough gross profit percentage. We simply cannot keep going on a gross profit of 20 per cent — we need at least 50 per cent, and 200 per cent or 300 per cent is not uncommon. If our circumstances are so competitive that we cannot charge a high enough margin, we should leave the industry and seek a more lucrative outlet for our talents.

The important point about gross profit percentage is that it should be the same from year to year (i.e. it should be a constant) unless we ourselves are doing something to make it change (like introducing more efficient methods of working). Always compare this year's ratio with last year's. Suppose last year we were making 75 per cent gross profit percentage. What can have happened to cause the decrease? It can only be something within the Trading Account. What could it be?

(a) It could be the manager/manageress stealing the sales money.
(b) It could be some member of staff stealing the sales money. Who, on the staff, is looking like a million dollars these days? It could be our million dollars he/she is looking like!
(c) It could be that stocks are down because of (*i*) theft by the staff or (*ii*) theft by customers or (*iii*) 'passing-out' (giving of stock to friends and relations).
(d) It could be increased purchase prices which have not been passed on as increased selling prices to customers.
(e) It could be stock losses due to poor buying (perishables thrown away or slow-moving stock sold at marked-down prices). It could be skylarking in the crockery department. Anything that means a lower stock means a lower gross profit, and hence a lower gross profit percentage.

The rate of stock turnover. The rate of stock turnover can be found using either of two formulae:

$$\text{Rate of stockturn} = \frac{\text{cost of stock sold}}{\text{average stock at cost price}}$$

$$\text{Rate of stockturn} = \frac{\text{net turnover}}{\text{average stock at selling price}}$$

The point is that the two figures used must be in the same form — either both at cost price or both at selling price.

Using the cost price figures from Tasty Sweets we have:

$$\text{Rate of stockturn} = \frac{£42,500}{\text{average stock}}$$

$$\text{Average stock} = \frac{(\text{opening stock} + \text{closing stock})}{2}$$

$$= \frac{£5,250 + £4,500}{2}$$

$$= \frac{£9,750}{2}$$

$$= £4,875$$

$$\therefore \text{Rate of stockturn} = \frac{£42,500}{£4,875}$$

$$= 8.7 \text{ times a year}$$

Whether 8.7 times in a year is a reasonable rate of turnover or not depends upon the type of goods being sold. It gives us a better picture if we turn the figure into another related figure, namely the amount of time the average stock is on hand before it is sold. We can do this by dividing the rate into the number of days, weeks or months in the year. Thus:

$$\frac{12}{8.7} = 1.4 \text{ months an average item is in stock}$$

$$\frac{52}{8.7} = 6.0 \text{ weeks an average item is in stock}$$

$$\frac{365}{8.7} = 42.0 \text{ days an average item is in stock.}$$

Whether the sweets dealt in by this trader would be in a satisfactory condition after about 6 weeks in stock is a matter for management to ponder.

(b) *Profit and Loss Account ratios.* Here the important ratios are:

    (i) The net profit percentage

    (ii) The expense ratios

Net profit percentage. The formula is:

$$\text{Net profit percentage} = \frac{\text{net profit}}{\text{turnover}} \times 100$$

$$= \frac{£49,050}{£138,000} \times 100$$

$$= \frac{4,905}{138}$$

$$= 35.5\%$$

Comments on this percentage. Net profit percentage can vary enormously between firms according to the type of industry concerned and the competitive state of the industry. One wants the return one earns from risking one's capital in business to be higher than the 8–10 per cent one could earn from a safe investment in a building society or a gilt-edged security. 35 per cent is well above this level.

What was the net profit percentage last year? If we know that it was 38.5 per cent, we could ask ourselves why it has fallen this year. Provided the gross profit percentage has remained more or less the same, the fall in net profit percentage must be due to something within the Profit and Loss Account. Has a particular expense item risen considerably in the current year? We can find out by taking out expense ratios (see below). Has some source of profit we enjoyed last year (other than gross profit) fallen considerably, or even ceased to be earned for some reason? We can look at these situations. For example, if Rent Received has fallen because we had to use rooms formerly let off for our own expansion, there is nothing we can do to recover the sums lost. If we have failed to pursue possible profits we should take steps to recover them in the coming year.

Expense ratios. Expense ratios are those where we relate

particular expenses to turnover, to arrive at a percentage. Thus the salaries ratio is found by the formula:

$$\text{Salaries ratio} = \frac{\text{Salaries paid}}{\text{Turnover}} \times 100$$

$$= \frac{£27,640}{£138,000} \times 100$$

$$= \frac{2,764}{138}$$

$$= \underline{20.0\%}$$

20 per cent of our turnover was used up in salaries: suppose last year the figure was 16.5 per cent. Clearly there is a problem here. Some people collect employees, because it makes them feel powerful if they have a little empire of 'hangers on'. If extra staff have been appointed with little real effect on the expansion of the business (an increased turnover) we should want to know 'Why?'. If every expense ratio is calculated and compared with the same ratio in previous years we shall be able to pinpoint areas where action is necessary. If we cannot avoid the increases in overheads we must pass the increases on to our customers by raising prices.

The most useful expense ratios are:
  (*i*) Wages and salaries as a percentage of sales.
  (*ii*) Bad debts to sales.
  (*iii*) Discount allowed to sales.
  (*iv*) Certain selling expenses, in particular advertising, expressed as a percentage of sales.

8. Balance Sheet ratios

The interpretation of a company's or firm's Balance Sheet can reveal much about the state of health of the business to an accountant. We are familiar with many terms that enter into the discussion of any Balance Sheet, fixed assets, current assets, current liabilities, etc. Using the simple Balance Sheet below we will extend our knowledge a little by learning some of the important ratios.

BALANCE SHEET OF 'TASTY SWEETS' AS AT
31 DECEMBER 19_9

19_9	£	19_9	£
Fixed assets		*Capital*	
Premises	68,000	At start	43,332
Plant and machinery	28,500	Add net profit 49,050	
Motor vehicles	13,820	Less drawings 18,750	
Furniture, etc	9,250		30,300
	119,570		73,632
Current assets		*Long-term liabilities*	
Stock	6,500	Mortgage 50,000	
Debtors	1,850	Bank loan 5,000	
Cash at bank	5,214		55,000
Cash in hand	738		
		Current liabilities	
	14,302	Creditors	5,240
	£133,872		£133,872

(a) *Working capital ratio or current ratio.* Working capital is the capital that is left over to run the business after the fixed capital has been used to purchase the fixed assets.

The best definition of working capital is:

Working capital = current assets – current liabilities

In the case of Tasty Sweets Balance Sheet it is:

Working capital = £14,302 – £5,240
= £9,062

The more useful management figure is:

$$\text{Working capital ratio} \quad = \quad \frac{\text{current assets}}{\text{current liabilities}}$$

$$= \quad \frac{£14,302}{£5,240}$$

$$= \quad 2.7$$

There are sufficient current assets to pay the current liabilities 2.7 times.

The chief use of working capital is to keep the business working, pay wages, buy more raw materials or goods for re-sale, etc. Shortage of working capital is one of the chief problems of businesses, for these reasons. It is the working capital (particularly the cash in hand and the cash at the bank) which we use to pay off our current liabilities, i.e. our creditors. If we have insufficient working capital to pay our creditors, one who cannot be paid may start legal proceedings against us and we may finish up in the bankruptcy courts. Buying too many fixed assets and leaving ourselves too few current assets is called *over-trading*. Traditionally a reasonable ratio was 2:1, i.e. current assets being twice the current liabilities. Nowadays, however, there are many variations of this figure. It is considered wise to look closely at the composition of current assets, particularly the amount of stock compared with debtors. To see what this implies we need to consider the *liquid ratio*.

(b) *Liquid ratio* (sometimes termed quick ratio or acid test ratio) is the ratio of liquid assets to current liabilities. Liquid assets normally include all debtors and cash. Sometimes only those debts due and expected to be paid immediately are taken. It is a good test of solvency and should be at least 1:1 so that there is immediate cover for the payment of current liabilities.

The acid-test ratio formula is:

$$\text{Acid test ratio} = \frac{\text{current assets} - \text{stock}}{\text{current liabilities}}$$

it is:

$$\text{Acid test ratio} = \frac{£14,302 - £6,500}{£5,240}$$

$$= \frac{£7,802}{£5,240}$$

$$= \underline{\underline{1.5}}$$

There are sufficient liquid funds to pay the current liabilities 1.5 times.

This is a satisfactory liquid capital ratio. Accountants hold that with our liquid assets we should be able to pay all our creditors, i.e. the liquid capital ratio should be at least 1.0. However, just suppose the figures had had rather more stock in them. Say:

	£
Stock	10,500
Debtors	2,850
Cash at Bank	214
Cash in Hand	738
	14,302

We should then have had:

$$\text{Working capital ratio} = \frac{14,302}{5,240} = 2.7$$

$$\text{Liquid capital ratio} = \frac{3,802}{5,240} = 0.73$$

Clearly we have not enough liquid capital to pay all our debts, because that requires a liquid ratio of 1, and there is some chance that we could get into financial difficulties.

(c) *Ratio of current assets to fixed assets.* This ratio attempts to show clearly how the capital of the business is divided between those assets which can easily be turned into cash and those which cannot. It is sometimes referred to as the ratio between fixed capital and working capital. Different types of businesses vary considerably as to the nature of this ratio, but it is useful for comparing different companies in the same industry.

In this case we have

Current assets : Fixed assets as £14,302 : £119,570
= 1:8.4

This is rather a high ratio of fixed assets and indicates that Tasty Sweets is in a rather illiquid position.

(d) *Ratio of loan capital to equity.* Where companies are concerned this ratio is normally referred to as the capital gearing of the company. It denotes the relationship between prior-charge capital and equity capital. Prior charge capital simply refers to capital obtained in such a way as to oblige the company to pay something for its use before Ordinary Shares can be paid a dividend.

At one time Preference Shares were included but they are now rapidly disappearing from the financial scene leaving only loans, whether debentures or unsecured loan stock, as prior-charge capital.

(i) *Low gearing.* Where Ordinary Shares (i.e. equity capital) exceed loans and the ratio is 1 to something more than 1, it is said that there is low gearing of the company's capital.

(ii) *High gearing.* Where loans exceed Ordinary Shares so that the ratio is 1 to something less than 1, it is said that a state of high gearing operates in the capital structure.

The same idea can be applied to sole traders and partnerships, in that a proprietor who does not contribute much capital personally, and does not plough back profits into the business to build up a reasonable capital stake in the business is always in a vulnerable position. Most of the profit achieved will be creamed off by the bankers or others supplying the finance. In our case the ratio is

$$\text{Loans : owner's capital as £55,000 : £73,632}$$
$$= 1 : 1.3$$

The 'gearing' is therefore on the low side and the proprietor has a reasonable stake in the business.

9. Financial ratios

Financial ratios seek to evaluate how the business is doing compared with other businesses and with alternative uses of the resources employed in it. Thus if the assets employed appear to be producing a poor return it might be better to seek some alternative, and more lucrative, use of them. Some of the chief ratios used are described below, but students are warned that different accountants argue for different definitions in this area, and those given may be found in slightly different forms elsewhere.

(a) *The return on capital employed* (ROCE) When we discover the return on capital employed we are to some extent comparing our business with other similar businesses (in so far as we can discover their figures). There are a variety of measures used (not everyone has the same ideas about what we should include under the term 'capital employed'). For example, if we look at any Balance Sheet it is a simple fact that whatever assets we have on the assets side have been obtained with the capital listed on the other side. For example, in the Balance Sheet of Tasty Sweets the total assets are worth £133,872. How have these been obtained? The answer is that the proprietor originally provided £43,332 and has also ploughed in profits earned worth £30,300, making the total of the proprietor's contribution £73,632. Then we also used capital from a building society or bank mortgage, and a bank loan totalling £55,000, and we managed to persuade creditors to lend us £5,240. All these various bits of capital financed the purchase of the assets.

It is usual to leave out the creditors (because to some extent anyway they are balanced up by the debtors on the other side who are using *our* capital to finance their business activities). It is also usual to average out the profits ploughed back and say, 'Well, really, we've only had the use of that capital for half the year on average'. A similar averaging process would be necessary if we borrowed the long-term liabilities at some time during the year. However, we will pretend both the Bank Loan and the mortgage have been used for the whole year.

The capital employed is therefore worked out as follows:

Capital employed = £43,332 + £15,150 + £55,000
  = £113,482

The return on capital employed is the profit we made in the year expressed as a percentage of that capital: this profit is £49,050. However, as we are counting the loan and the mortgage as part of the capital employed we must include the interest paid on these amounts as part of the profit — those figures were £575 and £5,250 respectively. This makes the full profit £49,050 + £350 + £5,250 = £54,650. Therefore we have:

$$\text{Return on capital employed} = \frac{£54,650}{£113,482} \times 100$$

$$= \underline{\underline{48.2\%}}$$

This appears to be a very satisfactory return — comparing it, for example with the same capital invested in gilt-edged securities where we might get about 9 per cent. It seems it is well worthwhile being in business!

(b) *Return on capital invested* (ROCI). A more subtle ratio, which applies more particularly to the proprietor, is to work out the return on capital invested. This term refers to the capital invested by the proprietor at the start of the year. As with all sophisticated ratios we have to think carefully about the figures we are using and perhaps adapt them if necessary. The profit earned was

£49,050 on original capital of £43,332 invested at the start of the year. However, to find out whether it has really been worthwhile being in business we have to see what extra benefit the proprietor is gaining. When we take up the opportunity of being self-employed we give up any chance of doing other things and these lost opportunities mean we have lost money. Thus, if we cannot now take a job, we have lost the opportunity to earn wages. We have also lost the opportunity of putting £43,332 in a safe bank account earning a high rate of interest. These losses are called the *opportunity cost* of being self-employed — the lost opportunities.

What were the opportunity costs to the proprietor of Tasty Sweets? We do not know, but let us imagine that the proprietor of Tasty Sweets could have earned £8,500 a year as the manager of a sweet shop, and could have invested his/her savings in a high interest account earning 9.5 per cent. The opportunity cost is therefore £8,500 + £4,117 (the interest calculated at 9.5 per cent on £43,332 if it had been invested instead of being used in the business). This means the extra profit actually earned by being in business is:

$$£49,050 - £12,617 = £36,433$$

Therefore the return on capital invested (ROCI) is:

$$\text{ROCI} = \frac{\text{net profit} - \text{opportunity cost}}{\text{capital at start}} \times 100$$

$$= \frac{£49,050 - £12,617}{£43,332} \times 100$$

$$= \frac{£36,433}{£43,332} \times 100$$

$$= \underline{84.1\%}$$

Clearly it is well worth while being in business.

(c) *Average collection period* is the time taken to collect money from the debtors. Naturally some debtors pay earlier than others so the average period must be taken.

There are two calculations normally undertaken — the first is simply:

$$\frac{\text{Sales per year}}{\text{Total debtors}}$$

Total debtors are difficult to quantify precisely but are often taken as the average of debtors at beginning of the period and debtors at the end. Thus:

Sales	£100,000
Debtors: opening	20,000
closing	30,000 an average of £25,000
thus	$\dfrac{£100,000}{£25,000} = 4$

This figure indicates that debtors are collected on an average four times a year and the average collection period is three months, i.e. 12/4 months.

As an alternative, the formula can be expressed as:

$$\frac{\text{Debtors x 52}}{\text{Sales}}$$

to give the number of weeks. In this example the figures would be

$$\frac{25,000 \times 52}{100,000} = 13 \text{ weeks}$$

(d) *Average payment period* refers to the time taken to pay the trade creditors and is very similar to the previous calculation.

Number of time creditors paid during the year is expressed as the fraction:

$$\frac{\text{Purchases per year}}{\text{Average creditors}}$$

or to find the average period taken in weeks use the formula:

$$\frac{\text{Creditors x 52}}{\text{Purchases}}$$

10. Construction of Balance Sheet from given data and ratios
From a few basic items and several ratios a Balance Sheet can be reconstructed as shown in the following example.

Example _____

Closing stock £6,000, sales £44,000, net profit £4,400, average collection period 6.5 weeks, current ratio 3:2, a net profit of 10 per cent of shareholders' equity at end. No appropriation of profit but at commencement of year Profit and Loss Account had a debit balance of £400. Creditors at end £10,000. Fixed assets and balance at bank also appear in the Balance Sheet.

First step is to find debtors.

Formula:

$$\frac{\text{Debtors} \times 52}{\text{Sales}} = 6.5, \text{ or Debtors} = \frac{6.5}{52} \times \text{Sales}$$

so Debtors $= \frac{6.5}{52} \times £44,000$, namely £5,500.

Next find total current assets from ratio 3:2. As Creditors = £10,000 current assets must be £15,000. Now find balance at bank: stock £6,000, debtors £5,500, i.e. £11,500. £15,000 − £11,500 = £3,500. Balance at bank is £3,500.

Find share capital and Profit and Loss Account balance.

Total equity is ten times profit of £4,400, namely £44,000.

Profit and loss Account credit balance is thus as follows:

Profit for year	£4,400
Less Debit balance	400
Balance at end	£4,000

Share capital must be balance of equity, namely £40,000.

Fixed assets are obtained as follows:

Equity £44,000 and creditors £10,000 =	£54,000
Less Current assets	15,000
Leaving for fixed assets	£39,000

The reconstructed Balance Sheet is therefore:

	£K		£K
Fixed assets	39	Share capital	40
Current assets:		Profit and Loss Account	4
Stock	6.0		
Debtors	5.5		44
Bank	3.5	Current liabilities:	
	15	Creditors	10
	£54		£54

Example

(involving Revenue Account and Balance Sheet):

Prepare a projected Trading, Profit and Loss Account and Balance Sheet as at 31 December. F. Green Limited started business on 1 January with an issued and fully paid share capital of £92,500. The company paid £17,500 for the goodwill of a business and £40,000 for fixed assets.

Plans for the year included the following.

(a) Net profit after charging £4,000 depreciation should be £15,000.

(b) Gross profit, 20 per cent of sales.

(c) All expenses (including depreciation) should be 80 per cent of gross profit.

(d) Stocks should be maintained at two months' trading. All trading was spread evenly throughout the year.

(e) The amount owing to the suppliers would be such as to give a current ratio of 5:2.

(f) All sales are on credit and customers pay promptly one month after date of sale.

First step is to find the sales.

Net profit of £15,000 is 20 per cent of gross profit.

Gross profit must be £75,000.

Gross profit 20% of sales.

Sales must be £375,000.

Cost of sales = £300,000, i.e. 80% of sales.

Stock which is two months' trading, namely £50,000.

The projected Revenue Account is as follows:

TRADING ACCOUNT FOR YEAR

	£K		£K
Purchases	350	Sales	375
Less Closing stock	50		
Cost of sales	300		
Gross profit	75		
	£375		£375

PROFIT AND LOSS ACCOUNT FOR YEAR

	£K		£K
Expenses	56	Gross profit	75
Depreciation	4		
Net profit	15		
	£75		£75

The projected Balance Sheet is as follows:

PROJECTED BALANCE SHEET

	£K	£K
Equity:		
Issued capital	92.5	
Profit and Loss Account	15.0	
		107.5
Fixed assets:		
Cost	40.0	
Depreciation	4.0	
	36.0	
Goodwill	17.5	
		53.5
Leaving working capital		
As current ratio is 5:2		
Current assets must equal	90.0	
Less Current liabilities	36.0	
		54.0
		£107.5

The only remaining item to ascertain is the balance at bank. As stock and debtors are known this is a simple process, namely:

	£
Stock	50,000
Debtors ⅟12 of £375,000	31,250
	81,250
Bank must be	8,750
Current assets	£90,000

It would be wise, however, to prove figure at bank, as follows:

	£	£	£
Proceeds of shares			92,500
Less Payments			57,500
			35,000
Proceeds of sales	375,000		
Less Debtors	31,250		343,750
			378,750
Expenses		56,000	
Purchases	350,000		
Less Creditors	36,000	314,000	
			370,000
Balance			£8,750

Progress test 28

1. What is the purpose of a cash budget? **(1)**

2. On what basis are the figures for a cash budget usually computed? **(2)**

3. What is meant by the usual cycle of receipts and payments? **(4)**

4. How are the following dealt with in the cash budget?
   (a) Depreciation.
   (b) Acquisition of assets. **(5)**

5. In what way do accounting ratios help in understanding business results? **(6)**

6. Describe and define 'current ratio'. **(8)**

7. What do you understand by capital gearing? **(8)**

8. What is low gearing? **(8)**

9. What is high gearing? **(8)**

10. What do the letters ROCE mean? **(9)**

11. State how the average collection period is calculated. **(9)**

12. Given average stock £6,000 and stock turnover 6, what is the cost of sales? **(10)**

13. Given cost of sales £300,000 and percentage of gross profit 20 per cent, what are sales? **(10)**

Specimen questions

1. A. Williams ran a successful business, but in order to maintain a high turnover figure it was necessary to allow extended credit to his customers. In order to obtain supplies promptly he had to deal with suppliers who only offered short-term credit. He was planning to expand turnover and was concerned that a cash flow problem might arise. He has asked you to prepare a forecast which he might present to his bank manager to support a request for overdraft facilities. He has given you the following information.

(a) Cash balance (in hand and at bank) at 1 July expected to be £2,400.

(b) Anticipated receipts from debtors will be half the value of sales made in the previous month, the other half being received two months after the sale.

(c) Suppliers will be paid one-quarter of a month's purchases in the month of purchase, the balance being paid the following month.

(d) Fixed expenses are expected to be £500 per month, paid in the month in which they are incurred.

(e)

	May	June	July	Aug.	Sept.	Oct.	Nov.	Dec.
Purchases		£14,000	£12,000	£20,000	£24,000	£26,000	£30,000	£15,000
Sales	£12,000	£15,000	£10,000	£20,000	£24,000	£28,000	£32,000	£30,000

You are required to produce a cash forecast based on the above information, covering the period July–December.

2. A. Hopeful Ltd proposed to commence a trading business on 1 January 19_1 and the following plans are made for the year.

(a) On 1 January, the company will acquire and pay for two freehold properties at a cost of £60,000 and £14,000 respectively, and furniture and equipment at a cost of £2,000.

(b) Sales will be £20,000 in each month except July, when they will amount to £80,000. The gross profit will be at a uniform rate of 30 per cent of selling price.

(c) An initial supply of goods will be purchased on 1 January at a cost of £8,000 and the stock will be maintained constantly at this level throughout the year.

(d) Trade creditors will be paid on the last day of the month in which the goods are purchased. Payments for all sales will be received on the last day of the month after that in which the goods are sold.

(e) Overhead expenses will amount to £6,000 in each month except July, when they will amount to £12,000. All expenses are to be paid on the last day of the month in which they are incurred.

Depreciation of fixed assets to be ignored.

You are required:

To calculate, by means of a cash budget, the minimum amount of Ordinary Share capital to be issued at par and fully paid up on 1 January 19_1 assuming that no shares of any other class are issued, so as to ensure that the company will not borrow money at any time during 19_1.

3. On 31 March the Balance Sheet of Schubert Ltd, retailers of musical instruments, was as follows:

	£		£
Equipment, at cost 2,000		Ordinary Shares of £1 each	
Less Depreciation 500		fully paid	2,000
	1,500	Unappropriated profit	1,000
Stock	2,000	Trade creditors	4,000
Trade debtors	1,500	Proposed ordinary	
Balance at bank	3,500	dividend	1,500
	£8,500		£8,500

The company is developing a system of forward planning and on 1 April supplies the following information.

(i)

Month	Credit sales £	Cash sales £	Credit purchases £
March (actual)	1,500	1,500	4,000
April (budgeted)	1,800	500	2,300
May (budgeted)	2,000	600	2,700
June (budgeted)	2,500	800	2,600

(ii) All trade debtors are allowed one month's credit and are expected to settle promptly; the trade creditors are paid in the month following delivery.

(iii) On 1 April, all the equipment was replaced at a cost of

£3,000; £1,400 was allowed on the old equipment and
a net payment made of £1,600. Depreciation is to be
provided at the rate of 10 per cent per annum.

(*iv*) The proposed dividend will be paid in June.

(*v*) The following expenses will be paid:

Wages £300 per month;
Administration £150 per month;
Rent £360 for year to 31 March next to be paid in April.

(*vi*) The gross profit percentage on sales is estimated at 25
per cent.

You are required to:

(a) prepare a cash budget for each of the months April,
May and June;

(b) prepare a budgeted Trading and Profit and Loss
Account for the three months ended 30th June.   (*IOB*)

4.   A. Trader had in stock on 1 July 600 articles costing £2.00
each. During the month he bought 1,800 more of these articles
at £2.40 each and sold 2,020 at £4.00 each, of which 20 of the
most recent items were returned. He sells stock on a first in,
first out basis. Draw up a statement showing the Gross Profit
earned and express the Gross Profit as a percentage of the
turnover.

5.   On preparing the Trading Account of R. Lyons, a retailer, for
the financial year ended 31 March 19_9, it was found that the
ratio of Gross Profit to sales was 15 per cent, whereas for the
previous financial year the corresponding ratio had been 25 per
cent. State, with your reasons, whether or not the following may
have contributed to cause the decline:

(a) The stock at 31 March 19_9 was undervalued.

(b) The cost of a new delivery van had been included in the
purchases for the year ended 31 March 19_9 and
charged to Trading Account.

(c) The sales for the year ended 31 March 19_9 showed a decline compared with the previous year.

(d) In both years R. Lyons and his family had been supplied with goods from the shop but the value of these goods had not been recorded in the books of the business.

(e) On the last day of the financial year an employee was successfully convicted of dishonesty with regard to the theft of takings from the tills.

6. A trader carries an average stock of £8,000 (valued at cost price) and turns this over five times a year. If he marks up his stock by 25 per cent on cost price, what is his Gross Profit for the year?

7. A trader carries an average stock valued at cost price of £6,250 and turns this over 14 times a year. If his mark up is 20 per cent on cost and his overheads came to £6,200, what is the Net Profit for the year?

8. M. Brown's current assets total £27,300 and his current liabilities total £8,500. Work out the working capital ratio, and comment on its adequacy.

9. R. Bird's current assets are as follows:

	£
Stock	15,500
Debtors	3,400
Cash at bank	5,800
Cash in hand	200

Her only liability is to a single creditor, £8,600. Work out (correct to two decimal places) (*a*) her working capital ratio and (*b*) her acid test ratio. Say whether each of these is adequate.

10. Here is M. Ross's Balance Sheet. You are to answer the questions below (with calculations if needed).

BALANCE SHEET AS AT 31 DECEMBER 19_9

19_9	£	19_9		£
Fixed assets		*Capital*		
Goodwill	2,000	At start		56,000
Premises	36,000	add Additions during year		2,000
Plant and Machinery	24,000			58,000
Motor Vehicles	4,000			
	66,000	Add Net Profit	16,600	
		less Drawings	7,200	
				9,400
				67,400
Current Assets		*Long-term Liabilities*		
Stock	9,192	Mortgage		10,000
Debtors	2,548			
Cash at Bank	2,762	*Current Liabilities*		
Cash in Hand	144	Creditors	3,228	
Payments in		Accrued		
Advance	176	Charges	194	
	14,822			3,422
	£80,822			£80,822

(a) What is the capital owned by the proprietor at the end of the year?

(b) What is the capital employed in the business? You should assume that profits were earned at an average rate throughout the year and that current liabilities are not part of the capital employed. The additions to capital were invested on 1 January.

(c) What is the working capital?

(d) Calculate the working capital ratio (correct to two decimal places).

(e) What is the liquid capital?

(f) Calculate the acid test ratio (correct to two decimal places).

(g) Work out the return on capital invested (correct to one decimal place) assuming that Ross could earn £9,000 a year in an alternative position with none of the responsibilities of a small businessman and could invest his capital at a rate of 10 per cent if he had no business to use it in. Comment on the results.

11. The following is the Balance Sheet of Brown Ltd at 31 December 19_2, and 31 December 19_3.

19_2		19_3	19_2		19_3
£		£	£		£
110,000	Fixed assets	105,000	100,000	Share capital	100,000
40,000	Stock	60,000	50,000	Retained profits	70,000
20,000	Debtors	30,000	20,000	Creditors	35,000
10,000	Cash	15,000	10,000	Proposed dividend	5,000
£180,000		£210,000	£180,000		£210,000

(*i*) The rate of stock turnover for the year (based on average stocks) was 12 times.

(*ii*) The ratio of gross profit to sales was 25 per cent.

(*iii*) An interim dividend of £5,000 was paid during the year (in addition to the £10,000 dividend outstanding at 31 December 19_2).

REQUIRED:

Your calculations, for the year 19_3, of the following:

(a) sales;
(b) purchases;
(c) net profit;
(d) total Profit and Loss Account expenses;
(e) return on shareholders' funds employed at start of year;
(f) average period of credit allowed to customers;
(g) average period of credit received from suppliers.

29

More difficult partnership matters

Admission of a new partner

1. Effect on the partnership

When a new partner is admitted the old partnership ceases to exist.

(a) Any *capital gains* made up to the date of admission of the new partner must therefore be *credited* to the *old partners* in the ratios in which *they* share profits and losses.

(b) Any *goodwill* built up by the old partners must also be *credited* to them in *their* profit-sharing ratios.

The methods of dealing with the above matters will take one of the following forms.

2. Goodwill recorded in the books

A Goodwill Account will be opened and the amount credited to the old partners in their profit-sharing ratios.

(a) *Debit* Goodwill Account; *credit* old partners' Capital Accounts.

NOTE: This goodwill may be written off to the Capital Accounts of *all* the partners (including the *new* partner), in which case the above entries will be followed by:

(b) *credit* Goodwill Account; *debit* the Capital Accounts of *all* partners in the *new* profit-sharing ratios.

3. Goodwill accompanied by revaluation of other assets

This method takes into account other capital gains.

(a) *Open a Revaluation Account.*

   (*i*) *Debit* the Asset Account with any *increase* in value; *credit* Revaluation Account.

   (*ii*) *Credit* the Asset Account with any *loss* in value; *debit* Revaluation Account.

   (*iii*) *Debit* Goodwill Account; *credit* Revaluation Account.

(b) *Transfer any profit on revaluation to the old partners' Capital Accounts. Debit* Revaluation Account; *credit* Capital Accounts in the *old* profit-sharing ratios.

(c) *If part of Capital is then withdrawn: credit* Bank Account; *debit* Capital Accounts.

(d) The Goodwill Account may again be written off to the Capital Accounts of *all* partners (*see* **2(b)** above).

4. The payment of a premium in cash by the new partner

The new partner may agree to pay a sum of money to the old partners for his share of the goodwill that they have built up.

(a) *Debit* Bank Account; *credit* Capital Account of *new* partner *with the amount of capital and premium introduced.*

(b) Transfer the Premium to the *old* partners in their *old* profit-sharing ratios: *debit* new partner's Capital Account; *credit* old partners' Capital Accounts.

5. Calculation of goodwill

The words *goodwill* and *premium* have both been used to denote a payment made by an incoming partner to share the profits of an existing business.

(a) *Goodwill* has been discussed earlier as an intangible but valuable asset. It is a 'right' similar to a patent or copyright but less clearly defined. It is really the right to enjoy super-profits either alone or in partnership with somebody else.

(b) *Super-profits* are simply those over and above the economic return for the labour and capital put into the business.

(c) *Simple calculation of super-profits.*

	£	£
Take profits earned or expected, say		15,000
Salary obtainable elsewhere	8,000	
Interest on capital in business, i.e. interest which could be obtained by investing elsewhere, say	2,000	
		10,000
Super-profits		£5,000

(d) *How long will super-profits last?* Nobody knows but competition suggests not longer than three to five years — say three years.

(e) *Value of goodwill* is capital value of £5,000 for say three years. This value can be calculated on an annuity basis or on the basis of the present value of the discounted cash flow (DCF) of £5,000 for each of three following years — say about £12,000.

(f) *Practical consideration.* Because the theoretical calculation includes so many unknowns, often in practice goodwill is valued on the basis of so many years of the average profits over a certain agreed figure.

Example

A and B admit C into partnership. It is agreed that goodwill is to be taken as two years' purchase of the average profits over £20,000 for the last five years.

The actual profits for the last five years were as follows: £24,500, £24,750, £26,000, £24,750, £25,000.

The aggregate goodwill profits will therefore be: £4,500 + £4,750 + £6,000 + £4,750 + £5,000, i.e. £25,000. Average profits will be £25,000 ÷ 5 = £5,000.

Goodwill will therefore be: £5000 x 2 = £10,000

Example

Sharpe and Keene who are in business as accountants, contribute capital equally and share profits equally, they decide to take Cutler into partnership as from 1 April 19__. Their Balance Sheet at 31 March 19__ consisted of freehold property £65,000, motor cars £14,000, office equipment £4,200, stock of securities £22,650, debtors £48,050, cash at bank £2,584 and client creditors £28,444. Sharpe had loaned the business £10,000 some time ago, and their Current Accounts showed Sharpe was owed £8,720 and Keene £6,320.

Before admitting Cutler it was agreed to revalue certain assets along the following lines:

Freehold property £80,000, cars £13,000, office equipment £5,500, stock of securities £23,500, debtors £47,500; and also to value the library at £500 (not at present on the books). This would be recorded as follows:

REVALUATION ACCOUNT

	£		£
Cars	£1,000	Freehold property	£15,000
Debtors	550	Office equipment	1,300
Balance c/d	16,100	Securities	850
		Library	500
	£17,650		£17,650
Capital Accounts:		Balance b/d	16,100
Sharpe	8,050		
Keene	8,050		
	£16,100		£16,100

Note that when revaluing assets we are concerned only with the 'difference' in value; thus cars are being reduced by £1,000, so we *debit Revaluation Account* and *credit Motor Cars Account*. On the other hand, freehold property is worth £15,000 more than its present book value, so we *credit* Revaluation Account and *debit* Freehold Property Account to record the *increase*. The Balance Sheet would now appear as follows.

BALANCE SHEET AT 31 MARCH 19_3

	£	£		£	£
Fixed assets:			Capital Accounts:		
Freehold property	80,000		Sharpe	59,550	
Motor cars	13,000		Keene	59,550	119,100
Office equipment	5,500				
Library	500		Loan Account:		10,000
		99,000	Current Accounts:		
Current assets:			Sharpe	8,720	
Stock of securities	23,500		Keene	6,320	
Debtors	47,500				15,040
Cash at bank	2,584				
		73,584	Current liabilities:		
			Creditors		28,444
		£172,584			£172,584

The partners are now ready to admit Cutler. Sharpe and Keene whose capital accounts both have credit balances of £59,550 on 1 April 19__, admit Cutler into partnership on the following terms.

(a) Cutler to bring in £20,000 as capital plus an additional sum of £12,000 as a premium for his share of the goodwill. This £12,000 to be withdrawn by Sharpe and Keene equally and used to reduce the balances on their Current Accounts.

(b) Prior to the introduction of Cutler, profits and losses have been shared equally between Sharpe and Keene. As from 1 April 19__, profits in the new partnership to be shared in the ratios of 3:3:1.

(c)   It is agreed that the partners' Capital Accounts shall be in proportion to their profit-sharing ratios: the adjustments to be made by additions of capital by Sharpe and Keene.

CAPITAL ACCOUNTS

	Cutler	Sharpe	Keene		Cutler	Sharpe	Keene
19_	£	£	£	19_	£	£	£
Apr. 1				Apr. 1			
Premium:				Balance b/d		59,550	59,550
	6,000			Bank	32,000		
	6,000			Bank		450	450
Balance c/d	20,000	60,000	60,000				
	£32,000	60,000	60,000		£32,000	60,000	60,000
				Apr. 2			
				Balance b/d	20,000	60,000	60,000

6.   Raising a Goodwill Account

Where the new partner is unable or unwilling to contribute an amount in cash as a premium for his share of the goodwill, an agreement may be reached under which the old partners take credit for the goodwill which they have built up, and this will be done by debiting Goodwill Account and crediting the old partners' Capital Accounts in their profit-sharing ratios.

This has the advantage for the old partners of additional interest on capital — where interest on capital is allowed under the agreement — plus, of course, additional capital to draw out on their retirement.

Sample question _____

On 1 April in the following year Sharpe, Keene and Cutler take into partnership their managing clerk Contango. Contango can bring in only £10,000 as capital, and it is agreed that a Goodwill Account of £28,000 be raised in the books of the partnership, and shared 3:3:1 among the three original partners.

The future profits of the new partnership of Sharpe, Keene, Cutler and Contango are to be shared in the ratios of 4:4:2:1, respectively, and the Capital Accounts of the partners are to be adjusted to the same proportions, such adjustment being effected by withdrawals or additions of capital as the case may be.

Show:
(a) the Journal entry giving effect to the creation of the Goodwill Account;
(b) the entries in the Capital Accounts of the partners.

Answer

JOURNAL ENTRY

			Being creation of goodwill on the admission of Contango as a partner.
Apr. 1 Goodwill Dr.	£28,000		
Capital:			
Sharpe		12,000	
Keene		12,000	
Cutler		4,000	
	£28,000	28,000	

CAPITAL ACCOUNTS

	Con-tango	Cut-ler	Shar-pe	Kee-ne		Con-tango	Cut-ler	Shar-pe	Kee-ne
	£	£	£	£		£	£	£	£
Apr. 1 Bank		4,000			Apr. 1 Bal. b/d		20,000	60,000	60,000
					1 Goodwill		4,000	12,000	12,000
Bal c/d	10,000	20,000	80,000	80,000	1 Bank	10,000		8,000	8,000
£	10,000	24,000	80,000	80,000	£	10,000	24,000	80,000	80,000
					Apr. 2 Bal. b/d	10,000	20,000	80,000	80,000

NOTE: The goodwill will now appear as an asset in the Balance Sheet of the firm.

7. Eliminating goodwill from the accounts

Some partnerships decide to write off the goodwill *immediately* the arrangements for the new partnership have been completed.

(a) When this is done, the *new* profit-sharing ratios are taken.
(b) In this way the *new* partner now bears part of the writing off of the goodwill.

Example

If Sharpe, Keene, Cutler and Contango decide to eliminate the goodwill of £28,000, then Contango, who did not share in the creation of the goodwill, would now suffer a loss of capital equal to one-eleventh of the goodwill figure of £28,000.

The Journal entry eliminating the goodwill would be:

	£	£	
Date Capital A/c's: Dr.			Being elimination of the goodwill of
Sharpe	10,182		£28,000 created on the entry of
Keene	10,182		Contango into the partnership.
Cutler	5,091		(Calculated to the nearest £1 as
Contango	2,545		agreed by the partners.)
To Goodwill		28,000	
	£28,000	£28,000	

The capital left would still be in the ratios 4:4:2:1.

Dissolution of partnership

8. Reasons for dissolution

When a partnership is dissolved the assets are disposed of, any profit or loss on the dissolution being shared between the partners in their profit-sharing ratios. A partnership may be dissolved for any one of the following reasons.

(a) On the expiration of the time fixed in the agreement for the length of the partnership.

(b) The death of a partner.

(c) The bankruptcy of a partner.

(d) Where ordered by the Court.

(e) When one partner gives notice to the others of his intention to dissolve the partnership.

(f) On conversion into a limited company to replace the existing partnership. In this case each partner will take shares in the new company in exchange for the capital held in the partnership.

9. Procedure followed at dissolution

The assets may be disposed of individually or the business may change hands as a complete unit. The proceeds are applied in discharging the liabilities of the partnership and in paying the partners according to certain legal or agreed priorities as follows:

(a) outside creditors: if not sufficient, then the rules of bankruptcy apply;

(b) amount of any loan made by a partner to the business;

(c) partners' capital;

(d) any profits on the realisation, including capital profits, in the partners' profit-sharing ratios.

10. Entries in books of account

The normal book-keeping procedure will take the following pattern.

(a) Transfer any balance on Current Accounts to the Capital Accounts.

> NOTE: Retain separate accounts for any *loans* made by partners to the firm.

(b) Open a Realisation Account: *debit* Realisation Account with the book value of assets (except Bank and Cash); *credit* the asset accounts concerned (closing the accounts).

(c) When the assets are sold; *debit* Bank or Cash and *credit* Realisation Account with the proceeds.

(d) Any assets taken over by a partner: *debit* partner's Capital Account; *credit* Realisation Account at agreed valuations.

(e) Any expenses on dissolution:

    (i) If paid: *debit* Realisation Account and *credit* Bank.

    (ii) If borne by a partner: *debit* Realisation Account; *credit* Capital Account.

(f) Pay off the creditors: *debit* Creditors; *credit* Bank. If discount is received: *debit* Creditors; *credit* Realisation Account.

(g) Pay off any loan due to a partner: *debit* Loan; *credit* Bank.

(h) The balance on the Realisation Account is now taken to the partners' Capital Accounts in their profit-sharing ratios.

(i) The available balance on the Bank Account should be equal to the balances on the partners' Capital Accounts. Capital Accounts are closed by transferring the amount due to each partner: *debit* Capital Accounts; *credit* Bank.

> NOTE: If a partner's capital account ends with a *debit* balance he will be expected to bring in cash to meet the deficiency. This will apply *unless* you are told that the partner is insolvent (*see* the Rule in *Garner* v. *Murray*, 11).

Example _____

Sharpe and Keene have now weathered the storms of business for a further ten years, during which time the other members have retired. They decide to dissolve the partnership on 31 March 19_4. The Balance Sheet immediately before the dissolution was as follows:

Fixed assets:	£	£	Capital Accounts	£	£
Freehold property	40,000		Sharpe	60,000	
Motor vehicles	6,500		Keene	40,000	
Office equipment	3,000				100,000
Library	400		Current Accounts:		
		49,900	Sharpe	1,250	
Current assets:			Keene	2,450	
Stock of securities	10,600				3,700
Debtors	49,800		Creditors		10,800
Bank	4,200				
		64,600			
		£114,500			£114,500

Sharpe and Keene now share profits in the ratios of 3:2 respectively.

The freehold property realised £55,000. Of the motor vehicles, one was sold for £800. Sharpe took over a Jaguar car at an agreed valuation of £1,100, and Keene took over the Bentley for £3,500. The office equipment was sold for £2,800 and the stock of securities realised £11,200. Book debts to the value of £13,200 were assigned to I. Bid for £12,500, and the balance of book debts were collected in full. The library was sold for £200, and the creditors accepted £10,360 in full settlement of their claims. The expenses of dissolution amounted to £325, and it can be assumed that all transactions took place on 30 April 19_4.

REALISATION ACCOUNT

19__		£	19__		£
Apr. 30			Apr. 30		
Freehold property		40,000	Bank (freehold property)		55,000
Motor vehicles		6,500	" (motor vehicle)		800
Office equipment		3,000	Cap. A/c Sharpe		1,100
Library		400	Cap. A/c Keene		3,500
Securities		10,600	Bank (office equipment)		2,800
Debtors		49,800	" (securities)		11,200
Bank (expenses)		325	" (I. Bid debtors)		12,500
Balance c/d		13,515	" (debtors)		36,600
			" (library)		200
			Creditors (discount rec'd)		440
		£124,140			£124,140
Capital A/c:			Balance b/d		13,515
Sharpe		8,109			
Keene		5,406			
		£13,515			£13,515

BANK ACCOUNT

19_	£	19_	£
Mar. 31 Balance b/d	4,200	Apr. 30 Creditors	10,360
Apr. 30 Realisation A/c:		Realisation A/c (expenses)	325
Property	55,000	Capital A/cs:	
Motor vehicle	800	Sharpe	68,259
Office equipment	2,800	Keene	44,356
Securities	11,200		
I. Bid (debtors)	12,500		
Debtors	36,600		
Library	200		
	£123,300		£123,300

CAPITAL ACCOUNTS

	Sharpe £	Keene £		Sharpe £	Keene £
Apr. 30			Mar. 31		
Realisation			Balance b/d	60,000	40,000
(Motor cars)	1,100	3,500	Current A/c's	1,250	2,450
Bank	68,259	44,356	Apr. 30		
			Realisation A/c		
			Share of profit	8,109	5,406
	£69,359	£47,856		£69,359	£47,856

11. The Rule in *Garner* v. *Murray* (1903)

A knowledge of the rule in *Garner* v. *Murray* is essential in partnership, since it is often a hunting ground for examiners searching to test a candidate's knowledge, hence the reason for including this aspect of partnership accounts.

(a) This rule, based on a decision given by Mr Justice Joyce in November 1903, lays down that the loss caused by the *default* of an insolvent partner is to be borne by the remaining partners in proportion to the last agreed balances on their Capital Accounts and *not* in the proportions in which they ordinarily share profits and losses.

(b) From an examination point of view you will apply this rule only when you are told that one or more partners is insolvent and unable to meet the ultimate deficiency on his/her Capital Account. In the normal course of events if a partner has a debit balance on his/her Capital Account, then he/she will be expected to bring in cash to make good the deficiency. The rule in *Garner* v. *Murray* applies therefore only when a partner cannot bring in cash to make good the *ultimate* deficiency.

NOTE: The insolvent partner must still be charged with his appropriate share of the profit or loss on dissolution, and it is the ultimate deficiency on the Capital Account which has to be apportioned between the remaining partners in proportion to the last agreed balances on their Capital Accounts.

Sample question

Williams, Jones and Smith were in partnership when on 31 December 19__ they decided to dissolve the partnership.

The Balance Sheet at that date was as follows:

	£		£	£
		Capital Accounts:		
Fixed assets	18,400	Williams	16,800	
Bank A/c	3,200	Jones	5,600	
Capital A/c: Smith	2,400			22,400
		Creditors		1,600
	£24,000			£24,000

The partners share profits and losses equally. The fixed assets were sold for £16,000, and the creditors discharged in full. *Smith was insolvent*, and unable to bring in cash to meet the ultimate deficiency on his Capital Account.

Show the Realisation Account, Bank Account and the Capital Accounts of the partners to record the dissolution.

Answer

REALISATION ACCOUNT

19__		£	19__		£
Dec. 31	Fixed assets	18,400	Dec. 31	Bank	16,000
			31	Capital Accounts:	
				Share of loss:	
				Williams	800
				Jones	800
				Smith	800
		£18,400			£18,400

BANK ACCOUNT

19__		£	19__		£
Dec. 31	Balance b/d	3,200	Dec. 31	Creditors	1,600
31	Realisation A/c	16,000	31	Capital A/c Williams	13,600
			31	Capital A/c Jones	4,000
		£19,200			£19,200

CAPITAL ACCOUNT — WILLIAMS

19__		£	19__		£
Dec. 31	Share of Loss on Realisation A/c	800	Dec. 31	Balance b/d	16,800
31	Smith; Share of deficiency $\frac{3}{4}$	2,400			
31	Bank	13,600			
		£16,800			£16,800

CAPITAL ACCOUNT — JONES

		£			£
Dec. 31	Share of Loss on Realisation A/c	800	Dec. 31	Balance b/d	5,600
31	Smith; Share of deficiency $\frac{1}{4}$	800			
31	Bank	4,000			
		£5,600			£5,600

CAPITAL ACCOUNT — SMITH

		£			£
Dec. 31	Balance b/d	2,400	Dec. 31	Williams: $\frac{3}{4}$	2,400
31	Share of Loss on Realisation A/c	800	31	Jones: $\frac{1}{4}$ (Share of deficiency)	800
		£3,200			£3,200

NOTE: You proceed with the dissolution in the normal way, taking any profit or loss to the Capital Accounts of *all* partners. The *ultimate* deficiency on the insolvent partner's Capital Account is then transferred to the Capital Accounts of the solvent partners in the proportions of the last agreed balances on their Capital Accounts.

Progress test 29

1. How does the admission of a partner affect the existing partnership? **(1)**

2. What are the main entries to record admission?

(a) When goodwill is recorded in the books? **(2)**
(b) When the new partner pays in a premium in cash? **(4)**
(c) When other assets have to be revalued? **(3)**

3. What is the main function of the Revaluation Account? **(3)**

4. Why is goodwill sometimes recorded in the books and then immediately eliminated? **(7)**

5. What are the essential features of the Rule in *Garner* v. *Murray* (1903), and when do you apply them? **(11)**

Specimen questions

1. Red and White are in partnership sharing profits and losses in the ratio of 3:2. The Balance Sheet of the partnership as at 30 April 19_2 is shown below.

	Cost	Accumulated depreciation	Net book value
Fixed assets:	£	£	£
Office equipment	1,500	500	1,000
Motor vehicles	7,000	1,400	5,600
	£8,500	£1,900	6,600
Current assents:			
Stocks		11,200	
Debtors		12,500	
Cash at bank and in hand		100	
		23,800	
Less: Current liabilities:			
Creditors		11,800	
Net working capital			12,000
Net assets			£18,600
Financed by: Capital			
Accounts:			
Red			12,000
White			6,600
			£18,600

It has been decided to admit Blue to the partnership as from 1 May 19_2. He will contribute £3,000 in cash as his immediate capital contribution; profits and losses are to be shared in the ratio of 6:3:1. The assets of the new partnership are to be revalued as follows:

Office equipment, £300; motor vehicles, £8,000; stocks, £12,000; debtors, £12,000; goodwill £10,000.

The partners do not intend to retain a Goodwill Account in the new partnership books, and goodwill is to be written off.

(a) Prepare the partners' capital accounts to record the above transactions; and

(b) construct the partnership Balance Sheet of Red, White and Blue immediately after the admittance of Blue on 1 May 19_2.

2. On 30 June 19_6 Campbell was admitted as a partner to the firm of Brown and Allen. He introduced £4,000 as capital and, as he could not immediately find additional moneys to pay for his share of goodwill, it was agreed to create a Goodwill Account for £32,000. Prior to his admission Brown and Allen shared profits and losses in the ratio of 3:1, but the new partnership profit sharing ratio was agreed at 3:2:1. Interest was allowed on capital at 8 per cent per year, before division of the residue of the profit. In the year under discussion this interest will be treated in two half-yearly instalments.

Because of pressure of business the actual entries for the admission of Campbell were not made immediately, his £4,000 capital merely being recorded in a Suspense Account.

No entries have been made for goodwill either, but it was agreed that a Goodwill Account should remain in the books, and be written off over the first four years of the new partnership.

At the year ended 31 December 19_6, the Trial Balance was:

	£	£
Capital at start of the year:		
Brown		40,000
Allen		27,000
Current Accounts at start of the year:		
Brown		5,900
Allen	1,169	
Drawings Accounts		
Brown	12,800	
Allen	11,600	
Campbell	7,000	
Suspense Account: Campbell		4,000
5 per cent loan: Brown		4,000
Interest on loan	200	
Purchases and Sales	47,300	161,400
Stock at 1 January 19_6	9,250	
Discounts Allowed and Received	440	950
Wages (Profit and Loss A/c)	31,120	
Lighting and Heating	860	
Rates	1,870	
Depreciation:		
Buildings		3,500
Vehicles		4,000
Buildings (cost)	83,000	
Vehicles (cost)	19,000	
Debtors and Creditors	12,300	3,730
Provision for Doubtful Debts		130
Bad Debts	150	
Vehicle Running Expenses	1,680	
Miscellaneous Expenses	3,471	
Bank	11,400	
	£254,610	£254,610

The following data is to be taken into account.

(a) Stock at 31 December 19_6 was valued at £14,200.
(b) Wages owing at 31 December 19_6 amounted to £80.
(c) Rates include £70 prepaid to 31 January 19_7.
(d) Depreciation is to be provided on the cost price of assets, buildings at 2 per cent and vehicles at 10 per cent. No new vehicles have been acquired during the year.

(e) The provision for doubtful debts is to be increased to 3 per cent of debtors.

(f) All revenues and expenses can be deemed to accrue evenly through the year.

(g) The goodwill will be written down by an appropriate amount for the half year to date, from the profits earned in the second half of the year.

You are required to prepare:
  (*i*) the Journal entries in relation to Campbell's admission as a partner;
  (*ii*) the Trading, Profit and Loss and Appropriation Account for the year ended 31 December 19_6, and a Balance Sheet as at that date.

3. Olmec, Aztec and Inca have been in partnership for some years sharing profits and losses 2:2:1 respectively. The area has been declining in prosperity and on 31 July 19__ they decide to dissolve the partnership and realise what they can on the assets. The Balance Sheet on that date is as follows:

BALANCE SHEET AS AT 31 JULY 19__

Fixed Assets			*Capital Accounts*		
Premises		68,000	Olmec		56,500
Fixtures and fittings		8,000	Aztec		33,500
Motor vehicles		13,250	Inca		3,000
		89,250			93,000
Current Assets			*Long- term Liabilities*		
Stock	19,274		Useful Finance Co.		14,850
Debtors	2,635				
		21,909	*Current Liabilities*		
			Creditors	2,365	
			Bank overdraft	944	
					3,309
		£111,159			£111,159

The premises were sold for £50,500. Fixtures and fittings for £1,750. Motor Vehicles £6,250—but one vehicle was retained to be taken over by Olmec for his own use at a valuation of £1,350. Stock realised £8,650 and £425 of the debtors proved to be impossible to collect. The Useful Finance Co imposed a charge of £650 for agreeing to the early repayment of the long-term loan, and the creditors were settled in full for £2,282. Expenses of dissolution were £1,854. You are asked to show the Realisation Account, the Bank Account and the Capital Accounts of the partners. Inca has only £1,024 available, which is banked, and the rule in *Garner* v. *Murray* is to apply to the balance of his deficit on Capital Account, using the balances of Olmec's and Aztec's capitals as shown above. Calculations correct to the nearest £1.

30
Limited liability companies: issue of shares

1. Introduction

Limited liability companies are formed under the Companies Acts 1985–89. The identity of the individual is lost in that of the company, which becomes on incorporation, a legal person with perpetual succession, a distinctive name and the right to sue and be sued in its own name. The Acts lay down certain requirements to which companies must conform.

2. Company requirements

These are extremely numerous, and only a brief mention can be made of a few of the most important.

(a) *Memorandum of Association.* This is, in effect, the company's charter which must state:

   (*i*) the name of the company;
   (*ii*) the registered office situation (in England, Scotland or Wales);
   (*iii*) the objects for which the company was formed (the activities the company can undertake);
   (*iv*) liability of the members: whether limited by shares or by guarantee;
   (*v*) the share capital: details of shares and their classification.

(b) *Articles of Association.* This document regulates the internal affairs of the company, dealing with such matters as the shareholder's right to call meetings, the appointment of directors, etc.

(c) *Certificate of Incorporation.* The legal authority of the company to operate, which must be displayed in the registered office.

(d) *A registration number.* This is stated on the Certificate and must be reproduced on all stationery and publications.

(e) *A board of directors.* Directors must be appointed to conduct and accept responsibility for the affairs of the company.

(f) *A Secretary* to act on behalf of the Board of Directors in dealing with legal and financial requirements. Only members of authorised professional bodies can be appointed as secretary of a public company.

(g) *Annual Return.* Each year details such as shares issued, names of shareholders, directors and secretary, must be sent to the Registrar of Companies. These details are given on a special form called an *Annual Return* and when sent, it is 'filed', and becomes a matter of public record.

3. Shareholders and members

These are the owners who provide funds for the capital of the company. This capital is divided into stocks and shares. New capital is issued as shares but may later be consolidated into stock.

(a) *Stock* is part of the company's capital such as £150.45p of stock.

(b) *Shares* are *units* of the company's capital. Each unit can be transferred from one owner to another, but it *cannot be divided into fractions.*

(c) *Stock units* are similar to shares, and were important when shares had to be numbered but are now very little used.

> NOTE: Stock has also lost its significance as far as equity capital is concerned. The term is now used for loans, i.e. loan stock whether of companies, the Government or Local Authorities.

4. Main classification of shares

(a) *Ordinary Shares,* sometimes called *Equities* (since they have equal voting rights), do not carry a fixed rate of dividend and depend entirely on profits for a dividend.

(b) *Preference Shares* always carry a fixed rate of dividend, although, depending on the profits, a dividend is paid in priority to any dividend paid to the Ordinary shareholders. Different classes of Preference Shares are as follows (percentage rates used may vary).

> (*i*) *Cumulative 7 per cent Preference Shares* means that any arrears of dividend will be paid before ordinary shareholders receive a dividend. This is a common type of preference share.

(*ii*) *Non-Cumulative 10 per cent Preference Shares.* If profits in any year are insufficient to pay a preference dividend and the Directors resolve to pass the dividend, then that dividend is lost for all time.

(*iii*) *Participating 8 per cent Cumulative Preference Shares.* These are entitled to 'participate' in an extra dividend beyond the 8 per cent when profits are very good. The exact amount would depend on the terms of the issue.

(*iv*) *Redeemable 6 per cent Preference Shares* are shares which the company has authority to repay or 'redeem'. Certain legal requirements apply, e.g. repayment must either be out of profits or the proceeds of a new issue of shares.

(c) *Deferred Shares.* These only receive a dividend after the ordinary shareholders have received a stated minimum. The exact level and the rights of Deferred shareholders (e.g. their voting rights) depend upon the terms of the issue.

5. Denomination of shares — par value — nominal value

Each share is given a certain value at which it would normally be issued. This is called the par value of the share and any variation from this value is a premium (if the value rises), or a discount (if the value falls), e.g. if shares having a par value of 25p were issued at 30p they would be issued at a premium of 5p per share.

Shares can be of any denomination but those of £1 each are the most convenient for student discussion.

6. Loan capital

This term is really a misnomer, since a loan *to* a business can never be capital *of* a business. The term implies that the funds made available in this way will be available for a very long time for use by the company. It consists of long-term loans made to the company and repayable in fifteen to twenty years' time or even longer, e.g. a company might issue loans dated 2011/2016. This means that the loans can be repaid in 2011 if the company so desire, but they must be repaid by 2016.

7. Types of loans

(a) *Secured loans.* This means that people lending money to the company have a legal charge on the assets of the company. Such a charge may be one of the following.

(i) *Fixed charge* on a specific asset. When the charge is on property it is called a *mortgage*.

(ii) *Floating charge* on all the other assets of the company.

(b) *Debentures* are a form of secured loan where the interest and repayment terms are set out in a document called a *Trust Deed*. The deed usually gives the right to appoint a *receiver*, if the interest and repayment terms are in arrears. The receiver appointed would take over control of the company from the directors and run it for the benefit of the Debenture holders.

(c) *Unsecured loans.* For example, 10 per cent Unsecured Loan 1996–99. Holders receive interest and repayment rights as stated. In the event of the company going into liquidation they have no special rights, being in the same legal position as trade creditors.

(d) *Convertible Loan Stock* (this can be secured or unsecured). Holders have a right to convert into Ordinary Shares on certain agreed terms, e.g. holders of £100 10 per cent Convertible Loan Stock 1990/94 may have the right to convert into 160 Ordinary Shares of 25p each at a certain time. This can be after a certain date, say after 1 May 2000, or it could be for limited periods, say during the month of March only in the year 2000.

(e) *Variable Rate Stock.* The rate of interest varies with an indicated rate, which itself might be an accepted market rate or the Treasury Bill Rate. Thus we might have a Variable Treasury Stock which paid interest at $\frac{1}{2}$ per cent above the average Treasury Bill Rate for the preceding 3 months.

8.   Types of companies

(a) *Private companies.* Only two members are required as a minimum and the shares are not freely transferable. Only persons approved by the directors may become shareholders, and the shares are not dealt in on any Stock Exchange.

(i) *Limited liability.* If the members of the company are protected by limited liability, a copy of the Balance Sheet and Profit and Loss Account must be included with the Annual Return.

(ii) *Unlimited liability.* No restriction on the financial

obligation of the members applies if the company decides not to file its accounts with the Annual Return.

(b) *Public companies.* Require a minimum capital of £50,000 and invite the public to subscribe for shares either by means of a prospectus or a comprehensive newspaper advertisement containing financial and other information about the company, as required by the Companies Acts. The abbreviation PLC (Public Limited Company) must be shown after the company's name.

(*i*) *Listed or quoted companies* are those who have submitted further information to the Stock Exchange and been given a quotation. The shares have a market price and may be freely bought and sold at or near this price on the Stock Exchange.

(*ii*) *Not-listed or unquoted companies* are those who do not enjoy the privilege of a Stock Exchange quotation but shares may be transferred to anybody at an agreed price. The difficulty is often finding a buyer and in order to cater for this an Unlisted Securities Market has been established.

9. Significance of limited liability

Limited liability and the separate legal capacity of the company enable the shareholders who provide the capital to limit their liability to the extent of their shares, ie. they are not liable to make good any losses of trading and cannot be forced to pay creditors. They can only lose their original contribution.

Apart from any guarantees, the only people who can be compelled to contribute are those who have agreed to pay so much for a certain number of shares but have not yet done so. i.e they have shares on which there are unpaid calls.

Under normal circumstances the only liability of members is to pay the cost of their shares and no more. That is really the meaning of limited liability. This places the creditors of a company in a vulnerable position and explains why Parliament has enacted that the name of a company must end in the word Limited, or Public Limited Company, or its Welsh equivalent.

10. Classification of capital

Every company must have:

(a) An *authorised share capital*, sometimes called the registered or nominal capital, i.e. that which the company takes authority to issue to the public, showing the division into different classes of shares.

(b) An *issued share capital*. That part of the authorised capital which has been issued to its members.

(c) *Called-up capital* is the amount of the capital actually 'called' or demanded from those persons who have offered to subscribe to the company's capital. These persons are called shareholders or members.

(d) *Paid-up capital* is the amount of capital actually paid to the company.

  (i) When all the money due on the shares has been received by the company the shares are said to be fully paid up.

  (ii) When the shares should have been fully paid but in fact all have not been paid, the shares are said to be fully called up.

The difference between fully paid and fully called up shares is due to the existence of certain calls in arrears, i.e. some subscribers are in arrears with paying their calls to the company.

If only a few of the calls have actually been made the shares are said to be partly called up or partly paid up. Sometimes only some of the calls have been made, e.g. 10,000 shares of £1 each: 75p called up = £7,500. If all the £7,500 has been paid, the shares would be described as partly paid. *Note* that the shareholders are still liable to pay 25p on each share.

11. Raising capital

Many businesses grow from sole traders to partnerships to private companies and eventually to listed public companies. Such businesses would use different methods at different times to raise capital.

(a) *The role of merchant banks*. When companies wish to obtain large amounts of capital they enlist the aid of a merchant bank. It is the merchant bank which acts as an issuing house and issues the shares on behalf of the company. The merchant bank will often guarantee the issue, i.e. underwrite the issue. This is a form of 'insurance' which ensures that the company will succeed in obtaining the capital even if the merchant bank have to purchase some of the shares themselves.

(b) *Placing of shares.* Sometimes one large investor, e.g. an insurance company or a pension fund will take most or all of the shares issued, i.e. a 'placing' of shares takes place.

(c) *Issue to the general public.* This may be either direct or through the intermediary of a merchant bank. In the latter case the merchant bank acquires the shares first and then issues them to the public. This is termed an *offer for sale*. For purposes of illustration it is assumed that the company issues direct to the general public.

12. Issue of shares

When shares are issued on the understanding that they are payable by instalments, the following points should be borne in mind.

(a) When the public apply for shares they send in a sum known as the application money. This does not guarantee that they will receive shares and can be returned to unsuccessful applicants.

(b) When the directors allot the shares it signifies acceptance of the offer made by the public to subscribe for the shares, and now a binding contract exists between the company and the subscriber. Hence the importance of the date of the allotment letter.

(c) *Entries in books of account.*

    (*i*) On receipt of application money: *debit* bank; *credit* Application Account.

    (*ii*) On sending the allotment letter: *debit* Application Account; *credit* Share Capital Account (with the application money). *Debit* Allotment Account; *credit* Share Capital Account (with the amount due on allotment).

    (*iii*) Sums returned to unsuccessful applicants: *debit* Application Account; *credit* bank.

    (*iv*) Excess application money retained on account of allotment: *debit* Application Account; *credit* Allotment Account.

    (*v*) On receipt of the amount due on allotment: *debit* bank; *credit* Allotment Account.

    (*vi*) Allotment money outstanding: *debit* Calls in Arrears Accounts; *credit* Allotment Account.

NOTE: Sometimes a single account called an Applications and

Allotment Account is used, in which case all the above entries would appear in the one account.

(*vii*) On making a 'call': *debit* Call Account; *credit* Share Capital Account.

NOTE: All calls are dealt with in this way.

(*viii*) When the 'call' money is received: *debit* bank; *credit* Call Account.

(*ix*) 'Call' money outstanding: *debit* Calls in Arrears; *credit* Call Account.

NOTE: The debit balance on the Calls in Arrears Account is shown in the Balance Sheet as a deduction from the Issued Share Capital.

Sample question

Bright and Breezy Ltd, whose authorised share capital is £50,000 divided into 200,000 Ordinary Shares of 25p each, issue 100,000 shares to the public on the following terms: 5p per share on application; 10p per share due on allotment; first call of 5p on 3 September, and second and final call of 5p due on 5 October.

Applications were received for 120,000 shares on 17 July and allotment made on 3 August, on which date excess application money was returned to unsuccessful applicants.

All instalments were received five days after the due dates.

Show the Ledger accounts recording the above transactions in the books of Bright and Breezy Ltd and an extract of the Balance Sheet at 31 October 19__.

BANK ACCOUNT

19__	£	19__	£
July 17 Application	6,000	Aug. 3 Application	1,000
Aug. 8 Allotment	10,000	Oct. 31 Balance c/d	25,000
Sept. 8 First call	5,000		
Oct. 10 Second and final call	5,000		
	£26,000		£26,000
Nov. 1 Balance b/d	25,000		

APPLICATION ACCOUNT

19__	£	19__	£
Aug. 3 Bank	1,000	July 17 Bank	6,000
Share capital	5,000		
	£6,000		£6,000

ALLOTMENT ACCOUNT

19__		£	19__		£
Aug. 3 Share capital		£10,000	Aug. 8 Bank		£10,000

ORDINARY SHARE CAPITAL ACCOUNT

19__		£	19__		£
Oct. 31 Balance c/d		25,000	Aug. 3 Application		5,000
			Allotments		10,000
			Sept. 3 First call		5,000
			Oct. 5 Second and final call		5,000
		£25,000			£25,000
			Nov. 1 Balance b/d		25,000

FIRST CALL ACCOUNT

19__		£	19__		£
Sept. 3 Share capital		£5,000	Sept. 8 Bank		£5,000

SECOND AND FINAL CALL ACCOUNT

19__		£	19__		£
Oct. 5 Share capital		£5,000	Oct. 10 Bank		£5,000

BALANCE SHEET AS AT 31 OCTOBER 19__

	£		£
Current assets:		Authorised capital:	
Balance at bank	25,000	200,000 Ordinary shares of 25peach	50,000
		Issued capital:	
		100,000 Ordinary shares of 25p each fully paid	25,000
	£25,000		£25,000

The authorised share capital must be shown on the Balance Sheet. When this is the same as the issued capital the expression 'authorised and issued Capital' can be used as the heading.

13. Journal entries

As examiners often ask candidates to record the issue of capital in Journal form, all the entries will be repeated as they would appear in the Journal.

Example

19__	£	£	
July 17 Bank (Dr)	6,000		Being 5p per share
Application A/c		6,000	received on application for120,000 Ordinary Shares this day.
Aug. 3 Application A/c (Dr)	1,000		Being return of 5p per
Bank		1,000	share on 20,000 un-successful applications.
Aug. 3 Application A/c (Dr)	5,000		Being allotment of shares
Allotment A/c (Dr)	10,000		on this day, 10p per
Share Capital A/c		15,000	share due on allotment.
Aug. 8 Bank A/c (Dr)	10,000		Being amount received on
Allotment A/c		10,000	allotment.
Sept. 3 First Call A/c (Dr)	5,000		Being first call of 5p per
Share Capital A/c		5,000	share on 100,000 shares.
Sept. 8 Bank A/c (Dr)	5,000		Being amount received on
First Call A/c		5,000	the first call.
Oct. 5 Second and Final Call A/c (Dr)	5,000		Being second and final call of 5p per share on
Share Capital A/c		5,000	100,000 shares.
Oct. 10 Bank A/c (Dr)	5,000		Being amount received on
Second and Final Call A/c		5,000	the second and final call.

14. Calls in arrear

If in the previous example a subscriber for 4,000 shares failed to pay his final call the appropriate entries in the Ledger and in the Balance Sheet on 31 October 19__, would be as follows:

NOTE: The issued capital is now described as "fully called".

Example

SECOND AND FINAL CALL ACCOUNT

19__	£	19__	£
Oct. 5 Share Capital	5,000	Oct. 10 Bank	4,800
		31 Calls in arrears	200
	£5,000		£5,000

CALLS IN ARREARS ACCOUNT

19__	£
Oct. 31 Final Call A/c	£200

BALANCE SHEET (EXTRACT) AS AT 31 OCTOBER 19__

	£
Authorised capital:	
200,000 Ordinary Shares of 25p	
each	50,000
Issued capital:	
100,000 Ordinary Shares of 25p	
each fully called	25,000
Less: Calls in arrears	200
	£24,800

---

15. Calls in advance

Many people of varying temperaments subscribe for shares, and while some folk are very slow in paying, others are quick off the mark and on occasions even make payments before they are actually due.

Where such a situation occurs, there will be a credit balance on the Instalment Account. It is usual to transfer this balance to a 'Calls in Advance' Account. It appears on the Balance Sheet immediately below the issued capital.

When the call is actually made the amount due on the particular instalment is credited to the Call Account and debited to Calls in Advance Account.

Sample question _____

Again using the previous example, assume that A. Quick, who had subscribed for 10,000 shares, paid the whole of the amount due on his shares with the first call.

Show the position as it would appear at 30 September and also the Second and Final Call Account, again assuming that a subscriber for 4,000 shares failed to pay the final call.

FIRST CALL ACCOUNT

	£		£
Sept. 3 Share capital	5,000	Sept 8. Bank	5,500
30 Calls in advance	500		
	£5,500		£5,500

CALLS IN ADVANCE

	Sept. 30 First call	£500

BALANCE SHEET (EXTRACT) AS AT 30 SEPTEMBER 19__

	£
Authorised share capital:	
200,000 Ordinary Shares of 25p each	50,000
Issued capital:	
100,000 Ordinary Shares of 25p each,	
20p called	20,000
Calls in advance	500
	£20,500

SECOND AND FINAL CALL ACCOUNT

	£		£
Oct. 5 Share capital	5,000	Oct. 5 Calls in advance	500
		10 Bank	4,300
		31 Calls in arrears	200
	£5,000		£5,000

CALLS IN ADVANCE

Oct. 5 Second and final call	£500	Oct. 1 Balance	£500

NOTE: At 30 September the 20p was called and this fact was stated on the Balance Sheet.

16. Shares issued by established companies

Because of the prosperity of some companies their shares are worth more than the amount originally subscribed and their market price would exceed their par value. Such shares are said to be quoted at a premium.

From time to time companies may wish to raise additional capital by issuing more shares, and if a company's existing shares of a par value of 25p are quoted at 45p this fact would have to be taken into account when fixing the price at which new shares would be issued. The directors of the company would realise that they could get more than 25p although they might not be able to get quite 45p for the shares.

17. Rights issue

The directors may decide that the existing shareholders should have first claim to the new shares and accordingly issue the shares at par or at a concessionary price of, say, 40p in the full knowledge that the shareholders will benefit. Such an issue is called a rights issue, as the existing shareholders have a right to take up so many shares, say one for five held.

18. Issuing shares at a premium

The directors may decide that it is wise to obtain as much cash as possible for as few shares as possible. In other words, for every 25p share capital on which dividends are calculated the directors may ask and get 40p. In other words, they issue shares at a premium.

A separate account called 'Share Premium Account' must be opened. The balance of this account must be shown separately on the Balance Sheet until it is utilised for one of the few purposes sanctioned by the Companies Acts.

19. Procedure for recording the issue of shares at a premium

The issue of shares at a premium follows the normal procedure for issuing shares except for the instalment that includes the premium (the premium is always payable with a particular instalment).

NOTE: The premium is credited to a Share Premium Account and debited to the Call Account to which it refers.

Sample question _____

The directors of Bright and Breezy Ltd decide to issue 50,000 shares of 25p at a premium of 10p per share. Applications, together with 15p per share, were received on 1 April. Allotments were made in full on 1 May, and the balance due on the shares, including the premium, was received on 8 May.

Show by means of Journal entries the issue of the shares and the Balance Sheet as at 31 May.

19__	£	£	*Narration*
Apr. 1 Bank A/c (Dr)	7,500		Being 15p per share on
Application A/c		7,500	application for 50,000 shares.
May 1 Application A/c (Dr)	7,500		Being allotment of 50,000
Allotment A/c (Dr)	10,000		shares of 25p each
Share Premium A/c		5,000	issued at a premium of
Share Capital A/c		12,500	10p per share.
May 8 Bank A/c (Dr)	10,000		Being receipt of allotment
Allotment A/c		10,000	instalment including the premium of 10p per share on 50,000 shares.

BALANCE SHEET (EXTRACT) AT 31 MAY 19__

Issued capital:		£
150,000 Ordinary Shares of 25p each fully paid		37,500
Share premium		5,000

20. Bonus shares or scrip issue

(a) When profits are retained in the business and are used for expansion purposes it is obvious that the profits are no longer available for distribution to the shareholders since they are no longer represented by liquid assets, but by fixed assets. It is desirable to recognise this change by the issue of *bonus shares*. Bonus shares are issued to existing shareholders by means of capitalising reserves, that is reserves are used to increase the number of issued shares. No money passes at all but the shareholders do receive share certificates. Often the arrangement is referred to as a paper or scrip issue.

(b) *Share Premium Account.* Provided all legal requirements are complied with and necessary resolutions passed the directors can use the balance on Share Premium Account for issuing bonus shares to the ordinary shareholders.

Example _____

On 31 December 19__ the directors of Bright and Breezy Ltd having complied with all the necessary requirements use the credit balance on the Share Premium Account to issue Bonus Shares at the rate of two new shares for every fifteen shares held.

SHARE PREMIUM ACCOUNT

19__		£	19__	£
Dec. 31 Share Capital Account		£5,000	Mar. 31 Balance b/d	£5,000

SHARE CAPITAL ACCOUNT

19__		£	19__	£
Dec. 31 Balance c/d		42,500	Mar. 31 Balance b/d	37,500
			Dec. 31 Share Premium	
			Account	5,000
		£42,500		£42,500
			Jan. 1 Balance b/d	42,500

BALANCE SHEET (EXTRACT) AT 31 DECEMBER 19__

Issued share capital:
170,000 Ordinary Shares of 25p each fully paid up   £42,500

Progress test 30

1. What are the main characteristics of limited liability?   (9)

2. What is the difference between Ordinary Shares and Preference Shares?   (4)

3. What is meant by:
    (a) authorised, registered or nominal capital;
    (b) issued capital;
    (c) called-up capital;
    (d) paid-up capital?   (10)

4. Why are instalments due on shares referred to as 'calls'?   (10)

5. Why is an Application Account opened before a Share Capital Account?   (12)

6. How are calls in arrears shown in a Balance Sheet?   (14)

7. What is a Debenture?   (7)

8. What are the characteristics of Convertible Loan Stock? **(7)**

9. When are shares normally issued at a premium? **(16)**

10. What is a 'rights issue'? **(17)**

11. What are the legal requirements for issuing shares at a premium? **(18)**

12. What is a 'scrip issue'? **(20)**

Specimen questions

1. A limited company offered 50,000 Ordinary Shares of £1 each at £1.15 per share, payable 75p per share on application on 1 March 19__ and 40p per share on allotment a month later.

Applications were received for 60,000 Ordinary Shares. On 15 March 19__ application moneys were returned to persons who had applied for 5,000 shares and to whom no shares were allotted, while the other applicants had their applications scaled down by a total of 5,000 shares.

All moneys payable on allotment were received, except that one shareholder failed to pay the amount due on his 300 shares applied for and allotted. Record the above transactions in the company's Cash Book and Ledger, and show the necessary Journal entries.

2. X Ltd decided to issue 200,000 Ordinary Shares of £1 each at a premium of 10p per share payable as follows:

(a) 25p per share on application;
(b) 35p per share (including the premium) on allotment;
(c) the balance three months after allotment.

On 1 April 19_ applications were received for 240,000 shares. On 8 April applications for 168,000 shares were accepted in full, and applicants for 64,000 shares were allotted one-half of the number for which they had applied; excess application money being used to reduce the amount due on allotment. On the same date deposits were returned to applicants for 8,000 shares. On 20 April all money due on allotment was received.

The amount due from the shareholders for the balance of the share issue was received on 31 July, with the exception of the amount due from O. Franks, the holder of 300 shares.

Show the entries necessary to record the above matters in the company's Bank Account and Ledger, balancing off at the end of October 19__ .

3. Expanding Ltd has an authorised capital of £2 million. Already in issue are 500,000 7 per cent Cumulative Preference shares of £1 and 1,000,000 Ordinary Shares of 75p each. It published a prospectus in connection with issuing the remainder of its authorised capital, as further ordinary shares of 75p at a price of £1.25. 25p per share was payable on application (due by 1 October 19_1), the balance on or before 31 December 19_1.

£3 million was received with properly completed application forms and all applications were scaled down pro rata, with the excess money being applied first towards the amount due on allotment and any further excess being returned. By 31 December 19_1 all amounts due had been received. Present the journal entries (including cash) recording all aspects detailed above.

4. On 31 May, XY Ltd had a registered capital of £25,000 divided into 20,000 7 per cent Preference Shares of 50p each (all issued), and 60,000 Ordinary Shares of 25p each (40,000 issued).

After payment of all dividends the Profit and Loss Account has a credit balance of £3,175.

Trade creditors amount to £3,500 and £300 mortgage loan interest is outstanding.

The company owns the following assets:

	£
Premises at cost	30,000
Machinery and plant at cost	20,000
Stock	5,000
Debtors	1,600
Cash and bank	1,500

Provisions have been created for doubtful debts, £125, and for depreciation of plant and machinery, £7,000. The premises are mortgaged for £24,000.

Set out the Balance Sheet as it would appear on 31 May.

5. Strok Ltd. an old-established company with an authorised capital of £250,000 Ordinary Shares of £1 each, decides to revalue its assets to bring them into the accounts at current values. The summarised Trial Balance prior to revaluation was:

	£	£
Issued capital, fully paid		200,000
Freehold Building	80,000	
Plant and Machinery	206,563	
Creditors		86,752
Bank		163,487
Stock	97,835	
Debtors	65,841	
	£450,239	£450,239

The valuation revealed a surplus over book values of £65,268 on buildings and £30,737 on plant.

It is proposed to capitalise the majority of the surplus by distributing as a bonus issue one Ordinary Share for every five shares held, and one 6 per cent Preference Share of £1 for every four shares held.

Following this distribution it is proposed to improve company liquidity by issuing 135,000 more ordinary shares of £1 at a price of £1.25 each. Part of this will be a rights issue available to existing ordinary shareholders on a 1 in 5 basis using the revised capital after the revaluation. The rest will be offered to the general public. A total of 75 pence per share is due on application, which includes the premium. The balance is payable after three months. All the rights are taken up, and other applications are received for 100,000 shares. Surplus application money for excess shares is returned and all money due on the first and final call is received except for the instalment on 1,000 shares allotted to one institutional investor.

To effect these proposals, the authorised capital is increased. The total cost of the issue made is £3,425.

Show:

(a) the necessary Journal and Cash Book entries;
(b) the Balance Sheet upon completion.

31
Sinking funds

Sinking funds are usually discussed in more advanced books on accountancy. However, questions on this subject do appear in examinations covered by this book so sufficient material has been included to cover this requirement.

1. Provisions

A provision is an amount set aside for a specific purpose. In 21:5 it was stated that when a provision is made the Profit and Loss Account is debited and the Provision Account itself is credited.

2. Effect of making a provision

If the Profit and Loss Account is debited with the amount of the provision, then the profit available for distribution must be less than it otherwise would be and it usually follows that the cash actually distributed is less. Hence the making of a provision has the effect of retaining cash in the business.

Unfortunately, in practice, cash which has been retained in the business as a result of a provision has a tendency to be used for purposes other than that originally intended. The most likely such purpose is the expansion of the ordinary business activities; the purchase of more stock for re-sale, etc.

3. Sinking funds

In order to ensure that *cash* is available for the specific purpose required, a sum of money equal to the amount of the provision is earmarked by being invested outside the business so that *under normal circumstances it cannot be used for other purposes*. The chief characteristic of a sinking fund is that the amount charged to the sinking fund is invested and allowed to accumulate, any dividends or interest from the investment being reinvested so that the fund grows.

4. Calculation of annual appropriation

The amount required to be set aside each year to accumulate to a fixed sum is obtained from annuity tables which state clearly the sum required each year at a given rate of interest for a fixed period of time.

Example _____

If £1 is put aside each year for three years and the rate of interest is 10 per cent the following would apply.

	£
Amount set aside at end of 1st year	1.00
Interest at end of 2nd year	0.10
Amount set aside at end of 2nd year	1.00
	2.10
Interest at end of 3rd year	0.21
Amount set aside at end of 3rd year	1.00
Total set aside and interest	£3.31

If the £1 is set aside each year for three years and allowed to accumulate at 10 per cent per annum the amount at the end of three years would be £3.31.

If, however, one wants to know how much is required to be set aside each year for three years to amount to exactly £3 the annual sum would be found by dividing 3 by 3.31,

$$\text{thus} \quad \frac{3}{3.31} = £0.90634$$

So if £0.90634 is set aside each year it will amount to £3 (assuming a compound rate of interest of 10 per cent). In order to find how much is required to be set aside each year to amount to £1 the amount would be $\frac{0.90634}{3} = £0.30211.$

_____

5. Total required

Naturally in practice a much larger amount is required and annuity tables which express the annual instalments as decimals of £1 are available for this purpose, a short abstract of which is as follows:

Annual sum required each year to produce £1 at the rates shown

Years	3%	5%	10%
3	0.32353	0.31721	0.30211
5	0.18835	0.18097	0.16380
10	0.08723	0.07951	0.06275

Once the amount required is known the annual instalment is simply obtained by multiplying the decimal by the amount required.

Example

Goodtime Ltd has issued £60,000 6 per cent Debentures at 98 ten years ago. As they are due to be redeemed at par in three years' time it was decided to make out of profits an annual appropriation sufficient to provide the amount required in three years' time. The annual amount set aside was based on the assumption that the money invested could earn 10 per cent interest.

Steps to be taken.

(a) Find the appropriate annual sum for the period in time in years (in this case 3) and percentage (in this case 0.30211) then multiply this by the total required at the end of the period, i.e. £60,000. This gives the annual sum £18,127.

(b) Open a Sinking Fund Account: *debit* Appropriation Account; *credit* Sinking Fund Account with this annual sum.

(c) Open a Sinking Fund Investment Account: *debit* Sinking Fund Investment Account; *credit* bank with exactly the same amount as the annual sum.

NOTE: This is the amount of cash which has been retained in the business as a result of the debit of the Appropriation Account figure.

(d) At the end of the second year when interest is received on the investment, *debit* bank, *credit* Sinking Fund Account.

(e) At end of the second year *debit* Sinking Fund Investment Account, *credit* bank with an amount equal to the annual instalment *plus* the interest earned during the previous year.

(f) Continue the same operation each year, i.e. always *credit* the sinking fund with interest received and reinvest with the next year's annual instalment.

(g) The exercise is now complete and there appear two balances of exactly the same amount but which have different characteristics, i.e. a credit balance in the Sinking Fund Account and a debit of the same amount on the Sinking Fund Investment Account.

SINKING FUND ACCOUNT

	£		£
Year 2		Year 1	
Dec. 31 Balance c/f	38,067	Dec. 31 Appropriation Account	18,127
		Year 2	
		Dec. 31 Bank (interest for year)	1,813
		Appropriation A/c	18,127
	£38,067		£38,067
Year 3	£	Year 3	£
Dec. 31 Balance c/f	60,000	Jan. 1 Balance b/f	38,067
		Dec. 31 Bank (interest for year)	3,806
		Appropriation A/c	18,127
	£60,000		£60,000
		Year 4	
		Jan. 1 Balance b/f	60,000

SINKING FUND INVESTMENT ACCOUNT

	£		£
Year 1		Year 2	
Dec. 31 Bank	18,127	Dec. 31 Balance c/f	38,067
Year 2			
Dec. 31 Bank	19,940		
	£38,067		£38.067
Year 3	£	Year 3	£
Jan. 1 Balance b/f	38,067	Dec. 31 Balance c/f	60,000
Dec. 31 Bank	21,933		
	£60,000		£60,000
Year 4			
Jan. 1 Balance b/f	60,000		

Normally the investments would now be realised for cash and if, as it is hoped, exactly the amount expected is obtained there would be £60,000 available to redeem the debentures. Sometimes the last instalment is not invested but used to increase the cash obtained from realising the instalments.

The £60,000 would be repaid to the debenture holders thus:

DEBENTURES ACCOUNT

Year 4		Year 4	
Jan. 1 Bank	£60,000	Jan. 1 Balance	£60,000

The net result of the exercise is that there is now a credit balance on the Sinking Fund Account of £60,000 instead of a credit balance of that amount on the Debenture Account.

6. Profit and loss on realisation of investments

If the investments realise more or less than the book value of the investments the profit or loss is transferred to the Sinking Fund Account. Note that this is one instance of a direct entry between the two accounts.

Example _____

On 1 January 19__, the balance on the sinking fund of a company was £165,000 represented by investments amounting to a similar figure. It also had outstanding £180,000 7 per cent Debentures. During the year to 31 December 19__, the undermentioned transaction took place:

(a) half-year Debenture interest was paid on 30 June;
(b) sinking fund investments were sold on 15 December and realised £187,000.

Income from investments received during the year amounted to £15,000 and this was not reinvested. The Debentures were refunded on 31 December 19__ together with a half-year's interest.

It is intended to redeem the Debentures on 31 December and you are required to give the appropriate accounts.

SINKING FUND INVESTMENT ACCOUNT

19__		£	19__		£
Jan. 1 Balance		165,000	Dec. 15 Bank		187,000
Jan. 1 Sinking Fund A/c					
Profit on					
investments		22,000			
		£187,000			£187,000

SINKING FUND ACCOUNT

19__		£	19__		£
Dec. 31 Balance c/f		202,000	Jan. 1 Balance		165,000
			Dec. 31 Bank interest		15,000
			Sinking Fund Invest-		
			ment A/c		22,000
		£202,000			£202,000
			Dec. 31 Balance b/f		£202,000

7% DEBENTURES ACCOUNT

Dec. 31 Bank		£180,000	Jan. 1 Balance b/f		£180,000

DEBENTURE INTEREST
£

19__
June 30 Bank (Gross) £6,300
Dec. 31 Bank   £6,300

Progress test 31

1. Why are sinking funds considered necessary? **(3)**

2. In what ways do they differ from normal provisions or reserves? **(3)**

3. How is the annual appropriation calculated? **(4)**

4. What are the main entries in the Sinking Fund Investment Account? **(5)**

5. How is interest on investments dealt with? **(5)**

6. How are profits or losses on sale of investments dealt with? **(6)**

Specimen questions

1. Security Ltd issued £50,000 9 per cent Debentures at 97 on 1 January 19_0 redeemable at par on 31 December 19_5. No redemptions took place in the intervening five years.

The company maintained a sinking fund for redemption of the Debentures, and on 1 January 19_5, the balance of this fund was £42,800. There was an equal amount invested in gilt-edged securities shown in the books at cost. No further securities were purchased in 19_5.

On 31 December 19_5, the sinking fund investments were sold for £43,300. On the same day, a final appropriation of £4,300 was made to the sinking fund from profits, interest of £2,900 was received on sinking fund investments and the debentures were redeemed.

Show the relevant accounts for the transactions in 19_5. (Ignore interest paid on debentures.)

2. Fox Ltd issued £275,000 6¼ per cent Debentures at par in 19_1 which were redeemable at 103 on 30 September 19_9. In accordance with provisions in the Debenture trust deed, annual appropriations had been made out of profits to a sinking fund, to provide for the redemption of the Debentures. The appropriations had been invested annually on 30 September together with the sinking fund investment income received in the year ended on that date.

On 1 October 19_8, the following balances appeared in the company's books.

(a) Sinking Fund Account £173,570 represented by investments (at cost) amounting to a similar figure.
(b) 6¼ per cent Debentures £180,000 (balance remaining after cancellations authorised by the Trust Deed).

During the year ended 30 September 19_9, the undermentioned transactions had taken place.

(a) On 31 March 19_9, a half-year's debenture interest was paid.
(b) The sinking fund investments were sold and the proceeds amounting to £185,640 were received on 12 September 19_9.
(c) The income from sinking fund investments received during the year amounted to £11,200 and was not invested but retained in view of the impending redemption of the debentures.
(d) The Debentures were repaid on 30 September 19_9, together with the half-year's interest due thereon.

You are required to write up the following accounts for the year ended 30 September 19_9, as they would appear in the ledger:

(i) 6¼ per cent Debentures;
(ii) sinking fund investments;
(iii) sinking fund.

3. You are required to write up the Sinking Fund Account, the Sinking Fund Investment Account and the Leasehold Property Account in the ledger of H Limited during the three years ended 31 December 19_4. H Limited has decided to provide for the renewal of a three-year lease, which was originally acquired on 31 December 19_1 at a cost of £40,000, by setting up a sinking fund. An annual appropriation of profit is made on 31 December in each year (commencing in 19_2) and the money is invested in chosen securities. The interest on the securities and any profit or loss on the sale of the securities are to be taken to the Sinking Fund Account.

The transactions during the three years were as follows.

		£
19_2 Dec. 31	Appropriation of profit of	12,000
	This amount was invested in securities.	
19_3 June 30	Securities originally cost £3,800 were sold for	3,500
	The proceeds of sale were re-invested.	
19_3 Dec. 31	Appropriation of profit of	12,000
	Interest received on securities of	1,400
	These two amounts were invested.	
19_4 Mar. 31	Securities originally costing £1,800 were sold for	2,000
	The proceeds of sale were re-invested.	
19-4 Dec. 31	Interest received on securities of	2,900
	This amount was not invested.	
	All securities were sold for	25,200
	This amount was not invested.	
	Appropriation of profit of such an amount as would bring the Sinking Fund Account to the amount required for renewal (£40,000) not invested.	
	Old lease was written off.	
	Purchase of new lease for	40,000

Funds flow statements of limited liability companies

1. Sole traders' and companies' capitals

Companies differ from sole traders in their capital structure, and consequently when we attempt to draw up a statement about a company's sources and applications of funds during a year we need to know the finer points about the company's capital structure and pattern of activities. Some of these points are made clear below. In the case of a sole trader the expression *capital* is used to denote the extent of the owner's financial interest in the business. It is measured by the difference between total assets and total external liabilities. Normally the capital in this context is made up of money originally put into the business plus retained profit.

As applied to companies the expression *capital* denotes the issued shares originally subscribed by the shareholders and increased by further issue of shares.

2. Retained profits and reserves

Retained profits of companies are treated as revenue reserves. They may be allocated from the Appropriation Account to a particular reserve such as Plant Replacement Reserve or to a General Reserve – the chief use of which perhaps is to equalise the dividend as between good and bad years. There is also usually a balance on the credit side of the Appropriation Account which is an unappropriated reserve. A Balance Sheet may be displayed in such a way as to show the ordinary shareholders' total interest in the company, but reserves are never added to the issued capital unless they are made the subject of a bonus issue of shares – which makes them permanent capital of the business.

3.   Asset revaluation and reserves

Reserves reflect the owners' financial interest in the business, in excess of the issued capital of the company. Sometimes reserves arise as a result of revaluation of assets.

Example _____

If premises which cost £60,000 are revalued to £75,000 the additional £15,000 still belongs to the owners but it is not part of the issued capital, and as such is shown as a reserve. It is a *capital reserve*, a term which implies that it may not be distributed as dividend to the shareholders even if funds were available to make this possible. The theory behind this is that these profits have been made in a way outside the 'objects clause' of the company's Memorandum of Association. Other capital reserves are Share Premium Account and Profits Prior to Incorporation Account (where profits have been made by a company before its Certificate of Incorporation was issued). Companies may not make profits before they come into existence.

Note that where a reserve has been created by revaluation there is no effect at all on the cash flow.

_____

4.   Profit on sale of asset

Occasionally a profit on a sale of an asset is taken direct to a reserve, instead of going to the Profit and Loss Account. Again such reserves do not involve an inflow of cash and should be ignored. (The proceeds of the sale of the asset do involve an inflow of cash.)

5.   Share premium reserve

Where shares are issued at a premium, the excess of the par value of the issued capital is credited to a *share premium reserve*. During the year that this is credited, it forms part of the proceeds of the issue of shares and is brought into the cash inflow.

6.   Discount on debentures

Occasionally debentures are issued at a discount. Often the amount of the discount is shown as a *fictitious* asset. During the year of issue the amount of the discount must be deducted from the issued debentures so that only the actual proceeds of the issue are shown as the net inflow of cash.

7.   Fictitious assets

When discount on shares or debentures is shown as an asset it is sometimes termed a fictitious asset. It is not really an asset but simply classified as such because of legal formalities. Formation expenses and expenses of shares issued are in the same category.

Prudence suggests that such assets are written off in the Profit and Loss Account as soon as possible. In the year in which they are written off, profits are reduced. However, no outflow of cash has resulted from this particular item; hence an adjustment is needed for the figure of retained profit (similar to depreciation).

8.   Goodwill, patents and trade marks

These are often referred to as intangible assets. Although there is nothing to see for them they are of value. However, their value often declines and this loss of value is written off in the Profit and Loss Account. Again no outflow of cash is involved so an adjustment is required to the figure of retained profit.

9.   Dividends

These are similar to the drawings of a sole trader in that they represent the amount withdrawn by the shareholders.

It is important to remember that the actual payments for the year are shown, not necessarily the amount charged in the Appropriation Accounts.

If *proposed dividends* are included they must *not* be shown in the current year. Often however the proposed dividends for the previous year are paid in the current year when they would be included in the Sources and Application Statement.

10.   Corporation tax

The amount actually paid during the year is included. In most examples this will not be the same as the amount included in the Appropriation Account. In other words, as with dividends, the amount owing for the year is completely ignored.

Provisions for corporation tax and also provisions for dividends shown on the Balance Sheet are completely ignored.

11.   Miscellaneous outgoings

(a) *Repayment of redeemable Preference Shares* during the year would be treated as an outflow of cash, again allowing for the premium where applicable.

(b) *Repayment of Debentures* during the year would also be treated as an outflow of cash.

12. Net profit

Where full final accounts are given in the question it is wise to take the figure of net profit appearing in the Profit and Loss Account. All items shown in the Appropriation Account should be treated separately. However, in many questions only two successive years' Balance Sheets are given so often a complicated exercise is required to find the figure of net profit.

Example

From the summarised Balance Sheet of B.S. Low Ltd, as at 31 December 19_2 and 19_3 prepare a Funds Flow Statement for the year 19_3.

	19_2 £	19_3 £		19_2 £	19_3 £
Freehold property	47,500	59,250	Issued share capital		
Machinery			Ordinary Shares	45,000	60,000
Less Depreciation	31,735	38,535	10% Preference Shares	15,000	15,000
Goodwill at cost	–	3,750	Share premium	–	3,000
Stock	4,210	13,500	Reserve	–	12,425
Debtors	3,980	5,400	Appropriation A/c	10,875	22,075
Bank	–	15,465	12% Debentures	–	10,000
Formation expenses	225	–	Bank overdraft	5,300	–
Discount on Debenture	–	100	Creditors	5,475	6,000
			Proposed dividend on:		
			Ordinary Shares	4,500	6,000
			Preference Shares	1,500	1,500
	£87,650	136,000		£87,650	136,000

NOTES:
(1)   Profit is arrived at after charging depreciation of £4,600.
(2)   The reserve of £12,425 represents:
    (a)   revaluation of Freehold Properties;
    (b)   profit on sale of Machinery which had a book value at 31 December 19_2 of £1,400.
(3)   No freehold property was bought or sold during the year.
(4)   The Balance Sheets are presented in a form intended to help with the problems of preparing Funds Flow Statements. They do not necessarily conform with the requirements of the Companies Acts.

DETAILED WORKINGS

(a) *Find the net profit*, since this is one source of funds. £

	£
Appropriation Account balance at end	22,075
Less Balance at beginning	10,875
Retained profit for year	11,200
Add Proposed dividends	7,500
Net profit	18,700
Add Formation expenses written off	225
	18,925
Add Depreciation	4,600
Inflow of cash resulting from profit	£23,525

(b) *Find proceeds of sales of machinery.*

	£
Amount of reserve	12,425
Less Arising from increase in value of property	11,750
Leaving balance due to the profit on sale of machinery	675
As the written down value of machinery sold was	1,400
The proceeds of sale must have been	£2,075

NOTE: As profit on sale is credited direct to reserve there is no need to adjust the figure of net profit.

(c) *Find acquisition of new machinery.* In some respects it is a little old-fashioned not to show separately provision for depreciation. However the method of adjusting depreciation in the Machinery Account is a useful examination technique which calls for an involved calculation to ascertain the amount spent on new machinery, as follows.

MACHINERY ACCOUNT		£
Balance at end		38,535
Add Depreciation for year		4,600
		43,135
Less Balance at beginning	31,735	
Less Asset sold	1,400	
		30,335
New machinery acquired		£12,800

(d) *Working capital movement* (disregarding cash balances)

19_3 Stock	13,500	
Debtors	5,400	
		18,900
Less Creditors		6,000
		12,900
19_2 Stock	4,210	
Debtors	3,980	
	8,190	
Less Creditors	5,475	
		2,715
Increase during year		£10,185

(e) *Debentures.* Net proceeds are £10,000 less discount £100 i.e. £9,900.

(f) *Share issue.* Proceeds consist of new issue of Ordinary Shares £15,000 plus premiums of £3,000, i.e. £18,000.

Solution

SOURCES AND APPLICATIONS OF FUNDS FOR YEAR TO 31 DECEMBER 19_3

Sources:	£	£
Net profit	23,525	
Proceeds of sale of asset	2,075	
Issue of Debentures	9,900	
Issue of Ordinary Shares	18,000	
		53,500
Applications:		
Dividend paid on Preference Shares	1,500	
Dividend paid on Ordinary Shares	4,500	
Machinery	12,800	
Goodwill purchased	3,750	
Increase in working capital	10,185	
		32,735
Unapplied funds available as increase in cash during year (from an overdraft of £5,300 to a favourable balance of £15,465.)		£20,765

Cash summary:	£
Balance at end	15,465
Add Overdraft at beginning	5,300
Improvement in cash	£20,765

NOTE: *Treatment of dividend.* Dividend should be shown as an outflow of cash only when actually paid. As there were proposed dividends of £6,000 for 19_2, this amount must have been paid in 19_3. Hence the dividend shown in the Sources and Applications of Funds Statement.

---

13. Statement of Standard Accounting Practice No. 10

Chartered accountants are now obliged to prepare a funds flow statement for businesses with a turnover of more than £25,000. Guidelines are issued as under the following.

(a) *Specific items to be included.* Special mention is made of the following items to be included:

(*i*) dividends paid;

(*ii*) acquisition and disposals of fixed and other non-current assets;

(*iii*) funds raised by increasing medium- or long-term loans or the issue of capital or expended in repaying medium- or long-term loans;

(*iv*) increase or decrease in working capital sub-divided into its components and movements in net liquid funds.

(b) *Form of statement.* While any recognised form of Sources and Applications Statement will be accepted, the example given in the Standard includes two novelties:

(*i*) tax paid is shown as a separate item and any accruals of tax ignored;

(*ii*) the Statement shows the increase or decrease in working capital and then shows the breakdown of that working capital, including cash.

A typical statement meeting requirements is shown on p.438.

STATEMENT OF SOURCES AND APPLICATION OF FUNDS

	This Year £K	Last Year £K
Source of funds:		
Profits before tax	1,430	440
Adjustments for items not involving the movement of funds		
Depreciation	380	325
Total generated from operations	1,810	765
Funds from other sources		
Issue of shares for cash	100	80
	1,910	845
Application of funds:		
Dividend paid	400	400
Tax paid	690	230
Purchase of fixed assets	460	236
	1,550	866
Increase/decrease in working capital	360	(21)
Increase in stocks	80	114
Increase in debtors	120	22
Decrease/increase in creditors (excluding taxation and proposed dividends)	115	(107)
Movement in net liquid funds		
Increase/decrease in cash	(5)	35
Short-term investments	50	(85)
	360	(21)
Change in net liquids funds	£45	£(50)

NOTE: *Net liquid funds* are defined as cash at bank, in hand and short-term investments held as current assets, *less* bank overdrafts and other borrowings repayable within one year of the accounting date.

Progress test 32

1. In what respects does a cash flow statement of a limited company differ from that of a sole trader? **(1–2)**

2. Does any revaluation of an asset affect the cash flow and, if so, how?   **(3)**

3. When shares are issued at a premium, how is the premium dealt with?   **(5)**

4. Does the writing off of formation assets or other fictitious assets affect the cash, and, if so, how?   **(7)**

5. When Debentures or redeemable Preference Shares are repaid, what amounts are included in the cash flow statements?   **(11)**

6. How are dividends paid dealt with?   **(9)**

7. How is the acquisition of goodwill by a company treated in a cash flow statement?   **(8)**

Specimen questions

1. The Balance Sheets of W. Limited in 19_3 and 19_4 are as follows:

	31.3._3	31.3._4		31.3._3	31.3._4
	£K	£K		£K	£K
Motor Vehicles, at			Issued Share Capital	100	100
cost less depreciation	96	60	Retained profits	12	44
Stock at or below cost	60	100	9% Debentures		24
Debtors	62	64	Bank Overdraft	25	
Bank		12	Creditors	81	68
	£218	£236		£218	£236

Prepare a Funds Flow Statement for the year 19_3 to 19_4.

2.

A COMPANY
BALANCE SHEETS – 31 DECEMBER

	Year 1 £K	Year 2 £K		Year 1 £K	Year 2 £K
Property at cost	–	20	Share Capital	25	25
Motor Vehicles at cost	30	35	General Reserve	20	25
Less: Depreciation	6	13	Profit and Loss		
	24	22	Account	7	3
Stock	15	25	Secured Loan		6
Debtors	15.5	16	Bank Overdraft		3
Cash	18	–	Creditors	20.5	21
	£72.5	£83		£72.5	£83

PROFIT AND LOSS APPROPRIATION ACCOUNT
FOR YEAR 2

	£K		£K
Transfer to general reserve	5	Balance brought forward	
Dividends	12	from previous years	7
Balance carried forward		Net profit for year	13
to next year	3		
	£20		£20
		Balance b/f	3

Prepare a Funds Flow Statement for Year 2, and reconcile this with the working capital at 31 December, Years 1 and 2.

3. Summarised Balance Sheets of Gryphon Ltd, yacht builders and chandlers, for the year ended 31 December 19_0 and 19_1 appear below.

	19_0 £	19_1 £		19_0 £	19_1 £
Buildings	300,000	300,000	Share Capital	300,000	450,000
Bank	43,440	4,860	Capital Reserves	150,000	–
Debtors	86,100	98,300	Profit and Loss A/c	81,780	106,260
Plant**	189,600	222,960	Corporation Tax	102,300	95,160
Stock	75,540	84,700	Creditors	60,600	59,400
	£694,680	£710,820		£694,680	£710,820

**Movements on Plant Account opposite

Movements on Plant Account:

	Cost	Depreci- ation	Net book value
	£	£	£
Balance at 31 Dec. 19_0	327,000	137,400	189,600
Add:			
Purchases	72,960		
Depreciation for the year		32,700	
	399,960	170,100	229,860
Less Sales	65,400	58,500	6,900
Balance at 31 Dec. 19_1	£334,560	£111,600	£222,960

A profit of £12,000 on the sales of plant had been credited to the Profit and Loss Account.

Corporation tax paid during the year to 31 December 19_1 was £102,300.

Account in as much detail as possible for the change in the bank balance between 31 December 19_0 and 31 December 19_1, in a Statement of Sources and Application of Funds for the year ended 31 December 19_1.

4. The following are the summarised Profit and loss Accounts of L.J. Ltd, a small trading company, for the years 19_4 and 19_5, and the Balance Sheets at the end of each of these years.

PROFIT AND LOSS ACCOUNTS FOR THE
YEARS ENDED 31 DECEMBER

	19_4		19_5	
	£	£	£	£
Gross profit		54,000		50,000
General Expenses	24,200		42,000	
Depreciation of Motor Vans	800		1,500	
Loss on sale of Motor Vans			4,800	
Interest on loan			1,600	
Directors' fees	8,000		8,000	
		33,000		57,900
Net profit/loss		21,000		−7,900
Balance of profit/loss b/f		800		21,800
Balance of profit/loss c/f		£21,800		£13,900

BALANCE SHEETS AT 31 DECEMBER

	19_4		*19_5*	
Authorised and issued	£	£	£	£
share capital:				
£1 Ordinary Shares				
fully paid		40,000		40,000
Balance of Profit and				
Loss A/c		21,800		13,900
		61,800		53,900
Loan (secured on				
freehold)		–		20,000
Trade creditors		12,400		26,150
		£74,200		£100,050
Freehold properties		35,000		35,000
Motor vans, at cost	14,000		30,000	
Less Depreciation	6,400		1,500	
		7,600		28,500
		42,600		63,500
Stock in trade		16,450		11,450
Trade Debtors		9,100		21,450
Bank		6,050		3,650
		£74,200		£100,050

The motor vans were entirely replaced by new vehicles on 1
January 19_5.

Prepare a statement showing the Sources and Applications
of Funds during the year 19_5.

Limited companies: published accounts

1. Introduction

Due to the separation of ownership and management, plus the limited liability of shareholders, there is a legal requirement for companies to publish accounts. This protects:

(a) the shareholders, who require information on how the directors have managed their funds during the year; and

(b) the creditors, who need to establish the creditworthiness of a company before advancing it money, or supplying goods or services.

Where a company is a public company, able to appeal to the general public for funds and with its shares quoted on the Stock Exchange and freely transferable, there is every justification for legislation to ensure that the public are fully informed about the company's affairs.

2. Disclosure requirements

The accounting and disclosure requirements are mostly contained in the 1985 Act but both the 1985 and the 1989 Act are important.

Directors are required to prepare annual accounts which must be circulated to each shareholder, and must also be filed with the Registrar of Companies who will then make them available to the general public for inspection.

(a) Every limited company must prepare full statutory accounts for circulation to shareholders. Small and medium-sized companies may file modified, i.e. less detailed, statutory accounts with the Registrar of Companies.

(b) Such companies must meet at least *two* of the following requirements to be exempted, and must be private companies:

		Small company	Medium-sized company
(*i*)	turnover	<£2m.	<£8m.
(*ii*)	Balance Sheet total	<£975,000	<£3.9m.
(*iii*)	average number of employees	<50	<250

These figures may be up-dated from time to time.

(c) The detailed exemptions in general terms are as follows:

small companies: no Profit and Loss Account required; a less detailed Balance Sheet required;

medium-sized companies: less detailed Profit and Loss Account; but a full Balance Sheet required.

The idea of these exemptions is to excuse small and medium-sized companies from the need to reveal details (particularly turnover) which would make them vulnerable to takeovers by large and aggressive competitors.

3. Format of accounts

The 1985 Companies Act lays down four alternative formats for the Profit and Loss Account, and two alternative formats for the Balance Sheet. Little discretion is allowed in the layout and naming of items in these formats.

In effect there is only one format for the Balance Sheet, which may be presented either vertically or horizontally, thus technically making two formats. Similarly there are only two formats for the Profit and Loss Account, which again may be presented either vertically or horizontally so technically making four formats.

Before looking at one of these formats in each case students might appreciate a few comments on the historical development of accounting presentations. The simple and logical presentation is in horizontal style (i.e. the same style as an account with a left-hand side and a right-hand side). The Balance Sheet was invented by Simon Stevin of Bruges in 1536 and called by him a Statement of Affairs, but unfortunately when he extracted his

Balance Sheet he crossed over the sides, putting Assets on the right and Liabilities on the left. Other nations quickly corrected this error, but in the United Kingdom Parliament enacted it into law in the Companies Act of 1856 where companies were required to produce a Balance Sheet in Simon Stevin's incorrect style. This thus became the 'traditional British Style'.

Later the accountancy bodies, for reasons nothing to do with accounting but to do with the greater amount of space available on the paper, adopted the vertical style, as a more sophisticated presentation. There is really nothing to be said for adopting the vertical style, which is much more difficult for laymen to understand than the ordinary 'account' style. Since the accounts which follow are in vertical style students can judge this for themselves. It requires quite a degree of accountancy knowledge in the Profit and Loss Account to move from the turnover in vertical style to the final balance on the Appropriation Account, as shown in our example. The greater length of line available to the printer can be achieved (if it is necessary at all) with the horizontal style by printing the accounts across a double page, with the 'debit' side on the left and the 'credit' side on the right. The accounts of any large European company will show this.

To return to the enacted formats, and illustrating the vertical style we have:

Example

Pro forma Final Accounts and Balance Sheet based on one format:

(NOTE: Trading items are incorporated in the format. Explanations of various items are given in the numbered notes.)

Note (1) This, as explained on p.448, is a written statement of the company's accounting policies (or changes in policy — such as a change in Depreciation — introduced in the current year).

GOOD PASSES PLC
PROFIT AND LOSS ACCOUNT FOR THE YEAR ENDED 31
MARCH 19_4

Notes		£K	£K
(2)	Turnover		660
	Cost of sales		420
	Gross profit		240
	Distribution costs	80	
	Administrative expenses	95	
			175
(3)	Operating profit		65
(4)	Other income		6
			71
(5)	Interest payable		3
(6)	Profit on ordinary activities before tax		68
(7)	Taxation		24
	Profit on ordinary activities after tax		44
(8)	Extraordinary items		4
			40
(9)	Transfer to reserves		4
			36
(10)	Dividends		12
	Unappropriated profit for the year		24
	Unappropriated profits brought forward		56
	Unappropriated profits carried forward		£80

GOOD PASSES PLC
BALANCE SHEET AS AT 31 MARCH 19_4

Notes	£K	£K	£K
Fixed assets:			
(11) Intangible assets			7
(12) Tangible assets			528
(13) Investments			140
			675
Current assets:			
(14) Stocks		95	
(15) Debtors		218	
(16) Investments		–	
Cash at bank and in hand		71	
		384	
Creditors: amounts falling due within one year:			
(17) Debenture loans	–		
(18) Bank loans and overdrafts	–		
(19) Other creditors	93		
Corporation tax	21		
Proposed dividends	12		
Advanced corporation tax payable	5		
	131		
Net Current Assets:			253
Total assets *less* current liabilities			928
Creditors: amounts falling due after more than one year:			
(20) Debenture loans		–	
(21) Bank loans and overdrafts		40	
(22) Other creditors			
Corporation tax		24	
			64
Provisions for liabilities and charges		–	
Deferred tax		–	
(23) Other provisions		–	
Net assets			£864
Capital and reserves:			
(24) Called up share capital		600	
(25) Share Premium Account		120	
(26) Revaluation reserve		60	
(27) Other reserves		4	
Profit and Loss Account		80	
			£864

(28) See p.453

4. Notes to the accounts

These are appended to the final accounts and are cross referenced to the numbers shown in the accounts and Balance Sheet, as above.

(1) Accounting policies. Give details of the company's accounting policies on accounting conventions i.e. historic cost, etc., depreciation, stocks, research and development, deferred taxation, etc.

(2) Turnover.

(a) Give definition of turnover.

(b) Give analysis of turnover between each class of business and each geographical market.

(3) Operating profit. Disclose the following items charged in arriving at operating profit.

(a) Depreciation.

(b) Hire of plant and machinery.

(c) Auditors' remuneration.

(d) Exceptional items.

(e) Staff costs (including directors), analysed as follows:

    (*i*) wages and salaries;

    (*ii*) social security costs;

    (*iii*) other pension costs;

and give the average weekly number of employees during the year analysed into categories.

(f) Directors' remuneration, analysed as follows:

    (*i*) fees;

    (*ii*) other emoluments (including pension contributions);

    (*iii*) pensions to former directors;

    (*iv*) compensation for loss of office.

If over £60,000 in total (including pension contributions), give:

    (*i*) the emoluments of the chairman;

    (*ii*) the emoluments of the highest paid director if more than the chairman; and

    (*iii*) the number of directors whose emoluments fall within rising bands of £5,000.

(The last three items exclude pension contributions.)

(g) Senior employees. Show the number of employees (excluding directors) with emoluments over £30,000 a year, in rising bands of £5,000.

(4)   Other income. Disclose the following:

(a) rental income, if material; and
(b) income from investments, analysed between listed and unlisted securities.

(5)   Interest payable. Disclose amounts analysed between:

(a) all loans and overdrafts repayable within five years; and
(b) all other loans.

(6)   Profit on ordinary activities before tax. Give analysis of profit attributable to different classes of business.

(7)   Taxation. UK corporation tax, £24K, based on profits for the year at 35 per cent. No adjustment for the previous year.

(8)   Extraordinary items. The redundancy payments fund.

(9) Transfers to reserve. £4K for the year out of profits.

(10) Dividends. Proposed dividend of 2 per cent on the Ordinary Shares.

(11) Intangible assets:

	£K
Development costs	1
Patents and trade marks, etc.	2
Goodwill (purchased 10 Jan. 19_4)	4
Total	£7

(12) Tangible assets.

	Freehold £K	Leases more than 50 years to run £K	Leases less than 50 years to run £K	Plant and equipment £K	Total £K
Cost or valuation:					
Balance b/fwd	200	40	60	396	696
Additions				74	74
Revaluation	60				60
Disposal					
Balance c/fwd	260	40	60	470	830

	Freehold £K	Leases more than 50 years to run £K	Leases less than 50 years to run £K	Plant and equipment £K	Total £K
Balance b/fwd	260	40	60	470	830
Depreciation:					
Balance b/fwd	—	10	32	214	256
Provision for year	—	2	4	40	46
Revaluation					
Disposals					
	—	12	36	254	302
Net book value	£260	£28	£24	£216	£528

Where property is revalued during the year, the name of the valuers, their qualification and the basis of valuation must be given.

(13) Investments.

	Investments other than loans £K	Loans £K	Own shares £K	Total £K
Balance b/fwd	100	40	—	140
Additions				
Revaluation				
Disposals				
Balance c/fwd	£100	£40	—	£140

Investments other than loans (balance c/fwd):

	£K
Listed	90
Unlisted	10
	£100

The market value of the listed investments is £55K.

NOTES: If any investments represent more than 5 per cent of the share capital of a company, the name of the company must be disclosed, together with the percentage of the shares held and the country of incorporation.

Investments like these which are shown as fixed assets must be investments in subsidiary and associated companies, which cannot be disposed of without losing control of the subsidiary, or influence with the associated company.

(14) Stocks.

	£K
Raw materials and consumables	20
Work-in-progress	15
Finished goods and goods for resale	60
	£95

(15) Debtors.

	£K
Trade debtors	210
Other debts	–
Called up share capital not paid	–
Prepayments and accrued income	18
	£228

(16) Investments. As for note (13).

(17) Debenture loans falling due within one year. Give details of the rate of interest, terms of repayment, security, and values for each Debenture. (If this results in a statement of excessive length give a general indication only.)

(18) Bank loans and overdrafts falling due within one year. Give the same details as for Debentures.

(19) Other creditors falling due within one year.

	£K
Trade creditors	81
Bills of exchange	–
Other taxes and social security	8
Accruals and prepaid income	4
Other creditors	–
	£93

(20) Debenture loans falling due after more than one year. Details as for note (17). Give analysis between loans and instalments of loans repayable within three years and over five

years. For Debentures issued during the year, give details including the reasons for the issue.

(21) Bank loans and overdrafts falling due after more than one year. Details as for note (18). Give analysis between amounts repayable within five years and over five years.

(22) Other creditors falling due after more than one year. Details as for note (19).

(23) Other provisions. Details are required as follows:

	Pensions	Corporation tax	Other provisions	Total
Balance b/fwd				
Movements during the year				
Balance c/fwd				

(24) Called-up share capital.

	Authorised	Allotted	Called-up
Ordinary Shares of £1 each	1,000K	600K	600K

(25) Share Premium Account.
Balance at 1 April 19_3 £120K

There have been no movements during the year.

(26) Revaluation reserve, £60K. No provision has been made for any capital gains liability, which may arise on the realisation of the freehold property. In the directors' view it is considered that any realisation would take place in the distant future, by which time tax legislation could change considerably.

(27) Other reserves.

	Opening balance £K	Movement during the year £K	Closing balance £K
Capital redemption reserve	–		–
Reserve for own shares	–		–
Reserves provided for by Articles of Association	–		–
Other reserves	–	4	4
Total	–	£4	£4

(28) Any other financial commitments. Contingent liabilities: details and amounts. Capital expenditure: a general indication of the type of expenditure and the amounts, analysed as follows:

(a) contracted but not provided for;
(b) authorised but not contracted.

Pension commitments for which no provision has been made: give separate details for pension commitments to past directors. Any other financial commitments not provided for which are relevant.

Progress test 33

1. Published accounts protect the interests of and provide information to two main parties. Who are they? **(1)**

2. Where would you check on the legal requirements for disclosure in published accounts? **(2)**

3. What are the general exemptions for published accounts? **(2)**

4. What requirements need to be satisfied in order to obtain exemptions? **(2)**

5. Briefly outline the alternative formats for the Profit and Loss Account. (Refer to Sch.4 of the Companies Act, 1985)

6. How many different types of profit are disclosed in the Profit and Loss Account? **(3)**

7. How are creditors grouped in a Balance Sheet? **(3)**

8. Under what heading are proposed dividends shown in a Balance Sheet? **(3)**

9. In the notes to the accounts, how is the directors' remuneration analysed? **(4)**

10. What information must be supplied in relation to tangible assets? **(4)**

Specimen question

1. Eric & Frank PLC is a company operating several furniture stores whose authorised capital is £1 million in Ordinary Shares of £1 each, of which 700,000 have been issued, are fully called and fully paid. The following is the Trial Balance at 31 December 19_6 before making any final adjustments:

	Dr £K	Cr £K		Dr £K	Cr £K
Ordinary capital		700	B/fwd	1,780	1,120
Profit and Loss A/c		156	Stock	280	
Dividend (interim)	18		Purchases	920	
Equipment	60		General expenses	11	
Motor vehicles	165		Audit fees	20	
Freehold property	900		Motor expenses	128	
Depreciation:			Bank interest	24	
Equipment		24	Trade creditors		90
Motors		85	Accrued charges		6
Salaries and wages	520		Debtors	280	
Rates, heating and			Sales		1,990
lighting	65		Rents income		38
Advertising, etc.	41		Bank overdraft		220
Expenses of letting	11		Corporation tax	21	
Provision for bad					
debts		5			
Revaluation reserve		150			
C/fwd	£1,780	£1,120	Totals	£3,464	£3,464

ADDITIONAL INFORMATION:

No dividends have been paid in earlier years but this year an interim dividend of £18K was paid and it is proposed to pay a final dividend of the same amount.

Salaries and wages, £520K, includes all amounts paid to directors and is made up as follows:

	£K
Chairman and managing director	65
Assistant managing director	31
Chief accountant	35
Company secretary	32
Departmental manager	16
Two non-executive directors at £6K each	12
Other salaries	96
	287
Wages	233
	£520

The freehold property had been revalued at the end of 19_5. Of the figure shown in the Trial Balance it is considered that only £250K related to the site itself, the remainder representing the value of the building. Starting from January 19_6, depreciation at the rate of 2 per cent per annum is to be charged on the building.

Equipment and motor vehicles are included at cost. During the year £10K was spent on new equipment. There were no disposals during the year. Using the straight line method, depreciation at the rate of 10 per cent on equipment and 20 per cent on motor vehicles, calculated on the closing balance, is to be charged.

Included in motor expenses is a sum of £15K for the hire of a removal van to help out in the busy season.

The closing stock is valued at £320K using the FIFO method of valuation.

Corporation tax on the profits for the year should be provided in the sum of £95K. The figure in the Trial Balance is made up as follows:

	£K
Balance b/fwd (the amount provided in 19_5 accounts)	50
Corporation tax paid during the year	71
As per Trial Balance	£21

The provision for bad debts is to be made equal to 5 per cent of debtors.

Expense allocation:

Cost of sales = Cost of goods sold plus wages

Distribution = Expenses relating to motor vehicles, advertising and bad debts provision

Administration = All other expenses including depreciation of equipment and property

REQUIRED:

Produce in a style suitable for publication a Profit and Loss Account for the year to 31 December 19_6 and a Balance Sheet as at that date. (You may like to attempt this question, checking your answer against the solution.)

34

Principles of accounting and SSAP

1. The principles of accounting

We are coming to the end of a long and difficult book which covers all the elementary and intermediate accounting needed by students of this subject. We must conclude, by extracting the principles which lie behind the many things we have learned. Students might feel that it may have been a better idea to start with the principles and then learn how they are applied in practice but that is not the way that these things are worked out. Almost any body of knowledge starts with the collection of simple pieces of data and ideas and the gradual accumulation of enough knowledge and experience to extract clear principles from them. Now we know how to keep books, and could run any business we care to start, or to seek employment in, we can see how the background theory forms a framework for everything we do. Accounting is now regarded as a discipline with an organised body of knowledge and a purposeful objective. There are three fundamentals of accounting theory:

(a) postulates;
(b) principles;
(c) concepts.

2. Accounting postulates

These are underlying assumptions which are generally accepted as valid. Examples:

(a) *Accounting data and reports* have validity and usefulness for widely different purposes.
(b) *Economic activity* is undertaken by identifiable enterprises which constitute units of accountability.

(c) Accounting is primarily concerned with the effect on an enterprise of its *exchange transactions* with other firms or individuals.

(d) Transactions are in terms of a stated or implied *money price* and this provides a basis for accounting measurement and analysis.

3. Accounting principles or conventions

These are basic propositions which express significant relationships in accounting. They are a generalisation of theory and accordingly tend to be universalised, i.e. they apply to all enterprises. They include the following.

(a) *Recording*. This is needed to provide reliable information concerning the economic activity of the enterprise.

(b) *Measurement*. Transactions should be recorded at their money price in order that these data may be recorded in a reasonably homogeneous and objective manner.

(c) *Classification*. Accounting records should accumulate and classify the financial data in such a manner as will facilitate their use for analysis, interpretation and reporting.

(d) *Modification*. To reflect progress and changes in the enterprise, status modifications of transactions may be required and should be recorded in a manner which is clearly evident in the accounting records.

(e) *Reporting*. Reports reflecting the progress and status of the enterprise should be prepared and made available to the owners and other interested parties.

4. Accounting concepts

These are formed primarily through observation and are established by agreement. They are defined as broadly based assumptions which underlie the periodic financial accounts of business enterprises. The most important of these concepts may be listed as follows:

(a) business entity and stewardship;
(b) transactions and duality;
(c) assets;
(d) liability;
(e) capitals, revenue and net worth;

(f) money as the unit of account;

(g) going-concern;

(h) accruals;

(i) prudence;

(k) ownership and equity.

5.   The concept of business entity

This concept holds that a business for accounting purposes is a separate unit distinct from all other units, and from the owner of the business. This may not be the case in law, although we know that limited companies and other incorporations (organisations given the status of persons by Royal Charter or Act of Parliament) are separate personalities. Sole traders and partners are not separate entitities in law from the businesses they own, but for accountancy purposes it is convenient to regard the business records as separate from the personal affairs of the sole trader or partners, until that moment when the profits have been calculated and the sole trader takes them as his/her reward for the enterprise shown, or the partners share them in the agreed manner.

The accountant therefore includes an expense in the records of a business if it is a business expense incurred in the process of manufacturing, trading or giving service to the customers. If this is not the case the expense is disallowed, since it is for the personal benefit of the proprietor.

Arising from the concept of business entity is the concept of stewardship. The owner, or owners, being separate from the business, the persons running it must act as stewards on behalf of the owner(s) and must account in a proper manner to him/her/them. In the case of sole traders they will, no doubt, exercise personal control, but partners may specialise and the partners must be mutually responsible for the affairs of the business. With companies the directors have the responsibilities of stewardship towards the shareholders, who are not permitted by law to take an active interest in the affairs of the business unless they are themselves directors.

6.   The concepts of transactions and duality

Since business is about exchange transactions with other businesses and the general public, the accountant conceives all business activity as a succession of transactions, each of which involves the business in some contractual way with one (or possibly more than one) other party. Since the records of the business are maintained in such a way as to keep track of both sides of every transaction we must have a double-entry on every transaction. This is the concept of duality, which holds that every transaction will involve one account being debited and another account being credited. We know that the rules for these entries are:

Debit the account that receives goods, or services, or money.
Credit the account that gives goods, or services, or money.
This can be abbreviated to 'debit the receiver, credit the giver'.

7. Assets

The concept of an asset should be sufficiently precise so that for accounting purposes assets can be distinguished from non-assets and be identified as belonging to a specific enterprise.

The chief feature of an asset is that it is purchased for long-term use in the business and thus makes an enduring contribution to the profit-making capacity of the business. The boundary line between short-term and long-term is one year.

8. Liability

The concept of a liability is that someone external to the business entity (and this includes the proprietor under the concept of business entity described in 5 above) is owed money by the business. Liabilities may be current (payable within one year) or long-term (payable over a number of years according to some clear contractual arrangement). The capital of the proprietor is in a special (very long-term) category, only being repayable when the business ceases to trade or at the death of the proprietor or partner concerned. Companies do not die, though they can be wound up either voluntarily or by order of the Court, when the capital and reserves available will be returned to the shareholders after other claimants have been satisfied.

9. Capital, revenue and net worth

Capital in its strictest meaning in accountancy refers to an accumulation of assets made available for use in the business by the proprietor, or proprietors, or the shareholders. If this capital is in money form it is referred to as 'money capital', but at the start of any business it is usual for at least some other assets to be brought in, motor vehicles, tools, etc. and these are listed on the assets side of the Balance Sheet, and their total value appears as 'capital' on the liabilities side, that total being the amount owed back to the proprietor (the capitalist).

The term 'capital' is widely mis-used – for example companies often call funds raised by debentures as 'loan capital'. A loan can never really be 'capital'. It is also customary to refer to groups of assets as forms of the capital that made their purchase possible. Thus fixed assets are commonly referred to as 'fixed capital' and current assets are referred to as 'working capital'. Current assets in cash form, or readily turnable into cash, are often called liquid capital.

The term 'capital expenditure' denotes expenditure on assets that last longer than a year and consequently permanently increase the profit-making capacity of the business.

The term *revenue* denotes income of the business, whether it be the proceeds of sales, or fees earned, or income received as the result of some business activity such as 'Rent Received' from a sub-tenant or 'Commission Received' on some one-off transaction. Since revenue receipts must be set against expenses in determining the profits of the business the term 'revenue expenditure' is used for all expenses which must be set against income to find the 'net income' or 'profits' of the business. Firms which do not trade (and consequently do not produce a Trading Account) often call their Profit and Loss Account by the term Revenue Account, it being the place where income (revenue) is set against expenditure (revenue expenditure) to find the profit.

The boundary line between capital expenditure and revenue expenditure is one year. Revenue expenditure is expenditure whose usefulness to the business is of short duration. Where revenue expenditure is of benefit for more than one year (for example, repairs and redecorations) they may be the subject of an adjustment at the end of the financial year, with some portion of the expense being carried forward to the next year.

Net worth refers to the interest of the proprietor in the business. On Day 1 of the business when the Opening Balance Sheet is prepared this will of course be the same figure as the capital contributed by the proprietor, but in subsequent years it may be increased by profits ploughed back into the business, or decreased by losses suffered. The term 'net' worth implies 'net of liabilities to external creditors, whether long-term or short-term'. Thus on a Balance Sheet showing assets of £50,000 financed partly by a bank loan of £20,000 and trade credit of £2,000 the net worth of the business to the owner would be £28,000.

10. Money as the unit of account

One of the attributes of money is that it can be used as a meduim of account. It is a universal measure of value which can give meaning to the value of any asset. One of the reasons why inflation is considered to be such a menace to civilised societies is that it makes money unsatisfactory as a unit of account. It destroys savings — there is a sad story about a Polish miser who saved all his life and denied himself many luxuries to accumulate wealth, which he eventually exchanged for one bread roll in the inflation after the First World War. The Accounting Standards Committee (*see* SSAP below) laboured for several years to produce a **Statement of Standard Accounting Practice** about inflation accounting, but it proved to be 'more honoured in the breach than in the observance' because accountants hesitated to discard ordinary concepts of money as a unit of account — and anyway inflation declined.

11. The ' going-concern' concept

The 'going-concern' concept holds that the assets of a business which is a going-concern may be valued at their worth to the business in its normal activities, whatever they may be. The usual basis is 'cost price less depreciation to date'. Should the accountant drawing up the annual accounts of the business be aware that it is the intention of management to cease trading and there is no intention to sell the business as a going-concern, or if the business is about to go bankrupt, the value of the assets would be viewed differently. The assets of a gone-concern may be worth much less than their book value, depending on the market for second-hand assets of that sort. The preparation of accounts on a 'going-concern' basis implies that the Revenue Account and Balance Sheet are prepared on the assumption that there is no intention to liquidate or curtail significantly the scale of operations.

12. The 'accruals' concept

The 'accruals' concept holds that the final accounts of a business should be prepared in such a way that all the revenue receipts that have accrued due to the business for the trading period under review shall be brought into account, and that all the revenue expenditure that has accrued due and is payable shall similarly be taken into account. Accounts which are prepared on an accruals basis give the 'truest and fairest view' of the business (a phrase taken from the Companies Act 1985) because they not only take into account every penny earned in the year and every penny expended (thus giving a true profit figure), but they also give a perfectly accurate Balance Sheet (showing every asset owned and every liability owed). Revenue and costs are matched with one another as far as their relationship can be established and dealt with in the Trading and Profit and Loss Accounts to the period to which they relate. (The opposite of accruals is the cash basis concept when income is only recognised on the receipt of money and costs only considered on the payment of money.)

13. Objectivity, materiality and consistency

These concepts are very important. The 'objectivity' concept holds that the accountant should view the business from the point of view of a dis-interested and unbiased outsider, viewing the business from afar. The accounts should not be prepared from the viewpoint of an interested, and therefore biased, member of the firm or company. In this way the true facts of the business can be seen.

The 'materiality' concept holds that if a figure is of material importance it should be revealed as a separate figure, either in the accounts or in a note to the accounts. If a figure is so tiny that it is not really in any way significant then it is immaterial and may be grouped in with other figures. Thus a company which has a word processor might merge it in with Office Equipment as an immaterial item. On the other hand a company that has loaned £1 million to several hundred customers should not lump in with those loans a £10,000 loan made to a director of the company. Although the loan is relatively small the fact that it is made to a director is a significant point, and it should not be hidden but should be disclosed as a separate figure.

The concept of consistency holds that from year to year the

accounts should be prepared in the same way unless there is some good reason for a change of accounting policy, in which case the reason for the change should be explained. As accounts are compared one year with another, the basis of the comparison is weakened if different policies (for depreciation perhaps, or in the treatment of reserves) are used. Consistent accounting policies enable outsiders to compare the company's records over the years confident that they are getting a correct view of the progress of the business.

14. Prudence

The prudence concept holds that business people should always act cautiously in all aspects of their business activities. In accountancy terms this means that revenue and profits are not anticipated, but taken into account only when realised in cash or the ultimate receipt of cash can be assessed with certainty. On the other hand, provision is made for all known liabilities whether the amount of these is known with certainty or is a best estimate in the light of the information available.

In certain types of business prudence is of great importance in the wider activities of firms and companies. For example the Bank of England regularly queries the 'prudential policies' of banks and other financial institutions to ensure they do not get into illiquid positions where depositors' finances might be at risk. Similarly in insurance the underwriters at Lloyds have clear limits on the amount of risk that may be covered on any particular ship, or destination.

15. Ownership and equity

The concepts of ownership and equity are related. The term ownership is synonymous for sole traders with 'net worth' (*see* 9 above). The same applies to partnerships except that the 'net worth' of the business to the partners collectively is shared between them in the manner revealed by the balances available to them on their respective Capital and Current Accounts. The term 'equity' refers to the interest in a company of the Ordinary Shareholders (those who do not draw a fixed rate of dividend on their shares). The student will remember that the Ordinary Shareholders' Equity includes not only what they contributed in capital originally but also all profits ploughed back into the business as reserves of various sorts. This explains why shares originally issued at par are often valued on the Stock Exchange well above par, or (if losses have been suffered) well below par. Remember though that other factors like expectations influence prices on Stock Exchanges.

16. Statements of Standard Accounting Practice

It was mentioned earlier that clear statements of accounting principles and the theory of accounting did not develop until centuries after the practical business of book-keeping had achieved wide use. Nothing illustrates this better than the fact that the various leading accountancy bodies did not get together until as late as 1969 to set up an Accounting Standards Committee to consider the various problems which they all faced. The procedure adopted is to circulate 'discussion documents' initially calling for views on the matter under discussion. A sub-committee of leading minds then draws up an 'exposure draft', which is a detailed proposal for a common policy on the matter, and this, after modification eventually becomes an SSAP (Statement of Standard Accounting Practice). In the explanatory foreword to the first SSAP, it was stated that:

'The Council (of the English Institute of Chartered Accountants) expects members who assume responsibilities in respect of financial accounts to observe accounting statements (SSAPs)'.

Even so, it has not always been possible to devise an acceptable solution to a particular problem and some SSAPs have been withdrawn and others are disregarded by at least some accountants who claim that the proposals are inapplicable for various reasons to the industry in which they operate. Space does not permit a full discussion of SSAPs, though relevant ones have been taken into account at various points in this book.

The full text of the Standards is available in the handbook *Accounting Standards* published by the Institute of Chartered Accountants in England and Wales, PO Box 433, London EC2 2BJ. Phone them on 071 628 7060 to find the current price and send cash with your order.

The basic accounting concepts are also laid down in IAS 1, the

International Accounting Standard, *Disclosure of Accounting Policies*, which applies to international financial statements issued on or after 1 January 1975.

The full list of SSAPs is as follows:

SSAP 1 Accounting for the results of associated companies (revised);

SSAP 2 Disclosure of accounting policies;

SSAP 3 Earnings per share (revised);

SSAP 4 The accounting treatment of government grants;

SSAP 5 Accounting for VAT;

SSAP 6 Extraordinary items and prior year adjustments (revised);

SSAP 7 (Provisional) Accounting for changes in the purchasing power of money (withdrawn January 1978);

SSAP 8 The treatment of taxation under the imputation system in the accounts of companies;

SSAP 9 Stocks and long-term contracts;

SSAP 10 Statements of source and application of funds;

SSAP 11 Accounting for deferred taxation (withdrawn October 1978);

SSAP 12 Accounting for depreciation (revised);

SSAP 13 Accounting for research and development (revised);

SSAP 14 Group accounts;

SSAP 15 Accounting for deferred taxation (revised);

SSAP 16 Current cost accounting (withdrawn);

SSAP 17 Accounting for post Balance Sheet events;

SSAP 18 Accounting for contingencies;

SSAP 19 Accounting for investment properties;

SSAP 20 Foreign currency translation;

SSAP 21 Accounting for leases and hire purchase;

SSAP 22 Accounting for goodwill (revised);

SSAP 23 Accounting for acquisitions and mergers;

SSAP 24 Accounting for pension costs.

Other items included in the publication are:

SORP 1 Pension Scheme Accounts;

SORP 2 Accounting by charities (including a guide for the smaller charity).

(A SORP is a Statement of Recommended Practice.)
Exposure Drafts currently under discussion include:

ED 42   Accounting for 'Special Purpose' Transactions;
ED 43   Accounting of Government grants;
ED 45   Segmental reporting;
ED 46   Disclosure of related party transactions.

Clearly we are moving into difficult areas beyond the scope of the present volume.

Progress test 34

1. What are the three fundamentals of accounting theory? **(1)**

2. What do you understand by: (*a*) measurement; and (*b*) classification? **(3)**

3. Distinguish between: (*a*) recording; and (*b*) reporting. **(3)**

4. Explain the meaning of: (*a*) accruals; and (*b*) prudence. **(12 and 14)**

5. What does SSAP 5 provide for? **(16)**

Specimen questions

1. Explain the concept of business entity. Why is it important in (*a*) sole trader accounts (*b*) limited company accounts.

2. What is the concept of duality? Explain the dual nature of the following transactions:
   (a) The purchase of an asset for cash.
   (b) The trading in of an old vehicle for a new vehicle, the balance being paid by cheque.
   (c) The payment of wages by bank giro transfer.
   (d) The writing off of a partially bad debt on which a final payment of £50 has been received from the liquidator of a company.

3. Explain the term 'net worth' as applied to a sole trader at the end of a highly successful first year in business.

4. What is the difference between a going-concern and a gone-concern in accounting terms?

5. Give two examples of items you would consider material in preparing the Balance Sheet of a jobbing builder, and two you would consider immaterial.

6. 'If a business invests in shares, and the market value of the shares increases above cost then, until and unless the business sells them, no profit is made. If the business invests in stock for resale, and the market value of the stock falls below cost then the loss is recognised even though no sale has taken place.'

'If a business undertakes an intensive advertising campaign which will probably result in increased sales (and profit) in succeeding years it will nevertheless usually write off the cost of the campaign in the year in which it is incurred.'

Explain the reasoning behind the application of accounting principles in situations such as these and discuss the effect on the usefulness of accounting information in relation to users' needs.

35

The computerisation of accounting

1. Why computerise accounting?

The vast majority of accounting activities are routine entries in the accounts, and by the time we reach this final chapter we should be thoroughly familiar with them. A glance back to Fig. 2.1 (*see* pages 17–18) will remind students of the countless debit and credit entries that make up the double entries for the Creditors Ledger, the Sales Ledger, the Nominal Ledger and the Private Ledger. All these entries are very simple, routine matters. It follows that they are very easy to computerise, since computers are very good at doing routine tasks that occur over and over again. From the earliest days of computerisation the writing of programs for accounting activities was given priority, and almost every aspect of accounting has now been covered by software packages of many sorts. It is impossible to describe them all but, to set the scene, we describe one or two of them.

2. Computerised solutions to accounting problems

The following solutions have been developed:

(a) *The small business package.* For very small businesses, especially those that mainly deal in cash, and do not have large numbers of debtors and creditors, there are simple systems, such as *Simplex Plus*. These can keep all the records a business needs, including VAT records, up to Final Accounts level. They consist of a set of programs, each of which can be called into the computer when required, and by a series of user-friendly prompts the entries required can be made. A user-friendly system is one that prompts the user at each stage to give the information which the computer needs, and checks to make sure there is no possibility of error. For example, it might say, 'You are asking me to write off T. Smith's Account as a bad debt. Is this correct? Yes/No.' On pressing the Y key, you are then asked 'Are you sure? Yes/No.' If you answer again by pressing the Y key, the account of T. Smith will be cleared. Our example, *Simplex Plus*, is available from Micro-Retailer Systems Ltd, Bridge House, Brook Street, Macclesfield, Cheshire, SK11 7AR (Tel: 0625-615375), (Fax 0625-612546).

(b) *The business software package.* While this seems to be a very general term which could apply to every type of software for the business user, it is used here in a special way. It implies software for small and medium-sized firms, which is able to do all the book-keeping described in this book and has a reasonable capacity — say up to 1,000 debtors' accounts and 1,000 suppliers' accounts. One of the best examples of this type of software (described later) is the *Sage Sterling* software, available from the Sage Group PLC, Sage House, Benton Park Road, Newcastle-upon-Tyne, NE7 7LZ (Tel 091-201 3000), (Fax 091-201 0308).

(c) *Up-graded business software.* These packages offer more sophisticated business software, suitable for the very largest organisations and all levels of accounting activity. For example, the Sage package *Sterling +2* offers four products, designated Book-keeper (B), Accountant (A), Accountant Plus (A+) and Financial Controller (FC). These offer successive stages of sophistication, right up to multi-company facilities. *Sage Sovereign* is at an even higher level, offering multi-company and multi-currency facilities.

(d) *Specialist packages and other solutions.* There are many people who require specialist packages only, in such fields as job-costing, the retail trade, stock control, etc. Formerly such users would have software written to suit their own particular needs, but today almost all aspects are covered by appropriate software which can be obtained by contacting the trade outlets. Many small and medium-sized firms solve their accounting problems by using a large computer bureau which has a mainframe computer and is prepared to sub-contract some of its spare capacity to client users. One such firm is The Accounting Centre, Elscott House, Arcadia Avenue, Finchley Central, London, N3 2JE (Tel: 081-349 3191).

These are the types of solution the computer offers to book-keeping problems, and it is helpful if we look at some of them in greater detail.

3. *Micro Simplex Plus* — a small business package

Micro Simplex Plus is a computerised version of the *Simplex* manual book-keeping system which has been in use by small traders since 1917 and still has some 200,000 small business users.

Micro Simplex Plus works off a series of programs stored on a floppy disk, which can be loaded on to hard disk if required. Of course, when the system is first set up, a certain amount of initial data has to be fed in. For example, we need to enter the details of the company or organisation. We need to enter the headings under which expenses are to be classified, such as rent, rates, light, heat, postage, motor expenses, etc. We need to enter details of suppliers and, if new suppliers are taken on from time to time, we shall open accounts for them at that time. Keeping the records up to date is called 'System Housekeeping'.

Once the system is fully set up, every day the program starts up by showing the main menu, which reads as follows:

Main Menu
1. Enter and View Information
2. Print information to Screen/Printer
3. Prepare VAT Return
4. Prepare Profit and Loss Accounts
5. System Housekeeping
6. Retail Sales Ledger
7. Re-start Micro Simplex Plus

To select the menu we require, we can press any of the keys 1 to 7. The most likely key we shall need to press is 1, because that enables us to enter our transactions. We may wish

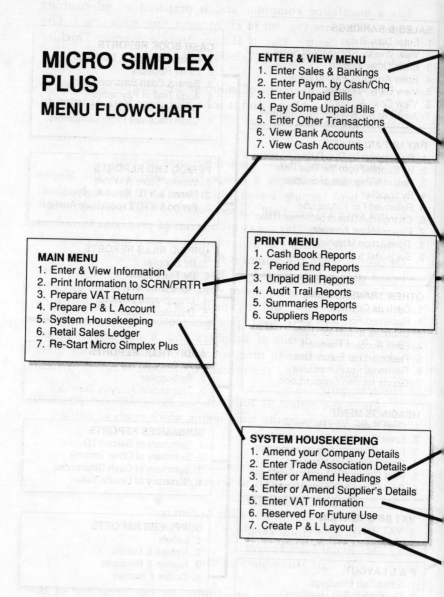

Figure 35.1 *The programs for Micro Simplex Plus (Courtesy of Micro-Retailer Systems Ltd)*

SALES & BANKINGS
1. Enter Daily Sales
2. View Weekly Summary of Sales
3. Enter Other Income
4. Enter Amounts Paid to Bank
5. View Bank Accounts
6. View Cash Accounts
7. Amounts Received from Customers

PAY UNPAID BILLS
1. By Supplier by Due Date
2. By Supplier upto the Due Date
3. Resume Payment of Suppliers
4. By Supplier
5. Reserved For Future Use
6. Change due Date or Settlement Disc.
7. Payments on Account
8. Transaction Matching
9. Set/Reset a Disputed Invoice

OTHER TRANSACTIONS
1. Cash as Counted
2. Reserved For Future Use
3. Cheques written for Cash
4. Bank Account Transfers
5. Reserved For Future Use
6. Reserved For Future Use
7. Goods for own Consumption

HEADINGS MENU
1. Enter Sales Dept Headings
2. Enter Goods for Resale Headings
3. Enter O/Heads & Exps Headings
4. Print Sales Dept Headings
5. Print Goods for Resale Headings
6. Print O/heads & Exps Headings

VAT INFORMATION
1. VAT Rates
2. Select your VAT Scheme

P & L LAYOUT
1. Sales Sub Headings
2. Overheads Sub Headings

CASH BOOK REPORTS
1. Sales, Receipts & Bankings
2. Other Receipts
3. Bank & Cash Balances
4. Audit Trail of Payments
5. Cheques Issued Report
6. Cash Received From Customers

PERIOD END REPORTS
1. Weekly Sales Analysis
2. Period & YTD Sales Analysis
3. Period & YTD Expenditure Analysis

UNPAID BILLS REPORTS
1. By Supplier
2. By Transaction
3. Aged Creditors
4. Unapproved Invoices
5. Disputed Invoices

AUDIT TRAIL REPORTS
1. All Transactions
2. By Supplier
3. Transaction Analysis Summary

SUMMARIES REPORTS
1. Summary of Sales YTD
2. Summary of Other Income
3. Summary of Cash Differences
4. Summary of Goods Taken

SUPPLIERS REPORTS
1. Labels
2. Names & Details
3. Names & Balances
4. Codes & Names

to enter sales, or to enter amounts paid to the bank, or to pay an unpaid bill, etc, but all of these options are available as activities if we press key 1. A further range of menus is shown in Fig. 35.1. The reader can follow through this further range of activities. There are 85 of them altogether, so that even in this simplest of all layouts there are 85 activities which the computer can perform. The reader will appreciate that, despite the simplicity of the system, it gives an excellent coverage of small business accounts, including all the necessary records, the VAT records for any of the 12 special retailers' schemes, the calculation of the profits and an audit trail which records every entry made. An independent survey by the magazine *What PC?* found it to be a very solid package, 'which does a thorough job of helping the small business keep track of all its sales and expenses; its VAT, profitability and cash flow'.

4.   *Sage Sterling* accounting software

Sage Sterling is a range of accounting software which covers all the principal accounting applications for which the average business proprietor uses a microcomputer. The general structure of *Sage Sterling* covers the following aspects:

> Sales Ledger
> Purchases Ledger
> Nominal Ledger (which includes the Cash and Bank
>   Accounts)
> Payroll
> Stock Control
> Sales Order Processing
> Purchase Order Processing
> Job Costing
> Management Reporting
> Utilities (this includes the layouts of documents,
>   verification of entries and the program's back-up
>   facilities)

The software offers a complete 'one-step' accounting system, so that all necessary double-entry book-keeping routines are taken care of automatically, with transactions

THE SYSTEM

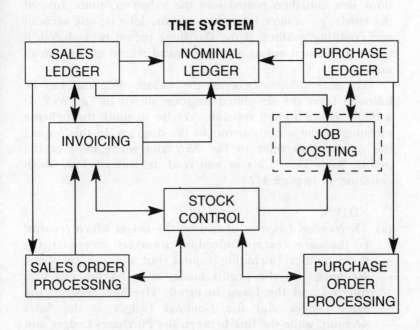

NOTE: Job costing is not integrated in *Sage Sterling*, but is included in the slightly more sophisticated *Sage Sovereign*.

Figure 35.2 *The 'Sage Sterling' System*

entered immediately into all the relevant ledgers. A one-step system implies that items do not need to be entered in a Day Book first and then posted into the ledger accounts. Instead the entries go at once into the accounts, debiting one account and crediting another. If the Day Book record is produced, it is merely printed out as a chronological record of the entries made.

The interlinkages between the various programs can be followed from the simplified diagram shown in Fig. 35.2. It actually makes a good revision exercise to think through the meaning of the various arrows in the diagram. In this respect the notes below refer to Fig. 35.2 and revise most of the points. Study Fig. 35.2 now and read the notes below, which continue on to page 477.

NOTES:
(a) *The Nominal Ledger* is, of course, the ledger which records: (*i*) the assets (except individual customers' accounts); (*ii*) the liabilities (including capital, but not the suppliers' accounts; (*iii*) the profits made; and (*iv*) the expenses suffered and the losses incurred. The link between the Sales Ledger and the Nominal Ledger is the Sales Account, while the link between the Purchases Ledger and the Nominal Ledger is the Purchases Account. Note that in computerised systems Returns In and Returns Out are handled on the Sales Account and Purchases Account respectively, and do not need separate Sales Returns and Purchases Returns accounts.
(b) *The Sales Ledger* is, of course, that part of the ledger where the individual debtors' records are kept. Each debtor has an account which is debited with goods received and any charges, such as carriage. It will be credited with any returns or allowances, and with any payments made or discount allowed. While these entries are going to affect the Nominal Ledger in the Petty Cash Account, Bank Account, Discount Allowed Account, etc, the *Sage* system also enables us to handle all the sales order processing. This involves not only invoicing but related activities like credit note production, to deal with returns and allowances.

It also affects stock control, because stocks move out – or return – in the normal course of marketing.

(c) *The Purchases Ledger* is very similar to the Sales Ledger, except that now we have the records of all our suppliers (the creditors) on a data bank. The computer now controls all the purchase order processing, which is concerned with obtaining estimates or quotations, placing orders when negotiations reach a satisfactory stage and receiving the goods (which affects the stock control levels). In *Sage Sterling*, the costs are handled for costing purposes by a special costing package, but in *Sage Sovereign* this package is integrated into the system to feed the costs directly into the costing system. The completion of jobs requires a link with the Sales Ledger as customers are invoiced for finished goods (or work completed).

(d) Of course, our diagram is a little incomplete, because the one box 'Nominal Ledger' covers a multitude of activities, for example the Cash Book activities, the Petty Cash system, the payroll and the financial areas of capital, loans, loan repayments, dividends, etc. Some extra details about these are given in the sections which follow.

(e) To conclude, we can see how the network of programs fits together to solve every accounting problem.

5. A typical pattern of menus: the Payroll

The reader will get some idea of the number and variety of programs that have to be written to computerise each section of the work if we take one part of it — the payroll — and consider the various programs. We can do little more than list them, because space is limited, but the reader can 'think through' what is involved in each set. The main menu reads:

1. Employee details
2. Processing payroll
3. Statutory sick pay
4. Statutory maternity pay
5. Government parameters
6. Company details

If we look at each of these separately, we have the following sub-menus:

1. Employee details
1. Amend details
2. Add a new employee
3. Remove an employee
4. P11 Deduction Card
5. Absence report

The first of these requires a separate sub-menu:

1. Full details
2. Personal details
3. Table selections
4. Bank/P45 information
5. Cumulative values

2. Processing payroll
1. Enter payments
2. Payment summary
3. Cash analysis
4. Cheque analysis
5. Giro analysis
6. Average earnings
7. Payslips
8. Print giros
9. Print cheques
10. Comps min-payment (a program about contracted-out schemes)
11. Collector of taxes
12. Update records

This is perhaps enough to show the reader how many programs are required if a difficult matter like the payroll is to be handled successfully by computer. We may just list the remainder:

3. Statutory sick pay: 6 programs
4. Statutory maternity pay: 2 programs

5. Government parameters: 7 programs
6. Company details: 8 programs

This gives a total of 45 programs to computerise the payroll.

6. The efficiency of the computer: the *Sage* Sales Ledger

It is one thing to keep routine records of one's debtors and to know at any given moment how much the debtor owes. It is quite another thing to understand in every detail the position of each debtor. For example, a debtor owes us £500. Is it a current debt, or an aged debt? Is it a large debt for him/her, or is it a sign of reduced interest in our products (the account normally has much bigger balances)? How much of the debt is VAT, rather than sales? Should we be instituting 'debt-chasing' procedures against the debtor? Has the debtor been behind with payments before?

If we move on to another level, we could ask the following questions:

(*i*)   What is the activity in each product?
(*ii*) What is the activity in each territory where our sales force operates?
(*iii*) What is the cash flow inwards position?
(*iv*) How can we revitalise dormant accounts?

We could not expect an ordinary book-keeper to analyse the entries made and answer such problems, but because of the computer's speed and continuous activity it can find the time to do so. The following features of the *Sage* Debtors Ledger give us some idea of the computer's efficiency:

(a) It can handle an unlimited number of accounts.

(b) It keeps a full record of every customer, and his/her history as a debtor.

(c) It knows the customer's credit limit, and the balance on each customer's account.

(d) It produces a Sales Day Book in chronological order, and an Aged Debtors list.

(e) It automatically posts every entry to all the relevant accounts, i.e. both the customer's account and the Sales Account in the Nominal Ledger.

(f) It extracts the VAT for onward transmission to Customs & Excise Department.

(g) It can handle part-payments.

(h) It can handle pre-payments and accruals.

(i) It can detect overdue accounts.

(j) It can handle refunds.

(k) It can handle dishonoured cheques.

(l) It can write off bad debts.

(m) It can handle contra entries (where a debtor is also a supplier, and one account can be off-set against the other).

(n) It can correct errors.

(o) It can handle depreciation.

(p) It can handle order acknowledgements.

It will print out a report on:

(a) Aged debtors.

(b) Customer year-to-date turnover.

(c) Departmental sales.

(d) Non-active accounts.

It will print out:

(a) Promotional letters.

(b) Debt-chasing letters.

(c) Invoices.

(d) Statements and remittance advice notes.

(e) Lists of debtors.

(f) Labels for all customers (for a mail shot perhaps).

The reader will see that such a range of activities makes *Sage Sterling* a good investment.

7. Documentation by computer

At this point it is convenient to see how documentation is handled by the computer. These examples are taken from the extremely user-friendly *Sage Sterling +2* software. As shown in Fig. 35.3, organisations can have stationery showing their own logo, in their own choice of colours and typefaces. Invoices, statements, remittance advice notes and correspondence therefore give a 'house' image which can look totally professional.

8. Management reporting

If the last two sections show what the computer can do to help control and manage a particular section of the work, it is trivial compared with what the more sophisticated computer systems can offer by way of management information. We may list these reports as follows:

(a) *Standard reports.* Each ledger produces a number of standard reports which all businesses require; for example, the reports from the Sales Ledger, listed in Section 6 above. Similarly, the Creditors' Ledger will produce an Aged Creditor Analysis, a Year-to-date Turnover for each creditor, a Purchases Day Book and a list of creditor balances. The Nominal Ledger will print out a Trial Balance when requested; a 'quick ratio' report (*Sterling Version 5* only); a budget variance report; a complete audit trail; a Day Book of Journal entries; and Control Account histories for debtors, creditors, bank, petty cash and VAT.

(b) *Management information.* A Report Generator program provides skeleton report formats which can be personalised to the organisation concerned by setting appropriate parameters. For example, column headings can be changed to suit an organisation's particular needs; items can be selected to suit the business; sub-totals, sorting levels and appropriate percentages, etc, can all be made to serve the precise requirements of management. Line graphs, bar charts, etc, can be designed to bring out particular features. Finally, for the very largest businesses, multi-company accounts can be prepared and consolidated.

At this point we are clearly moving into areas which are beyond the scope of this book. Students are urged to seize every opportunity to advance their knowledge and understanding of computerised accounting, which is clearly a powerful tool in the hands of any qualified person. There are,

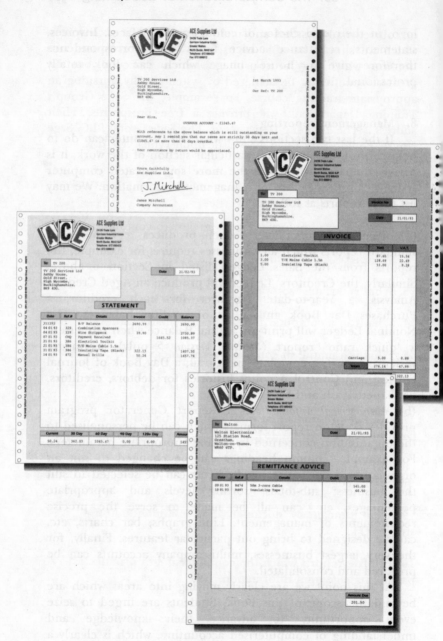

Figure 35.3   *Computerised documentation from Sage*

of course, many systems and many aspects within each system which we should be able to use. Most software houses run hot-lines which may be consulted when in difficulty, but the greatest benefit can be achieved by systematically pursuing an appropriate training course. For example, the Sage Group's Training Department will provide a free prospectus. Their address is The Training Department, The Sage Group PLC, Sage House, Benton Park Road, Newcastle-upon-Tyne, NE7 7BR.

Progress test 35

1. Why are accountancy activities so easy to computerise? **(1)**

2. What is a 'small business package'? **(2)**

3. What is business software? **(2)**

4. What can a computer bureau do for small businesses? **(2)**

5. What is a menu, in computer terminology? **(3)**

6. How do we select an item on a menu? **(3)**

7. List five programs that would need to be written to computerise a payroll. **(5)**

8. List four reports that might be produced automatically on the Sales Ledger. **(6)**

9. What is meant by 'documentation in a unique house style'? **(7)**

10. List five reports which the computer might produce as part of management information. **(8)**

Specimen questions

1. Write short notes (5–8 lines) about each of the following:

(a)	programs	(b)	aged debtors
(c)	contra entries	(d)	software
(e)	hardware	(f)	menu

2. What is meant by a 'user-friendly' system?

3. What is meant by 'upgrading' a system?

4. What is system housekeeping?

5. What is meant by 'year-to-date' turnover?

Appendix 1
Solutions

The following abbreviations have been used:

BD, bad debts; BDP, bad debts provision; BS, Balance Sheet totals; Crs, creditors; Depn, depreciation; Drs, Debtors; GP, gross profit; NP, net profit; TB, trail balance totals.

Other abbreviations are indicated against chapter headings.

Chapter 1
Cap., capital.
1. (a) £54,550 (b) £7,950 (c) £1,940 (d) £ 42,000 (e) £18,560
2. (a) £81,665 (b) £19,130 (c) £2,605 (d) £16,525 (e) £98,190 (f) £42,390
3. Cap. (b) £8,440 (c) £8,440 (d) £8,460 (e) £8,390
4. (a)(b) and (c) Cap. (d) Revenue.
5. Capital employed at start = £15,000; £8,000 from Brown and £7,000 from creditors. The capital of Brown then changes as follows: (a) £12,000 (b) £12,000 (c) £11,200 (d) £11,400

Chapter 2
1. R. Keen: Cash balance, £910; Bank balance, £23,400; Trial Balance totals, £36,290.
2. T. Rooke: Cash balance, £1,963.50; Bank balance, £11,921.50; Trial Balance totals, £89,541.60.
3. Alice Wood: Cash balance, £913.25; Bank balance, £13,342.63; Trial Balance totals, £87,479.85.

Chapter 3
1. GP, £9,064; NP, £7,376; BS totals, £74,256.
2. (a) £46,917; (b) £45,609; (c) 54.76 per cent.
3. GP, £84,696; NP, £71,497; BS, £100,139.

4.　(a)(*i*) £50,000. (*ii*) £80,000. (*iii*) 60 per cent. (*iv*) $37\frac{1}{2}$ per cent.

(*v*) $12\frac{1}{2}$ per cent. (b) NP £15,868.

Chapter 4

1.　GP, £114,170; NP, £65,896; BS, £118,547.
2.　GP, £115,346; NP, £61,885; BS, £148,106.
3.　GP, £114,257; NP, £75,051; BS, £106,267.

Chapter 5

1.　(a) FIFO, £140; (b) LIFO, £120; (c) -£20.
2.　GP, (a)(*i*) £910; (*ii*) £535; (*iii*) £760; (b)(*i*) £825; (*ii*) £450; (*iii*) £675.
3.　£21,450
4.　£4,720.
5.　£78,733
6.　(a) 60 per cent. (b) 20 per cent. (c) £30,976 (d) 4.5 times.
7. E: £6,400; F: £14,400; G: £12,000; Total £27,200 if R takes the shop. Set against £26,000 loss of income and a saving of rent £2,400 the overall benefit would be £3,600.

Chapter 6

Progress test 6 1.(a) As in text; (b) Sales Day Book; Dr F. Smith, Cr Sales A/c; (c) Purchases Day Book; Dr Purchases A/c, Cr T. Jones; (d) Cash Book; Dr Cash A/c, Cr Sales A/c; (e) Purchases Returns Books; Dr M. Lampard, Cr Purchases Returns A/c; (f) Journal Proper; Dr R. Matthew, Cr Bank A/c; (g) Cash Book; Dr MV Expenses, Cr Cash A/c; (h) Cash Book and Petty Cash Book; Dr Petty Cash Book, Cr Bank A/c.
2.　PDB: Total £808.70; Purchases, £735.18; VAT, £73.52
SDB: Total, £2,327.16; Sales, £2.115.60; VAT, £211.56
SRB: Total, £3.96; Sales Returned, £3.60; VAT, £0.36
Questions 1. Trial Balance total, £296.11. Debits: WS, £187.69; Purchases, 36.80; Sales Returns, 71.62; Credits: Sales, £242.25, Novo, £40.48; VAT, £13.38.
2.　(a) Trial Balance total £1,280.20; VAT A/c Credit balance of £73, output tax owing to HM Customs.
3.(a) Sales, £10,620; VAT, £1,030 (Credits), Debits: PS £6,600; LG £2,970; RD £1,760; BM £320.

Chapter 7

1. Cash balance, £1,020.68; Bank, £5,503.90; VAT, £324.17 Dr £26.20 Cr; Discounts £8.81 and £2.25.
2. Cash Balance £1,337.90; Bank, £2,629.27; VAT, £352.02 Dr £18.00 Cr; Discounts, £1.00 and £19.79.
3. Balance, £9.36; restored imprest, £90.64.
4. Balance £1.00; restored imprest, £79.00.

Chapter 8

1. Revised CB balance = £780.
2. Revised cash balance, £3,395; Final Bank Statement figure, £3,212.
3. Revised Cash Book, £1,500.
4. (*i*) Cash Book balance, £112, (*ii*) Bank Statement balance, £234.
5. Cash Book balance: Overdraft of £234.
6. Revised Cash Balance, £352 Bank Statement shows overdraft of £291.

Chapter 9

No answers supplied. Students should follow the text.

Chapter 10   Drgs = Drawings.

1. Cap. £51,610; Totals, £51,930.
2. (a) Debit P. Brown, credit R. Brown; (b) Debit Motor Vehicles A/c, credit T. Edmunds A/c; (c) Debit Cash A/c, credit Commission Received A/c; (d) Debit Typewriters A/c, credit Reliance Typewriter Co.
3. Profit increase of £1,342.
4. (a) Drgs. Debit £69; Sales A/c Cr, £69; (b) MV A/c Dr, £1,340, MV Expenses A/c Dr £48 Loss on sale of MV A/c Dr, £30, Bank A/c Cr, £1038, MV Ac Cr, £380. (c) Bad Debt A/c Dr, £100 Bank A/c Cr, £100; (d) Employee Loan A/c Dr, £100, Capital A/c Cr, £100.
5. (a) Premises Dr, £65,000, Water rates Dr £325, Rent Receivable Dr, £480, Bank A/c credit, £65,658; Rates Cr, £147. (b) Repairs Dr, £120, Drgs Dr £54. Bank Cr, £174. Rent Dr, £100. Bank Cr, £60. Repairs Cr, £40.
6. (a) Sale plus VAT to F. Brown. (b) Payment of wages and adjustments for PAYE and National Insurance. (c) Transfer of

GP to P & L A/c. (d) Acceptance of bill of exchange by N & Co. Ltd, to settle their account.

Chapter 11

1.   Rent and rates, £8,480. Rent receivable, £905.
2.   Stationery, £350. Salaries, £20, 100. Rates, £1,800. Insurance, £220.
3.   Property, £196,350. Profit on sale, £10,600. Property expenses, £2,022, Rent receivable, £34,064.
4.   GP £57,870. NP, £20,940. BS totals £211,800.
5.   GP £26,581. NP, £23,145. BS, £26,589.

Chapter 12

1.   BD Cr, £548, BDP, Dr, £548; Cr, £468. Bal., £420, P & L A/c Dr, £468.
2.   BDP Cr, £180, P & L A/c Dr, £180.
3.   BD A. Silkin, £50; H. Symons, £36. Bank A/c Dr, £36, Bad Debts Recovered A/c, £36.
4.   (*a*) P & L A/c Dr, £188; BDP Dr £220, Cr £188. Balance £208. BS Drs, £2,600 - £208 = £2,392.

Chapter 13

1.   Depn, £240; Final balance, £2,080.
2.   Depn, £1,500 per annum; final balance, £10,000.
3.   Depn, Yr 1, £4,324; Yr 2, £3,243; Balance at start of year 3, £9,728.
4.   Depn, £4,450.
5.   Loss 19_2, £78. Profit 19_3, £25. Machinery cost £8,800, *less* depn provision £2,160. Bal., £6,640.
6.   Vehicles, £12,210. Depn, £2,250. Loss on disposal, £530.
7.   Vans £17,400. Depn, for year, £5,800; Bal. on Depn A/c, £6,800. Profit on van 1, £300. Loss on van 3, £2,000.

Chapter 14

1.   Original Balance Dr, £10.   2. See text.
3.   Profit, £40,728.75   4. See text.
5.   Dr side; £12,810; £8,417; £27,994; £2,804; £14,957; £5,430; £45,000. Cr side: £28,400; £83,704; £5,308.

Chapter 15

Mfg., manufacturing; P., profit; RM, raw materials
1.   (a) Mfg. P., £37,300, GP, £102,250; (b) Prime Costs, £161,950.

2. (a) RM, £84,583; (b) Pr. Costs, £179,331; (c) cost of M. Goods, £225,697; (d) Mfg. P., £74,303; (e) £149,245; (f) £123,363.

3. Mfg. P., £116,221. GP, £114,684. NP, £206,688.

4. Pr. Costs, £74,700. Mfg. P., £92,350. GP, £96,380. BS, £227,770.

Chapter 16

1. GP A: £99,480; B: £40,080; NP: £129,250.

2. Mfg. P.A; £162,500; B: £108,000; A: 118.2 per cent; B: 104.3 per cent.

3. GP H: £133,480; E: £65,815; NP H: £72,707 - Commission £3,635; E: £1,007 – Commission £50; Balance Sheet totals £140,663.

Chapter 17

1. Drs, £42,310. Crs, £27,654.

2. Drs, £19,420. Crs, £17,030.

3. Drs, £8,338. Crs. £6,915.

4. Total, £24,248. Archer, £135. Attwood, £621. Bragg, £50. Charles, £513. Others in total, £22,929.

Chapter 18

1. GP, £94,675; NP, £80,891; Fixed assets, £112,402; Current assets, £29,062; Capital, £96,663; Long-term liabilities, £38,365; Current liabilities £6,436.

2. GP, £70,011; NP, £34,885; BS totals, £138,207.

3. GP, £124,257; NP, £71,646; BS totals £144,611.

Chapter 19

1. Brown, Cr, £2,344 Fawcett. Cr, £9,444 Southlands, Dr, £486.

2. Andrews: Cr £12,920; Banfield: Dr £3,395.

3. GP, £96,196; NP, £71,440; Current Accounts R. £23,580 credit; L. £16,660 credit; BS totals £95,646.

4. NP £85,680; Current Accounts M. £29,500 credit, £13,980 credit; BS totals £145,980.

Chapter 20

S, Surplus; D, Deficit, BS, Balance Sheet.

1. D, £17; BS, £315; Acc. Fund £312 at close.

2. S, £24. BS, £53,910.

3.   Bar profit, £18,368. S, £16,146. BS, £60,322.
4.   Bar profit, £8,050. S, £196. BS, £18,108.

Chapter 21

App., appropriation account.
1.   GP, £122,287. NP, £59,905 App., £4,045 BS £150,008.
2.   App., £27,970. BS, £228,470.
3.   GP, £132,218. NP, £71,262. App., £1,440. BS, £141,940.
4.   GP, £92,440. NP, £47,120; App., £4,940; BS totals, £72,940.

NOTE: Loss on sale of machine = £100. Machinery value £24,350 less depreciation £4,305.

Chapter 22

1.   GP, £69,172; NP, £50,637; BS, £65,625; Sales were £98,612 and Purchases, £28,560.
2.   GP, £44,720; NP, £30,905; BS £58,630; Sales, £77,920; Purchases, £36,170.
3.   GP, £50,251; NP, £39,492. BS, £46,810; Sales, £67,648; Purchases £16,318.
4.   GP, £35,882; NP, £21,670; BS, £29,262; Sales, £43,990; Purchases, £9,475

Chapter 23

GW, goodwill.
1.   Vendor's price, £105,682; GW (Final figure) £19,264; CB, £14,138; BS, £121,500.
2.   Capital Reserve on Formation, £17,500; Bank, £20,887; BS totals, £117,500.
3.   GW (written off), £5,400. GP, £88,860. NP, £65,670. App., £270; Bank, £86,210; BS totals, £167,340.
4.   GW, £3,000. Profit on dissolution, £12,900. BS totals, £78,000.

Chapter 24

CS, Cash settlement. P, Profit
1.   P, £25,810; CS. Matt pays Prize £51,246.
2.   P, £3,444; CS. Powell pays Johns £2,102.
3.   P, £308; CS. Antony pays Crespel £1,274.

Chapter 25

1.   Profit, £4,168; Sight draft, £7,396.
2.   Profit, £5,572; Sight draft, £7,089.

3. Profit, £62,62υ; Sight draft, £111,180.

Chapter 26

Sh'wgs., shortworkings; WO, written off.
1. Sh'wgs.: 19_4, £500; 19_5, £250. WO, £250, 19_6.
2. Sh'wgs., 19_2, £300. 19_3, £100 WO. 19_4, £100.
3. 19_1, £4,000. 19_2, £1,600. WO, 19_3, £800.
4. (a) over the four years they total £72,500. (b) over the four years they total £23,000. (c) WO, £500 in Year 19_4.
5. NP, £24,483; BS totals, £3,948.

Chapter 27

A. Acq., assets acquired; Adj. P., Adjusted Profit; Dec., decrease; Drgs., drawings; Inc., increase. Drs Debtors.
1. Sources of funds: NP, £10,500. Crs, £1,000. Dec. in cash, £10,500. Applications: A. Acq., £20,000. Stock, £1,000. Drs, £1,000.
2. Sources of funds: Adj. P., £30,000. Crs. £10,000. Drs, £3,000. Dec. in cash, £11,000. Applications: Drgs., £24,000. A. Acq, £15,000. Stock, £15,000.
3. Sources of funds; Adj. P., £16,700. Crs, £400. Dec. in cash, £16,600. Applications: Drgs., £10,000. Loan, £10,000. A. Acq., £10,000. Stock, £2,500. Drs, £1,200.
4. Adj. P., £24,300. Sale proceeds, £5,000. Dec. in cash, £15,200. Inc. in cred. £1,000, Drgs., £15,000. A. Acq., £7,500. Loan repaid, £13,000. Inc. stock £4,000; Inc. debtors £6,000.

Chapter 28

OD = overdraft.
1. OD commence in August and rise to £7,850 in December.
2. 152,000 O. Shares of £1 each.
3. OD, £3,110. GP, £2,050. NP, £435 (after £100 loss on sale).
4. Gross profit = £3,440; gross profit percentage = 43 per cent.
5. (a) Yes — undervalued closing stock increases the cost of sales and reduces the profit, and hence the gross profit percentage. (b) Yes — including a motor vehicle in purchases increases the cost of sales as in (a) above. (c) No — decline in sales should not affect the ratio, which is a constant. (d) Possibly. These goods reduce the stock and consequently affect the gross profit percentage as in (a) above. However, since it happened

last year too, it would only affect the gross profit percentage if
the quantity of goods taken was greater this year than last year.
(e) Yes — theft of sales money reduces the sales figure and
consequently the gross profit.
6.   £10,000 gross profit.
7.   £11,300 net profit.
8.   Working capital = £18,800; working capital ratio = 3.2.
This is more than adequate.
9.   Working capital = £16,300; working capital ratio = 2.90;
acid test ratio = 1.09. Both are adequate.
10.   (a) £67,400; (b) £72,700; (c)£11,400; (d) 4.33; (e) £2,208; (f)
0.65; (g) 3.1 per cent. The extra profit hardly seems worth the
effort and risk. Perhaps there are non-monetary satisfactions.
11.   (a) £600,000. (b) £470,000. (c) £30,000. (d) £120,000. (e) 20
per cent. (f) 2 weeks approx. (g) 3 weeks approx.

Chapter 29
1.   Cap. A/cs: Red, £13,200; White, £8,400; Blue, £2,000.
2.   Cap. A/cs: Brown, £64,000; Allen, £35,000; Campbell,
£4,000; Current A/cs: Brown, £38,940; Allen, £8,618; Campbell,
£1,827 (debit) GP, £119,050. NP, £76,400. BS totals, £158,368.
3.   Loss on realisation, £42,870; Capital Loss of £4,550 shared
Olmec £2,856, Aztec £1,694.

Chapter 30
Questions 1, 2 and 3. Follow the text.
4.   BS totals, £50,975.
5.   BS totals, £551,007; Share capital, £375,000 plus £50,000.
Ordinary Shareholders' Interest in the company, £414,255.
Preliminary Expenses, £3,425.

Chapter 31
1.   Profit on sale, £500. S. Fund, £50,500.
2.   Profit on sale, £12,070. S. Fund, £196,840.
3.   19_3 loss, £300. 19_4 profit, March £200: loss Dec £100; App.
£11,900.

Chapter 32
Wk'g cap., working capital. Inc. = increase. Adj. = adjusted.
1.   Sources: Adj. NP, £68K. New Debentures, £24K = £92K:

Applications: Inc. in Working Capital = £92K.

2. Sources: Adj. NP, £20K. Loan, £6K Dec. in cash, £21K = £47K. Applications: Dividend, £12K Property, £20K Vehicles, £5K. Wk'g cap. Increase of £10K = 47K.

3. Sources: Adj. NP, £140,340. Plant sales, £18,900. Dec. in bank, £38,580 = £197,820. Applications: New plant, £72,960. Corp. tax paid, £102,300. Inc. in wk'g cap., £22,560 = £197,820.

4. Sources: New loan, £20,000; Sale proceeds, £2,800; Dec. in wk'g cap., £6,400; Dec. in bank, £2,400 = £31,600.
Applications: Van, £30,000; Adj. loss, £1,600 = £31,600.

Chapter 33
1. Initial Journal entries and calculations.

	Dr £K	Cr £K
Depreciation: property	13	
Provision for depreciation		13
Depreciation: equipment	6	
Provision for depreciation		6
Depreciation: motor vehicles	33	
Provision for depreciation		33
Bad debts: Profit & Loss A/c	9	
Provision for bad debts		9

COST OF SALES

	£K
Opening stock	280
Purchases	920
	1,200
Less Closing stock	320
Cost of goods sold	880
Wages	233
	£1,113

DISTRIBUTION EXPENSES

	£K
Motor expenses	128
Provision for depreciation	33
Advertising	41
Increase in bad debts provision	9
	£211

ADMINISTRATION EXPENSES

	£K
Salaries	287
Rates, etc.	65
Audit fee	20
General expenses	11
Depreciation:	
Property	13
Equipment	6
	£402

ERIC AND FRANK
PROFIT AND LOSS ACCOUNT FOR THE YEAR ENDED
31 DECEMBER 19_6

Notes		£K	£K
	Turnover		1,990
	Cost of sales		1,113
	Gross profit		877
	Distribution costs	211	
	Administration expenses	402	
			613
(3)	Operating profit		264
(4)	Other income		27
			291
(5)	Interest payable		24
(6)	Profit on ordinary activities before tax		267
(7)	Taxation		116
	Profit on ordinary activities after tax		151
(8)	Dividends		36
	Unappropriated profit for year		115
	Unappropriated profit b/fwd.		156
	Unappropriated profit c/fwd.		£271

BALANCE SHEET AS AT 31 DECEMBER 19_6

Notes

		£K	£K	£K
	Fixed assets:			
(9)	Tangible assets			964
	Current assets:			
(10)	Stocks		320	
(11)	Debtors		266	
			586	
	Creditors: Amounts falling due within one year:			
(12)	Bank overdraft	220		
(13)	Other creditors	96		
	Corporation tax	95		
	Provision for dividend	18	429	
	Net current assets			157
	Net Assets			£1,121
	Capital and reserves:			
(14)	Called up share capital			700
(15)	Revaluation reserve			150
	Profit and Loss Account			271
				£1,121

NOTES TO THE ACCOUNTS

(3) Operating profit is arrived at after charging the following items:

	£K
Depreciation:	
Property	13
Equipment	6
Motor vehicles	33
	52
Hire of motor vans	15
Audit fee	20
Directors' remuneration	108
The Chairman (who is highest paid director)	65

Directors' remuneration		*Employees whose remuneration exceeded £30K*	
£5,001–£10,000	2		
£30,001–£35,000	1	£30,001–£35,000	2
£60,001–£65,000	1		

(4) Other income:

	£K
Rents income	38
Less Expenses of letting	11
	£27

(5) Interest payable:
Amount paid on bank overdraft
(repayable within 5 years) £24K

(7) Taxation:

Corporation tax:	£K
Under-provision for 19_5	21
Charge on current year's profit, i.e. 19_6	95
	£116

(8) Dividends:

	£K
Interim paid	18
Final proposed	18
	£36

(9) Tangible assets:

	Freehold property £K	Equipment £K	Motor vehicles £K	Total £K
Cost or valuation b/f.	900	50	165	1,115
Additions	–	10	–	10
	900	60	165	1,125
Depreciation:				
Balance b/f.	–	24	85	109
Charge for the year	13	6	33	52
	13	30	118	161
Net book value	£887	£30	£47	£964

(10) Stocks valued at cost or net realisable value whichever is the lower. Cost has been taken on a FIFO basis.

	£K
(11) Trade debtors	280
Less Provision for Bad Debts	14
	£266

(12) Bank overdraft: state nature of security (assume on freehold property).

(13) Other Creditors:

	£K
Trade creditors	90
Accrued charges	6
	£96

(14) Called up share capital:
700,000 Ordinary Shares of £1 each, fully paid £700K

(15) Revaluation reserve: £150K arising from revaluation of the Freehold property in 19_5. As there is no intention of disposing of this property in the foreseeable future, it is considered unnecessary to make any provision for capital gains taxation.

Chapter 34
Re-read text if in any difficulty.

Chapter 35
Re-read text if in any difficulty.

Appendix 2
Examination technique

1. Suggestions to students working on their own

(a) Skill will come only with practice; after careful reading, study with a pencil in hand working and reworking problems.

(b) Concentrate on understanding the principles involved; most mistakes are made because basic principles are forgotten. It is essential to revise constantly.

(c) Neatness and presentation of work in a suitable form are essential in examinations, and nearer to the time of the examination test your ability to work out set problems within a time limit.

(d) Read the questions *carefully* to make quite sure that your know exactly what you are required to submit.

(e) Do not be discouraged if a question takes you longer to complete than you expect, but do come back to the question and rework it.

2. Examination preparation
In preparing for examinations it is essential that:

(a) you check through the syllabus to ensure that you have covered the topics laid down by the examining body;

(b) having covered the syllabus, you work through a number of *recent* papers set by the body concerned. It cannot be emphasised too strongly that really thorough work on past papers, if combined with confidence that the whole syllabus has been covered, pays dividends on examination day. The student who discovers that he/she can answer all the questions asked is in a very happy position.

3. Approach

When working through past papers, and in the examination itself:

(a) read through the paper *carefully* to get a general idea of the scope of the paper. Move on to the next question when you have sized-up the previous one – for example 'Oh, it's a Flow of Funds question for a Limited Company!'

(b) *start* by tackling the short questions which from your general survey of the paper appear to present you with the least amount of difficulty;

> NOTE:
> (*i*) This is important, since *one* question successfully completed in good time, gives confidence to tackle the rest of the paper.
> (*ii*) From working past papers you should have a good idea of how long *you* take to complete a question.

(c) before working a question *read it through carefully* to get the sense of the question and to ensure that you give the answer asked for;

> NOTE: This again is important — many able candidates can so easily do more work than is necessary or leave out part of the information asked for in the question.

(d) avoid spending too much time on one answer, thus leaving others incomplete. In the examination itself it is always useful to divide the total time allowed, allocating it in parts to the questions on the paper, e.g. four questions on a 2½-hour paper might be allocated 20, 30, 35 and 65 minutes respectively. Remember especially that if you do get hopelessly bogged-down on a question it is better to abandon it and do the other questions, returning to it if time allows at the end.

4. Pre-examination revision

The most useful form of revision is the working of past examination papers, and to build confidence in one's ability to tackle papers the following steps are suggested.

Step I. Practice by working the paper in *rough*, tackling it simply as an arithmetical exercise purely for the purpose of obtaining the 'answer' in the shortest possible time, at the same time taking care to avoid 'silly' mistakes.

This tends to build confidence in those students who doubt their ability to obtain the answer.

Step II. Confident that you can *work* the questions, you must now concentrate on working them within the time allowed for the examination, at the same time setting out the work *neatly* and in *detail* on the type of paper normally provided at examinations in Accounts.

5. Reworking

By all means come back to a paper and rework it — without reference to your previous effort — until you have completed it, when you can compare results.

Index